Anthropological Archaeology

ANTHROPOLOGICAL ARCHAEOLOGY

GUY GIBBON

Columbia University Press
New York *1984*

Library of Congress Cataloging in Publication Data
Gibbon, Guy E., 1939–
Anthropological archaeology.

Bibliography: p.
Includes index.
1. Social archaeology.   2. Ethnoarchaeology.
I. Title.
CC72.4G53   1984   930.1   84-4321
ISBN 0-231-05662-1 (alk. paper)

Columbia University Press
New York   Guildford, Surrey

*Clothbound editions of Columbia University Press books are
Smyth-sewn and printed on permanent and durable acid-free paper.*

For Ann

Contents

Preface   ix

Chapter 1 Anthropological Archaeology and the Study of   1
Human Behavior
WHAT IS ANTHROPOLOGICAL ARCHAEOLOGY?   1
ALONG THE RESEARCH FRONTIER   14
THE PLAN AND CONTENT OF THE BOOK   28
SUMMARY   29
SUGGESTED READINGS   31

PART ONE   BACKGROUND

Chapter 2 The Cycle of Science   35
PHASES OF RESEARCH   35
ARCHAEOLOGICAL RESEARCH DESIGNS   60
SCIENCE AS A LEARNING PROCESS   66
SUMMARY   69
SUGGESTED READINGS   71

Chapter 3 Strategies of Research   73
STRATEGIES OF INVESTIGATION, EXPLANATION,
   AND INTERPRETATION   74
METHODOLOGICAL PRINCIPLES AND RULES   93
SUMMARY   99
SUGGESTED READINGS   101

Chapter 4 The Model-Building Process   102
WHAT ARE MODELS?   103
THE ART OF MODEL BUILDING   115

AN EXAMPLE OF MODEL BUILDING   125
SUMMARY   131
SUGGESTED READINGS   134

PART TWO   ANTHROPOLOGICAL ARCHAEOLOGY AS
           CULTURAL HISTORY

Chapter 5   Reconstructing Interpersonal Relationships and
                 Symbolic Thought at the Community Level   139
                 IDENTIFYING MEANINGFUL UNITS OF SPATIAL
                    ANALYSIS IN THE SETTLEMENT   140
                 NONSPATIAL APPROACHES TO COMMUNITY
                    SOCIAL ORGANIZATION   150
                 THE POLITICAL SYSTEM   163
                 THE WORLD OF SYMBOLIC THOUGHT: THE
                    IDEOLOGICAL SUBSYSTEM   169
                 SUMMARY   175
                 SUGGESTED READINGS   177

Chapter 6   Coping with the Natural Environment on   180
                 the Community Level: The Technoeconomic
                 Subsystem
                 DIFFERENT MEANINGS OF THE TERM
                    ENVIRONMENT   182
                 THE PROBLEM OF DETERMINING WHICH
                    RESOURCES WERE EXPLOITED   183
                 THE BIOCULTURAL INTERFACE: THE HUMAN
                    POPULATION   204
                 SUMMARY   217
                 SUGGESTED READINGS   219

Chapter 7   Analysis and Interpretation at the Regional and   220
                 Interregional Levels
                 SOME MODELS FOR SETTLEMENT PATTERNS   221
                 MODELING THE RATE OF INTERACTION
                    BETWEEN COMMUNITIES   241
                 RECONSTRUCTING TECHNOECONOMIC
                    SYSTEMS   245
                 SUMMARY   262
                 SUGGESTED READINGS   265

Chapter 8   Processes That Promote Sociocultural Change   267
   HOW SHOULD CHANGE BE STUDIED?   267
   MODELING CHANGE IN SOCIOCULTURAL
      SUBSYSTEMS   271
   THE GROWTH OF SETTLEMENT HIERARCHIES   290
   TOTAL SOCIETY SIMULATION   298
   SUMMARY   302
   SUGGESTED READINGS   304

PART THREE   ANTHROPOLOGICAL ARCHAEOLOGY AS
             SOCIAL SCIENCE

Chapter 9   Cross-Cultural Comparisons   311
   PROBLEMS OF CROSS-CULTURAL COMPARISON   313
   SOME CROSS-CULTURAL COMPARISONS   325
   EVOLUTIONARY THEORY AND COMPARATIVE
   ARCHAEOLOGY   337
   SUMMARY   349
   SUGGESTED READINGS   351

Chapter 10   Formalizing Archaeological Theories   352
   PARTS OF A THEORY   354
   PRINCIPLES OF THEORY CONSTRUCTION   362
   EVALUATING THEORIES   369
   TWO AXIOMATIC SKETCHES   371
   SUMMARY   382
   SUGGESTED READINGS   384

Chapter 11   Is a Science of Archaeology Impossible?   385
   CONCEPTIONS OF THE NATURAL AND SOCIAL
      SCIENCES   387
   CAN ARCHAEOLOGISTS DISCOVER LAWS?   396
   IS A SCIENCE OF ARCHAEOLOGY IMPOSSIBLE?   406
   SUMMARY   412
   SUGGESTED READINGS   414

   Glossary   417
   References   429
   Index   449

Preface

Archaeology is fascinating because it explores the foundations of human development. In fact it is the only social science that explores human behavior primarily through the material culture of social groups. *Anthropological Archaeology* introduces the reader to some of the problems that stimulate anthropological research in archaeology and to the concepts, language, and techniques used by archaeologists in conducting that research.

Anthropological Archaeology has been written with certain goals in mind: to make readers aware of the significance of regularities in the arrangement of archaeological materials; to describe and provide examples of the behavioral processes that contribute to the arrangement of these materials; to develop critical attitudes toward archaeological reconstructions; to define the major concepts, language, and techniques used by anthropological archaeologists; and to extend the reader's knowledge of the problems and methodology of social science. The attitude adopted throughout the book is one of benign skepticism: it still remains to be seen whether the accomplishments of anthropological archaeology will ever match the bolder proclamations of the field. Nevertheless, this tension between wishful thinking and objective possibility makes anthropological archaeology such an exciting enterprise today.

Introductory-level texts commonly gloss over troubling issues and make it seem as if knowledge in the field is more secure than it actually is. That approach is not adopted here. Instead it is assumed that it is just these troubling issues that advanced students of archaeology are interested in. In many instances the text does not commit itself to one view or another. Each reader must reach his or her own conclusion. Nor does the book pretend to present all aspects of anthropological archaeology. For instance, some topics that form the core of many introductory books, such as excavation, dating, and curation, are largely ignored. The emphasis throughout is on the methodological problems and potential of reconstructing the culture and way of life of past peoples through their material remains. Definite decisions have been made, too, on how anthropological archaeology should be presented. For example, a set of basic trends that define anthropological archaeology is proposed, an ideational interpretation of the culture concept is adopted, and anthropological archaeology is considered a science.

Professional archaeologists will recognize that *Anthropological Archaeology* relies primarily on the work of others; readers are urged to seek out these primary sources, which are listed in the text and as Suggested Readings at the end of each chapter. Although many of these authors have received their training in departments of anthropology, one can adopt the anthropological approach in archaeology without being in an anthropology department or having been trained in one, and being there does not make one an anthropological archaeologist. As will become clearer in chapter 3, anthropological archaeology is regarded here as a somewhat fuzzy research program, a plan of study, that one can decide to adopt only some of the time.

I hope that the text will be useful to both those archaeologists oriented toward the collection and analysis of data and others concerned primarily with model building and the conceptual basis of archaeology, for, as I will demonstrate, the disparate activities of modern archaeologists fit together into a larger, coherent enterprise.

Anthropological Archaeology

CHAPTER ONE

Anthropological Archaeology and the Study of Human Behavior

Anthropological archaeology has been discussed in a number of major syntheses, of which the most widely read are the Binfords' *New Perspectives in Archeology* (1968), Leone's *Contemporary Archaeology* (1972), and Watson, Leblanc, and Redman's *Explanation in Archaeology* (1971). This book offers a personal view of what anthropological archaeologists are attempting to achieve and of the methodological and conceptual problems that accompany these goals. Fortunately or unfortunately, depending on your viewpoint, anthropological archaeologists do not share a single, unified way of thinking about archaeology or the past. Therefore, this essay on the anthropological approach to archaeology reflects, as any similar introduction must, the experience, interests, and philosophical convictions of the author.

What is Anthropological Archaeology?

Few archaeologists agree entirely on what anthropological archaeology is or should strive to be. Nonetheless, certain generally agreed-upon trends have motivated the approach. These include (1) the adoption and redefinition of the culture concept; (2) a synthesis of cultural ecology, structural-functionalism, and cultural materialism; (3) the emergence of a new set of assumptions about the proper goals of archaeology and about its subject matter; (4) the acceptance of a new conception of the scientific method; and (5) a surge in the borrowing of theories, methods, and techniques from other fields.

Each of these trends, along with their implications for the pursuit of archaeology, is briefly examined in this section.

Black Boxes, Culture, and the Systems Approach

In North America the roots of anthropological archaeology extend back into the nineteenth century. Ethnographers and archaeologists, as well as linguists and physical anthropologists, were leading expeditions from the great museums of the country to record the vanishing life-ways of the American Indian. Archaeologists soon found that Old World historically based interpretive schemes such as Christian Thompsen's three-age sequence could not be usefully applied to the organization of their accumulating archaeological discoveries. Not only was an indigenous historical tradition generally lacking, but the aboriginal habitation of the continent appeared relatively recent. As a result, they began to adopt the emerging interpretive concepts of their colleagues in the new discipline of anthropology.

Most anthropologists study groups of living people and attempt to interpret or explain their behavior. Among the many questions that puzzle them is why social groups differ from one another in their traditional patterns of social relations, subsistence, and religious beliefs. Many social, psychological, and religious theories have been proposed to explain these differences. Although early anthropologists did not use this particular metaphor, they tended to think of human social groups as if they were "black boxes" that reacted to external stimuli in patterned ways according to unobservable codes or sets of instruction defining their range of appropriate responses. As observers, anthropologists could record the existence of external stimuli such as seasonal changes in habitat, chance personal encounters, or the birth of a baby, and the resulting behavioral response of members of the social group to these stimuli. What they could not observe was the hidden mechanism in the black box that interpreted and acted upon these stimuli to produce "proper" behavior. Since the mechanism is not observable, the unit of analysis—the social group—is opaque (that is, an impenetrable black box), and the code that governs the mechanism must be guessed at by carefully comparing stimuli with patterned behavioral responses. Obviously, according to this belief, similarities and differences between social groups are the result of similarities and differences in the wiring of their black boxes. To interpret or explain the behavior of groups of people, then, is to learn the code or set of instructions that govern their behavior.

Anthropologists have called these codes or sets of instructions cultures and, collectively, culture. Although culture has remained a fuzzy concept in anthropology, it has become the central organizing concept of the discipline. One of the traditional goals of anthropology has been to describe the cultures of all human societies and to explain why they differ in some respects and are similar in others. Obviously, how the culture concept is defined will influence how this disciplinary task is perceived, as well as the kind of information that is collected during field research, the way in which it is ordered for study, and how it is interpreted.

Sir Edward Burnett Tylor, the author of the first general anthropology textbook written in English and one of the founders of academic anthropology, defined culture in the following manner: "Culture . . . taken in its wide ethnographic sense is that complex whole which includes knowledge, belief, art, morals, law, custom, and any other capabilities and habits acquired by man as a member of society" (1871:1). Tylor's definition captures the meaning of culture as it has been traditionally used by anthropologists in the English-speaking world. According to this view, a culture consists of the patterned, repetitive ways of thinking, feeling, and acting that are socially acquired by the members of a particular society or segment of a society. In this traditional sense a culture is a code for living plus patterned behavioral responses—both ideas and acts.

Other anthropologists have restricted the meaning of culture exclusively to mental grammars—to the rules for feeling, acting, and speaking shared by the members of a particular society. These rules are regarded as a kind of grammar of behavior that people learn in much the same manner in which they learn the grammar of their language. By abstracting the underlying sets of rules that presumably channel human behavior into acceptable, patterned forms of cultural activity, these anthropologists think that they will be able to interpret and predict the actions of the people they study.

Anthropological archaeologists in North America have in general adopted Tylor's broad definition of culture (e.g., Sharer and Ashmore 1979:24). However, they were strongly influenced in the first half of the twentieth century by the normative or ideological interpretation of culture described in the paragraph above, an interpretation derived from the Boasian tradition of American anthropology. According to this interpretation, patterned behavior in human groups is the result of the existence of sets of shared rules or norms for behavior. Even though some individuals might occasionally deviate from these norms, social pressures such as gossip, kidding, economic sanctions, and social ostracism generally restrict their behavior to a range tolerated by their society. Since most behavior is regulated by norms, whether it involves interpersonal relationships, the construction of houses, or the manufacture of tools, archaeologists should in principle be able to infer the behavioral norms of past societies from the repetitive patterning of materials in archaeological sites. Given this argument, anthropological archaeologists concentrated their efforts during the first half of the twentieth century on reconstructing norms and identifying "archaeological" cultures. These cultures were then usually arranged taxonomically according to the degree of their shared norms, as in the Midwest Taxonomic System (table 1.1; McKern 1939). Since the appearance of new norms was explained at this time by tracing the diffusion through space of ideas, and by innovations or chance discovery, a tremendous amount of effort was devoted to locating the origin of the city, food production, the use of fire, and other episodic events, and to tracing their dispersal throughout the world.

During the last three or four decades, social and cultural anthropologists have in general continued to view cultures as ideational systems, as systems of ideas such as cognitive systems, structural systems, or symbolic systems (Keesing 1974). Anthropological archaeologists, on the other hand, have in general shifted their emphasis to that part of the broader traditional definition of culture which corresponds with culturally informed behavior and its material by-products—to the life-ways of past communities (p. 75). Some anthropological archaeologists have even written at times as if cultures are patterns *of* behavior in human communities rather than patterns *for* behavior. A cultural anthropologist, Marvin Harris, has expressed this perspective: "The culture concept comes down to behavior patterns associated with particular groups of peoples, that is to customs or to a people's way of life" (1968:16). This portion of the physical world (behavior and its material by-products) has been called, metaphorically, the behavioral stream, the stream through time of actual observable behavior and the changing configurations of matter that result from this behavior. Scientists who study the behavioral stream are now called behavioral scientists, and, because of their shifting interests, many anthropological archaeologists now identify themselves with the behavioral sciences (Schiffer 1976).

One important result of this shift in emphasis among anthropological ar-

Table 1.1 An Example of the Midwest Taxonomic System: A Classification of Late Prehistoric Cultures in Minnesota

Period	Pattern	Phase	Aspect	Focus	Some Components
Late Woodland	Mississippi	Upper	Oncota	Orr	Rushford / Hogback
				Blue Earth	Humphrey / Bartron
		Plains	——	Silvernale	Silvernale
			——	Cambria	Cambria
			——	Great Oasis	Great Oasis Lake
	Woodland	Lake Michigan	Headwaters Lakes	Blackduck	Blackduck / Osufsen
			Red River	Arvilla	Arvilla, N.D. / De Spiegler, S.D.
			Mille Lacs	Kathio	Aquipaguetin Island
				Malmo	Malmo / Kern
			Rainy River	Laurel	Smith Mound #4 / McKinstry
Middle Woodland			So. Minn. Effigy Mound	——	Fox Lake
				——	——
		Hopewellian	——	Howard Lake	Anderson
				——	Tudahl
Early Woodland		——	——	La Moille	La Moille
Archaic					

SOURCE: Wilford 1955, table 6. Reproduced by permission of the Society for American Archaeology from *American Antiquity* 21(2):130–142.

chaeologists was a change in attitude toward their subject matter. Traditionally, the remnants of tools, houses, carts, and other artifacts of human activity were viewed as objects or things with an importance of their own: they were material instantiations of norms. Now they were viewed as social documents that were a source of information about relations and variability within past life-ways. One studied the material remains of past human activity in order to understand and explain extinct human behavioral *systems*. With this shift the concept of system became, therefore, a key concept in anthropological archaeology. If cultures are viewed as complex systems, as aggregations of things and events joined in interaction and interdependence to form integrated wholes, then the relationships among their parts are as important as the parts themselves. The result is a potentially powerful new perspective from which to view behavior in human communities (Plog 1975).

Thinking about past human social groups in terms of complex systems has had three basic advantages for archaeologists. First, the system concept promotes comprehensibility; the concept of system is an organizing device that provides a mental picture of the behavior and material products of social groups. Second, the system concept encourages holistic thinking; a system by definition is an aggregation of things and events joined in interaction and interdependence that forms an integrated whole. Third, thinking in terms of systems generates hypotheses about sociocultural and environmental units and their interrelationships.

Cultural Ecology, Cultural Materialism, and Structural-Functionalism

Cross-cutting definitions of what culture is are diverse interpretations of the purpose of culture, of what it does if it does anything at all (Hatch 1973). Cultures have been viewed, for instance, as abstracted sets of rules and a body of knowledge that does not "do" anything or, in a slightly more utilitarian manner, as a frame of reference of life in human communities. Each of these views and others are based on assumptions that anthropologists find useful in studying human beings in social settings. Because different sets of fruitful assumptions are possible, it is entirely unlikely that concepts like culture have a single, correct definition, what the philosopher Karl Popper (1970) has called an essence. Rather, various definitions serve different purposes and prove useful or not. As a result, the interpretations of concepts tend to change as disciplines shift their focus of inquiry. Such a change occurred in anthropological archaeology in what it was thought culture does when a normative view of culture that focused on entities shifted to a systems approach that stressed interrelationships.

A decidedly utilitarian interpretation of culture began to gather momentum in anthropological archaeology by the early 1960s. According to this interpretation, a culture is a human group's means of adapting to its natural and social environment. As Lewis Binford, the leading proponent of the new perspective, wrote: "Culture is an extrasomatic system that is employed in the integration of a society with its environment and with other sociocultural systems" (1965:205). Like other organisms, humans must adjust to their natural environment and to other organisms. Although chance and other variables must be taken into consideration, cultural similarities and differences are primarily determined by the histories of adaptations. From this perspective, an explanation of the patterned, repetitive ways of thinking and acting of members of a society would not be complete or even particularly useful without some understanding of the people/land adaptation that had been made.

A research program—a plan of study—for examining extinct human societies developed within anthropological archaeology in the 1960s and 1970s around the systems concept and this utilitarian interpretation of culture. The theoretical foundation of the program was a synthesis of three deep-rooted anthropological approaches to the study of human societies: cultural ecology, structural-functionalism, and cultural materialsim. *Cultural ecology* is the view that sociocultural systems are adapted for exploiting particular portions of their environment through the use of certain technologies, and that the form of a sociocultural system is in large part determined by the ecological conditions to which it is adjusted.

From this perspective, the physical environment is considered an immensely elaborate natural system composed of animals, plants, inanimate objects, and their interrelationships. Since communities cannot possibly exploit their environment fully, each develops a patterned relationship with only some resources and competitors. These choices define a position within the web of the natural environment that has been called an ecological niche. From the perspective of cultural ecology, sociocultural systems are complex adaptive systems that can be partially defined by the web of relations—the ecological niche—they have spun. As cultural ecologists, anthropological archaeologists attempt to trace and to account for these relations. This perspective is a very practical one for archaeologists, for it involves collecting categories of independent information on animals, plants, the landscape, and natural resources that are reasonably easy to obtain from the archaeological record.

Cultural ecology identifies the main determinants of sociocultural change as the ecological conditions to which these systems are adapted. *Cultural materialism* is the supplementary view that among these conditions technoenvironmental change is the most basic determining factor in cultural evolution. This view is based in part on the observation that technological subsystems articulate more closely with the environment than do other sociocultural subsystems. As cultural materialists, archaeologists attempt to trace the presumed causal connections running from ecological systems through technology and its organization in economic systems to the sociocultural system and culture itself.

Cultural ecology, cultural materialism, and the systems approach share the assumption that sociocultural systems are sets of units connected by functional, causal, and other types of relations. The third approach in this synthesis, *structural-functionalism,* is a set of assumptions about the nature of these relations. According to this view, each unit and relation helps maintain the cohesiveness and integrity of the whole system, while the whole functions to supply the biological needs of individual human beings. Since sociocultural subsystems are interlinked, a change in one will induce changes in the others: like strands in a spider's web, when one is disturbed, the others will vibrate. As structural-functionalists, archaeologists attempt to unravel the function of the units that make up sociocultural systems and to determine how these systems are maintained as structural wholes.

The utilitarian view of culture evident in the synthesis in anthropological archaeology of cultural ecology, cultural materialism, and structural-functionalism meshes nicely with the systems approach, for the synthesis emphasizes relations and processes among entities rather than entities themselves. As a result, cultures have come to be viewed as systems with structure and function; as wholes whose wholeness is more important than their fragmented parts.

A New Set of Working Assumptions

There are many extradisciplinary and rarely discussed reasons why these shifts in emphasis occurred in anthropological archaeology. Some of these reasons are the growing importance in the western scientific ethos of a systems perspective, process metatheory, quantification, and a new conception of science. Whatever the determinants of this shift were, they were accompanied within anthropological archaeology by the adoption of a new set of working assumptions and new goals. Anthropological archaeology is said to have three main goals (Binford 1968a): (1) the study of culture history, (2) the reconstruction of past life-ways, and (3) the investigation of those processes that maintain and transform sociocultural systems. Anthropological archaeologists have always shown an interest in each of these goals, although each has varied in importance from one time period or school of archaeology to another.

Cultural historical reconstruction dominated anthropological archaeology during the first half of the twentieth century. Archaeological sites and their contents were described, classified, and arranged within spatial-temporal or taxonomic frameworks; local variability and idiosyncracies in artifact form and spatial distribution were generally ignored; and the normative view of culture was adopted. At the time this was a pragmatic and understandable emphasis. The nineteenth century had been a period of unrestrained speculation: American aborigines were thought by quite reputable people, for example, to be a long-lost tribe of Israel, Viking offspring, or survivors of the sunken continent of Mu. These fanciful speculations were largely a response to a general dearth of knowledge about the spatial-temporal and cultural relationships of archaeological sites throughout the world. The new goal of the early twentieth century was the collection and description of facts and the construction of controlled chronologies. Through the efforts of these early cultural historians, the initial chronologies for many areas of the world were established and the antiquity of human life greatly expanded.

Cultural historical reconstructions dwindled in importance in the early 1950s for at least three reasons. First, the basic spatial-temporal sequences for many of the geographic regions of primary interest had been worked out in broad outline. Second, new dating techniques, especially the invention of radiocarbon dating by Willard Liddy in 1949, made the ordering of archaeological material along the dimension of time a less challenging intellectual activity. Third, archaeologists as anthropologists, at the prodding of their anthropological colleagues (Steward and Setzler 1938; Taylor 1948), became increasingly dissatisfied with "merely" describing and ordering the contents of archaeological sites. Cultural historical reconstruction as generally practiced was not necessarily wrong: it was simply inadequate for answering questions about human behavior and culture process. The result was a shift during the 1950s and most of the 1960s to a new research emphasis that had as a goal the creation of plausible accounts of extinct life-ways. Among the important questions at the time were: How did past societies exploit their natural habitat? How were their settlements organized? How could past life-ways be reconstructed?

Two basic assumptions formed the intellectual underpinnings of this new emphasis: (1) the archaeological record contains valuable insights into human behavior as it once existed in the past, and (2) cultures are adaptations to ecological and environmental factors. According to the first assumption, the contents of archaeological sites are social documents that can be "read" to interpret the institutions and life-ways of past societies. The second assumption, often interpreted to mean that external environmental factors produce sociocultural change, resulted in the recording of many new varieties of data. Large-scale interdisciplinary research teams were organized to reconstruct the vegetation, climate, animal life, geology, and soils of past environments. Animal bones, seeds, pollen grains, and other surviving ecofacts were regularly collected for the first time in archaeological excavations. During this shift in disciplinary goals anthropological archaeologists began to regard human behavior and sociocultural systems rather than artifacts as their main concern; to emphasize relationships between social processes and material remains; and to redefine archaeology as the study of behavior and its by-products as objectified in the archaeological record.

The most recent shift in emphasis in anthropological archaeology was a natural extension of the earlier goals of the discipline. Constructing pictures of past life-ways is still, after all, just description. Armed with a new conception of science (a conception described in the next section of this chapter), many anthropological archaeologists sought to "explain" past life-ways, to know *why* some sociocultural systems rapidly change, for example, while others remain stable for long periods. During the 1960s and 1970s, a process metatheory came to dominate the discipline as archaeologists increasingly attempted to explain the stability and change of sociocultural systems by delineating those processes that had constrained and channeled the structure of these systems. Earlier archaeologists had not ignored processes and explanations, for environmental change, universal evolution, diffusion, invasion, migration, and other processes actually abound in earlier reports as explanations of change and stability in prehistory. What was new was (1) the systematic study of processes from a systems perspective, (2) the growing importance of other processes such as population pressure, social restrictions, chance variability, and the effect of feedback between sociocultural subsystems, and (3) the realization that still other processes distort the relationships between the archaeological contexts studied by archaeologists and the systemic contexts that are the indirect objects of their studies.

Although archaeologists are primarily interested in the processes that form and transform past sociocultural systems, their subject matter is the material remains of these systems—the pottery fragments, stone flakes, and crumbled

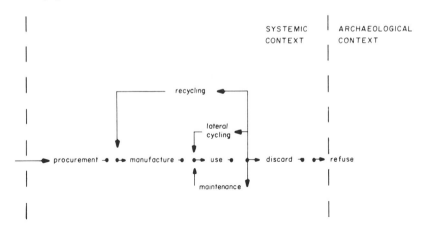

Figure 1.1   The flow of durable materials from the systemic to the archaeological context. Key: ---- system under analysis; - - opportunity for storage or transport. Source: Schiffer 1972. Reproduced by permission of the Society for American Archaeology from *American Antiquity* 37(2):156–165.

house foundations that exist in the present. A fundamental conceptual distinction exists between those remains that are collectively called the *archaeological context* and past sociocultural systems or the *systemic context* (figure 1.1; Schiffer 1972, 1983). The systemic context is made up of past sociocultural systems, their web of interrelationships, and their position along the dimension of time. Archaeologists cannot directly observe past sociocultural expressions of cultures or the processes that maintained and eventually changed them: they must infer their existence from the study of the patterns of spatial relationships of their surviving material remains. Although these remains were once a part of past behavioral systems, they are now elements of the archaeological record. Since the archaeological context has been formed by processes that deposit materials from sociocultural contexts and by the transformation of these materials in both form and spatial location within soil matrices, archaeologists are faced with the formidable methodological problem of unraveling the distortion that these processes cause in our perception of the systemic context.

A New Conception of Science

It is a relatively simple matter to outline the time of the changes that have occurred in anthropological archaeology (e.g., Binford 1962; Deetz 1965), but a much more complex one to account for them. Why did attention swing so obviously toward new methodologies, theories, and techniques? Why was there a growing interest in a more scientific methodology, with all that this implies in the way of careful measurement and theory building? Although sweeping changes in the ethos of western science must again be taken into consideration, within the discipline anthropological archaeologists felt a dissatisfaction with the intellectual content of archaeology, with the value of its contributions to society. An undercurrent running through the literature of the 1960s and 1970s is the call for more scientific and precise methods of analysis and a body of theory better able to relate archaeological materials to the concerns of everyday life. The "revolution" in anthropological archaeology that purportedly transformed the discipline was inspired in part by a genuine need to make archaeology more scientific and by a concern to develop a body of theory.

In their quest for a scientific identity, many anthropological archaeologists adopted the deductive-nomological model of science of the logical empiricists or positivists (Gibbon 1980). Among the theses of this conception of science are (1) the hypothetico-deductive approach (the strategy of science that deduces testable consequences from hypotheses and confronts them with data); (2) the covering-law model of explanation (the model in which all sufficient explanations involve the deductive subsumption of events to be explained under propositions consisting of hypothetically assumed general laws of nature and initial conditions); (3) the operationalist-instrumentalist interpretation of scientific concepts and theories (in which the meaning of concepts is determined by their mode of measurement and theories represent handy fictional stories rather than depictions of what actually happens in reality); (4) the belief that there is an essential unity of scientific method (a "logic of science") among all natural and social sciences; (5) an emphasis on the search for laws; (6) the belief that explanation and prediction represent the principal aims of science; (7) the view that scientific theories and explanations are primarily systems of logically arranged statements; (8) the demand for relevance in research; (9) the equation of laws with relational statements expressing observable regularities; and (10) a belief in autonomous facts that serve as a means of objectively evaluating theories. Many readers will find at least some of these statements meaningless. Therefore, many of these theses are developed more fully in subsequent chapters.

Logical empiricism entered anthropological archaeology only in a general sense, rather than as a well-thought-out plan of study. For this reason, many of its most fundamental theses were never entirely comprehended or formally developed. Nonetheless, only against the background of logical empiricism do many of the fundamental concepts and endeavors of anthropological archaeology in the 1960s and 1970s become intelligible. Even though the connection is not always immediately obvious from this brief introduction, the following characteristics of anthropological archaeology in the 1960s and 1970s indicate the essential indebtedness the discipline owes to the logical empiricist conception of science: (1) adoption of the hypothetico-deductive approach (Hill 1970a; Fritz and Plog 1970; Watson, Leblanc, and Redman, 1971:22, 47; Leblanc 1973:200; Plog 1974:12–25); (2) acceptance of the covering-law model of explanation as both a standard and a goal of scientific inquiry (Spaulding 1968, 1973; Fritz and Plog 1970; Watson, Leblanc, and Redman, 1971:4–10; Plog 1974:14); (3) belief in the methodological unity of science (Watson, Leblanc, and Redman, 1971:26, 56; Watson 1973); (4) the demand for relevance in research (Fritz and Plog 1970:411–412; Fritz 1973); (5) the belief in autonomous facts that serve as a means of objectively evaluating theories (Spaulding 1968:38; Watson, Leblanc, and Redman, 1971:31); (6) a powerful emphasis on method; (7) the use of symbolic logic, mathematization, and quantification; (8) the equation of laws with relational statements expressing observable regularities; (9) emulation of the alleged methods of the natural sciences; (10) the belief that testing is primarily a matter of predictive success; (11) the view that archaeology has progressed both historically and logically from description to theoretical explanation; and (12) the correspondence between the language of logical empiricism and the language of archaeological theory. Many archaeologists hoped that they would be able to implement more rigorous research strategies capable of achieving the emerging goals of their discipline by following the logic of science as revealed in the writings of the logical empiricists.

Borrowed Theories, Methods, and Techniques

Some of these emerging trends, especially the adoption of a systems approach, a logical empiricist conception of science, and the synthesis of structural-functionalism, cultural ecology, and cultural materialism, resulted in the massive and relatively rapid borrowing of theories, methods, and techniques from other disciplines. Moreover, as in the other social sciences, external developments in technology during the 1950s, especially the development of the computer, made available, comparatively suddenly, many new aids that were seemingly appropriate for this type of analysis. Anthropological archaeology has not been changing in a vacuum: it is very much a product of the time and place in which it has emerged. The trend toward the use of quantification, the concern with theories and principles, the preoccupation with process and prediction, have all been evident for some time in social science research. In a very real sense archaeology has become more sophisticated because science has become more sophisticated. The computer has had a considerable impact on archaeological inquiry in several ways. First, computers can store and handle huge amounts of data. Second, they are able to manipulate data in complex ways to test hypotheses and build mathematical models. And third, they force researchers to visualize and design the tests and models they wish to construct at the beginning, rather than at the end, of a project. The expense of running a computer forces one to consider much more carefully what she is trying to show and thus exactly what things she should measure to show it. The computer imposes discipline, and as a result, analysis in the social sciences has become methodologically sounder. One indication of this trend is the increasing importance of formal research designs throughout the social sciences. Whether a study of the history of the development of anthropological archaeology eventually demonstrates a causal relationship between these events or not, the computer has been a powerful impetus in archaeology in the swing from a descriptive to a processual approach.

Related to the development of computer usage in archaeology has been the greatly expanded use of inferential statistics and mathematical modeling, both of which have opened new research possibilities in anthropological archaeology. Accompanying these trends and partly dependent on them were new theoretical developments in other disciplines, such as locational theory in geography and ecological theory in biology. When these were coupled with internal advances in archaeology, especially the adoption of some of the many goals of sociocultural anthropology, the result was a tremendous impetus for a new archaeology.

Along the Research Frontier

The past two decades have witnessed one of the more significant upsurges in both fundamental thinking and methods of approach that archaeology has witnessed. Like all disciplines, archaeology is dynamic rather than static. Archaeologists are constantly exploring new approaches to the archaeological record and assessing their more traditional methods and techniques. My aim is to explore the new opportunities presented by current trends and equally to assess their limitations. In this section some of the problem areas in the major trends discussed in the last section are reviewed. These areas of uncertainty, debate, rethinking, and stimulation are either new opportunities or pitfalls along the research frontier of anthropological archaeology.

Anthropological archaeology today as a general approach to the study of the material remains of past social groups is based on a number of assumptions. Each of these assumptions is closely identified with one or more of the trends that I have been discussing. Although not all anthropological archaeologists share all of these assumptions, they seem as a whole to characterize the approach. Five of the most fundamental of these assumptions are: (1) culture is a human group's means of adaptation and the principal organizing concept in understanding past human groups; (2) sociocultural systems are composed of interdependent parts that cannot be fully understood apart from their whole; (3) sociocultural systems are complex adaptive systems whose web of relations is primarily determined by technology and its organization; (4) most of the data relevant to creating plausible reconstructions of all parts of extinct sociocultural systems are preserved in the archaeological record; and (5) anthropological archaeology is a social science and, consequently, should be concerned with the explanation of human behavior and sociocultural change as well as with the development of laws and general theory. Hidden within each of these assumptions are formidable problems for the anthropological archaeologist.

The Culture Concept

How modern anthropologists define their traditional conceptual tool, culture, channels and constrains their approach to a number of classic anthropological questions: How have cultures developed and what forces shape them? How are cultures learned? How different and unique are cultures? Do universal patterns underlie diversity? What is cultural description?

As we have seen, anthropological archaeologists now emphasize that part of culture composed of habits, customs, institutions, and other patterns *of* behavior, while sociocultural anthropologists have conceptualized culture as a system of knowledge or a shared code of meaning *for* behavior. Obviously, these contrasting views lead to markedly different answers to the classic questions of anthropology. An archaeologist describes a culture, for example, by reconstructing the subsistence economy, technology, social organization, demography, religious practices, the flow of exchange, and other components of the life of human beings in society; sociocultural anthropologists describe the same culture by detailing the ideational codes lying behind this realm of observable events. For the latter, "real" cultural entities are conceptual norms, symbols, and meanings; for the former, they are the artifacts, body movements, and patterns of "things" that exemplify them. According to sociocultural anthropologists, archaeologists have really been asking, How do ways of life change and what shapes the form they take in particular settings? How different—and how similar—are ways of life in different times and places? How do human groups organize and sustain their social life? How do human biology, the natural environment, and other cultures affect life in a community?

The diverging interests of anthropological archaeologists and most other anthropologists can be made clearer by borrowing Karl Popper's idea (1972:106–190) that the world is composed of three distinct but real realms which we will call culture, mind, and physical environment (figure 1.2); this conceptual framework will eventually aid us in understanding some of the other fundamental methodological and conceptual problems of contemporary archaeology, too. Here culture is composed of rules of behavior, language, mathematical systems, the "thought" content of books, and other ideas; the mind is formed of conscious and unconscious states, dreams, and thoughts; and the environment is made up of physical actions and objects, such as stones, atoms, human bodies and body movements, speech acts, and the instantiation of knowledge in books and works of art, as well as tools, houses, and settlement patterns.

These realms interact with and influence one another. For instance, culture in this ideational sense clearly influences one's thoughts and dreams, and, through the intended and unintended consequences of culturally informed activity, the physical environment. Changes in the physical environment, such as glacial surges or overpopulation, nearly always lead to the creation of new thoughts that affect the content of culture. And human thought processes may eventuate in new conceptions of the physical environment and lead to the invention of new tools, myths, and rules of behavior; these thoughts elaborate and change the content of culture and, therefore, the patterned activities of individuals.

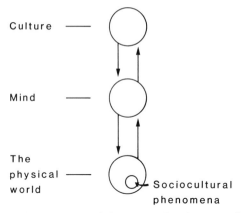

Figure 1.2 A simplified diagram of the interaction between three realms of the world.

In this very schematic conception, segments of the traditional concept of culture are separated. Although some of the content of the mind and the physical environment are influenced by the content of culture, this content is not considered part of the content of culture itself. Tools, works of art, speech acts, and many body movements represent culturally informed behavior or its by-products but not actual items of culture. The culture concept has been narrowed to language, norms of behavior, and other systems of ideas. While most sociocultural anthropologists continue to concentrate on the study of culture in this ideational sense, anthropological archaeologists have in general concentrated on patterned behavioral activities and their by-products, that is, on the life-ways of people living in groups.

David Bidney (1953:32) has called the failure to distinguish between conceptual ideals and the practices or customs they condition the positivistic fallacy. To understand change and diversity, human action and human social relations, we must understand both the rules of the game and patterns of life of communities. Following Ward Goodenough, Keesing (1974:81–83) has sought to untangle this conceptual muddle by distinguishing between a culture and a sociocultural system. Culture in this conceptualization refers to ideational designs for living, patterns of shared meanings, and systems of knowledge and belief. This definition corresponds, of course, to modern views of culture as an ideational system. Sociocultural systems, on the other hand, "represent the social realizations or enactments of [these] ideational designs-for-living in particular environments" (p. 82)—that part of the traditional concept of culture now emphasized by archaeologists. Sociocultural systems are objective, empirical realities that can be studied by the methods of the natural sciences. In this sense they are fruitfully regarded as complex living systems in the cybernetic sense, as systems within which complex circuits connect ecological, demographic, ideational, and other subsystems.

These systems rather than culture are subject in some way to natural selection, are adaptive or maladaptive, for natural selection works on behavior rather than on shadowy mentalistic formulations such as culture. Even though cultures provide a grammar for behavior and information input into sociocultural systems through their ideational component, cultures themselves in this view are not part of sociocultural systems. Nonetheless, cultures are crucially important subsystems of ways of life in environments that cannot be ignored. Besides being codes for knowing and acting, they may well be the fount of important principles or universals of being human that are obscured by the substantive stuff of culture (Geertz 1965). Such a model of culture enriches our understanding of change and adaptation and helps us balance overly simplistic ecological/adaptationist models.

This distinction between culture and sociocultural system benefits archaeology in several ways. First, it helps sort out the elements and principles of past cultures. As Keesing notes:

> A settlement pattern is an element of a sociocultural system, not an element of a cultural system in this sense. (The same conceptual principles might yield densely clustered villages or scattered homesteads, depending on water sources, terrain, arable land, demography, and the peaceful or headhunting predilections of the neighboring tribe.) A mode of subsistence technology similarly is part of a sociocultural system, but not strictly speaking part of a cultural system (people with the same knowledge and set of strategies for subsisting might be primarily horticulturalists in one setting and primarily fishermen in another, might make adzes of flint in one setting or shells in another, might plant taro on one side of a mountain range or yams on the other side). (1974:82)

Second, it reshuffles and sharpens the questions that archaeologists ask about the past: How are the complex circuits of sociocultural systems interconnected? How does information ramify through them? How do homeostatic processes and directional change operate? How do ideational systems operate in this process of adaptation and change? How snugly are the cultural and sociocultural realms interrelated? How are ideas about choosing postmarital residence related to increased population or increased agricultural production? Are changes in subsistence strategy always the result of external (environmental) perturbations or can they be the consequence of the working out of the internal logic of an ideational system? And so on. But this more sophisticated model of culture raises formidable—perhaps intractible—problems that have lain dormant in archaeology. Some of the questions posed above are obviously very difficult for archaeologists to answer, for instance. As we will learn in Part Three, the culture concept may well represent an insurmountable barrier to the realization of an explicitly scientific archaeology as presently envisioned.

The Systems Approach

Since sociocultural systems can be treated as if they are cybernetic systems, anthropological archaeologists are able to employ the analytical framework associated with the systems approach. As we know by now, some archaeologists claim that the systems approach is the theoretical orientation that will liberate anthropological archaeology from the fetters of a "thing" orientation and make it respectable among the social sciences. However, the systems approach comes encumbered with a set of metaphysical assumptions that raises further problems for the anthropological archaeologist. For example, the world is viewed as a complex living system in which individuals, social groups, and institutions are dynamically interrelated actors involved in continuing processes of decision making. This implies that the nature, purpose, and meaning of any actor or action can only be understood in relation to a field of forces involving other actors and actions.

These assumptions imply other well-known statements of system theory, such as "The whole is greater than the sum of its parts"; "Systems exist as organized sets of relationships that 'behave' to perform some function"; and "Changes in one subsystem will cause changes in other subsystems." Since the systems approach is one of the major pillars holding up the foundation of anthropological archaeology, it is germane to ask, What is a system? What is the systems approach? Perhaps most fundamentally, what are the potentialities and limitations of the approach in anthropological archaeology?

One definition of a system is "a set of units with relationships among them. The word 'set' implies that the units have common properties. The state of each unit is constrained by, conditioned by, or dependent on the state of other units" (Miller 1965:200). According to this definition, systems are

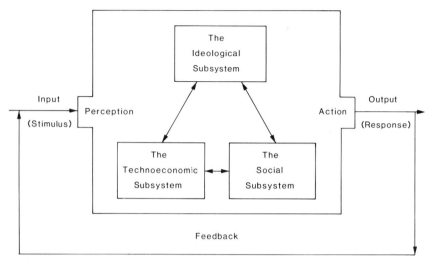

Figure 1.3   A simple system with feedback.

composed of units and relations (figure 1.3). The units form the structure of the system, and the relations are the processes that coordinate the units to make the system an organized integral whole that, because of its possession of organization, is greater than the sum of its parts. These interunit organizing relationships often act indirectly through chains of relationships that must be untangled by careful investigation. Units such as technology and religion that appear unrelated superficially actually influence each other in often subtle ways in many societies. Since the state of each unit in a system is constrained by, conditioned by, or dependent on the state of other units in the system, the relationships are causal, functional, or normative.

Systems can come in any size or degree of complexity. For example, a plant cell, a supermarket, the United States economy, and the universe have all been profitably regarded as systems. Every one of these systems can also be thought of as being composed of increasingly smaller and less complex systems on the one hand and of being a component of increasingly larger and more complex systems on the other. As Beer has stressed:

> The universe seems to be made up of sets of systems, each contained within one somewhat bigger, like a set of hollow building blocks. Just as it is always possible to expand the system to a scope of wider perspective, it is also possible to cut down the system to a smaller version. (1959:10)

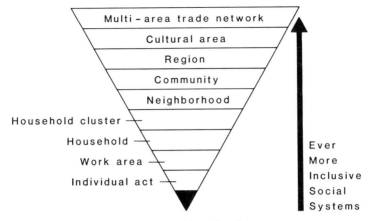

Figure 1.4 Hierarchies of social systems.

In archaeology, a household and a neighborhood are smaller level systems within a sociocultural system that in turn is a component of regional and continental systems (figure 1.4).

A primary problem of the systems approach is abstracting systems from reality. In anthropology this problem has usually been resolved in terms of function or purpose; units of reality that interact to produce a particular end product are definable as systems. As a result, the relationships between the units have tended to be conceptualized as input-output or role-function linkages. For example, a subsistence system may be defined as those units or subsystems of a system required to produce food. This system would include demand, plant and animal resources, technology, transportation, exchange, and labor. In general, systems are conceptualized in terms of the roles necessary for the performance of some function.

Once the systems approach is defined, attention focuses on changes in a system's variables, with variable being "any of the system's properties that can be measured, such as the number, size, spatial arrangement or rates of change of the units in the set" (Miller 1965:203). In the subsistence example, the size, sexual composition, and permanence of procurement units may be chosen for study. These would be explained in terms of the spatial attributes and other properties of the subsystems of the subsistence system: how much food is procured, and where and when, obviously depends on spatial and temporal variations in the demand for food, in its accessibility (which is in turn partially dependent on technology), in the shape and capacity of the transport system available to the procurement units, in the initiative of the procurers, and in the supply of labor.

This set of roles necessary to explain the variables of the subsistence subsystem is termed the environment of that subsystem, and the values assumed by the variables in which the states of these environmental subsystems are expressed are termed the parameters of the system. These latter variables are distinct from the variables of size, sexual composition, and permanence of procurement units that are the focus of interest. The parameters are usually largely dependent on factors operating outside the system itself. The object of the exercise is to define a set of units and the functional relationships between them so that the values of certain attributes of one of that set of units, termed variables, can be "explained" by the values that are independently assumed by attributes of the other units, termed parameters. This requires that *all* relevant parameters be included, that *all* relevant roles be identified, and that the attributes of those roles that affect the variables be evaluated. The system must be analytically closed so that the values of variables and parameters (the state of the system) at any one instant can be represented as a single valued function of the initial state of the system and the time coordinate. This is often accomplished by closing an analysis around the conjoint system of a set of variables and the parameters of its environment.

The study of the structure of the functional linkages of a system is called synchronic analysis. Diachronic analysis, on the other hand, is concerned with the mechanisms rather than the structural end products of changing subsystem relationships. It attempts to trace the origins of particular elements of the system and their interrelations and then follow the evolution of the way they function, cutting across a successive series of synchronic pictures of the systems. The central concept in both of these forms of analysis is that of process. Simply stated, the concept of process contains the idea of a flow of events, happenings. A particular type of process, such as diffusion, refers to a repetitive pattern of similarly organized flows of matter, energy, or information. In the process metaphysics that underlies the systems approach, the universe is regarded as made up of "things" in complex hierarchies of smaller and larger flow patterns. "Things" are self-maintaining or self-repeating features of the flow with a certain invariance, even though matter, energy, and information are continually flowing through them. Examples are a city, the shapes of clouds, and the flame of a candle. In process philosophy, objects have become systems of interacting, interpenetrating part-processes and systems relativistic, processual objects.

The sets of relationships between events or decisions that are generated by processes are called structures or patterns. They can be static three-dimensional configurations such as the spatial arrangement of artifacts in a site, a more or less stable structure moving through time (like a swarm of bees or the oscillating state of a sociocultural system), or the gradual systematic elaboration of a settlement system. Processes such as feedback, adaptation, and adjustment operate to stablize and preserve systems like these or to change, elaborate, or dissolve them. Today processes such as invention, adjustment to changes in the natural environment, the spread of ideas, population crowding, and residence practices are generally thought to provide adequate explanations of the phenomena archaeologists study. The task of the contemporary archaeologist is to identify the processes (the flows) that have formed and transformed the patterns they isolate in the archaeological record and infer to have existed in past sociocultural systems.

The systems approach is not devoid of fundamental limitations and problems. In applying the systems approach, archaeologists must grapple with problems raised by this approach's emphasis on organization, complexity, and analytical closure, by the numerousness of parameters that must be included in an analysis of any set of variables, and by the multidirectional and often direct, yet ordered, links between parameters and variables. Let us consider the implications for archaeological research of a few of these problems.

The Problem of Closure. The problem of realistically closing the systems we wish to study in science is by no means easy to resolve. This problem is particularly acute in archaeology, where most of the systems that are isolated are spatial assemblages. Among the questionable assumptions of the regional approach that underlies many of these studies are (1) that the degree of interaction in a system is related to spatial proximity; (2) that the interactions that are relevant to any given problem are spatially discrete; and (3) that the system and its environment of parameters can be closed within the same spatial boundary. As Gouldner has noted, "The notion of interdependence, so crucial to the concept of a system, needs to be taken as problematical rather than given if a systems model adequate to the analysis of social behavior is to be developed" (1967:155). One of the basic research problems of the systems approach is the identification of degrees of "system-ness" or "entitation" (Buckley 1967:42); in general, realistic systems cannot be isolated by arbitrary a priori definitions. Archaeologists cannot simply assume the existence of a system or that the phenomena they are interested in are a part of it. The qualitative recognition of the important systems of a people or a field of study is prior to and far more important than their measurement.

The Problem of Systems Duality. All social systems contain "things" and "images of things" (Miller 1965). The former are linked by and articulated around flows of matter and energy, and the latter by flows of information. In the earlier discussion of the culture concept, "things" was equated with sociocultural system and "images of things" with culture. An archaeologist applying the systems approach must still grapple with the implications of the culture concept, for an understanding of the images and information flows that inform a model of a social system is fundamental to the understanding of the behavior of that model. For example, the perceived environment is a concept entirely separated from the real environment yet related to the real environment and of fundamental importance in understanding a people's adjustments to that environment.

The Problem of General Theory. The models of systems theory are working models rather than abstract models. Such models are not primarily aimed at the formulation of generally applicable theory. They "are used to make us more aware, as we examine specific societies at specific times, of the links by which they are tied together" (Mills 1967:180). Systems theory and the systems approach are not to be confused with general systems theory, which is concerned with attempts to derive deductively theories that transcend empirical reality. General systems theory is concerned with "formal theoretical statements of the properties of different types of system [with] the emphasis . . . on theories of systems rather than the systems themselves" (Conacher 1969:157). Therefore, the systems approach will only contribute indirectly to the formulation of the general theories that many anthropological archaeologists see as the central objective of their view of archaeology.

The Numerousness of Variables, Parameters, and Linkages. As mentioned earlier, the systems approach requires that all relevant variables, parameters, and linkages of a system be identified and included, that all relevant roles be identified, and that the attributes of those roles that affect the variables be evaluated. For this reason, the successive development of systems models nearly always involves an elaboration of variables, parameters, and linkages relevant to a particular situation.

Problems with Functionalism. The systems concept is essentially functional. But much that is actually done in archaeology is not concerned with functioning systems but with the artifacts of systems, with the purely formal study of the distribution of artifacts, sites, land forms, and so on. Although "living systems create and live among their artifacts" (Miller 1965:223), artifacts are not, of themselves, systems. Thus, as long as archaeology is primarily concerned with assemblages of artifacts and their distributions, it is difficult to see how a systems approach can be realistically adopted. Only when archaeologists become concerned with the explicit study of the functioning of the artifacts and other components of past sociocultural systems is a systems approach relevant. In other words, the systems concept is irrelevant to a large and flourishing component of archaeology. Besides this problem, there are other fundamental difficulties with functionalism that are not limited to the systems approach alone.

Functionalism

As Jarvie (1965, 1967) has stressed, functionalism in anthropology is both a method of studying societies and a theory about how societies work. In our earlier introduction to structural-functionalism, this approach was defined as a set of assumptions about sociocultural systems. In sociocultural systems, every unit and relation helps maintain the cohesiveness and integrity of the whole system, while the whole functions to supply the biological needs of individual human beings. This view raises the basic research question, What is the function of, for example, a cultural practice or an institution? It has led to assertions that certain traits (say a certain population size) will be associated with certain other traits (such as a certain form of economic structure) because they "function" effectively together; they help form a cohesive, integral, and adaptively effective sociocultural system. Functionalism has been criticized from several directions, however. The harshest criticisms have claimed that functionalism provides unsatisfactory explanations and a too restrictive view of the nature and working of sociocultural systems.

As a method, functionalism explains social events and institutions by specifying the function they perform in a society. The explanatory adequacy of this approach is based on many of the theoretical assumptions about the way societies work that we have reviewed above. But are functional explanations satisfactory or even valid explanations? If one adopts the covering-law model of explanation, as many anthropological archaeologists have, in which the explanandum (that which is to be explained) is deductively derivable from statements of theory and statements of fact (the explanans), then functional explanation does not satisfy the requirements of a nontrivial, scientific explanation. Although the covering-law model of explanation is considered more fully in chapter 3, a simple example will serve our purpose here. Let us consider the problem, Why did the Dakota harvest wild rice? As premises in the explanans we might maintain that:

(L_1) People in all societies must have sustenance.
(C_1) The only way to do so in Dakota society was by harvesting wild rice.

The conclusion logically follows that

(E) The Dakota harvested wild rice.

While the logical form of this explanation is valid, the initial condition (C_1) is obviously false. Nevertheless, the word *only* must appear in C_1 or the conclusion will not be logically valid. If harvesting wild rice is only one possible way of obtaining sustenance among the Dakota, we have not explained why the Dakota chose wild rice harvesting rather than some other subsistence practice. Of course, the strength of this argument depends on one's view of what constitutes a valid or satisfactory explanation.

A second body of criticism has been directed at many of the assumptions that underlie the functionalist view of how societies work and at the apparent inability of functionalism to explain social change. For instance, functionalism conceives of societies as coherent and consistent wholes. By embracing harmony, however, it ignores conflict and dysfunction. Even a quick glance at the morning newspaper will cast doubt on this harmonious view of society. Functionalism implies that societies are goal-directed, that they have a teleological character. Finally, "functions" are often the unintended consequence of human actions rather than the result of purposal deliberation. Although an understanding of these side effects contributes to our understanding and explanation of how a society as a whole works, it does not explain the specific institutions that we are studying.

How, then, are we to regard such assumptions as "A function exists for every action and institution" and "Past societies contain no nonfunctional elements"? The first statement is an unfalsifiable, metaphysical assertion, while the second is falsifiable but almost certainly false. If functionalism is taken to be a theory about the actual nature of societies, as stated it is clearly false. Why, then, does functionalism continue to have a strong appeal in anthropological archaeology?

Positivism

Positivism has often been regarded as the leading movement in western philosophy in the first half of the twentieth century. However, the mood of the philosophy of science has been definitely antipositivist since the early 1960s. The debates involved in the demise of positivism have been complex. However, the direction of the criticisms of positivism can be illustrated by briefly reviewing the attacks on two of its most basic tenets, the belief in a rock-hard observational base and the assumption of the methodological unity of the sciences.

Auguste Comte, who introduced the term *positivism*, meant by *positive* something physical or observable rather than something speculative or metaphysical. According to positivists, to be meaningful, scientific terms, sentences, and theories had to be grounded in the rock-hard observational base—in facts. This assumption of a theory-neutral, independent, observational base was most severely criticized by antipositivists. Since their arguments are developed more fully in chapters 2 and 11, it simply can be stated here that antipositivists rejected the assumption of the theory-neutrality of observation and with it a realm of uninterpreted basic facts. This conclusion, if sound, questions the very possibility of an objective, neutral, observationally controlled science of archaeology. For instance, if the language of science is laden with anthropomorphisms and metaphors, what are facts? If the dichotomy between facts and theories can no longer be maintained, and if knowledge is conceptualized, and in this sense subjective, in what sense are tests meaningfully objective? If reality is unknowable, what role does the concept of empirical test play in contemporary science?

These criticisms eventually led to criticism of the deductive conception of science advocated by leading positivists and adopted by many anthropological archaeologists. Antipositivists were particularly critical of the covering-law model of explanation and the idea of a logic of science. With the demise of the positivist conception of science, the very thesis of the unity of science came under attack, too. Some critics maintained that the logic of the social sciences must be different, because of the element of human consciousness, from the logic of the natural sciences. Others have sought to maintain a general conception of social science as an objective, rational inquiry that aims at true explanatory and predictive knowledge of an external reality without being positivist (Thomas 1979). For all of these reasons, anthropological archaeologists are being forced to reformulate their conception of the scientific enterprise.

The Plan and Content of the Book

Anthropological Archaeology is arranged in a logical order, proceeding from a discussion of general methods and methodology in Part One, to the analysis and interpretation of sociocultural systems and their change in Part Two, to an examination of the potential and feasibility of general theory in anthropological archaeology in Part Three. Throughout, emphasis is placed on the emerging conception of anthropological archaeology as the study of past dynamic sociocultural systems. Each chapter includes a selection of further readings, much of it more advanced than the material contained in the book.

The examples in each chapter have been chosen with several criteria in mind. Each is intended to be a clear example of some principle, or set of principles, concerning the subject matter of the chapter. Each is intended to be interesting to read and understandable to the nonspecialist; as a result, more recent and often more advanced examples have not always been chosen. Finally, the examples were chosen to reflect my own interests, which include prehistoric archaeology, Europe and North America, the history of ideas, and the philosophy of social science.

If a middle-level text of this nature has one fundamental goal, it is to start the reader grappling with the methodological and substantive problems of a discipline or school of thought. This chapter has introduced some basic problems in anthropological archaeology. Still other problems exist with such concepts as intention, measurement, general theory, cultural ecology, and cultural materialism. Few if any of these problems are resolved here. I hope that the reader will begin to lose the image presented by introductory texts that anthropological archaeology is a trouble-free approach with a bag of tricks that is inexorably leading to truths denied an earlier generation of archaeologists. Like all disciplines, archaeology is dynamic rather than static. Archaeologists, as mentioned earlier, are constantly exploring new approaches to the archaeological record and assessing their more traditional methods and techniques. It is a feel for the excitement of this dynamic mode of inquiry that I hope to present here.

Summary

Chapter 1 presents a current definition of the anthropological approach to archaeology, introducing some methodological and substantive problems of the discipline while establishing it as a dynamic mode of inquiry. The approach is based on the adoption and redefinition of the culture concept. While the traditional goal of anthropology has been to describe cultures of all human societies and to explain their differences and similarities, the particular definition of culture affects how this task is perceived, what information is collected, and how it is ordered and interpreted. Social and cultural anthropologists have viewed cultures as ideational systems, but anthropological archaeologists now concentrate on human behavior and sociocultural systems, viewing artifacts not as material instantiations of norms but as social documents providing information about relations and variability within past life-ways. They undertake a systematic study of processes from a systems perspective stressing interrelationships. In the 1960s and 1970s this perspective developed as a synthesis of the views of cultural ecology, structural functionalism, and cultural materialism. Its stress on interrelationships provides organization, encourages holistic thinking, and helps generate hypotheses.

Recent concern to make the discipline more scientific and to develop a body of theory has resulted in the adoption of the deductive-nomological model of the logical empiricists (positivists), stressing the hypothetico-deductive approach, the covering-law model of explanation, unity of scientific method, relevance in research, and a belief in autonomous facts. This has in turn resulted in an increased borrowing of theories, including a trend toward the use of quantification, concern with theories and principles, and preoccupation with process and prediction.

From a research standpoint, the following assumptions are characteristic of anthropological archaeology as a general approach to the study of material remains:

1. Culture is human groups' means of adaptation and the principle organizing concept in understanding past human groups.
2. Sociocultural systems are composed of interdependent parts that cannot be understood apart from the whole.
3. Sociocultural systems are complex adaptive systems whose web of relations is primarily determined by technology and its organization.
4. Most data relevant to reconstructing extinct sociocultural systems are preserved in the archaeological record.
5. Anthropological archaeology is a social science concerned with the explanation of human behavior and sociocultural change as well as with the development of laws and general theory.

Although the distinction between culture and sociocultural systems helps sort out the elements and principles of past cultures and sharpens questions about the past, the systems approach presents problems of closure, systems duality, general theory, numerousness, and variable parameters and linkages, so that it is useful only in explicit study of the functioning of artifacts and other components of past sociocultural systems. Functionalism neither satisfies the requirement of nontrivial scientific explanation nor explains social change. The positivist approach presents problems in both its rock-hard observational base and in its assumption of a methodological unity of the sciences.

The last section presents a plan for the book's presentation of these issues in detail.

SUGGESTED READINGS

Extensive lists of readings helpful in understanding the nature and development of anthropological archaeology can be found in W. Rathje and M. Schiffer's *Archaeology* (New York: Harcourt Brace Jovanovich, 1982), M. Joukowsky's *A Complete Manual of Field Archaeology* (Englewood Cliffs, N. J.: Prentice-Hall, 1980), R. Sharer and W. Ashmore's *Fundamentals of Archaeology* (Menlo Park, Calif.: Benjamin/Cummings, 1979), and F. Hole and R. Heizer's *An Introduction to Prehistoric Archeology* (New York: Holt, Rinehart and Winston, 1973). Among the journals that publish articles with an anthropological archaeology perspective are *American Antiquity, American Anthropologist, Anthropological Archaeology, Antiquity, Current Anthropology, Journal of Field Archaeology,* and *World Archaeology;* a list of other archaeological journals can be found in M. Joukowsky's *A Complete Manual of Field Archaeology* (Englewood Cliffs, N.J., Prentice-Hall, 1980), pp. 544–546.

There are many different views of anthropological archaeology. Some of these views and several critiques are:

Bayard, D. T. 1969. Science, theory, and reality in the "New Archaeology." *American Antiquity* 34:376–384.

Binford, L. R. 1972. *An Archaeological Perspective.* New York: Seminar Press.

——1983. *Working at Archaeology.* New York: Academic Press.

Binford, L. R., ed. 1977. *For Theory Building in Archaeology.* New York: Academic Press.

Binford, S. R. and L. R. Binford, eds. 1968. *New Perspectives in Archeology.* Chicago: Aldine.

Deetz, J. 1970. Archeology as a social science. *Bulletin of the American Anthropological Association* 3:115–125.

Dumond, D. 1978. Science in archaeology: The saints go marching in. *American Antiquity* 42:330–349.

Dunnell, R. 1979. Trends in current americanist archaeology. *American Journal of Archaeology* 83–84:437–449.

Flannery, K. V. 1967. Culture history v. cultural process: A debate in American archaeology. *Scientific American* 217:119–122.

——1973. Archeology with a capital "S." In C. Redman, ed., *Research and Theory in Current Archeology,* pp. 47–53. New York: Wiley.

Flannery, K. V. ed. 1976. *The Early Mesoamerican Village.* New York: Academic Press.
——1982. The golden marshalltown: A parable for the archaeology of the 1980's. *American Anthropologist* 84:265–278.

Gumerman, G. and D. Phillips, Jr. 1978. Archaeology beyond anthropology. *American Antiquity* 43:184–191.

Hole, F. and R. Heizer. 1973. *An Introduction to Prehistoric Archeology.* New York: Holt, Rinehart and Winston.

Johnson, L. 1972. Problems in "avant garde" archaeology. *American Anthropologist* 74:366–377.

Klejn, L. 1973. Marxism, the systemic approach, and archaeology. In C. Renfrew, ed., *The Explanation of Culture Change,* pp. 691–710. London: Duckworth.

Knudson, S. 1978. *Culture in Retrospect: An Introduction to Archaeology.* Chicago: Rand McNally.

Kushner, G. 1970. A consideration of some processual designs for archaeology as anthropology. *American Antiquity* 35:125–132.

Leone, M., ed. 1972. *Contemporary Archaeology.* Carbondale and Edwardsville: Southern Illinois University Press.

Longacre, W. 1970. Current thinking in American archaeology. *Bulletin of the American Anthropological Association* 3:126–138. Washington, D.C.

——1973. Current directions in southwestern archaeology. In B. Siegel, ed., *Annual Review of Anthropology* 2:201–219. Palo Alto, Calif.: Annual Reviews.

Martin, P. 1971. The revolution in archaeology. *American Antiquity* 36:1–8.

Rathje, W. and M. Schiffer. 1982. *Archaeology.* New York: Harcourt Brace Jovanovich.

Redman, C., ed. 1973. *Research and Theory in Current Archeology.* New York: Wiley.

Redman, C., M. Berman, E. Curtin, W. Langhorne, N. Versaggi, and J. Wanser, eds. 1978. *Social Archeology: Beyond Subsistence and Dating.* New York: Academic Press.

Salmon, M. 1976. "Deductive" vs "Inductive" archaeology. *American Antiquity* 41:376–381.

——1978. What can systems theory do for archaeology? *American Antiquity* 43:174–183.

Schiffer, M. 1978. Taking the pulse of method and theory in American archaeology. *American Antiquity* 43:153–158.

Sharer, R. and W. Ashmore. 1979. *Fundamentals of Archaeology.* Menlo Park, Calif., Benjamin/Cummings.

Spaulding, A. 1973. Archeology in the active voice: The new anthropology. In C. Redman, ed., *Research and Theory in Current Archeology,* pp. 337–354. New York: Wiley.

Sterud, E. 1978. Changing aims of americanist archaeology: A citations analysis of American Antiquity—1945–1975. *American Antiquity* 43:294–302.

Thomas, D. H. 1979. *Archaeology.* New York: Holt, Rinehart and Winston.

Watson, P. J., S. Leblanc, and C. Redman. 1971. *Explanation in Archeology: An Explicitly Scientific Approach.* New York: Columbia University Press.

Woodall, J. N. 1972. *An Introduction to Modern Archeology.* Cambridge, Mass.: Skenkman.

PART ONE

Background

The goal of any science is the investigation, understanding, and explanation of sets of empirical phenomena, such as the movement of the planets, patterned human behavior, and the spatial distribution of artifacts. If archaeology is ever to become a science, its repertoire of research tools must involve more than description, classification, and analysis. These processes by themselves cannot explain empirical phenomena. Other, interpretive, processes are also necessary. At present, the best available method for bringing together conjectures and ordered observations—ideas and facts—and testing how well they correspond is the scientific method. Science is best characterized by the critical attitude, the doubting and testing of knowledge, that results from this procedure. This procedure, too, accounts for the phenomenal success of science as a system of knowing.

The two main goals of the scientific method in archaeology are the accumulation of knowledge about past humans and the critical evaluation of this knowledge against new sources of relevant data. However, achieving these goals is not a simple and straightforward task. Contemporary archaeologists do not agree among themselves on a number of major issues that concern the scientific method and the manner in which it can be most effectively employed in archaeology. Among the contested issues are: Should the scientific method be initiated with observations of artifacts or with conjectures about them? How are archaeological facts best explained? Should archaeological research be directed toward historical reconstruction or social science studies? What is archaeological knowledge and how does it accumulate?

Chapters 2 through 4 explore possible answers to these and related questions. Chapter 2 introduces a view of the scientific method and the major phases of the cycle of science. Chapter 3 discusses strategies of research; these strategies concern choices that must be made between different types of investigations, different procedures for explaining and reasoning to hypotheses, and different points of view about nature, human beings, society, and culture. The modeling process, which is the focus of Part Two, is reviewed in chapter 4.

Part One is a short guide to many of the general problems of doing anthropological archaeology. It presents a framework for thinking about what is being done, why it is being done, and how what is being done fits in with other research in archaeology. The issues reviewed in the background chapters (and in chapter 11) are basic issues about anthropological archaeology as a system of knowing and not about specific methods and theories, which are the subject matter of Part Two and chapters 9 and 10.

CHAPTER TWO

The Cycle of Science

I will define a science as a community of scholars who share an approach to and an interest in a common subject matter. In general terms the goals of a scientific community are to describe, to predict, and to explain the properties of their commonly shared subject matter. Of course, the approach they share is the scientific method. This definition of science suggests that the concept of scientific method is unproblematic. Unfortunately, or fortunately, depending on your view, there is not at present a recognizable body of principles that constitute a universally applicable scientific method. Science means different things to different people. In fact, Paul Feyerabend (1975), a philosopher of science, maintains that the only clear principle in science today is "anything goes."

Although science and the scientific method remain ambiguous concepts, and *the* scientific method apparently does not exist, the main characteristics of the method can be instructively introduced by viewing it as a continuous, self-correcting, learning process. This ideal meaning is being referred to when the concept of scientific method is used in part one. This ideal framework will allow me to present a number of methodological issues and problems that are relevant to the archaeological enterprise today.

Phases of Research

The scientific method is like a cyclical puzzle-solving game. In anthropological archaeology the goal of the game is an ever deeper understanding of the culture and sociocultural systems of past human beings. The game of

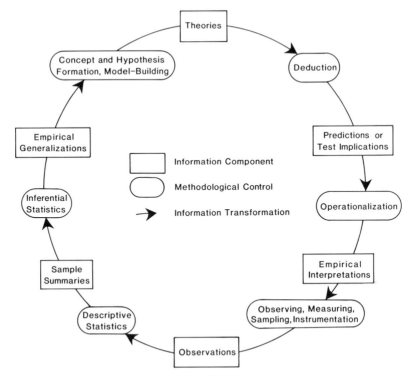

Figure 2.1   A schematic diagram of an idealized version of the cycle of science.

science is played by moving clockwise around the research cycle (figure 2.1). Like chess, science has pieces that can be manipulated. These pieces are observations, sample summaries, empirical generalizations, theories, predictions, and empirical interpretations (Groot 1969; Wallace 1971). These six pieces, which are represented by solid-line rectangles in figure 2.1, are *information components*. Like chess, rules and general guidelines exist for the proper movement of the pieces. In science these rules and general guidelines are called *methods*. Methods, such as defining, measuring, modeling, and sampling, transform one information component into another. The solid-line ovals in figure 2.1 indicate the main methods that control the course of the game of science. The scientific method consists, then, in the cyclical interplay between abstract notions and observable phenomena. In archaeology, information transformations typically link observations about the archaeological record to statements of generality about the universe to which the observational data are samples and, ultimately, to statements of extreme generality about systemic contexts.

Since the scientific method is cyclical, the process can be entered at any phase. Most anthropological archaeologists would begin a discussion of the cycle of science with theories or predictions. There are good reasons, nonetheless, for beginning with observations: observations are the boundary conditions of our body of beliefs; observations inject new information into the cycle of science; observations serve as tests of predictions; many archaeological research projects are initiated by making new observations on recently excavated material or existing collections; and the basic purpose of most research in archaeology is to account for the content and spatial variation of archaeological sites. One could even evoke authority and quote philosophers of science to support this choice. For instance, Norwood Russell Hanson claims that scientists "do not start from hypothesis: they start from data" (1958:70), and Quine and Ullian state with a metaphorical flair that "observation is the tug that tows the ship of theory" (1970:29). But the main reason for discussing observables first is to emphasize the gaping logical discontinuity that exists between recorded observations and their integration into theories. The belief in the existence of such a continuity once led in the narrow empiricist conception of science to the disparagement of conjecture and to the stifling of scientific inquiry. As we will see, controlled conjecture is an essential and creative component of the cycle of science.

Transforming Observations to Empirical Generalizations

If the goal of science is the investigation, understanding, and explanation of sets of empirical phenomena, a fundamental, unavoidable question is, What is a set of phenomena? For our purposes, it is sufficient to state that phenomena are things and events "out there" that we can observe. What archaeologists actually analyze and interpet are observations on these phenomena. What, then, we might ask, are observations? Are they independent objective facts about these phenomena as narrow empiricists once assumed or are they something less certain and more complex?

Since all information components in the cycle of science are interdependent, observations cannot be isolated, objective facts about the world. Like other information components, they are partly empirically determined and partly determined by our concepts, and thus by our perceptions of the phenomena we study. The implications of this statement have had a profound impact on twentieth-century conceptions of science. Since observations are statements formulated against a background of cultural expectations and archaeological traditions, theories in archaeology must be consistent with *assertions* about observations rather than with facts. What does this mean?

Phenomenal experiences (sights, sounds, smells, tastes, touches) are given meaning by conceptual frameworks like languages and theories. Since we learn many of these frameworks as small children, we tend to unquestionably accept them: we either forget or do not know that they are only ideas or notions about the world and its content. But even common observations such as length, volume, weight, and hardness must be interpreted by theories of measurement (Ellis 1968). Observations in archaeology, as in all sciences, are *interpreted* perceptual experiences; they are theory-laden, for they are always preceded by something theoretical, by some system of expectations (Feyerabend 1975). Idus Murphree's account (1961) of how changes in the concepts of progress and culture among early anthropologists eventually resulted in their seeing behavioral activities and artifacts in new and different ways in an interesting example of this process in action.

In theory, archaeologists are always able to make an infinite number of observations on any collection of artifacts. Observations, however, unlike perceptual experiences, are not immediately given. While archaeologists experience or are bombarded by perceptions, they must *make* observations. It should be obvious, too, that it is impossible to interpret and record every perceptual experience; the scale and complexity of the archaeological record are too large. Like other scientists, archaeologists must choose what observations they would like to make, what perceptions they would like to interpret. Clearly, what archaeologists do observe is always determined in part by an idea, no matter how vague and tentative, about what things are worth observing and what kinds of observations are worth making. In turn these ideas condition the methods appropriate for making observations. For instance, they determine whether a hand lens, a telescope, a caliper, or a weight scale is an appropriate observational device.

Ideally, observational decisions should be decided by the implications of tentative solutions to interesting problems. More commonly, the traditional units of observation learned from books and university training courses are adopted. Even in this case, however, some usually implicit idea or hypothesis still guides the selection of observations.

Observing and Measuring. Let us look more closely at observing and the concept of measurement. A sensible place to begin is with the basic question, What are data (singular, datum)? Data are not chairs, tables, artifacts, and archaeological sites, as some people believe. Data are observations that are made on these objects and on events by measuring their properties. In archaeology, data include such varied characteristics as name, number, length, degree, intensity, and distance to or from something else. Objects include artifacts, sites, social groups, human biological populations, and any other entity in archaeological or systemic context that can be treated as an object. Events are processes or activities, such as eating, erosion, diffusion, interaction, and conflict. What is considered an object or an event is determined by the framework and goals of a particular research project; for example, an atom or human group may be considered an object in one frame of reference and a system of interacting components in another (Blaut 1962).

In archaeology, observing is the careful and deliberate search for particular kinds of data. Sometimes the recorded observations of an archaeologist are the anticipated outcome of prior hypotheses and empirical interpretations; they are in a sense an output of the research process, an expected outcome of a well-thought-out research design. At other times, recorded observations are the result of exploratory research or do not conform to prior expectations: in these cases the process of observing is a fresh source of information, a wellspring of empirically based data that is a genuine input into the research process. For instance, unexpectedly uncovering the remains of a trading depot in an area may change the interpretation of other sites in the region and constitute a fresh input of information into a research project.

Whether they are anticipated or not, all observations are made through an instrument. Instruments involved in making observations in archaeology include calipers, chemical kits, cameras, measuring tapes, rulers, feature forms, notes, microscopes, and radiocarbon dating machines, as well as the technically unaided sensory organs—the eyes, ears, nose, tongue, and hands—of individual archaeologists. The sense impressions observed through an instrument are measured by comparing them with consciously or unconsciously recognized scales of value. This process "makes" an observation. Measurements are made by systematically comparing sense perceptions with sets of abstract symbols and by assigning one or more of these symbols to each perception or set of perceptions. Abstract symbols include words, numbers, letters, colors, and sounds. Sets of abstract symbols like these, along with the rules that govern their legitimate manipulation, form measurement scales or scales of value. *Measurement* may be simply defined as the application of a set of procedural rules for comparing sense impressions with a scale and for assigning symbols such as numbers, letters, or words to the resulting observations. In this sense the length of an artifact, its thickness, the shape of a feature, and the color of a soil stain are all observations made by comparing sense impressions with various scales. According to this interpretation, all observations in archaeology, as in all other empirically based disciplines, are measurements.

Because they are abstract, symbols that represent scale values can be manipulated in any legitimate manner permitted by the rules that govern the relationship between symbols within the scale. This possibility gives archaeologists and other scientists the opportunity to imaginatively explore the logical implications of a wide range of manipulations that are controlled and limited by relatively specific rules. We will see in subsequent chapters how archaeologists have explored imaginary worlds of the past through the manipulation of symbols.

Scaling provides the measurement standard against which sense impressions can be compared. The basic types of scales commonly used by archaeologists (the Campbell system) are the nominal, the ordinal, the interval, and the ratio. The properties of these scales differ, and it is these scalar properites that partly determine the statistical operations that can be applied to particular sets of data. These common scales underlie metric scales, color charts, weight scales, and other familiar scales that archaeologists rely upon during fieldwork and laboratory analysis. Measurement scales can be composed of a limitless range of symbols: heavy–light is a scale, as are the colors of the rainbow. Measurements report the properties of objects and events in terms of scale values: they report the value of variables in terms of a stated measurement scale. Understanding the most essential mathematical properties of scales is necessary for discovering how we can actively engage in the creative process of scale building in archaeology, for the type of scale we use determines the operations (logical, mathematical, and statistical) that we can legitimately use in drawing conclusions from our data.

Scales are commonly classified according to their logico-mathematical properties, the conventionally defined rules that govern the assignment and manipulation of their symbols. The four main logico-mathematical properties that are used in classifying scales are symbolic representation, rank, distance, and a point of natural origin. All scales share the basic property of

Table 2.1 Levels of Measurement in the Campbell System

Measurement Level	Symbolic Representation	Rank	Distance	Point of Natural Origin
Nominal	X			
Ordinal	X	X		
Interval	X	X	X	
Ratio	X	X	X	X

symbolic representation; they name or represent something. Therefore, the differences between types of scales must be defined on the basis of the additional logico-mathematical properties they possess (table 2.1). The number and variety of analytic models that can be used in describing the distribution of measurements of a single property and in analyzing relationships among different properties increase with each additional logico-mathematical property a scale possesses.

The *nominal scale* simply specifies the presence of an attribute or quality. It is a scale only because it possesses the most elementary property common to all types of scales: symbolic representation. The adjective *nominal* means "in name only." The names of archaeological sites or of projectile point types within a region are examples of nominal measurements. Each site and point type has only been symbolically represented with a name. We do not know, for example, how much larger one site is compared to another or even whether one site is larger than another.

Scales are used to measure general concepts, such as color, size, and length, that are capable of being logically subdivided into smaller divisions or subclassifications. But not all of these general concepts are normally represented on the nominal scale of measurement. Smaller divisions or subclassifications of properties of objects or events may represent either qualitative or quantitative differences among the objects or events. When the differences are only qualitative, but are clearly subcategories of a more general concept (red, green, and blue for the general concept of color, for example), the set of subcategories constitutes a nominal scale. Standard statistical terminology refers to these nonquantitative divisions of the dimensions of a concept as *categories.* On the other hand, quantitative divisions that can be calibrated are called *class intervals.* These intervals may represent nominal measures if they are assigned symbols, such as A, B, and C. However, class intervals are generally measures on more complex scales where their mathematical relationships become apparent.

To demonstrate the presence or absence of an attribute or quality of an artifact, for instance, is to only begin the process of measurement and analysis. Assigning nominal measures or names to properties of artifacts or other objects and events is in general but a prelude to mathematical manipulations of values on ordinal, interval, or ratio scales.

The *ordinal scale* builds on the nominal scale by adding the property of *rank* to that of symbolic representation. As in the nominal scale, the subcategories of the dimensions of a concept have been identified and named. In addition, the subcategories can now be arranged in a *rank order* because they represent different amounts of a property. For example, small, medium, and large sites are arranged in a rank order on the basis of the property of size. In this example a quantitative property has been introduced to relate the subcategories of the general concept of size to each other along a qualitative dimension. However, ordinal scales, such as small–medium–large and rich–poor, do not indicate how much larger or smaller one site is than another or how much wealthier one household is than another.

The *interval scale* adds the property of *distance* to that of symbolic representation and rank. When using an interval scale, we know not only that the categories belong on a single dimension and in a certain rank order, we also know how far it is between one point and another on the scale. We know how much larger or smaller one site is than another or how much wealth one household has compared to another. The magnitude of these differences is known because the intervals between subcategories on an interval scale are of equal distance. For instance, an interval scale for degree of hardness (Moh's scale) ranges from 1 to 10. On this scale the same amount of hardness is represented between points 1 and 2 as between points 7 and 8, although the amount of hardness is additive in a rank order. Our calendrical system and the Fahrenheit and centigrade systems of measuring temperature are classic interval scales. As you may have noticed, these examples, like all interval scales, have an arbitrary point of origin.

The *ratio scale* adds a *point of natural origin* to the other three logico-mathematical properties of scales. A natural origin fixes the location of the zero on a scale. Unless there is a natural (as opposed to an artificial or arbitrary) point of origin that determines the location of the zero on the scale, a valid ratio (2:1, for example) cannot be established by dividing one measurement by another. When we count the number of features in our excavation units, we are using a ratio scale, for zero or no features is a point of natural origin.

In narrower definitions of measurement, measurement is distinguished from *enumeration*. Enumeration involves simply counting the number of objects or events in a certain category. Nominal data, such as the number of pottery shards in a sample that have red interiors, can be counted. But measurement more narrowly defined involves specifying the amount of any clearly defined property possessed by an object or event. In this sense, concrete objects or events can be counted but they cannot be measured. What is measured is one of their particular properties (qualities or dimensions): the *length* of a projectile point but not the projectile point itself. In narrower definitions of measurement, then, nominal data and sometimes even ordinal data are not considered measurements at all. According to these definitions, nominal and ordinal measures are qualitative data in contrast to the quantitative data provided by interval and ratio scales. As the rate of constructing mathematical models that require precisely measured data has increased in anthropological archaeology, there has been a corresponding shift from identifying qualitative data to an emphasis on acquiring quantitative data.

Once a set of observations qua measurements has been made, two kinds of description are possible: description of pattern in the sample of actual observations and description of pattern in the finite universe of which the sample is a part. Description of pattern in the sample of actual observations is summarized through the methodological controls imposed by measurement, scaling, and descriptive statistics. *Descriptive statistics* display systematic order among observations: they reduce an apparently unwieldy mass of data to manageable proportions by displaying the interrelationships between categories of data. Typical examples of descriptive statistics are the average weight of three grinding stones, the range in length of twenty projectile points, and the most common house type in a site. It is here in the cycle of science that descriptive statistics play their nearly indispensable role. Sample summary is represented by a rectangle on the lower left side of figure 2.1. (Of course it is the symbols that represent individual observations that are compared, classified, and manipulated according to the rules of particular scaling systems. Observations themselves cannot be added, correlated, or listed as items in tables.)

Sample summaries or descriptions often form the bulk of archaeological reports. But a summary of a sample of observations is not a real information transformation. The information contained in a sample summary is merely a set of observations displayed in a more comprehensible and digestible manner. *How* samples are summarized is largely determined by specific tests of explanatory hypotheses or, less effectively, by traditional practices in archaeology.

The second kind of description, the description of pattern in the finite universe of which a sample is a part, is an information transformation. During this transformation, a conceptual leap is made to a new kind of information. This information consists of claims about finite universes that are incompletely known. These isolated descriptive statements, which are called *empirical generalizations,* are made through the process of induction to a denumerable set called a population from a smaller randomly selected set called a sample. The process expands sample descriptions to generalizations. Some empirical generalizations are inferences (reasoned guesses) about single properties of classes or types of artifacts or features. Examples include the *average* weight, the *range* in length, and the *number* of a class or type of artifact in an incompletely known universe, such as a partially excavated site. An even more useful type of empirical generalization is a statement about associations between properties of artifacts, features, sites, and ecofacts. The statement that a consistently high correlation between stone scraping tools and fish bones in a series of samples is also descriptive of the population from which they were drawn is an example.

Empirical generalizations are about the objective patterns that exist in populations of artifacts, settlements, houses, events, and so on. Inspired guesses are often made about the form of these patterns. Nonetheless, the most reliable method available for making accurate inferences to population patterns is statistical inference. *Statistical inference* is a process of reasoning from a sample description (a statistic) to a population description (a parameter) using the principles of probability. The main objective of statistical inference is to reach reasonable conclusions about finite universes when only samples are available for study. These inferential leaps to new kinds of information are controlled by the process of probability sampling, a process designed to determine the chance of error occurring in making inferences from a sample to a universe once a set of observations has been made. (One might say that the purpose of sampling procedures is to *systematically* establish relationships by empirical generalization.) The fundamental importance of probability sampling in inferential statistics is another example of the interplay of phases of the cycle of science; probability sampling is a methodological control involved in the transformation of empirical interpretations to observations.

Building Theories

Human curiosity may well be the inspiration for the very existence of archaeology. Throughout recorded history people have attempted to make sense of megaliths, artifacts, archaic human skeletons, and the bones of extinct animal species. As often as not these interpretations now seem bizarre. For example, in the eighteenth century, artifacts were identified as thunderbolts and fairies' darts; the skeletal fragments of archaic humans were considered the remains of misshapen or diseased individuals; and the massive bones of extinct megafauna were considered the remnants of escaped circus elephants (Daniel 1975). As bizarre as these answers seem, each was an attempt to make sense of the unfamiliar, the unknown, by placing it within the context of the familiar.

Conjectures about archaic human bones or artifacts—and their relationships—are called identities, explanatory hypotheses, culture histories, or scientific theories, depending on their complexity and purpose. In figure 2.1 this entire class of theoretical entities (along with concepts) is simply called theory for short. Theories in this sense are statements that interpret observations by using abstract terms and relationships.

One type of theory is an *identity*. The statement "This is a projectile point" interprets a stone artifact by identifying it with a class of tools called projectile points. The artifact is made sense of or accounted for by assigning it to a class of familiar tools and labeling it with the abstract universally applicable term *projectile point*. When we reason as in this example that A is a B or that A's are B we are making a statement of identity. Other statements are relational; they connect two or more abstract notions. For instance, after reviewing the literature on Bronze Age sites in southern Europe, we might conclude that "villages become more nucleated as the intensity of warfare increases." This statement connects two abstract notions, degree of village nucleation and intensity of warfare. Statements that relate two or more abstract notions are called *explanatory hypotheses*. In archaeology, explanatory hypotheses are generally post facto hypotheses, hypotheses about things and activities as they existed or occurred in the past.

Where do the ideas for identities and hypotheses come from? Are they just wild guesses or are they the logical outcome of some process of thought (Caws 1969)? Some philosophers, called rationalists, maintained that absolutely certain knowledge can be found through reason alone. Perhaps the best known of these philosophers are Plato, René Descartes, Aristotle, and Saint Augustine. The claims of the rationalists met with severe objections in the modern age, and today theories of knowledge tend to be grounded in principle to the empirical world of sense impressions (Montague 1925). Early empiricists such as Francis Bacon tried to develop systems of logic through which one could move with logical certainty from observations to theories. These attempts, too, have failed. Logical certainty does not exist in the transformation of empirical information components to theoretical ones because theoretical concepts cannot be directly understood from experience alone. Theoretical concepts are familiar terms used to think about the empirical assertions, the observations and generalizations, that we wish to explain and account for. They are more abstract and have greater scope than empirical terms, however: they refer to universals or to whole classes of abstract ideas or notions. Atom, force, gravity, culture, and society are abstract symbolic representations of a property or properties of classes of things or events. For this and other reasons, there is still no known logical machinery that links observations with theories with logical certainty. Theories *are* new kinds of abstract information. Their entry into the cycle of science must be controlled by the principles of concept formation, model building, and other appropriate methods.

If theoretical terms and hypotheses cannot be directly apprehended from experience alone, where do they come from? Albert Einstein (1934:15) thought that they were "free inventions of the human intellect." Others have also argued that theory does not result from empirical generalization (Willer and Willer 1973). In general these free inventions are borrowed from existing knowledge through the process of *inductive analogical argument* or through what the American philosopher Charles Peirce (1932 7:137) called *abduction*. Thought processes like abduction that connect observations with ideas or ideas with observations have also been called *abstractive* (Willer and Willer 1973). Although I am skirting the really tough issue of where new concepts come from, it is sufficient to know that empirical assertions are generally accounted for in archaeology by subsuming them under such familiar ideas as subsistence, population pressure, axe, scraper, and community, or such hypotheses as "Towns of similar size and location are found at similar distances apart" (the latter being a hypothesis borrowed from geography). It is here in the cycle of science that analogies and illustrative metaphors play their crucial role. Common sources of theoretical concepts and hypotheses in archaeology are sociocultural anthropology, history, the social sciences, and everyday experiences.

What is important to understand in this context is that theories are not formed by empirical categories that stand for sense impressions but by concepts that stand for ideas. The process of abstraction is not the same as the process of empirical generalization. The notion that if we somehow had all the facts about an archaeological assemblage we would be able to write an objective and scientific history of the sociocultural system that produced it is, according to this argument, a delusion. Of course, since all observations are theory-laden (and, therefore, in a sense, ideas), what is considered an idea or an observation will depend on the aim and the disciplinary context of a research problem.

In anthropological archaeology the abstract terms in identities and the relationships in hypotheses generally refer to properties and characteristics of systemic concepts, to such concepts as axe, projectile point, house, and degree of centralized political power. A shift has been made during this transformation from a focus on archaeological contexts to a focus on systemic contexts, from a discussion of sites and artifacts to a discussion of communities and tools. During this shift, models of some part of the systemic context are often formed through the process of abduction to account for the observations made on the archaeological record.

A *model* is an abstractive tool that connects theories with empirical data. The modeling process in this phase of the cycle of science is a playful, creative interlude in which processes are simulated and assumptions tried out; no commitment needs to be made to the view that *this* is what necessarily happened in the past. This process of abstraction establishes isomorphisms—correspondences—between empirical observables and theoretical unobservables. Because of the rapidly increasing awareness in archaeology of the pivotal role of models in abduction, the process of model building is discussed more extensively in chapter 4.

Culture histories and scientific theories are formed through the rigorous evaluation of models. Both scientific theories and culture histories make sense of the archaeological record by assigning significance or meaning to objects and events in archaeological context. Although both are forms of theory, their intent is markedly different. When archaeologists adopt the perspective of the historian, they endeavor to write coherent culture histories. Culture histories are about unique sequences of events, about particular peoples, cultures, or regions. They are stories of what life in a community was like or narrative accounts of specific sociocultural changes. By definition, they are bounded by the dimensions of space and time. Nonetheless, since they are intended to tell us *why* things happened as they did in the past, they are much more complex than natural history chronicles, which merely organize events in time.

Scientific theories concern general problems, such as the dynamics of sociocultural change or the movement of planets in space. The building blocks of scientific theories are universal hypotheses, which are declarative sentences unbounded by spatial or temporal restrictions. An example is "The greater the degree of group sedentism, the greater the amount of stored food." Notice that this hypothesis is truly universal: it is not restricted by any spatial or temporal qualifications. If the hypothesis is true, it should apply to any past, present, or future situation in which group sedentism increases. This would be so even if the domain of application of the hypothesis were restricted to hunter-gatherers, horticulturalists, or some other socioeconomic subcategory. Since hypotheses become laws or at least lawlike statements when they become well confirmed, scientists are generally more interested in hypotheses than in identities. And, since scientists strive to increase the scope of their knowledge, a goal of scientific research is to broaden the scope of hypotheses, to subsume an ever increasing number of classes of objects and events under the domain of a hypothesis or scientific theory.

Empirical generalizations differ from hypotheses in a number of defining characteristics. They are local, assertions about things quite close to experience, and always derived from inductive statistical reasoning. Although it is often difficult to distinguish between low-level hypotheses and empirical generalizations in some sciences, in anthropological archaeology empirical generalizations are generally about characteristics of archaeological contexts. Even this distinction is blurred in some instances, however, for empirical generalizations often have the form of a hypothesis in archaeology. For example, investigations of sites in a region may lead to the generalization $I_{AB} = P_{APB}/D_{AB}$, where P refers to site size, D to distance between sites, and I to expected relative numbers of shared items, styles, or features within the region. This statement suggests the universal hypothesis $I_{ij} = {}_iP_j/zD_{ij}$, where P refers to size of population centers, D to spatial distance between centers, and I to the degree of spatial interaction expected between any two population centers, i and j. Again, notice that scientific "laws" like this are invariant theoretical statements and not reflections of observed regularities.

Although it is often difficult for nonscientists to comprehend, science does not consist of statements about natural or sociocultural regularities. The regularities that anthropological archaeologists and other scientists can perceive are never invariant enough to justify the absolute connection of the equals sign used in theoretical statements (as we will see in chapter 11). In a sense, scientists work in ideal worlds, worlds with frictionless planes, absolute vacuums, economic people, and so on. As a result, they find it unnecessary to assume regularity in nature or in sociocultural systems. Laws are not found in the real world through the process of empirical generalization.

Scientific theories are formed by combining identities and interlinked universal hypotheses into coherent and logically consistent stories. These stories explain why certain events occur and will continue to occur in the future under certain circumstances. Like culture histories, scientific theories give meaning to facts and provide a measure against which exceptional and unusual events can be recognized. Archaeologists often begin the process of accounting for observed facts by establishing tentative hypotheses. As these hypotheses become well confirmed, they become statements of the order that may have existed in past systemic contexts. We might ask, however, why these statements hold? This is the principal question underlying the search for theory in the sciences. Scientific theories provide the justification for statements of regularities (laws) by showing that they follow logically from the theories themselves, that they are a part of a coherent pattern. Besides giving meaning to facts, theories provide a rationale, an explanation, or theoretical justification for relationships expressed in hypotheses or laws.

As in the other social sciences, scientific theories in archaeology are loosely organized and lack the rigorous structure of formal theories in the natural sciences. Chapters 10 and 11 consider what scientific theories and laws would look like in anthropological archaeology and whether their construction is a practical goal in the discipline today.

Testing Hypotheses

Every theory makes some prediction about the content of the world. For example, the identity "This is a projectile point" implies that a particular artifact was once bound to a shaft and propelled through the air when used. These two predictions are contained in the definition of *projectile point*. The hypothesis "Villages become more nucleated as the intensity of warfare increases" implies that nucleated villages will be present whenever and wherever villages and intensified warfare occur together. This prediction is a logical implication of the direct positive correlation between degree of village nucleation and intensity of warfare. Predictions are also derivable from culture histories and scientific theories. Assume, for instance, that a scientific theory consists of the two statements "The greater the degree of group sedentism, the greater the amount of stored food" and "The greater the efficiency of food production, the greater the degree of group sedentism." These two statements taken together imply the following prediction: "The greater the efficiency of food production, the greater the amount of stored food." This statement has been deduced from the theory (table 2.2).

One of the distinguishing features of anthropological archaeology in the last several decades has been the increasing incorporation of prediction of one sort or another in research designs. Predictions are derived from theories through the methodological control of deduction. In everyday theories many logically possible predictions are hidden in mazes of vague and only partially articulated hypotheses. The formalization process discussed in chapter 10 makes these hypotheses explicit and orders them in a systematic manner so that logical predictions become more readily apparent. At the same time, the deductive mode of reasoning is a check against the drawing of unwarranted statements. This source of error multiplies rapidly in importance as theories are more vaguely articulated. Like sample summaries, logical predictions are not true information transformations; predictions are already contained in the theories from which they have been deduced: they have been drawn out rather than transformed.

Table 2.2   Deductive Logic: The Syllogism

(A)		
All dogs are vertebrates	(premises)	All A are B
All vertebrates are animals		All B are C
All dogs are animals	(conclusion)	All A are C

(B)

The greater the efficiency of food production, the greater the degree of group sedentism
The greater the degree of group sedentism, the greater the amount of stored food

Therefore, the greater the efficiency of food production, the greater the amount of stored food.

Syllogisms are arguments that contain two premises and a conclusion. In A and B, above, the premises (logically) imply the conclusions. Therefore, if the premises are true, the conclusions must be true too.

How are claims to knowledge in science justified? What arguments are put forward to demonstrate the truth of theoretical statements such as "The greater the efficiency of food production, the greater the amount of stored food"? In science, knowledge claims are justified by devising confrontations between their consequences and fresh observational experiences. Many philosophers of science even maintain that scientific knowledge is defined in part by the possibility of its empirical refutation (see, for example, Popper 1969, 1970, 1972). One of the necessary characteristics of predictions in anthropological archaeology, then, is that they have test implications; that they say something about the archaeological record or its environmental context. For this reason, it is necessary to distinguish between two meanings of the word *true*. Theories in science are true (in a sense to be explained below) when their test implications are not falsified by empirical observations. These types of statements must be distinguished from logical statements that are contextually and thus necessarily true. Tautologies such as "If all neolithic societies have food production, and if this is a neolithic society, then this society has food production" are true by definition, in this case the definition of neolithic society. Here we have logical certainty without empirical utility. In science, however, we are interested in statements that have implications for the real world as we perceive it.

Predictions are often statements about the relationship between two or more ideas. When these statements are expressed in terms of correlations and associations, mathematical methods can be employed in the testing process. For example, the hypothesis "The greater the A, the greater the B" implies that it is reasonable to suppose that a significant mathematical relationship should be found between A and B. Or, if another theory implies that A and B are spatially connected, we can predict that the *expected* and *observed* distributions of A and B will be nearly identical. Statistical measures can be adopted, too, in this example to assess the goodness of fit between the expected and observed distributions. As chapter 3 will indicate, if the fit between the two distributions is reasonably snug, we can say that the hypothetical connection between A and B accounts for the distribution of whatever A and B represent in the observational world.

In archaeology, terms within test implications nearly always refer to characteristics of past sociocultural systems and human groups. Therefore, it is necessary to interpret the concepts and relationships in these statements in terms of phenomena on which observations can be made. A switch must be made during this phase of the cycle of science back to the archaeological context. This abstractive transformation raises challenging methodological and substantive problems in anthropological archaeology.

To connect abstract notions with observational data, the abstract notions must be given *empirical interpretations*. The meaning of an empirical interpretation can be more easily grasped if we think of a concept as having three parts: a name, a theoretical definition, and an operational definition. A theoretical definition gives meaning to a concept, a name labels it, and an operational definition indicates what is actually measured or observed when an instance of the concept is identified in the archaeological record. Since observations are the primary means in science of assessing the goodness of fit of a theory with the real world, all theoretical terms should ideally be given observational interpretations. As the tripartite division of a concept implies, operational definitions do not provide concepts with meaning; they are rules for empirically interpreting concepts and, therefore, ways of indirectly testing the truth or falsity of theoretical statements. Operational definitions provide the means by which the presence or absence of the things and events denoted by theoretical terms can be observationally detected or inferred. Because these things or events purportedly exist, or have some property, when the specified test conditions are carried out, the predicted results occur.

Social scientists share the names and theoretical definitions of many concepts. However, they *measure* or *operationalize* these same concepts using different operational definitions. For example, *matrilocality* is the name of a concept shared by both social anthropologists and archaeologists. One theoretical definition of the term is "postmarital residence that locates the married pair in the domiciliary group of the wife's mother." Social anthropologists can identify the practice of matrilocal residence by actually talking to married couples living in the domiciliary group of the wife's mother and asking directed questions. This direct approach is obviously not available to prehistoric archaeologists. An alternative operational definition of the term must be devised. One such definition that seems to apply to pre-European contact sites in North America is "a living floor area of the average house in a society of greater than 600 square feet" (table 2.3; Ember 1973). Another example is the concept *warfare*. A theoretical definition of warfare is "activity undertaken by a political unit to weaken or destroy another." In archaeology, "the presence of mutilated skeletons" is a simple operational definition of this term.

As the last example illustrates, operational definitions are frequently incomplete: they capture only part of the intended theoretical meaning of a

Table 2.3   Residence and Living Floor Area of Average House in Ember's
Sample 1

Patrilocal Societies	Living Floor Area (in Square Feet)	Matrilocal Societies	Living Floor Area (in Square Feet)
Aranda (Id 1, 1900)	30		
Azande (Ai 3, 1920)	42		
Aymará (Sf 2, 1940)	89		
Maori (Ij 2, 1820)	100		
Yahgan (Sg 1, 1870)	100		
Chukchee (Ec 3, 1900)	120		
Fang (Ae 3, 1910)	150		
Toda (Eg 4, 1900)	160		
Nambicuara (Si 4, 1940)	170		
Papago (Ni 2, 1930)	192		
Havasupai (Nd 3, 1880)	200		
Pukapukans (Ii 3, 1930)	210		
Tiv (Ah 3, 1920)	250		
Burusho (Ee 2, 1930)	288		
Rundi (Ae 8, 1910)	304		
Rwala (Cj 2, 1920)	500		
Lau Fijians (Ih 4, 1920)	511		
		Khasi (Ei 8, 1900)	600
		Miskito (Sa 9, 1920)	936
		Mandan (Ne 6, 1830)	962
		Tapirape (Sd 2, 1930)	972
Nootka (Nb 11, 1880)	2450		
Mean	326	Mean	868
S.D.	547	S.D.	179

SOURCE: Ember 1973, table 1. Reproduced by permission of the Society for American Archaeology from *American Antiquity* 38(2):177–181.
NOTE: Each society in the table is listed with its *Ethnographic Atlas* identification number and the zero year of the decade (as indicated in the atlas) to which our measure of floor area and the atlas rating of residence apply.

concept or relationship. Operational definitions like this are mere *indicators,* in the same manner as "the presence of exotic objects" (such as foreign flints, seashells, metals, obsidian, or amber) is merely an indicator of the presence of trade. For this reason, two or more indicators are frequently used to form a more complete empirical interpretation of a term. In our example, the indicators "defensive walls," "ditches," "towers," and "the presence of mutilated skeletons" together provide a more convincing operational definition of warfare than either one does by itself. If indicators like these are quantified, they can even be used to measure the intensity or degree of an activity besides merely denoting its presence in the past.

Moving from predictions to empirical interpretations in the cycle of science is a true information transformation. And, like the transformation from empirical generalizations to theories, it is an example of abstractive thinking: it connects concepts and relationships in theories by abstraction to empirical objects and events for at least some of their relevant scope. In this transformation two types of error are easily committed. The first is made when operational definitions measure only part of the intended meaning—the theoretical definition—of a concept. This type of error results in incomplete transformations and severely affects the testing process. Nevertheless, incomplete operational definitions are a common occurrence in archaeology for several reasons. First, operational definitions of theoretical definitions formulated by scholars working with living groups are often very difficult to conceive of in archaeology. For instance, what would be a complete operational interpretation in archaeology of such terms as *population pressure* or *degree of social interaction?* This problem has been compounded until recently by the practice in archaeology of not formulating operational definitions or of not making explicit those definitions that have been formulated. As a result, tests of predictions have rarely been directly and explicitly comparable to or additive to one another, for there has seldom been a guarantee that each was measuring the same thing.

The second type of error occurs when concepts have more than one widely used theoretical definition. Think of the many theoretical definitions of the concept *agriculture,* for example. If the definition is not made explicit, concepts having different empirical implications could be misleadingly compared as instances of the same concept. The effects of both types of error are most easily avoided or minimized by clearly stating the theoretical and operational definitions of concepts and relationships in theories.

Two Measurement Problems: Reliability and Validity. Let us look briefly at the problem of measurement error in greater detail. Methods of measurement cannot be approached uncritically. Measurement has its limitations, and it is subject to several sources of error. A familiar example is an error caused by an inaccurate measuring instrument, such as a caliper or a weight scale. A slightly less familiar example is the assignment of inappropriate symbols to nominal data. Mislabeling projectile point or other artifact types results in misleading counts. Many archaeologists are only now becoming aware of the potential magnitude of still other sources of measurement error. For instance, careful measurements of the properties of items in archaeological contexts are not necessarily meaningful measures of the properties of objects and events in systemic contexts. And inappropriate sampling techniques will almost certainly lead to inaccurate inferences about population parameters. Nearly all of these measurement errors can be studied under one of two very basic questions. These questions concern the reliability and the validity of measures.

The *reliability* of a measure is concerned with the question, Would two or more archaeologists measuring the same property on a series of objects (the length of a series of projectile points, for example) agree in their results most of the time? If they would, their procedures are reliable. The reliability of measurement procedures refers to their degree of precision, to the probability that, if repeated by the same or an independent observer, the measurement will give the same result. The smaller the range of values for a series of measurements, the more reliable or precise the measurements are. Measurements can be made more reliable by improving the instruments of measurement and in some cases by standardizing the procedures of measurement.

Making valid measures is a more subjective judgment. *Validity* is concerned with the question, Are we measuring (seeing, counting) what we think we are? The validity of a measurement is the extent to which the concrete indicators that are measured correspond to the concept archaeologists want to measure. Each of these questions, those concerned with reliability as well as with validity, should be asked of every measurement in archaeology.

Just why the validity of measurements is a methodological problem in archaeology can be more clearly grasped by separating measurements into three basic types: fundamental, derived, and fiat (Krantz et al. 1971:2). Measurements of an existing property of an object or event, such as length, height, or distance, are *fundamental measurements*. They are measures of easily observable and relatively simple general properties. *Derived measurements* are slightly more complex, for they are defined on the basis of relations between fundamental measures. A familiar example is the length-height ratio. *Fiat measurements,* or proxy measurements, as they are sometimes called, are the most complex measurements, for they are measurements of more elusive or abstract concepts, such as degree of social stratification, intensity of warfare, and extent of craft specialization (Fritz 1972). Of the three basic types of measurement, fiat measures are easily the most prone to problems of measurement validity and reliability.

Some of the problems involved in making valid and reliable fiat measures have already been illustrated with the concept of warfare. Let us consider how we might measure another concept, *socioeconomic status.* Socioeconomic status is an abstract and complex concept. We cannot simply place calipers around it and read a measure from a scale. An indirect measure is needed. An empirical interpretation can be formulated by selecting a set of characteristics whose values can be combined together into an index, which is taken to represent (by fiat) the complex abstract concept. In the case of socioeconomic status, measures are obtained by archaeologists along a number of dimensions, such as burial wealth, position within a cemetery, and degree of postpartum manipulation (see chapter 5). The status of individuals or families is then determined by arranging the combined values of the measure (the index) into a rank order.

Are these measures of socioeconomic status both valid and reliable? There are a number of reasons why there may be a low correspondence between the theoretical meaning of a concept and the values of an index designed to measure that meaning. A fairly common reason in archaeology is the ambiguous definitions of concepts. For example, determining whether the inhabitants of a prehistoric community were food producers or not will depend on what we mean by food producer, for this concept has a notoriously wide range of interpretations. A single index is unlikely to capture all of these meanings. Another common reason for low concept validity in archaeology is the lack of systematic evaluations of the validity of indices. As a result, poor measures are perpetuated. Finally, as mentioned earlier, it is often very difficult for archaeologists to devise valid measures of such abstract concepts as *socioeconomic status, family cohesiveness,* or *religious tolerance.*

A useful way of thinking about validity and reliability is to think of an imaginary scale ranging from 0 to 10 points. A measurement corresponding to 10 on the scale would represent identity between a concept and its measure: the measure repeatedly captures the entire theoretical meaning of the concept. A measurement on the other end of the scale would represent inconsistent measures or a complete lack of correspondence between the measure and what it was intended to represent. Most fundamental and derived measurements in archaeology fall near the upper end of this imaginary scale of validity and reliability, while the great majority of fiat measurements undoubtedly fall in the lower half of the scale. The reason for this discrepancy should be obvious. Fiat measures are indirect measures: they are measures of underlying variables that are also, at least in archaeology, poorly defined as well.

Empirical interpretations of concepts and relationships are transformed into observations through the methodological controls of instrumentation, scaling, and sampling. Instrumentation provides the means for making observations, and the instrument chosen depends on how accurate the observations are to be. Microscopes, vernier calipers, balance scales, radiocarbon counters, color charts, the unaided eye, hand lens, and cameras are typical instruments used to make observations in archaeology. Techniques for finding and excavating sites are also instrumental procedures. As mentioned earlier, scaling provides the measurement standard against which sense impressions can be compared. The last of the methodological controls, sampling, is essential in determining which of the many possible observations should be made. Sampling is a procedure for maintaining control over the *representativeness* of observations from some larger universe in the archaeological record. Appropriate sampling procedures thus must be chosen before observations are made. In general, the labor and cost of making measurements increases steeply as increasing accuracy is required.

The fit of theories with reality is evaluated by deducing hypotheses or other test implications and by transforming them into empirical interpretations that can be checked against the archaeological record. New observations are recorded, summarized, and transformed into empirical generalizations. Empirical generalizations are then compared for goodness of fit with previously formulated empirical interpretations and, by implication, test implications. If the tests demonstrate a satisfactory fit between observed and expected observations, a prediction is considered supported or confirmed. When the fit is unsatisfactory, a theoretical statement is rejected or altered in some manner to establish a more satisfactory correspondence. Science proceeds cyclically in this manner, constantly confronting conjectures and observations. As a result, most theories in disciplines are arrived at through the modification of already existing theories rather than through the origination of completely new abstractions.

In this phase of the scientific method, testing grounds abstract notions in archaeology to the real world of artifacts, features, ecofacts, and sites. But demonstrating that an identity, hypothesis, culture history, or scientific theory is true or false is often a complex and laborious enterprise that is bound to fail before it starts for at least four reasons. First, tests of general statements usually involve inductive inference, a generalization from particular cases to more inclusive and often more abstract universes. General statements, however, can never be completely tested. Take the proposition "The

greater the population pressure, the greater the intensification of food procurement practices" as an example. Every instance of a successful test of this
proposition provides the statement with some support, some degree of *confirmation*. Of course, every instance covered by the proposition cannot possibly be investigated. For instance, archaeologists cannot look into the future to determine whether all future cases also support the proposition. Nor
can they examine that part of the archaeological record that has been destroyed. Both of these examples show that at least some tests cannot be made.
This is a general problem in science, for most hypotheses have a form that
states or implies something about all or, at the very least, almost all instances of a kind. Since in practice it is impossible to observe all conceivable
instances, most theoretical statements, especially in scientific theories, can never
be fully confirmed: they can only be evaluated against available existing evidence.

The second reason testing is often inconclusive follows from the very nature of the act of observing. Observations are theory-laden. They are formulated against a background of cultural expectations and archaeological
tradition. This background affects the way in which we interpret perceptual
experiences and directs our attention to some sense impressions rather than
to others. A secure, objective, factual base against which we can test our
general notions does not exist. It is a mistake to assume the essential "give-
ness" of the archaeological record: changing theories can and have provided
truly new conceptions of archaeological reality or some part of it. Sellars
(1963) has called the belief in objective brute facts the Myth of the Given.

Testing is often inconclusive for a third reason: inappropriate methodological controls. Unsatisfactory fits between predicted and recorded observations may result from incomplete empirical interpretations, poor sampling
procedures, inappropriate inferential statistics, misleading artifact collecting
techniques, and many other sources of error that lead to the rejection of
true hypotheses and the acceptance of ones that are false. Here we do not
know if a conjecture is false or whether one of the methodological controls
is weak. This situation is exacerbated by the tendency among scientists to
protect their pet hypotheses from falsification by blaming any negative results in testing on weak or inappropriate methodological controls rather than
on an erroneous conjecture. The formalization process discussed in chapter
10 is one possible means of exposing ad hoc maneuvers like these.

Finally, as mentioned earlier, scientific laws are invariant theoretical statements, while statements about natural or sociocultural regularities are never

invariant enough to justify the absolute connection of the equal sign used in theoretical statements. Because of the ideal nature of scientific theories, philosophers of science called *conventionalists* regard theories of this type as merely computational devices, instruments that help us make correct and useful predictions about phenomena. Since they are only computational devices, they do not actually describe physical or sociocultural reality. Nor does it make sense to talk about their truth or falseness: they are either useful or they are not. Their value is primarily that of calculi that help us use and control things and events as they appear to us. Given this interpretation of scientific theories, we would not expect test implications and physical reality to conform in some strictly defined sense, although we could still talk about the fit of empirical generalizations and empirical interpretations as true or false. Conventionalism and other interpretations of theories are discussed in more detail in the first section of chapter 11.

For all of these reasons, the acceptance or rejection of theories is never conclusive in archaeology or in any other scientific discipline: scientific hypotheses or theories cannot be conclusively proven by any set of available data, no matter how accurate and extensive. At best we can evaluate our theories and justify our preference for one over another on the basis of available knowledge. Even though experience may show it to be wrong and require us to revise it, we provisionally assume the truth of that knowledge for practical purposes, for it is the least insecure theoretical information we have.

Trial Formulations

In actual research, archaeologists anticipate the results of their activities by making *trial formulations*. Trial formulations are usually imaginary explorations—thought experiments—which mentally trace the consequences of transforming one information component into another or of applying a particular methodological control. The process proceeds by asking, If I attempt this, what will be the effect on that? For instance, If I use this sampling technique, will I be able to make those inferences? Will that retrieval system allow me to make those observations? Trial formulations are also involved in the testing process. Here we could ask, Are these test implications easily testable? Are there convincing arguments of relevance that link these systemic context statements to specific archaeological observations? What would be a valid empirical interpretation of intensive agriculture? Does this test imply costly excavations that we cannot afford? In each trial the results of applying specific methodological controls are imaginatively recreated. In some cases *pilot studies* are actually carried out on a small scale to determine whether a methodological control will work or if certain sites are actually present, and so on. A determination is then made about the potential success or relevance of a particular research activity. The result is often the invention of new measurement scales, dating techniques, statistical tests, and other controls. When this proves impossible, the goals of the project must be adjusted to accomplish what is possible at that time.

Movement around the cycle of science varies widely in complexity and duration. In some cases it will be difficult to complete even one trip around the cycle because of incomplete data, inadequate measuring scales, and other barriers to successful information transformation. Some of these problems can be vitiated by breaking a complex problem down into a series of smaller, more manageable subproblems. The result is a complex, hierarchically organized research project that involves an intricate series of trial formulations on several levels of difficulty. As a rule this constant interplay between thought and action is rarely reflected in the archaeological literature, for reports are organized to summarize the results of this interplay and not the interplay itself.

Archaeological Research Designs

Research designs are sets of instructions or strategies of investigation that clarify the goals and guide the procedures of research projects. They accomplish their objective as mechanisms of control by serving at least three functions: (1) they delimit the goals of research projects by clarifying the actual questions that archaeologists and other scientists want answered; (2) they provide more focused approaches by determining through trial formulations which goals and procedures will most economically, effectively, and objectively answer the questions that have been posed; and (3) they minimize error through the use of appropriate sampling methods and standardized collection and excavation procedures and through the control of other extraneous variables that might adversely influence the outcome of a project. Research designs thus are concerned with strategies of reaching research objectives and of dealing with problems as they arise. Good designs generally extend from the initial clarification of the research problem to the final presentation of the results of the project. Although in many of the behavioral sciences research design is associated with formal hypothesis testing, the concept can be profitably applied to any type of investigation. Until recently, archaeologists have paid little attention to the problems involved in formulating formal research designs.

How do research designs guide the goals and procedures of research projects? Although error and ambiguity can never be completely eliminated from a research project, their effects can be minimized and research procedures focused by following a carefully thought-out blueprint or framework for research. This does not mean that subjective views and personal idiosyncracies can or should be eliminated in designing research: only that within these constraints the blueprint provides a route map for decision making. As mentioned in the preceding section, crucial decisions during many phases of a research project are made through the extensive use of trial formulations. For instance, we could adopt the tactic of generating hypothetical—and, we hope, plausible—data through simulation studies. This tactic allows us to ask, Would these data answer our research questions? If they do not, we might decide to alter the design or redefine the problem. When the implications of a problem are not carefully outlined, the crucial choices that must be made in the allocation of work effort, money, and other limited resources are often made ad hoc, to the overall detriment of a project.

During the development of a research design, it soon becomes apparent whether or not the conception of a research problem is too vague. In fact it often becomes painfully obvious that a problem is so vaguely worded that it offers little guidance in the formulation of a research design. Consider a research project whose goal is "the study of the interrelationship between a changing natural environment and sociocultural change in a region." This hazily formulated problem does not indicate just what it is about this purported relationship that is a puzzle: What about the natural environment is relevant to the problem? Should information about temperature and moisture be collected? Are soil types important? Are we to assume that the technoeconomic subsystem was most directly and severely affected by changes in the natural environment? Are we to assume that changes in the natural environment affected all cultural subsystems equally? Was the relationship between culture and environment deterministic? Stochastic? And so on.

Crucial decisions cannot be effectively made without clearly defined research problems. How else can we decide what observations should be made, how they should be made, whether they should be made at random, if an intensive study of a small sample would be more effective than a less intensive study of a larger sample, whether the analysis should be primarily quantitative or qualitative, which statistical techniques would be most effective, or whether a highly structured design would be more effective than a looser, more flexible design? Well-defined research problems suggest which methodological controls and procedures will be potentially important. Fuzzily defined problems tend to deflect research toward easily answered questions and away from tough decisions that must be made in measurement, sampling, definition, and modeling.

The ideal scientific investigation is a controlled experiment in which hypothetical relations among dependent and independent variables are tested. In experimental designs of this sort investigators are able to control and separately introduce some variables in order to observe their effect upon others. If the controlled experiment is a success, they will have demonstrated how regular occurrences are produced by the predictable interaction of the variables in question. By definition, experimental designs require at least one formal comparison of the relations between variables. But not all designs that satisfy this criterion are necessarily good designs. For instance, if S is an uncontrolled independent variable (say a specific past social structure), can archaeologists observe R (a portion of the archaeological record) and say that S caused R, that is, that S→R? In this "experiment" the outcome, the archaeological record, is studied and the independent variable, the S, is assumed. However, this design is clearly too simple and inadequate. The archaeological record, the R, might have been formed through the activities of human groups having different social structures. Or the observed spatial relationships between artifacts could be chance occurrences resulting from postdepositional processes. The archaeological record could have formed, without S, the presumed cause. In this case S→R is a poor experimental design. Methodological research in experimental disciplines is primarily concerned with developing sophisticated designs that minimize errors of this type.

Hypothesis-testing investigations in anthropological archaeology nearly always adopt ex post facto approaches. Research is ex post facto when the independent variables cannot be controlled and manipulated because they have already occurred. Since the social actions that archaeologists study have already taken place, inquiries must start with observations of the dependent variable (the archaeological record) and retrospectively examine a variety of independent variables (possible past social actions and postdepositional processes) for their probable effect on the dependent variable. Even though archaeologists assume that a large number of variables were operating in the past, they also assume that some of these variables were more relevant than others. Research designs are constructed to focus attention on these latter variables. The scope of the variables—whether they pertain to a cultural history or a scientific theory—determines the most appropriate testing procedure. For example, scientific theories and universal hypotheses are usually tested by the method of controlled cross-cultural comparison, a method that is discussed in chapter 9. Still, archaeologists can never assume that ex post facto thought experiments, no matter how rigorously designed, can approach the controlled situation of the laboratory.

Although experimental designs are possible in some areas of archaeology, anthropological archaeology is not an experimental science in a formal sense. It is basically an observational science whose subject matter (artifacts and sites) is both unique and finite in number, and whose investigative focus is not and cannot be limited to hypothesis testing. Artifacts and many other items can be brought back to the laboratory, where varied and repeatable observations are possible, but many observations must be made in the field and are nonrepeatable, for the process of excavation is destructive. Excavations cannot be repeated endlessly under varying controlled conditions. When archaeologists excavate, they assume an obligation, the obligation to retrieve as much information as possible. However, an unresolvable dilemma exists, for it is impossible to anticipate the kinds of observations that future developments in the discipline will require. For this reason alone, designs for research in archaeology where excavation is involved cannot be limited to hypothesis testing. Some provisions must be made for retrieving as much information as possible. Furthermore, since every site is unique and liable to contain surprising, unanticipated information, some provisions must also be made for disseminating this information within the discipline.

For all of these reasons, research designs in archaeology tend to be more flexible, open-ended, and cumbersome than designs in other disciplines: highly structured closed research designs are desirable only if they contribute to the effective solution of clearly defined problems. Multiple-phase research designs with built-in flexibility are more appropriate for many types of archaeological investigations. An example of a multiple-phase exploratory design that focuses on the selection of attributes, the construction of types of artifacts, and the analysis of their distribution in space is presented in the flow

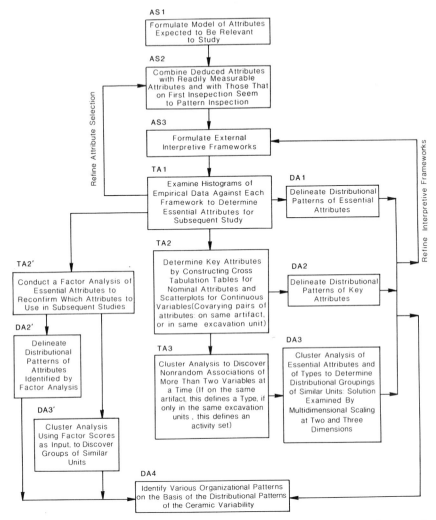

Figure 2.2 A flow chart of the steps involved in a multivariate, nested approach to artifact analysis. Source: Redman 1978, figure 8.3.

chart in figure 2.2. A general research plan designed to study the effects of a particular event (the independent variable) is outlined in table 2.4. This example illustrates the typical interdisciplinary effort that characterizes many recent research designs in archaeology. Archaeologists have always tended to approach broad problems through small-scale research projects (Struever

Table 2.4   A Research Design Model for Studying the Effects of Variable X Among Societies of Type A

I. Introduction
   a. Historical background: brief sketch of a culture of type A; situation prior to X; chronology of events
   b. Practical and theoretical significance of the research
   c. Brief summary of relevant studies and literature

 II. Statement of specific research goals
   a. Aspects of culture and social organization to be the focus of research (e.g., land use, subsistence)
   b. Specific hypotheses (if any) to be tested
   c. Definition of terms

III. Specifications of research operations
   a. Descriptions of intended research tools to be used as the basis for operational definitions of key terms in IIc
   b. Mention of general descriptive procedures as well as quantifiable research operations
   c. Mention of hypothesis-generating features of the initial research phase
   d. Description of interfering variables and how they will be controlled

IV. Research population and sampling procedures
   a. Methods to be used in delimiting communities or other populations to be studied (If the population is large, the methods of selecting and studying the representative sample should be specified here)
   b. Specification of control population—the group not experiencing the effects of experimental variable X (irrigation, population increase, etc.)

 V. Diagram of research design: Set up a plan in the form of a diagram in order to visualize the logic of data gathering operations. The diagram helps clarify points of research strategy. The diagram must provide the following:
   a. The prior situation in both experimental and control populations
   b. Clear evidence that X was introduced into one group and not the other
   c. Observations on dependent variables for both populations

VI. Analysis of results
   a. Types of statistics and/or other analytic techniques to be used
   b. Statement of types of results that would lead to the rejection of the hypotheses in IIb

VII. Significance of the results
   a. For a cultural history
   b. For theory in anthropological archaeology
   c. Additional advantages, including professional training, new techniques, and so on

---

SOURCE: Pelto 1970:295–296.

1968, 1971). But following the explosion in frequency of interdisciplinary and multidisciplinary studies that occurred simultaneously in North America, England, and the Soviet Union after World War II, projects have gradually become both more complex and multifaceted. The result has been the increasing formulation of designs that focus from their inception on shared and individual research goals that interlock in complex but complementary strategies.

Science as a Learning Process

What view of the scientific method emerges from this brief review of the cycle of science? How is the scientific method to be understood? One means of more clearly grasping just what the scientific method is about as it has been presented here is to contrast it with the *deductive* or *logical empiricist* conception of science. A methodological model for the social sciences based on the deductive or logical empiricist model of science has played an important role in the development of archaeology during the last quarter century. According to this model, science is supposed to be firmly grounded on rock-hard observational or factual data—pure descriptions—whose meaning exists independent of ourselves as observers and our changing world views. Pure facts are assumed to be uninfluenced by the hypotheses and theories that are introduced to explain them. In the classic deductive model of science, theories are conjectured or guessed at through a process of creative discovery. They are tested by being grounded in the secure observational base. During this process of justification, their consequences are deduced and compared with actual observations. The conjectures are falsified if there is a disagreement between predicted and observed facts. They are confirmed though not proven if there is agreement between them.

Serious doubts have been raised about the deductive or logical empiricist conception of science. Many of the radical dichotomies that characterize its structure, such as theory/observation, explanation/description, and discovery/justification, have been successfully challenged. Perhaps most importantly, the hard observational base upon which the model was grounded has been skillfully dissolved by perceptual experiments and the discovery of the importance of perceptual filters in decision making. All of these doubts taken together have undermined the usefulness of the model as an ideal guide to the research process. Science can no longer be viewed as an objective and value-free process.

Since the demise of the logical empiricist model of science, a single "best" conception of the process of science has not gained wide acceptance. However, a view of the scientific method as a continuous learning process has the advantage for the moment at least of avoiding the extremes of both deductivism, with its reliance on immutable facts, and a relativism in which "there is no external point of reference from which we can meaningfully ask 'what is really the case here'?" (Hesse 1976:94). This view also retains the objective and empirical character of science. In the learning process conception of science, observers are regarded as "receptors" who code perceptual experiences and produce initial data according to a "program" (a culture or school of thought, if you will). Perceptual experiences are necessarily transformed into interpreted observations during this process, for observers only "see" and "know" through cultural and theoretical filters. Once established, initial data are transformed through descriptive and inferential statistics, the modeling process, and other methodological controls to produce best-fitting theories (figure 2.3).

In the learning-process conception of science, observations are not linked with certainty to abstract terms and theories by tidy logical arguments. No

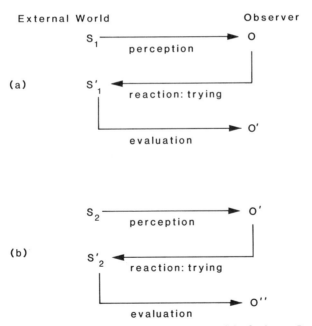

Figure 2.3 A simplified diagram of the learning model of science. In (a), an observation is made, carried through the cycle of science, and evaluated; the result may be a slightly different interpretation of the perception (O'). The process of confronting experience and a theoretical framework is continued in (b).

such guarantees exist. Science is an imaginative search for understanding and predictive capability that is guided by preconceptions, intuition, insight, luck, and personal critical judgment. Identities and hypotheses are commonly derived through the analogical extension of the observational language—by the intelligible appropriation of familiar systemic context concepts. Obviously, analogical reasoning and the metaphorical extension of everyday words play a particularly important role in the modeling process in archaeology, though archaeologists cannot always assume that the reasons for past activities are among their familiar concepts.

Testing in the learning process conception of science is consistent with empiricist theories of science in at least two ways (Hesse 1976; Groot 1969). First, testing involves an evaluation of the goodness of fit of expected and observed observations. Second, the testing process corrects our understanding of the structure and processes of the social and natural world in the past. In the testing process, predictions are deduced from theoretical statements; tests become possible when the concepts and relationships in predictions are transformed through abstraction into terms appropriate to the archaeological context; and new observations are made that may correct, modify, and extend identities, hypotheses, culture histories, and scientific theories. The learning-process conception of science departs significantly from empiricist conceptions of science in the testing process, too, for "facts" in the descriptive language are always considered potentially ephemeral interpretations that take at least part of their meaning from their conceptual arrangement. The popular notion that the sciences are bodies of established fact is entirely mistaken. For this reason alone, tests are never truly conclusive.

Science conceived of as a continuous learning process is not value-free objectivity. According to this view, knowledge of the prehistoric past will never be absolutely certain, for the rock-hard observational base of the logical-empiricists has been undermined. The realization that the observational base is dependent on cultural expectations, intellectual traditions, and other highly subjective elements should not surprise anthropological archaeologists: anthropologists have been aware for decades of the many subtle ways in which culture influences the perceptual experiences and thinking of human groups. Still, science is success-oriented and accumulative. The familiar dichotomies between theory and observation, explanation and description, and discovery and justification remain useful concepts, as long as we remember that facts, too, are also theoretical and explanatory in themselves and need justification. In this view, scientific systems represent flexible and hierarchical networks of interdependent meanings. They are not static like logical systems. Conceptual innovations, changes in cultural perceptions, and new discoveries continually modify both what is observed *and* the observable. In science, knowledge represents successfully tested conjectures within these self-organizing networks. While knowledge in this interpretation can never be final, it does gradually accumulate within intellectual traditions through time.

Summary

Chapter 2 introduces scientific method as a continuous, self-correcting learning cycle composed of information components (observation, sample summaries, empirical generalizations, theories, predictions, and empirical interpretations) interspersed with methodological controls. The logical gap between observations and theories necessitates controlled conjecture as a creative component in the cycle. To transform observations to empirical generalizations, archaeologists must first observe by measuring the properties of objects or events (compare sense perceptions with abstract symbols and assign symbols to the perceptions) in scale values. Nominal, ordinal, interval, and ratio scales show symbolic representation, rank, distance, and point of natural origin, respectively. Such sets of observations make possible sample description-displaying patterns within the sample, and empirical generalization-inferring patterns within the finite universe of which the sample is a part. The most reliable method for the latter is statistical inference using probability theory. Conjectures about archaic human bones or artifacts are classified as identities (class identification), explanatory hypotheses (statements relating abstract notions), cluture histories (sequences of events bounded by space and time), and scientific theories (universal hypotheses unbounded by space or time). Scientific theories are formed by combining identities and interlinked universal hypotheses into coherent and logically consistent stories. Theories enter the cycle controlled by concept formation, model building, inductive analogical argument, and other methods. The transformation means a shift from a focus on the archaeological record to a focus on past social systems.

Every theory makes a prediction, implying that it can be tested. The theory can be considered true if it is not falsified by empirical observations of the test. In archaeology, most implications refer to past systems, so abstract notions must be given empirical interpretations. Each concept consists of a name, theoretical definition, and operational definition. Errors arise when operational definitions measure only part of the intended meaning of a theoretical definition or when there is more than one widely used operational definition of a name. These can be compounded by problems of reliability and validity, which increase in the progression from fundamental to derived to fiat measurements. Empirical interpretations are transformed into observations through methodological controls of instrumentation, scaling, and sampling. In archaeology, empirical interpretations are checked against the archaeological record for goodness of fit. Trial formulations to determine potential success or relevance of a methodological control or information component are common in science. In the end, scientific theories may prove useful or not useful, but they cannot be conclusive.

Movement around the cycle of science is controlled by the systematic design of sets of instructions that clarify research goals, provide more focused approaches, and minimize error. Given the exigencies of excavation, multiple-phase flexible research designs are generally more appropriate than highly structured closed designs in anthropological archaeology.

This view of science makes use of data transformation through methodological controls to produce best-fitting theories, recognizing scientific systems as flexible hierarchical networks of interdependent meaning. It avoids the extremes of deductivism or relativism, recognizing that facts take meaning from their conceptual arrangements.

Suggested Readings

The scientific method has been discussed in numerous books. A variety of perspectives are presented in the following accounts.

Amedeo, D. and R. G. Golledge. 1975. *An Introduction to Scientific Reasoning in Geography*. New York: Wiley.

Blalock, H. M., Jr., ed. 1974. *Measurement in the Social Sciences*. Chicago: Aldine.

Bunge, M. 1967. *Scientific Research*. 2 vols. New York: Springer-Verlag.

Davies, J. T. 1973. *The Scientific Approach*. London: Academic Press.

Goldstein, M. and L. Goldstein. 1978. *How We Know: An Exploration of the Scientific Process*. New York: Plenum Press.

Gould, P. 1970. Is *Statistix inferens* the geographical name for a wild goose? *Economic Geography* 46:439–448.

Groot, A. D. de. 1969. *Methodology*. The Hague: Mouton.

Hanson, N. R. 1969. *Perception and Discovery, an Introduction to Scientific Inquiry*. W. C. Humphreys, ed. San Francisco: Freeman, Cooper.

Harré, R. 1965. *An Introduction to the Logic of the Sciences*. London: Macmillan.

—— 1970. *The Principles of Scientific Thinking*. Chicago: University of Chicago Press.

Kaplan, A. 1964. *The Conduct of Inquiry: Methodology for Behavioral Science*. Scranton, Pa.: Chandler.

A large and often contradictory body of literature awaits the reader interested in the philosophy of science. Besides the suggested readings listed below, the reader should become familiar with the journals *Philosophy of Science, Philosophy of Social Science,* and *British Journal for the Philosophy of Science.*

Achinstein, P. 1968. *Concepts of Science*. Baltimore: Johns Hopkins.

Bayard, D. T. 1969. Science, theory, and reality in the "New Archaeology." *American Antiquity* 34:376–384.

Brodbeck, M., ed. 1968. *Readings in the Philosophy of the Social Sciences*. New York: Macmillan.

Brody, B., ed. 1970. *Readings in the Philosophy of Science*. Englewood Cliffs, N.J.: Prentice-Hall.

Gibson, Q. 1960. *The Logic of Social Enquiry*. New York: Humanities Press.

Gunnell, J. 1975. *Philosophy, Science, and Political Inquiry*. Morristown, N.J.: General Learning Press.

Harré, R. 1972. *The Philosophies of Science*. New York: Oxford University Press.
Hempel, C. 1965. *Aspects of Scientific Explanation and Other Essays in the Philosophy of Science*. New York: Free Press.
—— 1966. *Philosophy of Natural Science*. Englewood Cliffs, N.J.: Prentice-Hall.
Keat, R. and J. Urry. 1975. *Social Theory as Science*. Boston: Routledge and Kegan Paul.
Kimmerman, L., ed. 1969. *The Nature and Scope of Social Science*. New York: Appleton-Century-Crofts.
Nagel, E. 1961. *The Structure of Science*. New York: Harcourt Brace Jovanovich.
Popper, K. 1970. *The Logic of Scientific Discovery*. New York: Harper and Row.
Ryan, A. 1970. *The Philosophy of the Social Sciences*. London: Macmillan.
Toulmin, S. 1953. *The Philosophy of Science*. New York: Harper and Row.

The problems of perception and "seeing" in science are discussed in:

Dretske, F. 1969. *Seeing and Knowing*. London: Routledge and Kegan Paul.
Frisby, J. 1979. *Seeing: Illusion, Brain, and Mind*. New York: Oxford University Press.
Hanson, N. R. 1969. *Perception and Discovery, an Introduction to Scientific Inquiry*. W. C. Humphreys, ed. San Francisco: Freeman, Cooper.
Hirst, I. 1965. *Perception and the External World*. New York: Macmillan.

The following articles illustrate several approaches to the construction of research designs in archaeology:

Binford, L. 1964. A consideration of archaeological research design. *American Antiquity* 29:425–441.
Daniels, S. G. H. 1972. Research design models. In D. Clarke, ed., *Models in Archaeology*, pp. 201–229. London: Methuen.
—— 1978. Implications of error: Research design and the structure of archaeology. *World Archaeology* 10:29–35.
Goodyear, A., L. Raab, and T. Klinger. 1978. The status of archaeological research design in cultural resource management. *American Antiquity* 43:159–173.
Redman, C. 1973. Multistage fieldwork and analytical techniques. *American Antiquity* 38:61–79.
Sabloff, J. and W. Rathje. 1973. Ancient Maya commercial systems: A research design for the island of Cozumel, Mexico. *World Archaeology* 5:221–231.
Tuggle, H., A. Townsend, and T. Riley. 1972. Laws, systems, and research designs: A discussion of explanation in archaeology. *American Antiquity* 37:3–12.

CHAPTER THREE

Strategies of Research

The principal goal of the scientific method in archaeology is the construction of logically consistent and well-supported theories, for at least three reasons. First, theories are conceptual frameworks that give perceptual experiences meaning. Second, they are systems of expectations that guide archaeologists in choosing what to observe in the archaeological record. Third, they are meant to be descriptions and explanations of actual human behavior in the past rather than mythical or other imaginary reconstructions. Theory building in archaeology is more often than not the product through time of many people rather than of one person, for individual archaeologists tend to emphasize particular phases of the cycle of science, such as site excavation, experimentation, theory building, or quantitative testing. The first section briefly reviews six general types of investigations in which archaeologists participate, strategies of explaining and of reasoning to hypotheses, and the divergent goals of culture historians and social scientists. All archaeologists must choose among these strategies of investigation, explanation, and interpretation.

The manner in which working hypotheses affect the structure and goals of research are discussed in the second section. Archaeologists, like other scientists, differ in the asumptions they explicitly or implicitly make about nature, human beings, society, culture, and other aspects of the world as we know it. These divergent sets of assumptions result in the development of competing plans for study or research programs that focus on different questions, problems, procedures, and solutions. Methodology is the logic of this process, and methodological debate in archaeology is about the appropriateness of various methods, techniques, and goals in the process. Understanding how research programs affect research strategies is an integral part of understanding the divergent goals and procedures of anthropological archaeologists.

Strategies of Investigation, Explanation, and Interpretation

Anthropological archaeologists differ in their strategies of investigation, explanation, and interpretation. In this section alternative strategies for accomplishing each of these goals are briefly reviewed with their implications for the design of research.

Type of Investigation

As chapter 2 stressed, the cycle of science is a whole, a cyclical system of inquiry whose goal is the acquisition of knowledge. Skill is required in both empirical research and theorizing, in model building and hypothesis testing. But many archaeologists emphasize only specific phases of the cycle of science in their own research. Some emphasize the bottom half of the cycle (figure 3.1), *empirical research* or analysis, and pursue problems of measurement or descriptive studies. Others emphasize the top half of the diagram

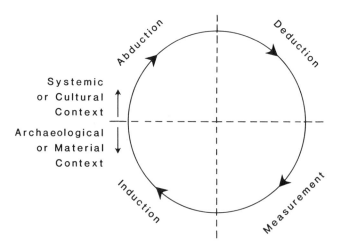

Figure 3.1   Ideal types of investigation.

and concentrate on *theorizing* or interpretation through the use of abductive or deductive reasoning. The cycle of science can also be sectioned vertically. Processes on the left side take place within what Hans Reichenbach (1951), a philosopher of science, referred to as a "context of discovery," while those operating on the right side take place within a "context of justification." Both measurement and abduction involve abstraction. As mentioned in chapter 2, abstraction in science moves from the observational level to the theoretical and back to the observational level. Thus, there is a continual abstractive process, phases of which may be performed by different archaeologists, that forms a dialectic through which theoretical statements may be modified or expanded to sharpen their explanatory power and to increase their scope of application.

Types of investigations emphasize various phases of the research cycle. Since the distinction between types of research is usually difficult to make in actual research projects, any classificatory system tends to be somewhat arbitrary. The following system of five categories has been chosen here for illustrative purposes: hypothesis testing, concept and instrumental investigations, descriptive studies, exploratory investigations, and interpretive and theoretical studies (Groot 1969:301–309). Even though each category could be expanded and subdivided still further, these five serve the purpose of introducing the major types of investigations that characterize research in anthropological archaeology.

Hypothesis Testing. In science, a hypothesis is generally considered a statement of relationship between two or more ideas whose truth or falsity is capable of being empirically evaluated. Ideally, hypotheses are derived from theories by logical deduction; that is, by implication from a set of theoretical statements. However, in developing disciplines or in advanced sciences, when new areas of research are being initiated formal interlinked sets of theoretical statements are rarely available from which hypotheses can be derived. Whether hypotheses are theoretically derived or isolated statements, the purpose of hypothesis testing as a research strategy is to compare the empirical implications of hypotheses with new observations. Enough has already been said about the testing process that these procedural details do not have to be repeated here.

Hypothesis testing is a valuable research strategy when new scientific theories or culture histories have been proposed. To evaluate the claims of the "stories," their empirical implications must be tested. Hypothesis testing is also a valuable strategy when isolated hypotheses or identities have been proposed to account for specific empirical properties and relationships. In this case an attempt is made to determine the extent of support for the statement before it becomes integrated into or the basis for a scientific theory or culture history.

The explicit formulation and testing of hypotheses has several other important functions in the cycle of science. First, archaeologists are compelled to be explicit and objective by specifying just what is being tested. Second, the testing process clearly indicates which hypotheses are so vaguely worded that they are empirically meaningless and, therefore, unfalsifiable. In fact the testing process is a mental apparatus that serves the valuable function in developing sciences like archaeology of distinguishing between true hypotheses, theoretical orientations such as the ecological approach, and vague generalities such as "Climatic change affects cultural adaptations."

Hypothesis testing commonly develops out of exploratory and interpretive-theoretical investigations. As a result, hypothesis testing as a dominant research strategy is more typical of mature disciplines. For this reason, most scientists regard an emphasis on hypothesis testing as an enormous methodological advance over other types of investigation, especially descriptive studies.

Instrumental-Nomological Investigations. The goal of instrumental-nomological investigations is to use or develop measurable theoretical constructs: to construct, standardize, and validate *instruments* of measurement. It makes little sense to include the concept *interaction* in a research design, for example, until an actual measure of interaction is available. An instrument in this sense is very broadly defined. Instruments are generally thought to be something mechanical, such as a microscope or telescope. But instruments can be verbal as well (Fritz 1972:136–137), as mentioned in chapter 2. One type of instrument is a measurement system and the technological equipment necessary to make accurate measurements using the system. Familiar examples of measurement systems are the decay rates of radioactive materials, the metric system, and the Munsell color scale. Instruments for making measurements within these systems include radiocarbon dating machines, rulers, and Munsell color charts. The history of science has recorded many instances of sudden progress in a discipline after the appearance of new systems and instruments of measurement. In archaeology a particularly striking example of this phenomenon occurred after the invention of radiocarbon dating in 1949.

Instrumental-nomological investigations also include experimentation with theoretical and operational definitions of concepts and relationships. Example in archaeology include Naroll's work (1962) on an instrument to measure population size and Robbins' measure of the relative permanence of settlement patterns (1966:3). Inappropriate and inadequate operational definitions can easily stymie the growth of a discipline like archaeology for a number of reasons. As mentioned earlier, a falsified hypothesis can be protected by arguing that the validity of its empirical interpretation is low, that it poorly defines and measures the theoretical meaning of the hypothesis for which it is an interpretation. Here an abstractive error has been made, an error of interpretation. Another defense is to argue that the reliability of testing devices is low, that they do not produce consistent results from site to site. Because there can be no guarantee that the same thing is being measured when measuring instruments are inconsistent or ambiguous, the results of investigations cannot be meaningfully compared. Finding valid and reliable empirical interpretations of concepts in archaeology is often such a formidable task that a separate instrumental-nomological investigation is justified. Recent attempts to produce a valid empirical interpretation of the concept *matrilocal residence* is an interesting and instructive example of this type of investigation in anthropological archaeology (Longacre 1970; Stanislawski 1973).

Anthropological archaeologists have only begun to explicitly grapple with the complex problems raised by the concepts *validity* and *reliability*. Since the construction and testing of theoretical statements are blocked when accurate instruments of measurement are poorly developed or absent, instrumental-nomological investigations are becoming increasingly popular in anthropological archaeology, a discipline whose measurement systems generally span both the systemic and archaeological contexts. It cannot be too forcefully stressed that the development of accurate instruments of measurement of both the verbal and mechanical type is essential to the continuing growth in sophistication of the discipline.

Descriptive Studies. The goal of descriptive studies in archaeology is generally the systematic description and classification of a sample of the archaeological record. In this type of investigation the main methodological controls are sampling, mechanical instruments of observation, and descriptive and inferential statistics. The statistics of samples and the parameters of universes are typically estimated in descriptive studies through the processes of categorization, counting, computation of association and dispersion, and other statistical controls (Thomas 1976; Doran and Hodson 1975). This information is then generally summarized in tables and graphs. Classic examples of largely descriptive studies are A. V. Kidder's (1932) study of artifacts from the American Southwest and Squier and Davis' (1848) report on the mounds of the Mississippi River Valley.

Descriptive studies in archaeology are comparable to ethnographic descriptions by sociocultural anthropologists. They are fact-finding expeditions that tell us what is on hand archaeologically. Tests of prestated hypotheses and the formulation of new hypotheses, except at the simplest level of the identity of artifact or site function, are absent. Sites are excavated or surveys carried out with a minimum of prediscussion. Only then is an attempt made to account for what was found.

In archaeology, descriptive studies are often called natural history chronicles. They answer the questions What, Where, and When: What objects and events occurred where when? Since their objective is not to explain why things happened as they did, they require less reflective thought. For many archaeologists, descriptive studies lack the stimulation of hypothesis testing, for there is nothing to falsify or confirm; there is no risk. As a result they are generally considered less respectable than other types of investigations, in particular hypothesis testing and model building. This widespread bias is shared by many behavioral sciences, especially in the United States. But descriptively oriented studies play their essential role in the research process just by stating what, where, and when. The descriptive phase in a research project, whether it is ever reported or not, is an essential link in the cycle of science. It establishes a base from which theories can be formulated. In fact neglect of this phase in the past has often led to the formulation of untimely and immature hypotheses, to the fabrication in North America, for instance, of mysterious races of mound builders, giants, and wandering Vikings (Wauchope 1962).

As might be expected, descriptive studies are particularly common and relevant during the initial exploration of the archaeological resources of a region. The danger lies in allowing fact collection to become an end in itself once these initial phases have been completed. The eventual result is the perpetuation of diffuse objectives, the inability to identify relevant facts, inefficient observation, the recording of those traits that are most self-evidently quantifiable, and the stockpiling of numbingly dull descriptive studies. Nonetheless, to the unwary afflicted with *descriptitis,* there never seem to be enough accurate facts. To these baleful souls, the larger the sample, the more extensive the different kinds of measures and things measured, and the more empirical generalizations that are generated, the better a study is assumed to be. *Systematic empiricism,* the overemphasis on data collection and analysis, is a pseudoscience, for it neglects other essential phases of the cycle of science (figure 3.2; Willer and Willer 1973). Still, in proper perspective, to observe before theorizing *is* a valuable objective in the initial exploration of unknown regions. After all, observations are the stuff about which theories are built.

Exploratory Investigations. Exploratory investigations account for sample summaries and empirical generalizations by generating identities and hypotheses. This objective places exploratory studies between descriptive and hypothesis-testing investigations in the cycle of science. Even though exploratory investigations are a form of empirical investigation, they contain an element of playful model building that is rarely described in archaeological reports. Prior expectations, vaguely formulated theoretical orientations, and even explicit biases generally dominate the exploratory process, a process considered by many to be the most creative phase of the cycle of sci-

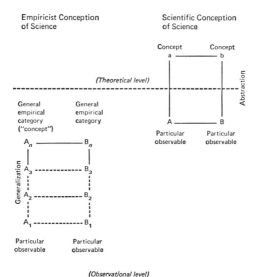

Figure 3.2 Systematic empiricism. An overemphasis on data collection and analysis (on the left) compared with the cycle of science (on the right). Source: Willer and Willer 1973, figure 5.

ence. Although the identities and hypotheses that are the products of exploratory studies are intended to provide us with some idea of what existed or happened in the past, rigorous testing of these ideas is not a function of the exploratory process. The products of exploratory investigations do not have to be well supported, just suggestive and stimulating. They are products of an initial process of discovery, not of justification. In fact they may be so vaguely worded or empty of empirical implications that their testability remains highly dubious. Therefore, the outcome of an exploratory investigation is never conclusive, and it generally remains of little value unless confronted with new observational data.

The process of obtaining hypotheses from the facts without, at the outset, having any particular theory or model in mind has been called abduction by Charles Peirce (1932, vol. 7, book 2). What motivates the process is a desire to explain an interesting set of facts. For example, an archaeological report may record the distribution of artifacts and features at a site, and end at that point. What is now needed is some idea of the underlying principles that produced the distribution. This objective is approached through imaginative guessing. The source of ideas adopted at this point in the cycle of science is generally decided by research bias. For instance, an archaeologist with her primary training in environmental archaeology is likely to abduce quite different hypotheses than an archaeologist with a social structural orientation. Still, each will usually be able to abduce one or more hypotheses that seem to fit or make sense of the known data.

The generation of hypotheses and identities in the cycle of science serves a number of useful purposes. As mentioned earlier, they provide initial interpretations of sample summaries and empirical generalizations. For this reason, they are particularly common when there is little available theory or where natural history chronicles have dominated archaeological investigations. Here they represent a "let's see what will happen if . . ." approach that characterizes what Stephen Toulmin (1953) has called the natural history stage of scientific development. They are valuable in challenging entrenched interpretations, too, for the availability of multiple working hypotheses is an effective deterrent to the too ready acceptance of untested or only partially tested interpretations (Chamberlain 1897; Feyerabend 1975). The generation of exploratory hypotheses also plays an indispensable role in the testing of widely accepted theories.

Exploratory investigations have proceeded along many different pathways in archaeology. One of the most common approaches today is the manipu-

lation of data bases using statistical techniques to discover significant relationships between variables. An example of one such technique is factor
analysis. In this technique the strength of the relationship between variables
is expressed in a matrix of correlation coefficients. Factors are then determined that best account for the correlations using as few linear combinations of variables as possible. In archaeology, interpreted factors have been
used to suggest the possible existence of tool-kits, work-activity areas, artifact types, and other clusterings in the systemic context. An example of this
procedure is discussed in chapter 5. Another common procedure is the exploration of a range of as-if hypotheses based on existing theories. For instance, I developed an exploratory interpretation of the processes leading to
the growth and decline of some Mississippian cultures in the American
Midwest by adopting a model of state development and decline. The purpose of the study was to suggest a range of as-if hypotheses that would account for the archaeological materials being studied and that would open
up interesting new avenues of research (Gibbon 1974).

Interpretive and Theoretical Studies. Existing sets of data, hypotheses,
identities, and other types of established information are synthesized in new
ways in interpretive and theoretical studies. The new synthesis usually involves the adoption of a new theoretical point of view, for the goal of this
type of investigation is to derive new relations and to suggest new interpretations. Lewis Binford's interpretation (1968b) of post-Pleistocene adaptations by groups of hunter-gatherers and their resulting preadaptations to a
life-way organized around horticultural activities is a classic example. Interpretive and theoretical studies are especially important when coherent and
well-supported theories are lacking or when the explanatory value of a particular point of view is being demonstrated. In some instances existing hypotheses may be too limited in scope or too complex and, therefore, too
difficult to test, or both. In these situations trial formulations are performed
to arrive at the simplest or the most easily tested hypotheses. Like exploratory investigations, the products of interpretive and theoretical studies are
tentative and inconclusive; they must still be tested. For this reason, they
are theoretical rather than empirical.

The call in archaeology today for more hypothesis and theory building is
a call for an increased emphasis on interpretive and theoretical studies. Interpretive-theoretical studies force archaeologists to think through the processes that may have been at work in the past in an area. They focus atten-

tion on a manageable number of ideas and they concentrate observation on selected phenomena only. As a result, archaeologists approach excavations or surveys with some idea of what to look for and of why they should expect to find predicted phenomena. According to this ideal, an excavation or survey is no longer an exploratory groping after significant relationships. It has now become an experiment designed to test the validity of a set of previously thought-out hypotheses.

When combined with hypothesis testing, interpretive-theoretical studies or exploratory investigations are called the *hypothetico-deductive* (HD) *approach* (figure 3.3). The formation of isolated hypotheses is the research objective, and the cycle of science is initiated at this information component. The researcher examines the available data, frames an interpretive hypothesis to explain them, examines the consequences of the hypothesis, and tests these consequences against additional data. Many scientists regard the hypothetico-deductive approach as *the* scientific method, for it involves the framing of a hypothesis and the testing of knowledge. However, this is a too restrictive view of science: all types of investigation play their indispensable role in the cycle of science. Other overly narrow emphases on particular types of investigation, such as systematic empiricism (Willer and Willer 1973) and operationalism (Bridgman 1927; Campbell 1957) have produced equally limited views of science.

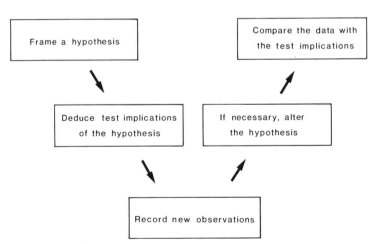

Figure 3.3 A simplified diagram of the hypothetico-deductive approach.

These five types of investigations are somewhat arbitrarily separated, as mentioned at the beginning of this section. However, they do demonstrate the variety of research activities that are integral phases of the cycle of science. And they do demonstrate that archaeologists have the opportunity of entering the research process at a variety of points in ongoing projects. Information components that are the products of one researcher are frequently the starting points of new projects initiated by others. Innovations in sampling techniques or scaling devices, models borrowed from other disciplines, and new empirical interpretations of key concepts frequently stimulate archaeologists to attempt to transform already existing information components. As a result, movement around the cycle is more often than not a product of the archaeological community than of single individuals. It cannot be too strongly emphasized that no phase of the research process is more important than another, for the process is a cycle, a continuous interaction between abstract notions and the archaeological record.

Explanatory Strategies

Strategies of research can be sectioned in other ways besides types of investigations. We have claimed, for example, that the goal of the scientific method in anthropological archaeology is the acquisition and accumulation of knowledge about past peoples and their cultures. Important heuristic tools for the acquisition and accumulation of knowledge are the processes of describing, abstracting, explaining, and predicting. The surprisingly complex processes of describing and abstracting have already been discussed in chapter 2. In this section the concepts *to explain* and *to predict* are briefly examined. Since there is no consensus as to what is an acceptable strategy of explaining or predicting, to explain and to predict have remained controversial concepts in contemporary archaeology as in the other social sciences. This controversy will be introduced by concentrating on to explain and ideal philosophy of science explications of this concept.

What is an explanation? Most archaeologists would probably agree that an explanation accounts for or resolves some puzzling aspect of an object or event. Agreement ends here, however, for the value of an explanation depends on what one is willing to accept as an explanation, and that varies widely. The main debate concerns the proper form of an explanation and whether explanations even have proper forms. A subsidiary debate has focused on what "to resolve a puzzle" means. As we shall see, one's position in these debates can dramatically affect one's research goals and strategies.

Deductive Explanation. Some archaeologists have argued that the only valid means of explanation in anthropological archaeology as in any science is deductive explanation (e.g., Spaulding 1968; Fritz and Plog 1970; Watson, Leblanc, and Redman 1971). Puzzling aspects of events or objects are accounted for or explained in deductive explanations by showing that they are the expected outcomes of prior knowledge. The explanation is made possible through a logical form of argument that subsumes some puzzling aspect of the world under a network of premises that includes laws or lawlike statements and statements of initial conditions.

A classic example of deductive explanation is *deductive-nomological* (DN) explanation (e.g., Hempel 1965; Hempel and Oppenheim 1948). In part A of table 3.1, $L_1, L_2, \ldots , L_r$ refer to laws or lawlike statements of universal theoretical scope or to universal empirical generalizations. Simple examples are "Whenever A then B" and "The greater the A, the greater the B." $C_1, C_2, \ldots , C_k$ are initial conditions or particular circumstances that de-

Table 3.1   Deductive Explanation

A. Ideal Form of a Deductive-Nomological Explanation
$L_1, L_2, \ldots , L_r$

	explanans

$C_1, C_2, \ldots , C_k$

E   explanandum

B. Sketch of a Deductive-Nomological Explanation
   L_1 A population will adopt a more productive but labor intensive subsistence system when population pressure reaches critical point K.
   C_1 X is an agricultural population.
   C_2 The population of X increased until the critical population pressure K was reached.
   C_3 More intensive (and therefore more productive) agricultural techniques were known to X.

   E   X adopted a more labor intensive but productive agricultural system.

C. Sketch of a Deductive-Statistical Explanation
   L_1 Suicide rates (S) vary inversely with the degree of integration of domestic society (I). ($I = 1/S$)
   C_1 There are two groups, one of married, one of unmarried people.
   C_2 Married people are more integrated.

   E   There is a lower suicide rate among married people than among unmarried people.

limit the domain of applicability of the law or lawlike statements. These two sets of statements are called the premises or *explanans* of the explanatory argument. E represents what is to be explained, or the *explanandum*. The explanandum can be some puzzling aspect of an object or event, or it can be a law or lawlike statement. E is explained by demonstrating, deductively, that it necessarily follows from or is implied by the initial conditions (the $C_1, C_2, \ldots, C_k$) and laws (the $L_1, L_2, \ldots, L_r$). If the premises are true, the single line separating E from the other statements implies that E *must* necessarily have occurred or be true. In a deductive-nomological explanation, then, description, even if followed by classification, cannot explain the manner in which artifacts are distributed or any other empirical phenomenon. The phenomena to be explained must be subsumed under generalizations or laws that possess predictive capabilities, and the primary task of the anthropological archaeologist is to discover these laws or generalizations and their limiting conditions. Part B in table 3.1 is an example of a deductive-nomological explanation.

Another form of deductive explanation is *deductive-statistical* (DS) explanation. This type of explanation has the same general form as a deductive-nomological explanation, except that the explanandum and the lawlike statements in the explanans are probabilistic or statistical statements. Again, the explanandum can be some puzzling aspect of an object or event, or it can be a law or lawlike statement. An example of a deductive-statistical explanation in which statistical laws are being explained is contained in part C of table 3.1.

Deductive-nomological and deductive-statistical explanations are called covering-law explanations because both subsume or cover the explanandum under a universal statement that expresses a contingent, or factual, connection of which the explanandum is an example. *Inductive-statistical* (IS) explanation is a weaker form of covering-law explanation, since the explanans does not guarantee the truth of the explanandum (table 3.2). $P_1, P_2, \ldots, P_n$ in part A of table 3.2 are sentences stating empirical or probabilistic laws; they are inductive laws because they state inductive inferences. In part C of table 3.2 the empirical laws are suggested by regularities of identity within a class of observed objects. The first statement (P_1) is a strong inductive inference derived from a sample summary of a site. The second statement (P_2) is a weaker inductive inference derived from the proportion of artifacts of type A known from all excavated sites of an archaeological culture. The initial conditions and the law statements provide some support for the conclu-

Table 3.2   Inductive Statistical Explanation

A. Ideal Form of an Inductive-Statistical (IS) Explanation		
$P_1, P_2, \ldots, P_n$	probabilistic laws or lawlike statements	premises
$C_1, C_2, \ldots, C_n$	statements of antecedent conditions	
E	description of the empirical phenomenon to be explained	conclusion

B. Explaining Change in a Systemic Context
   P_1 The probability that a population adopts a more productive but labor intensive subsistence system is proportional to the population pressure on the subsistence base.
   C_1 X is an agricultural population.
   C_2 The population of X increased to the point where pressure was exerted upon the available subsistence resources.
   C_3 The population of X is familiar with more intensive (and therefore more productive) agricultural techniques.

   E   The population of X adopted a more productive but more labor intensive agricultural system.

C. Explaining the Contents of Archaeological Site Z
   P_1 90% of all swords in village Y of culture X are Type A.
   P_2 The probability that swords in a village of culture X will be type A is .9.
   C_1 The excavated component is an archaeological expression of a village of culture X.
   C_2 The artifacts being studied are the remains of swords.

   E   90% of the swords found in the excavated component of site Z are of Type A.

sion in the argument, but the support is only partial for two reasons. First, the explanandum and the law statements in the explanans are probabilistic or statistical statements, as in deductive-statistical explanations. Second, as the double lines separating E from C and P statements indicate, the relationship between the premises and the conclusion is based on the uncertainties of inductive inference, instead of deductive necessity. Therefore, belief in the initial conditions and laws does not necessarily imply belief in the conclusion, only a reasonable expectation: although the argument is basically deductive in structure, the statements contained within it do not necessarily (that is, logically) supply the conclusion.

Even though inductive-statistical explanations can lead to false conclusions, this weaker form of covering-law explanation is often defended pragmatically because it produces hypotheses from which testable consequences can be deduced. Furthermore, scientists who look upon deductive explanation as the only valid means of explanation in science regard inductive-statistical explanation as a necessary if insufficient conceptual tool during the early phases of the development of a science. As a science matures and well-supported law statements and an adequate knowledge of initial conditions become available, more rigorous forms of explanation are naturally adopted. Debate still rages over the historical accuracy of this developmental view of explanation in science. A few of the arguments in the debate are reviewed in chapter 11.

Deductive explanations supposedly show us why things are as they are—how they came to be as they are now or were in the past. This form of explanation provides answers to why-questions through the process of deductive reasoning: if the premises of a valid argument are true, certain things or events must *necessarily* follow or have followed. A degree of certainty is implied that is not a characteristic of inductive explanations or of the other explanatory strategies discussed in the following paragraphs. For this reason, deductive explanation is regarded by its proponents as a valuable and essential goal of the scientific process and an end product that contributes to the growth of knowledge in science. The pivotal question is, of course, whether sufficiently well-supported law statements and an adequate knowledge of initial conditions presently exist in anthropological archaeology or in any other social science. Are there lawlike statements in the social sciences that have enough empirical support to qualify as nontrivial laws? If there are, do we know the specific circumstances within which they are operative? Negative answers to these questions would force us to prematurely adopt poorly supported premises or to accept logically weaker forms of explanation, such as inductive-statistical explanation, if we accept the developmental view of covering-law theorists. Many of these weaker forms of explanation have been called explanation sketches by Hempel (1965) because of their deductive incompleteness. According to Hempel, for anthropology, history, sociology, and other "immature" disciplines to mature, they must transform these sketches into more rigorously deductive forms. However, this conclusion is predicated on an acceptance of the covering-law model of explanation.

Alternative Strategies of Explanation. Other scholars have adopted alternative strategies of explanation for a number of reasons. First, the covering-law form of explanation introduces criteria of valid explanation that are unrealizable at the present time in the social sciences. If the criteria were seriously adopted, explanation would be impossible. Second, some scholars maintain that society is not law-governed or at least that law statements are not necessary for valid explanations. Third, some philosophers of science argue that the covering-law form of explanation is, after all, only an ideal model; in fact, it is not even a very successful model of explanation, for, among other things, it does not typify explanation in the physical sciences (Morgan 1973; Achinstein 1971).

Two alternative strategies of explanation are reason giving and what-explanations. Sociocultural anthropologists frequently provide *reason-giving explanations* by discussing why a person or a group of people thought that an action or belief was correct or proper. Reason-giving explanations tend to answer such general questions as "What was their intention in doing that?" (in addressing their mother in a particular manner, for example). In one form of reason-giving explanation, *practical inference,* the explanatory argument has the following schema: A intends to bring about p; A considers that he cannot bring about p unless he does x; therefore A sets himself to do x (Wright 1971:27). For obvious reasons, few archaeologists have offered reason-giving explanations, R. G. Collingwood (1964, 1966) being a notable exception. Can prehistoric archaeologists, at least, ever hope to explain if true explanations in the social sciences must refer to the motives, intentions, and dispositions of people and to the reasons they have, or are alleged to have had, for their behavior? How could archaeologists ever test the premises of reason-giving explanations? The implications of these questions, questions that challenge the very idea of a science of anthropological archaeology, are discussed in greater detail in chapter 11.

What-explanations explain by making clear what something is or by showing how something fits within a sequence of events. This strategy of explanation does not logically entail (necessarily) the phenomenon to be explained or tell us, deductively, why things are as they are. But it does help us understand a puzzling situation by providing information that satisfies our curiosity. Simple examples of questions that what-explanations answer are Can you tell me what this is? and Can you tell me what happened here? These questions are commonly answered in this mode of explanation by redescribing a thing or an event within some theoretical framework. In archaeology this framework is generally composed of objects and events within a systemic context, and the items or events to be explained are properties of the archaeological record. For example, chert flakes and pottery shards are explained by redescribing them as knives and fragments of jars, or a site is explained by redescribing it as a market or a butchering station. In these examples a shift has simply been made from a language that describes physical objects in the archaeological record to a language that describes items in systemic context.

Common varieties of what-explanations include *narrative explanations* (what happened here and in what order), *teleological explanations* (what goal was this action directed toward), and *pattern explanations* (what sort of pattern was this object or event a part of) (Taylor 1970). Pattern explanation is probably the most widely used strategy of explanation in anthropology today. In a pattern explanation, a fact or even a low-level generalization is explained by convincingly demonstrating its place in a pattern. The pattern can be a social system, an organism, a theory, a picture, a story, or any other collection of related elements. The more richly networked the complex of relations, the more effective the explanation. Table 3.3 illustrates the schema of one model of pattern explanation, the systems model (e.g., Meehan 1968; Tuggle, Townsend, and Riley 1972).

Most pattern explanations in archaeology are based on ethnographic or historical analogues and purport to explain the presence or persistence of a trait or characteristic in a society by relating the function of that trait to the survival or smooth functioning of the society. For instance, why did archaeological culture A have what appear to have been seasonal group ceremonies? Because regular ceremonies provided social cohesion to a loosely knit cultural group whose members were widely scattered throughout much of the year. Other pattern explanations are what-if explanations that present a chain of plausible inferences that link the archaeological record and an interpretation. What if, for instance, the people who once lived at site A were middlemen in an obsidian trading network. If they were, would it not be reasonable to expect to find obsidian concentrated in unusual amounts in storage rooms or other facilities? Unusual amounts of obsidian were found concentrated in several unique facilities unassociated with domestic equip-

Table 3.3 The Systems Model of Explanation

Ideal Form of a Systems Explanation

$$\begin{bmatrix} V_1, V_2, V_3, \ldots, V_n \\ R_1, R_2, R_3, \ldots, R_n \end{bmatrix} \mathord{\rbrace} \Phi$$

In the ideal form, Vs represent relevant variables and Rs represent rules interconnecting the variables, Φ any logical entailment of the system (that is, any conclusion that may be deduced from the system by applying the rules of inference), and $\rbrace$ an "if . . . then" relationship.

ment at site A. Therefore, there is reason to believe that the people who once lived at site A were middlemen in the obsidian trade. A plausible chain of reasoning has been made from the what-if assumption to the observationally available data, although the chain is not deductively valid and no direct appeal has been made to a law or empirical generalization.

Even though reason giving and what-explanations are the most common explanatory strategies in anthropology today, their explanatory sufficiency has been questioned. Covering-law theorists claim, for instance, that what-explanations do not explain the presence of specific events or objects because they do not show why the systems or patterns of which they were a part, rather than others, were present and operated as they did. Other questions have been raised, too. For example, if reason-giving and what-explanations explain by satisfying curiosity, will an explanation that satisfies one person's curiosity necessarily satisfy another's? In science, should a satisfactory explanation really be relative to individual personalities? How do you demonstrate that a closed abstract pattern is empirically meaningful? Are not patterns just heuristic abstractions that are invented to help us understand puzzling aspects of the real world? Even if patterns are intended to be more than just heuristic abstractions, does not an element of logical circularity exist here, anyway? Finally, and most telling, are not reason-giving and what-explanations merely explanation sketches? As the discipline matures as a science, the laws and initial conditions that underlie these incomplete and unsatisfactory sketches will become apparent, or so it has been claimed.

The debate rages on. No one explanatory strategy has been universally accepted in anthropological archaeology or in any of the other social sciences. Since there is a variety of options, it becomes important to comprehend the implications of a strategy that is adopted. For example, by adopting deductive explanation and the covering-law model, archaeologists commit themselves to the search for well-supported lawlike statements and sufficient initial conditions. Should the strategy of reason-giving explanations be adopted, archaeologists would have to decide what to explain, the rational actions of individuals or human groups, or the unintended consequences (due perhaps to misinformation or incomplete information) of both individual actions and the actions of many individuals. Furthermore, they would have to determine how the intentions, motives, and purposes of prehistoric individuals could be plausibly reconstructed. By adopting the strategy of what-explanations, archaeologists become committed to the search for empirically meaningful patterns, the functions of traits, appropriate ethnographic models, and, in general, relations among elements in unique structures.

I have ignored the concept *to predict* until now, because definitions of the concept are affected by the form of explanation that one adopts. According to the symmetry thesis associated with the strategy of deductive explanation, explanation and prediction are usually symmetrical. An argument is an explanation if E is known; it is a prediction if the presence of E is only forecast from the implications of the explanans of the argument. For instance, the argument in part A of table 3.1 is an explanation. If we did not know that E had in fact occurred, we could still predict its occurrence from the information contained in the premises of the argument. In what-explanations, predictions point to what must be present if the pattern—a historical sequence or a social system, for example—did in fact exist. Of course, covering-law theorists who support the symmetry thesis find predictions formed in this manner incomplete and, therefore, unsatisfactory. Since the implications of these arguments affect strategies of theory construction in archaeology, they are examined in greater detail in Part Three.

History or Science?

Are anthropological aracchaeologists social scientists or historians? If they are either one or the other will their subject matter, methods, and objectives be different? Since there are no universally agreed on definitions of social science or history, these terms will be defined here as differing scientific strategies. This emphasis is consistent with the explication of the scientific method developed in chapter 2 and the relatively recent movement of history from its place among the humanistic studies to the ranks of the social sciences. The emphasis also raises a series of fundamental issues that are considered in some detail in chapter 11.

A broad, useful definition of a social science is a discipline concerned with explaining the behavior of groups of people through the explicit formulation and testing of explanatory hypotheses. Since explanatory hypotheses may refer to different levels of abstraction, different objectives within archaeology can be pursued. For instance, hypotheses can be designed to explain the behavior of members of a particular society, of a particular type of society, or of the species *Homo sapiens*. Archaeologists who concentrate on the description, explanation, and prediction of the behavior of members of a particular society are cultural historians. They are concerned with the uniqueness of individual archaeological cultures and with regional differentiation, with *idiographic* studies. Archaeologists who study more inclusive domains unbounded by temporal and spatial restrictions—all hunter-gatherer societies, for example—are social scientists, *sensu stricto*. Their main concern is *nomothetic* studies, the discovery of patterns that repeat themselves. These patterns enable them to deduce principles that apply to all human societies or to all societies of a specific type. The subject matter (artifacts, sites) and the methods of the cultural historian and the social scientist in archaeology are fundamentally similar. What does differ is their research objectives. These differing objectives lead to distinctive research strategies and the accumulation of different kinds of scientific knowledge.

As social scientists, archaeologists examine the archaeological record intent on discovering universal statements—ideally laws—that govern the behavior of human social groups under specific conditions. They are committed to formulating hypotheses and lawlike statements about domains of study more inclusive than particular societies: their objective as social scientists is valid *general* theory about human social and cultural behavior. For them, sites are a medium to be excavated and studied as a means of generating and testing ever more inclusive hypotheses and laws. As cultural historians, archaeologists find hypotheses and lawlike statements useful conceptual tools for making sense of specific archaeological cultures. Unlike social scientists, they are consumers rather than producers of universal and statistical statements that apply to domains greater than that of a particular culture or culture complex.

The objectives of cultural history and of social science are both legitimate goals in anthropological archaeology. Anthropological archaeology is a study of universalities and uniqueness, of unique cultures and of shared patterns of behavior. To borrow Rickert's distinction (1926), anthropological archaeology is both an individualizing and a generalizing science. In practice, archaeologists shift back and forth from one objective to the other, from idiographic to nomothetic studies. As a cultural historian, an archaeologist constructs cultural histories that make intelligible what went on in a particular cultural universe. As a social scientist, the same archaeologist searches for principles common to many different universes. The major parts of this book emphasize one or the other of these two objectives. Part Two focuses on individualizing studies, while Part Three concerns the generalizing objective of anthropological archaeology.

Methodological Principles and Rules

The scientific method is a cyclical series of activities that is aimed at confronting conjectures and observations. The argument has already been made that strategies of research—where one enters the cycle, what one is willing to accept as an adequate test or explanation, and so on—are not entirely objectively determined. Choices can and must be made. Every archaeologist makes these choices against a background of methodological principles and rules that they have either consciously or unconsciously adopted. Methodological principles and rules guide their choices by exhorting the adoption of particular worthwhile research questions, proper procedures, and acceptable answers. More often than not these principles and rules are untestable or at least untested tacit assumptions that lie hidden in our thinking.

A perusal of the major archaeological works of the past will demonstrate that the assumptions archaeologists make change through time (e.g., Trigger 1968). Many of these assumptions have closely mirrored the social milieu of the times, and, as society changed, the assumptions changed, too. Others, successful in one field of inquiry, have been transferred from field to field even though their usefulness in these new areas of application could not be predicted. Examples are the spread of teleological explanation until it came to typify much of medieval thought, the spread of mechanistic explanation during the rise of the natural sciences, and, more recently, the spread of systems explanation. Whatever their source, the assumptions or methodological principles that archaeologists adopt best characterize a school of archaeology or the archaeology of a period. In fact, part of the process of becoming an archaeologist is becoming enculturated with a set of methodological principles and rules. Understanding the dominant principles and rules of a period or of a school of archaeology is very important in answering basic questions like Why do or did they collect this rather than that kind of information? or Why do or did they find these rather than those problems interesting?

Many methodological principles concern the nature of being human or the fundamental structure of society, culture, and the natural world (see part

A of table 3.4). Others concern the strategies and goals of the scientific method itself (part B). These principles have a significant impact on the cycle of science, for they result in admonitions or strictures about what are acceptable procedures and what are not. The following statements are typical methodological rules: state everything as clearly as possible; be wholly

Table 3.4 Examples of Methodological Principles

A. Principles Concerning the Nature of Being Human or the Fundamental Structure of Society, Culture, and the Natural World
  1. All temporal changes observed by the senses are merely permutations and combinations of eternal principles (Plato).
  2. People are bad; people are good.
  3. People act more or less rationally (the assumption of rationality).
  4. Sociological and cultural materials can be reduced to psychological materials (George Homans).
  5. Nature is based upon rational principles.
  6. Society operates in accordance with fixed causal laws.
  7. The past is knowable.
  8. The course of historical events has a profound significance.
  9. The aim of history is moral instruction through the recounting of edifying tales.
  10. Divine revelation is a source of knowledge.
  11. Mental phenomena and overt behavior are irreducibly different sorts of things (Cartesian dualism).
  12. Social facts must be explained in social terms (Durkheim's maxim).
  13. The laws of the natural world remain constant.
  14. Culture is a hodgepodge of disparate and unrelated traits.
  15. Nature chooses simple systems.
  16. Only God could create a perfect world.

B. Principles Concerning the Strategies and Goals of Science
  1. Fact collecting of itself is insufficient scientific procedure.
  2. Nonempirical statements are meaningless (a principle of logical positivism).
  3. When accounting for phenomena do not multiply entities beyond necessity (Occam's razor).
  4. There is one scientific method common to all sciences, however diverse their subject matter (the methodological unity of science thesis).
  5. Anything goes (Feyerabend's maxim).
  6. Knowledge evolves through the amassing of facts.
  7. Theoretical statements should be capable of falsification (Popper's maxim).
  8. The history of anything constitutes a sufficient explanation of it.
  9. Since only the outer world counts, behavior rather than thought should be our object of study.
  10. Only experience can decide the truth or falsity of a factual statement.
  11. Scientific statements are causal; they consist of individual cases subsumed under hypothetically assumed general laws of nature (the covering-law position).
  12. Science is only a Glorious Entertainment (posed as a question by Jacques Barzun).

objective; do not rigidly accept authority as a source of proof; search for regularities and causalities. Other examples are listed in table 3.5.

An example will make the relationship between methodological principles and rules clearer. Consider the common view in anthropology and sociology that a society is a group of interdependent human beings. Among the methodological principles associated with this view are the following: the actions of members of a society are primarily determined by the patterns of behavior unwittingly established by the social group; all social phenomena are inherently relational; since human existence is dependent on relations with other people, people cannot be conceived of apart from society; all parts of a society fit more or less into a unified whole. Anthropologists and sociologists who adopt these principles are constrained to explain human behavior in terms of principles that pertain to the human group. Among the procedural rules that they might adopt are the following: always study people within specific historical structures; concentrate your research on patterns of behavior rather than on individual actions; do not assume an isolated individual, whose needs, abilities, or wants are regarded as independent of the social organization within which he or she lives or works.

Sets of methodological principles and rules can and do clash, for most are nonverifiable, a priori assumptions. The widely accepted modern view of society presented in a simplistic form above would seem strange to someone not enculturated within the twentieth-century rejection of the notion of individual responsibility. Victorians, for example, followed the principle that "uniqueness does not reside in the social whole but in the individual." A

Table 3.5   Example of Methodological Rules

 1. State everything as clearly as possible.
 2. Let facts speak for themselves.
 3. Do not rigidly accept authority as a source of proof.
 4. Search for regularities and causalities.
 5. Decide what to expect before observations are made.
 6. Gather facts without any preconception of what they may mean.
 7. Teach students the cold, hard facts.
 8. Build systems rather than make detailed studies of particulars.
 9. Do not use analogies as a source of proof.
10. View societies as unique wholes.
11. Tell it like it is.
12. Those theories should be given preference that can be most severely tested.
13. Those empirical theories should be given preference that have the highest empirical content.

number of methodological rules follow from this principle that clash with those presented above. For instance, "The characteristics of individuals rather than of group behavior should be the focus of investigations" and "Group behavior must be explained in terms of the individual." Obviously, the degree of interdependence between the individual and the social group that is now commonly assumed was not then a widespread assumption. A clear difference in research goals follows from the adoption of one or the other of these sets of principles.

Methodological principles and rules like those in the examples given above should be clearly distinguished from suppositions or hypotheses about actual empirical relationships in the real world. They are *conventions,* research tools, that might best be described as the rules of the game of science (e.g., Popper 1970). Some clearly involve substantive claims about what kinds of entities exist in the world, what relations obtain between them, and so on. For instance, they might postulate the existence of group behavior, systems, and cultures. In this manner they inform a science's conception of its proper subject matter. Others provide criteria for the selection, evaluation, and criticism of the problems and solutions arising within a science. Together these background assumptions constitute the metaphysical content of a scientific discipline.

The goals and research activities of anthropological archaeology are more easily comprehended by understanding the methodological principles and rules that underlie its theoretical foundations. Some principles have been shared by nearly all archaeologists for over a century and are rarely debated. These include:

—The study of history matters.
—Social relics exist.
—The past is knowable.
—Material culture, the physical, man-made remains surviving from the past, can be used as evidence about the past.
—The processes of the past were the same as those in operation at the present (the principle of uniformitarianism).
—People did things in the past for the same reasons they do things today (Roe's principle of cultural uniformity) (1976:64).

Other methodological principles have been adopted by many anthropological archaeologists and characterize processual archaeology. Some of these principles are:

—A sociocultural system is a unique whole.

—Sociocultural systems (as unique wholes) are composed of interdependent parts that cannot be fully understood apart from the whole (the doctrine of functionalism).

—Culture is a human group's means of adaptation.

—Sociocultural systems and ideologies are functions of their technological bases (the doctrine of cultural materialism).

—Culture is to be explained in terms of culture.

—There are predictable regularities in the social world.

—Society is law-governed.

—Data relating to the entire extinct cultural system are present in the archaeological record.

Still other assumptions once widely held within anthropological archaeology, such as "The patterning of material remains in an archaeological site is the result of the patterned behavior of the members of extinct societies," have been vigorously challenged within the discipline itself (Schiffer 1976).

Methodological principles such as these guide anthropological archaeologists in choosing research questions, problems, and procedures. For instance, the assumption that regularities exist in the social world provides a rationale for model building in archaeology today. Or, as a more extended example, if culture is considered a human group's means of adaptation to the environment, and sociocultural systems and ideologies are considered functions of their technological bases, an essential goal of archaeological research becomes the reconstruction of past environments and the technology of human groups. A program of exploratory and hypothesis-testing research will be initiated that includes the systematic collection of animal bones, seeds, pollen grains, and other ecofacts, and the careful examination of grinding stones, scrapers, storage vessels, sickles, and other food procurement and processing tools. A research goal will be the reconstruction of subsistence and settlement systems. Processual models of integrated sociocultural systems will be formulated. And so on. However, these procedures, which are effective for acquiring knowledge for this set of assumptions, are not necessarily effective if other sets of assumptions are adopted instead.

It is useful to think of schools of archaeology, such as processual archaeology, as *research programs,* programs for research that are founded on a core of essentially unchallenged methodological principles. Research programs are guiding forces in the cycle of science: they influence the manner in which archaeologists carry out their projects, determine what is archaeologically legitimate, determine the meaning of archaeology as it is taught in colleges and universities, guarantee its continuance, and even influence the evaluation of archaeological works. Puzzles, the definition of interesting concepts and data, and many other guidelines to research follow from these programs, for particular programs emphasize some goals, problems, and procedures to the exclusion of others. Research programs reflect conceptual approaches, theoretical orientations, or theories. Examples in anthropology include the ecological approach, structural-functionalism, and the evolutionary approach.

Research programs perform their function in science by presenting a plan or direction of inquiry. If it is assumed, for instance, that the controlled study of overt behavior is the only sound procedure for achieving reliable knowledge concerning individual and social action and that laws of human behavior exist and are subject to discovery, then study overt and publicly observable behavior or its by-products and seek behavioral laws (the behavioral approach). Or, in humanistic archaeology, if it is assumed that research should emphasize the great achievements of human beings, that classical civilization represents the highest level of human achievement, and that the purpose of the study of the past is to develop a desirable type of human being rather than just knowledge of the past, then emphasize the excavation of classical sites and the recovery of great works of art or other outstanding human achievements, as well as classical studies, methods of historical and philological criticism, the ideal of literary elegance, and personal growth. Although these brief sketches of behavioral and humanistic archaeology are clearly caricatures of research programs, they do demonstrate the prescriptive nature of the programs.

The research programs archaeologists adopt are theoretical-methodological stances, stances that inevitably influence the theoretical and operational definitions of their basic concepts. As a result, individuals committed to different programs, even though they may be interested in the same subject matter, region, and problems, often misunderstand one another and talk at cross-purposes. However, the recognition of fundamental differences between core principles and the ensuing debate between supporters of different programs have often stimulated the growth of archaeology in the past: new research programs then become the conventional wisdom of another generation of archaeologists. As archaeologists become aware of the heuristic value of research programs, they are more easily able to shift from one program to another as their research interests change.

Some philosophers of science have suggested that the coherence of research programs is a useful indicator of the maturity of a science or even whether a discipline is a science or not (Lakatos 1970). It is probably fair to conclude that research programs in anthropological archaeology remain loosely formulated. Nonetheless, all the arguments presented above do suggest that we should reject notions that research programs are inherent in the stuff of archaeology and embrace instead the assumption that groups, or schools, of archaeologists display a preference for one or another approach to the archaeological record. This assumption leads us away from the hopeless task of discovering philosophies *in* archaeology to the more rewarding task of finding the pervasive attitudes *toward* archaeology and the uses of archaeology that any one school or age displays.

Summary

Chapter 3 reviews a variety of research strategies from which archaeologists must choose when proceeding around the cycle of science. Among strategies considered are types of investigations, explanatory-predictive strategies, idiographic or nomothetic studies, and research programs. Even though science is a cyclical system of inquiry, individual archaeologists frequently emphasize particular phases of the cycle. Five characteristic types of investigations in archaeology are (1) hypothesis testing, (2) concept and instrumental investigations, (3) descriptive studies, (4) exploratory investigations, and (5) interpretive-theoretical studies. Archaeologists also have options in choosing among explanatory-predictive strategies. Among the ideal forms of explanation considered are deductive-nomological, deductive-statistical, inductive-statistical, reason-giving, and what-explanation.

The main issues involved in choosing an explanatory strategy concern the proper form of an explanation and what *to resolve a puzzle* means. If taken seriously, one's position on these issues may dramatically affect research goals and the selection of other research strategies. The history-science debate distinguishes between two additional distinctive and traditional objectives within anthropological archaeology: the examination of uniqueness and the search for generality. Social science and culture history are both defined as strategies of science. The first is a search for generality unrestricted by time and place. The second is an examination of uniqueness and the general at a particular time and place. Both objectives are legitimate and complementary strategies in anthropological archaeology.

Archaeologists choose among these competing strategies immersed in a body of largely tacit, metaphysical assumptions. These background assumptions concern the nature of the research process, society, culture, the natural world, and what *to be human* means. Sets of assumptions form research programs that guide the selection of suitable questions, proper procedures, and acceptable answers. Understanding how research programs affect research strategies is an integral part of comprehending the diverse goals and procedures of anthropological archaeologists.

Suggested Readings

The text has stressed the many forms of explanation that philosophers of science claim either exist in or at least should exist in any science. The merits of nearly all of these perspectives are discussed and debated in the following writings.

Borger, R. and F. Cioffi, eds. 1970. *Explanations in the Behavioral Sciences*. Cambridge: Cambridge University Press.

Brown, R. R. 1963. *Explanation in Social Science*. Chicago: Aldine.

Harré, R. and P. Secord. 1972. *The Explanation of Social Behavior*. Oxford: Backwell.

Korner, S., ed. 1975. *Explanation*. New Haven, Conn.: Yale University Press.

Levin, M. 1973. On explanation in archaeology: A rebuttal to Fritz and Plog. *American Antiquity* 38:387–395.

Morgan, C. 1973. Archaeology and explanation. *World Archaeology* 4:259–276.

—— 1974. Explanation and scientific archaeology. *World Archaeology* 6:133–137.

Salmon, M. 1975. Confirmation and explanation in archaeology. *American Antiquity* 40:459–464.

Salmon, M. and W. Salmon. 1979. Alternative models of scientific explanation. *American Anthropologist* 81:61–74.

CHAPTER FOUR

The Model-Building Process

Building models, especially formal mathematical models, is a popular research activity in the social and behavioral sciences for many reasons. Models simplify reality, conceptualize phenomena from different points of view, provide explanations, isolate problems for investigation, predict relationships, and give real-world relationships meaningful expression and integration. Although you may find this connotation of the term *model* somewhat unusual, we all inescapably employ and build theoretical models of one kind or another. What we regard as proper behavior and the research programs we adopt are examples of *mental models*. In archaeology, mental models are models *of* archaeology, such as the positivist, the idealist, or the processualist. *Operational models*, in contrast, are simplified, often idealized, interlinked guesses about the processes and objects that either now exist or have existed in the past. Operational models are models *in* archaeology, such as models of economic exchange, diffusion, or the spatial relationships of a set of artifacts. Since anthropological archaeology is an observational science, the process of building operational models allows archaeologists to creatively play with ideas, construct images, imaginatively manipulate variables, and regard archaeological phenomena in new and stimulating ways in order to understand why phenomena are as they are.

Chapter 4 introduces processes involved in building and evaluating operational models. The first section defines *model* and identifies a variety of types of models. The second section discusses the art of model building. The third provides an example of the model-building process. When the term *model* is used in these sections, only the operational meaning of the term is being referred to.

What Are Models?

Models are heuristic devices for structuring observations and thinking about human behavior. They play their most important roles in the cycle of science (1) during the interpretation of sample summaries and empirical generalizations and (2) in the testing of cultural histories and scientific theories. In this section the model concept is introduced by reviewing the characteristic traits and structure of models and some of the perspectives from which models have been defined.

The Function and Structure of Models

Models as Simplified Representations of Reality. Reality in archaeology refers to objects in archaeological context, such as artifacts and their spatial distributions, or to events and objects in past systemic contexts. Both of these realities are complex hodgepodges of empirical entities and shifting relationships. Even if we wanted to, we could never answer all questions that could be posed about these realities or reconstruct all of their many details, for they are too diverse and on too large a scale to comprehend as wholes. Models help us structure only some of these observations and think about only some aspects of past human behavior. They perform these functions by providing concepts only for those characteristics of the world in which we are interested. This is clearly a pragmatic procedure, for most of this detail is incidental to the problems and questions that are chosen for study. The results of these abstractions are often idealized pictures and representations of the incomprehensibly complicated realities that archaeologists study. In a sense, models are conceptual spotlights that illuminate only chosen aspects of reality.

Like all pictures and representations, models are simpler than the part of reality they are supposed to represent. Simplification through model building serves several purposes in the transformation of information in the cycle of science. First, by removing unnecessary incidental detail, simplification leads to a better understanding of a problem and its essential components. Second, by critically scrutinizing only selected aspects of reality, simplification makes gaps in knowledge glaringly obvious. Finally, by being selective, the simplifying process highlights potentially important relationships that might otherwise have been missed.

Since the relationship between a model and any empirical phenomenon is always focused and partial, it is possible to formulate several different models of various aspects of the same situation. Each of these alternative representations is generally useful for different purposes. Archaeologists, for example, commonly develop separate models of the social organization, the economic subsystem, and the political organization of a past sociocultural system from the same set of artifacts and sites. A cultural history is an eventual result of the synthesis of these models. In addition, since models are only as-if and partial representations, alternative models can be built to represent the same aspects of a given situation. For example, competing models can be built as trial explanations of the distribution of the same sites in a region. Part Two contains examples of this competitive use of the modeling process.

Models as Meaning Providers. Besides being a primary locus of representation and simplification in the cycle of science, models also give meaning to objects and spatial distributions in the archaeological record. They perform this function by interpreting the contents of the archaeological record in terms of familiar objects, systems, or processes, such as grinder, social system, and migration. Since experience has convinced us that the objects, systems, or processes that these terms denote do exist, it is not implausible to assume that they might have existed in the past as well; models gain their initial credibility through these kinds of plausibility arguments. In their role as meaning provider, models provide a context within which borrowed analogies and metaphors can be manipulated to create new interpretations and to suggest new lines of research. Models are perceptual sensitizers, devices that sensitize archaeologists to the possibility of looking at archaeological phenomena in sometimes new and interesting ways.

The Structure of Models. Models perform their interpretive and, ultimately, explanatory role in the cycle of science by providing a *rationale,* a *process,* and a *form* for interpreting observations. A model's rationale is the point of view, the picture of reality, or the basis of abstraction behind the selection of the concepts and process of the model. In anthropology, evolutionism, functionalism, and cultural ecology are examples of rationales or theoretical orientations toward social phenomena (e.g., Kaplan and Manners 1972:32–87). These points of view are not given in the data; they are not arrived at through a process of induction that leads unerringly from data to a correct interpretation. Instead, they are a form of mental experiment, an imaginative quest through the process of abduction that carries us "beyond the phenomena from which we began" (Toulmin 1958:38). Rationales are not selected to perceive reality as it really is, as piles of potsherds and stone flakes, but to transcend these observable archaeological materials to obtain a conceptualization of past sociocultural phenomena that provides an explanation for them. In Willer's words, the "most important characteristic of systematic abduction is the attainment of a consistent point of view toward the data, a point of view which will allow the unambiguous, logical, or mathematical statement of hypotheses." In a model with a number of possible hypotheses, "the consistency of a point of view or rationale as an organizing principle connecting the abduced relationships into a consistent model becomes more and more important" (1967:29). This is why the abduction of an internally consistent model requires the conscious use of one rationale or another.

Seeing observations from a point of view is a form of hypothetical as-if thinking. We might playfully ask, for example, What if the properties of electricity are like those of a fluid? What if a society is like an organism or a complex adaptive system? What if site A is the remains of a rice harvesting camp? The points of view expressed in these questions provide a rationale for abstracting only some phenomena and ignoring others. When functionalism is the point of view, for instance, only the concept of function and phenomena pertaining to it are relevant. Other phenomena pertaining to evolutionism, cultural ecology, or design styles are ignored. In this sense, a model abstracts only those parts of phenomena for which it provides concepts.

In addition to providing the basis for abstraction of models, rationales also provide the basis for deriving the process and form of models. Operational models differ most clearly from general models or conceptual schemes by their determinant processes, by the hypothetical relationships among concepts that follow from adopting a particular rationale. Determinant processes make the formation and structure of the concepts of a model understandable by showing how the model behaves. By going beyond mere abstraction to the generation of relationships among concepts, operational models gain the capacity to predict, postdict, and explain a wide diversity of phenomena. For example, if in constructing a model of the behavior of electricity we decide that the properties of electricity are like those of fluids, the processes of the model will (experimentally, at least) be considered the known laws of fluids. In this example the laws of fluids determine how the concepts of electricity should interact and what the structure of their relationships should be if the model is an accurate representation of the behavior of electricity. Or, if we decide that it is useful to think of societies as evolving like organisms, the processes of the model will be those same processes that have led more complex, functionally diverse, interdependent organisms to evolve from simpler, less diverse, less interdependent ones. Finally, if we decide that site A was a rice-harvesting site, the sequences of activities that went on in ethnographically recorded rice-harvesting camps are the processes of the model that we construct. The resulting sets of relationships among the concepts in these examples provide the form or structure of each model. For these reasons, the study of form or structure by itself is of very limited value: a generative mechanism or process is needed to show how the model behaves.

In summary, a model orders observations and minimizes perceptual confusion by organizing perceptions within a conceptual framework constructed by means of a rationale. It does this by representing observations by concepts and then ordering the concepts. The resulting structure and relationships of its concepts are the form of a model. An operational model also provides a process that makes the form of the model understandable by showing how it behaves. The form provides a systematic set of relationships between concepts and the process indicates how the relationships work. Because they have a form and process, models have a predictive capability and are able to generate anticipated relationships. Precisely for this reason, operational models are more than just clusters of concepts.

Models, Scientific Theories, and Culture Histories. Models should not be confused with scientific theories or culture histories. For the many reasons that have already been discussed, it is fruitful to think of some aspect of reality, some segment of the archaeological record, for instance, *as if* it could be explained by referring to the rationale, processes, and form of a model. To propose that a culture *is* an organism, however, is to propose a scientific theory. The organismic theory maintains that the organization and activities of human cultural groups can be explained by the principles that govern or the relationships encountered in organic systems.

Modeling, on the other hand, is a method for transforming information. Models playfully consider what is structurally possible and suggestive; theories suggest what is empirically probable. While models are only hypothetical representations that cannot be true or false by definition, theories are about what is or was. For this reason, models are only useful or they are not: they are not capable of actually explaining observations. Models only provide interpretive explanations, a basis for deterministic explanation that is not absolute and may be altered or displaced by others that have different structures and provide more effective explanations. The acceptance of a particular model is solely for practical purposes—for its isomorphism with empirical patterns and thus its effectiveness in providing an explanation for them.

Scientific theories and culture histories explain, while models are merely heuristic devices that help us arrive at explanations by providing a series of *trial* explanations. Once models are transformed to theories, human cultures are no longer regarded for certain purposes, for instance, *as if* they are organisms but *as* organisms. For all of these reasons, it is necessary to distinguish a model of or for a scientific theory or culture history from a scientific theory or culture history itself.

Types of Models

Models are constructed as heuristic devices to aid our understanding of the content, structure, and interactions of the three ontological realms of culture, mind, and the physical world. Not all models, however, serve similar functions or have the same degree of concreteness. On an abstract level, a culture can be thought of as a machine or an organism. On a more mundane level the spatial relationships of artifacts within a site can be modeled with distribution maps, stick figures, statistical formulas, and other simplified structural representations. A toy airplane is a model. So is the spread of contagious diseases when the abstracted structure and process of the spread are used to help us understand the spread of information. A statistical chart of the age distribution of a population is another kind of model, as is a mathematical formula. Since models serve multiple functions and have different degrees of concreteness, they can be classified from many different perspectives, each of which emphasizes certain characteristics of models to the exclusion of others. In this section, five classifications of models will be briefly introduced (table 4.1). These are material-formal, iconic-analogue-symbolic, a posteriori–a priori, static-dynamic, and real-abstract.

Table 4.1 Some Type of Models

1. Material	analogues for data or theories	
Formal	idealized descriptions of data	
2. Iconic	direct representations of properties of empirical phenomena	
Analogue	analogues for data or theories	
Symbolic	formal models composed of interconnected symbols, such as mathematical notation	
3. a priori	conceptual devices for developing theories that function in the context of discovery	
a posteriori	interpretations of existing theories that function in the context of justification	
4. Dynamic	models that involve changing forms through time	
Static	models concerned with one period or moment in time	
5. Real	models that are intended to be representations of the real world of the past	
Abstract	models of nonexistent, abstract worlds of words, numbers, signs, and symbols created by theoreticians	

Material and Formal Models. A basic categorization of models separates those that are *idealized descriptions* of data (formal models) from those that are *analogues* for data or theories that are being interpreted (material models) (Harré 1970; Hesse 1966). Material models incorporate as analogues ideas or images from one physical system to interpret another. In archaeology the pattern of spread of contagious diseases, ethnographically recorded subsistence patterns, and present-day tools provide analogies that have proven useful in interpreting artifacts and their distribution. Models that constitute idealized descriptions of data, that are abstractions of particular situations, are formal models. Formal models make no reference to any other physical analogue. A toy airplane is a simple formal model, as is a graph or table of numbers. The most sophisticated formal models are mathematical formulas. Mathematical formulas lack any empirical grounding or reference until the symbols of which they are composed are given empirical interpretation: otherwise their elements and relationships remain purely formal ones.

Iconic, Analogue, and Symbolic Models. Clarke (1972a, 1978) has discussed three basic classes of model, the iconic, the analogue, and the symbolic, that elaborate on the material-formal distinction. Iconic and symbolic models are formal models, while analogue models are material models. Each

Table 4.2　A Simple Iconic Model Without Process: The Material Composition of the Lithic Assemblage from a Site

	Waste		Tools		Total	
	No.	%	No.	%	No.	%
Quartzite	20	30	82	36	102	35
Chert	39	59	96	42	135	46
Other	7	11	51	22	58	20
Total	66	100	229	100	295	101

provides a different basis upon which a general rationale for model construction may rest. In addition, as one moves from iconic to analogue to symbolic models the degree of abstraction from reality increases. These distinctions provide particularly significant insights into the model-building process in archaeology.

An *iconic model* is constructed to directly represent properties of empirical phenomena by subjecting them to a transformation in scale or importance and emphasis. Thus the general rationale underlying iconic models is one of direct similarity to the subject of representation, and the process if present is abstracted from the subject itself and used to connect the concepts of the model. Since the process is intended to *directly* represent the behavior of the subject of representation, the process and resulting form of an iconic model are dependent on the number of properties abstracted and, therefore, on the number of points of similarity between the model and subject, as well as on the level of abstraction and type of transformation that has been made. Statistical tables, distribution maps, scatter diagrams, and hardward models such as miniature replicas of airplanes or engineering models of dams are iconic models. Most of the graphs in Part Two are examples of simple models of this type.

The simplest kinds of iconic model are those whose transformation has been limited to that of scale, size, or dimension. Toy trains, photographs, stick models of atoms, and kinship charts are examples. A photograph, for instance, transforms the characteristics of the subject of representation into two dimensions and usually reduces its size. However, typologies of ideal societal types, such as hunter-gatherer, subsistence farmer, chiefdom, and state are iconic models, too. Some iconic models, such as toy airplanes, are literally scale models. Toy airplanes are shaped like real airplanes, but they have been transformed in scale and constructed from different materials. They have some but not all of the characteristics of real airplanes. This is why they are called model airplanes. These differences in scale and material may be crucial or they may not be. If engineers are interested in the aerodynamic flow and stress of a plane's wings, a toy airplane in a wind-tunnel may be an appropriate research tool.

Iconic models frequently lack processes and are therefore incomplete operational models. A kinship diagram in which rules of relationship have not been specified is an example, as is a toy machine whose parts do not interact in a coordinated manner. Since a process or set of processes is absent, the models lack the predictive capability of operational models (table 4.2).

The definition of an *analogue model* is identical to that of a material model. Images, properties, and concepts in analogue models are derived by analogy from better known and more familiar situations. The images, properties, and concepts in the analogues are then allowed to represent the properties, processes, and structure of the subject being represented. Here the process and form of the model are borrowed from the analogue and are intended to be isomorphic with the structure and process of the abstracted properties of the subject. A basis for analogical argument and quantitative and qualitative prediction is provided by these apparent isomorphisms. The borrowing of suggestive metaphors and analogies is one way in which knowledge gained in one area of inquiry aids puzzle solving in other areas. In fact the heuristic possibilities contained in the process of borrowing are one of the most useful features of analogue models.

Harré's distinction (1970) between a *model,* the *source* of a model, and the *subject* of a model is helpful in more clearly delineating the components involved in building analogue models. In an iconic model the subject and the source of the model are the same. In an analogue model the subject and the source are different; the model is analogically related to the source and is an attempted representation of the subject. For example, the organismic model of society is based on an analogy with an organism. Here the subject of the model is the properties, processes, and structures of societies or institutions; the source of the model is an organism; and the model is a representation of this subject, analogically related to the source.

The construction of an analogue model is an excellent example of imaginative as-if thinking. What if, for instance, the rate of exchange of goods between communities is considered isomorphic with the varying strength of the attractive forces between planets? In this example the rationale is the likening of the properties of exchange among humans to those of gravity.

Although human exchange and gravity are generally considered dissimilar processes, by thinking with the model we might conclude that if a large and a small community (planet) are equidistant from a source (the sun), the greater rate of exchange (attraction) will occur with the larger community (planet). Furthermore, by applying the known laws of gravity that compose the processes of the model, we may even predict rates of exchange. Other well-known analogue models in anthropology are the organismic model, functionalism, and evolutionism. In fact, the history of anthropological explanations of social relationships and social structures in the United States has, for the most part, been the history of two of these analogue models, functionalism and evolutionism. Analogue models are very common in archaeology, especially those derived from ethnographic and historical situations. A familiar example is the invasionist-migrationist model, which dominated archaeological interpretation of culture change between the 1920s and the 1960s (e.g., Clark 1966).

In contrast to an iconic or analogue model, a *symbolic model* does not refer to any empirical phenomena at all. It is a formal model composed of interconnected symbols, such as mathematical notation. The symbols are integrated in a special calculus (a mathematical theory or a geometric system, for instance) that provides a set of logical rules for their combination and manipulation. These sets of logical rules provide the processes and forms of symbolic models. The general rationale of this type of model consists of allowing the calculus to represent a set of phenomena; some aspect of the real world is mapped onto the ready-made calculus by giving the symbols in the calculus real-world interpretations. Therefore, the source of symbolic models is sets of symbols, and the processes are the relations between the symbols as developed in the source itself. In a developed symbolic model, the structural relationships between the data that are the subject of the model are isomorphic with the logical relationships between the symbols in the calculus. Of the three types of model in this classification system, symbolic models are the most concise in construction and the most advanced because of their generally powerful but not rigid processes.

Symbolic models are based on abstract symbolic systems that lack empirical content, such as probability theory, game theory, and graph theory. The relationships among elements within these systems are purely logical, although they may be deterministic, statistical, stochastic, and so forth. A typical example of a simple symbolic system is figure 4.1A, which represents a two-variable linear relationship devoid of empirical content. In this abstract

A.   A two variable linear relationship

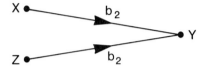

B.   A multiple variable linear relationship

Figure 4.1   Examples of symbolic systems.

symbolic system, Y is the dependent variable, since the distribution of Y depends on the distribution of the independent variable X, and b is a linear
coefficient that gives the value of Y for any value of X. The symbolic system
becomes a model when Y, X, and b are given empirical interpretations. For
example, Y could be interpreted as number of buffalo killed each year and
X as climate. This simple deterministic model can also be expressed by the
formula $Y = bX$. The symbolic system can be complicated by adding an
additional independent variable, Z. This transforms the symbolic system into
the multiple variable linear formula, $Y = b_1X + b_2Z$ (figure 4.1B). In this
example, Z might be interpreted as sophistication of technology. In both
examples the subject of the models is the empirical relationship between
number of buffalo killed each year and climate or climate and sophistication
of technology; the sources are the symbolic systems and the models are the
interpreted symbolic systems.

A Priori and A Posteriori Models. The distinction between a priori and a
posteriori models emphasizes the two major roles of the modeling process
in the cycle of science. A priori models are conceptual devices for developing theory. They function in the context of discovery by providing sets of
rules for ordering data, structural schema suitable for explanation, and images for the interpretation of archaeological phenomena. In general they are
conceptual aids for drawing conclusions about archaeological phenomena.
During this transformation of information archaeologists must determine
which model or models have the greatest potential for developing an accurate, comprehensive, and systematic culture history or scientific theory. A

posteriori models are interpretations of existing theory. Their function is to facilitate the testing process; they function in the context of justification. A posteriori models perform their function by simplifying the content and relationships among elements in complex culture histories or scientific theories. For instance, the spread of information in early urban societies can be compared to the spread of contagious diseases in order to arrive at testable implications. The simple mathematical formula for the spread of contagious diseases simplifies calculations and facilitates deduction. In the cycle of science, a priori and a posteriori models tend to be closely related, although their functions are clearly different. For instance, once the contagious disease model has been tested, it can be simplified or made more complex within the context of discovery. In this new, altered state the model now functions as an a priori model for the creation of a more effective or elaborate culture history.

Dynamic and Static Models. Another useful distinction between types of models is between those that are dynamic and those that are static. Dynamic models involve changing forms through time. Examples are the contagious disease model mentioned above and the stochastic model of agricultural advance discussed in the last section of this chapter. Static models are concerned with one period or moment in time. Examples are an aerial photograph or the Christaller settlement model examined in chapter 7. Chapters 5 through 7 of this book focus on static models, while chapter 8 is concerned with dynamic models.

Real and Abstract Models. The types of models that we have been discussing can also be separated into real and abstract categories. Real models are representations of the real world of the past, of what Kaplan (1964) has called the past-in-itself. Most modeling efforts in anthropological archaeology take as their main object of study particular societies, behavior that actually existed in the past, and events that can be verified. These efforts have resulted in the description and explanation of the archaeological record in many parts of the world. By contrast, abstract models are models of nonexistent, abstract worlds of words, numbers, signs, and symbols created by theoreticians. This type of model is a tool theoreticians use to test the operation of different hypothetical processes, as in counterfactual situations of what may have arisen under alternative conditions or in ideal sociocultural systems. These abstractions provide imaginary worlds against which their real-world counterparts may be measured and more fully understood. Abstract models are also essential tools in formulating scientific theories, for they are about general structures and processes independent of space and time. The distinction between real and abstract models is paralleled in the distinction between systems theory, or the systems approach, and general systems theory. The models of systems theory "are used to make us more aware, as we examine specific societies at specific times, of the links by which they are tied together" (Mills 1967:180), while the models of general systems theory are about the abstract forms and processes of general theory (Langton 1972).

Models may be classified into other categories besides those mentioned here. For example, the distinction between theoretical and empirical models emphasizes the degree of abstraction involved in model construction. Whatever classificatory system is used, research projects commonly build and manipulate more than one type of model, for models play a primary role in interpreting and testing theories by extending or completing them, by connecting them with experience, and by integrating them with other theories.

The Realist-Positivist Dispute

How is the correspondence between the process and form of the models discussed here and the process and structure of the phenomena they represent to be interpreted? Ideally, they are isomorphic, corresponding exactly in form and process. But is the correspondence one of *similarity* or of *identity?* From a realist conception of science, the modeling process is an attempt to depict and transfer actual forms and processes from one better known realm of study to another. The intended correspondence between the process and form of a model, and the process and structure of the phenomena it represents, is one of identity. On the other hand, in the positivist conception of science, models are typically regarded as heuristic aids that help one build or represent a scientific theory or culture history: the correspondence is always one of similarity of structure or process rather than of identity. Although the differences between a realist and a positivist conception of science are not more fully explicated until chapter 11, the correspondence issue is worth mentioning here, for it has far-reaching implications concerning the intent and nature of the model-building process.

The basis of the realist-positivist dispute is an epistemological disagreement, a disagreement over what can be known about the world. For the positivist, cultures, social structures, the subjective states of individuals, and underlying forms and processes may exist, but it is not the purpose of science to attempt to get behind the phenomena experienced through our sensory equipment. Underlying forms and processes are best regarded as shorthand concepts or useful analogues for helping us understand the patterned social activities of people living in societies. The correspondence between a model and the phenomena it represents is one of suggestive similarity only. When human cultures are compared to organic systems, for instance, their structural and processual similarities are being referred to rather than an identity in kind. Scientists model because the source of a model is usually more familiar and its form and process better understood. The structural and processual similarities of models and the phenomena they represent give models their predictive capability. Since similarities are being compared or explored, the characteristics of models and the phenomena they represent are never precisely the same: their correspondence is only partial. For the realist, models help us explain archaeological phenomena by making reference to underlying processes and forms that may have been actually involved in some aspect of the formation of the archaeological record. Although the substance of the subject and the source of a model may be different, their forms and processes are identical in a general systems or third world sense, depending on one's interpretation. Since realists make ontological commitments to unobservable entities, such as underlying structures, mechanisms, and essences, different phenomena may have an identity that positivists find mystical and metaphysical. Models are not just heuristic devices for the realist, but descriptions of actually existing and recurring forms and processes that underlie or are behind the phenomena being studied.

The Art of Model Building

Building models is a creative art in archaeology, an art requiring a combination of controlled comparison and bold conjecture. Fruitful models depend on skill in abstraction, derivation, and evaluation. *Abstraction* is the ability to imagine or recognize a correspondence between archaeological data and the form and process of a model or source; it is the ability to abstract from archaeological data to a model. Although skill in abstraction is essential to fruitful model building, it is a difficult skill to acquire, for human activity in the past was certainly complex and only some of this activity has been materialized in the archaeological record. Becoming familiar with a wide range of models and practical examples of their application is one route to skillful abstraction. Model builders also require skill at derivation. *Derivation* is the process of becoming aware of the significant implications of a model in both the context of discovery and the context of justification. Another essential skill in model building is *evaluation*. Not all models are equally fruitful; some in fact may be misleading and lead to a loss of time, effort, and money.

How are models constructed? Are there similar themes running through the construction of material and formal models that promote effective abstraction, derivation, and evaluation? Unfortunately, no model-building scheme can guarantee effective modeling. With this understanding, a series of idealized steps is introduced below for the development of models within the context of discovery, for exploratory research is the dominant type of investigation in archaeology today (figure 4.2). In this regard, the process of learning to build a priori models must be clearly distinguished from learning models, developing a posteriori models, or teaching models.

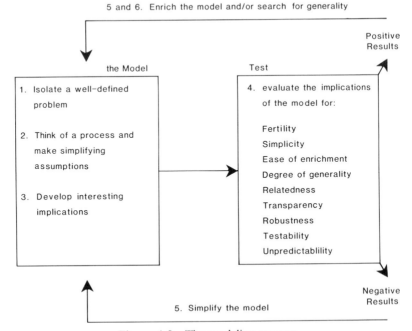

Figure 4.2 The modeling process.

Steps in the Modeling Process

1. Isolate a Well-Defined Problem. The first step in the modeling process is the isolation of a well-defined problem. Well-defined problems aid in clarifying the goals of the modeling process, determining what measures to use and what type of model to construct, recognizing when the modeling process has been successful, and, in general, guiding effective procedure. Most importantly, the isolation of a well-defined problem aids in the construction of meaningful hypotheses. Consider, for instance, the vagueness in archaeology of problem areas. Problem areas concern sets of observations, such as the covariation in space of specific artifact types, the pattern of distribution of sites in a region, or the varying spatial extent of vertically distributed components in a site. In many instances the problem is so complex that it has to be factored into simpler problems. For instance, in trying to model the dynamics of a past sociocultural system, it is easier to initiate the modeling process by focusing on fairly precise questions: Was the community zoned? How? What was the pattern of location of households? What processes led to social ranking? How did the subsistence system work? Each of these questions can then be studied and modeled separately and synthesized to create a consistent, comprehensive model of the sociocultural whole. Or, in examining an archaeological site, you might ask, Why are artifact types A and B spatially associated? What were these artifacts or features used for? Why is a particular artifact type distributed in this way rather than in the many other ways it could be distributed? In other words, how can we account for the properties and the spatial distributions of the content of archaeological sites?

In formulating a problem to initiate the modeling process, it is always helpful to establish a clear statement of deductive objectives: to define precisely what the model is to do. However, trial formulations involving later stages of the modeling process also aid in clarifying well-defined problems by indicating what is possible, fruitful, or interesting, for, as the model is developed, different possible objectives may become apparent. Frequently, the process of the developing model plays a key role here by suggesting ways in which the problem might, tentatively, at least, be made more specific and interesting.

2. Think of a Process and Make Simplifying Assumptions. As mentioned earlier, a good model is always a statement about a process, or a statement that has a sense of process or relationship. The second step in modeling in-

volves thinking of a process that might account for the observations made on the archaeological record and that might form a basis for the selection of properties for study. At this point in the modeling process, the model builder freely and imaginatively speculates about the processes that might have produced the facts. One way to put process into a model is to ask the question Why? One way to determine whether a model has a sense of process is to determine if relational statements can be derived from it. For example, imagine that model A contains the concepts *information spread* and *population density*. Can we forecast an acceleration of the rate of information spread if the density of population increases? Or take model B, which contains the concepts *rate of exchange* and *community size*. If community size doubles, can we predict the new rate of exchange? If we cannot, the models probably lack a sense of process.

Thinking about just any process will not do, either. In archaeology, generative processes with implications for the form and content of material culture in both systemic and archaeological context are obviously preferable to those that do not. Sometimes the pattern of distribution of artifacts and sites will themselves suggest a process. For instance, the distribution may be largely random, clustered, or regular. If it is highly regular, a competitive effect may be operating in the process. If the distribution is clustered, a contagious or distance-decay effect may be operating. If it is random, a variety of independent influences may be operating to produce in aggregate the effects normally obtained from a truly random process. At other times, ethnographic analogies or simple mathematical formulas may provide a process that could have generated the observed empirical distribution of artifacts and sites.

Since the subject of a model is usually very complex, it is often necessary to initiate the modeling process by making simplifying assumptions. The easiest way to accomplish this is to consider the subject simpler than it really is. For example, sites in a region may simply be thought of as dots on a map or a maze of complex interacting processes may simply be considered equivalent to a random force in their overall impact. Starting simple not only avoids the frustration of attempting to model an overwhelming amount of data, it gets things moving as well. The result is the invention of an imaginary model-world quite distinct from reality, but a model-world nonetheless that represents at least some of the observed facts. After deliberately omitting and distorting some aspects of a situation to build a simple conceptual model, we can then ask, How far off are we? How much in error is our model because of the simplifications we have made? This process of simplifying a situation to make it more easily solvable or understandable and then asking how closely the simplified but imaginary system approximates the real system is a characteristic feature of modeling. In general, archaeologists begin with very simple models and attempt to move progressively toward more elaborate models that more nearly reflect the complexity of the subject that is being represented.

Step two is a critical step in model building, for the conceptualization of the model is being formed. Here we ask, Should the concepts be treated in a continuous or discrete manner? Should time play a role in the model? Should the relationships be deterministic or nondeterministic, linear or nonlinear? Should the structure inherent in the relationships be represented by a word-picture or a mathematical formula? Are the variables measurable? Can we collect data for these variables? Numerous trial formulations are often involved in formulating the type of model that is desired at this step. An extensive knowledge of the phenomena for which the model is being constructed is obviously helpful here.

3. Develop Interesting Implications. Now develop interesting implications of the model. This is achieved by asking, What consequences does the model have? What does it imply besides the basic data that it was developed to explain? These implications or consequences are deduced from or, less formally, suggested by the model. Sometimes interesting implications can be developed by looking for situations where the form and process of a model have actually varied. Cross-cultural comparisons are a practical guide here. Exploring the implications of neutral analogies or correspondence is also a fruitful source of possible implications.

Model builders usually do not know the full range of characteristics of a model—of an analogue, for instance—that correspond with or most effectively represent the characteristics of the modeled situation. This ambiguity is a constant source of stimulation and hypothesis (Hesse 1966). Properties and formal structures shared by models and the phenomena they represent are *positive analogies* or *positive correspondences;* those not shared are *negative analogies* or *negative correspondences;* and those not known to be shared are *neutral analogies* or *neutral correspondences*. Neutral correspondences have interesting implications for research: they suggest additional shared properties and formal structures that aid in directing research and formulating hypotheses. Step three initiates the testing process, then, by deriving testable implications from a model.

4. Evaluate the Implications of the Model. The fourth step involves testing the implications drawn from the model. If the implications of the model are not supported by empirical tests, the process of model development begins again with the search for a fruitful process and form. This testing procedure guarantees a constant interplay between the real world of artifacts and sites and the model world that parallels the interplay between theories and the world of experience. As a general rule, testing the basic assumptions of a model is not a productive approach to validating a model, for the main assumptions underlying the model may be rejected prematurely at this stage of the modeling process. It is better to concentrate on testing the implications of the model elaborated in step three.

Some implications will seem interesting and even provocative, but they will not be easy to evaluate. Other tests will be too weak to indicate whether the model, the evaluative procedure, or both are at fault in the negative finding. In all of these procedures, models are tested by making predictions about observations yet to be made, as in the process of justification discussed in chapter 2. If the implications of the model are supported, we may decide to accept the concepts and relationships in the model as actually pertaining to the situation that is being studied. These tentative conclusions are then incorporated into a culture history or scientific theory.

5. Enrich or Simplify the Model. Following step four, the model will be considered a success or a failure. If it has not been successful, if its implications are not supported by empirical tests, the chances are that it is simply inadequate. If the core assumptions still seem intuitively correct, it can be simplified and run through steps one to four again. Models are simplified by (1) making variables into constants, (2) eliminating variables, (3) using linear relations, (4) adding stronger assumptions and restrictions, and (5) suppressing randomness. Simplifying a model still further can be a productive process, for an exploratory model does not have to be particularly accurate or contain much detail to generate interesting but testable implications.

The process of elaboration or enrichment involves just the opposite set of modifications and at least two sorts of looping or alternation procedures. The first loop entails an interplay between the deductive tractability of a model and the assumptions that characterize it. If it is not tractable or cannot be "solved," the assumptions may have to be altered. The second loop involves a continuous cycle of model modification and confrontation with data: each enriched version leads to a test that in turn leads to a new enriched model in a cyclical joust between conjecture and refutation. The second loop is initiated by asking, Were relevant variables omitted in the initial simplification? What else was omitted from the model that may be essential in deriving an adequate explanation of the real-world situation? New variables and relationships are now added. A rich source of inspiration is additional neutral correspondences or associations with previously well-developed logical structures, especially mathematical formulas. A general tactic is the adoption of a simple version of a logical structure as a starting point: increasingly more sophisticated versions are then employed as the modeling process moves around the loop. Sometimes startling analogies prove extremely stimulating, such as the comparison of cultural and organic systems or human population movements and the random bumping of gas molecules. Obviously, facility in modeling means to a large extent the selection and modification through testing of the basic assumptions that underlie models.

In adopting either strategy, archaeologists do not have to decide whether to record data or to develop a model first, for looping processes are involved: modeling is a process with looping dynamics very similar to the dynamics of the cycle of science. Regardless of where one enters the looping process, modeling is, ideally, an ever more specific and accurate cyclical procedure. Nonetheless, models cannot be endlessly enriched and elaborated until they attain an identity with reality. There is a limit to which one may go, often called the complexity dilemma or Bonini's paradox (Bonini 1963:136), for models become increasingly more difficult to understand as their assumptions and relationships are made more complex. In the end, "constructing a model as complex or more complex than reality is self-defeating" (Zimmerman 1977:30).

6. Search for Generality. Archaeologists interested in developing scientific theories move on to a sixth step in model building. In this step the goal is to search for generality, to broaden the model so that it becomes more general and abstract. Once again, in this phase of the model-building process it is more important to be creative than to be critical. Several tactics exist for accomplishing this goal. For instance, you can search for a more general model that includes yours as an implication. Or you can expand the domain of a model by eliminating terms that restrict its arena of applicability, such as proper nouns; we can talk, for example, of horticulturalists rather than the Winnebago or the Yanomamö.

Perhaps the most common tactic adopted in achieving generality is to consider a specific numerical instance of a problem and then to assign some symbols. A variable in a mathematical formula is found that corresponds more or less to each concept in the verbal model. The structural equation linking symbols in the formula provides the process and form of the mathematical model, as well as direct causal links between the concepts (figure 4.3). Establishing symbols is nearly always a key step in model development, for it forces the model builder to make statements about the model's assumptions and, if the numerical instance can be "solved," the steps in the solution can be generalized to other real-world contexts. At the very least this tactic provides a general expression of some of the obvious things that are noticed in a specific context. The next section contains an example of this tactic in the modeling process.

Once a numerical example has been translated into symbolic terms, the obvious can be written down, such as input-output relations, the flow of energy or information, or growth relations. Interesting deductive consequences are then often produced by experimenting with different values of the variables in the equation. If the assumptions of the model fail to achieve the desired results, we can always go back and modify or relax some of them and try again. The goal is to discover a set of assumptions that lead to a deductively tractable model: to do this typically requires a number of attempts.

Mathematical models have several advantages over strictly verbal models. For instance, mathematical models provide a logical structure that may reveal unforeseen implications, logical contradictions, a necessity for additional assumptions, and so forth, that are not obvious from an examination of a verbal model. In addition, mathematical models are not constrained by real-world physical properties. Since mathematical systems need not be true

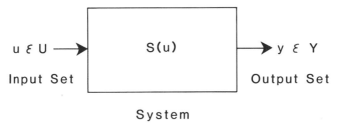

Figure 4.3 A simple mathematical model of a system. In the diagram the transformation between the input set (U) and the output set (Y) is represented by y = S(u).

to the world we live in, we can pretend that the flow of ideas obeys the laws of fluids, that settlements attract information in accordance with the laws of gravitation, or that the movement of settlements into a region conforms to the known laws of gases in a container. We may know that the system must be false. Nonetheless, it does have logical consequences that can provoke fruitful and stimulating evaluations at this stage in the search for generality.

From this point of view, mathematical systems are games, like chess. People invent games by specifying rules. Even though the rules can be easily changed, within the rules certain strategies are recognized as good. This game aspect of mathematics is particularly useful to archaeology, for archaeologists are trying to discover which hypotheses about the archaeological record work and which do not. The ability of mathematics to explore any world we choose to invent gives it its power; it is to archaeologists' advantage to think in terms of possible worlds, for the past still remains largely unknown. But the complexity of the real world cannot be ignored: eventually, it must be dealt with as realistically as possible. A model becomes less abstract and general and more realistic and specific as it is enriched in the looping process. A point is reached, however, as mentioned earlier, where it also becomes more intractable mathematically and it is less easy to untangle the multiplicative relationships of stochastic, discontinuous, and other variables in complex systems.

Evaluating Models

We have argued that operational models are either useful representations of empirical reaility or they are not. But what does *useful* mean? We already know that models are only meant to be hypothetical structures that show that, given certain assumptions and conditions, a particular view of the past is fruitful, insightful, and otherwise stimulating; they are not meant to be statements about what actually happened in the past, as are scientific theories and culture histories. In addition, there may well be an infinite number of models from which we can deduce the facts that we are trying to represent (this is an instance of the *deductive paradox*). Believing that there is only one correct model for the facts can only lead to frustration, confusion, and the stifling of creativity. For all of these reasons, models are most effectively evaluated from many perspectives, including their fit with reality, fertility, ease of enrichment, degree of generality, relatedness, transparency, testability, and unpredictability. A model's usefulness is thus evaluated along an array of dimensions, depending on its purpose and degree of maturity. For instance, in the early stages of model building, when new ideas are being tried out, a model's fertility, degree of relatedness, and other structural characteristics may be just as important as its fit with reality. All models do not have to be robust, transparent, or easy to enrich. A simple iconic model, such as a map of site distributions, that is low in fertility may still play an important role in a research project. Rigor, precision, and fit with reality can easily be overemphasized, when other traits, such as research fertility or unpredictability, may be more important.

Models are often evaluated in terms of their *fertility*, their ability to predict new facts correctly. Fertility is the richness of the variety of deductive consequences that the model produces. A fertile model produces a relatively large number of interesting predictions per assumption, for it has a form and a process that generates *behavior*. A model with low fertility generally lacks a sense of process and, therefore, a mechanism with behavioral implications. Models are also evaluated in terms of their *simplicity, ease of enrichment*, and *degree of generality*. Models should be relatively simple; they should contain as small a number of assumptions and variables as possible. They should also be easy to enrich or elaborate in attempts to approach the complexity of the real world. Moreover, models should be easily modified to extend their scope or domain; the greater the degree of generality of a model, the wider its domain of application, the more situations it will apply to, and the greater the variety of possible implications it will have.

Other characteristics that are useful in evaluating models are *relatedness, transparency, robustness, testability*, and *unpredictability*. Relatedness is the number of cases, hypotheses, or results a model brings to bear on a problem. Transparency concerns the immediacy of the intuitive confirmation of a model, the obviousness of its interpretation. The robustness of a model is its degree of sensitivity to changes in the assumptions that characterize it. A model should also be testable; it should make assertions about the real world that can be checked with new observations. Finally, a useful model often contains an element of unpredictability; an unpredictable model produces interesting and unexpected implications that are not immediately obvious from its assumptions. Discovering unanticipated and surprising implications frequently is the result of expressing models in mathematical terms, thereby making more obvious their deductive implications.

Many of the characteristics that are useful in evaluating models also point to the potential liabilities of model construction. One example is *excessive formalism*, the overreliance on logical form, symbols, and rigor at the expense of fertility and content; the result is an excessive concern with methodology. Another example is *misplaced concreteness*. It is easy to become so involved in constructing a model—model building is, after all, an intriguing intellectual puzzle—that one forgets that models are not scientific theories or culture histories; they are only as-if representations of empirical phenomena, methodological tools. Showing that the implications of a model are true or false does not imply that a theory is necessarily true or false; models are merely useful or they are not.

A natural hazard of analogical reasoning is *overidentification* with a model; here too many characteristics (negative correspondences) are erroneously transferred to and imposed on an interpretation of a real-world situation. An equally potential liability is *underidentification:* the model is too limited in scope because some positive correspondences have not been transferred from the source of the model; ideally, the form and processes of a model should coincide with the form and processes of abstracted real-world situations. Another liability is *misidentification:* data are made to fit or mirror a model that is really not applicable. The result is generally a distortion of the data base and a false representation of past behavior or of the properties of artifacts in the archaeological record. An example is the application of easy-to-use, faddish, and widely examined models rather than other models that are more appropriate to the goals of a research project. For instance, we might assume that people make environmental decisions to optimize their energy returns. In reality, however, they may be making safe rather than optimizing decisions, or they may be attempting to resolve spatial or environmental conflicts that we still do not comprehend. In this case we would be adopting an inappropriate rationale.

An Example of Model Building

The following example is based on a series of stochastic models for social processes proposed by David Clarke (1972a). Although the example is only a sketch, it does illustrate the representational function of models, the processes of enrichment and elaboration, and the application of technical symbols in model construction. The playful elaboration of a set of ideas that we see here characterizes most trips around the cycle of science, even though it is omitted for practical reasons from most examples in later chapters.

1. Isolate a Well-Developed Problem. Clarke had become intrigued with several features of Danubian I archaeology. First, archaeologists usually rep-resented the dispersal pattern of the settlements of these fifth-millenium B.C. European farmers by an east-west linear movement model, a model that can be displayed on a map by successive waves of increasingly more recent ra-diocarbon dates radiating outward from a core area or, more simply, by di-rectional arrows (figure 4.4). This simple iconic model is not entirely devoid of test implications. However, its fertility is low: even though it successfully represents the direction and magnitude of community movements on a con-tinental-millennial scale, it does not provide an adequate interpretative ex-planation of either the direction or magnitude of movement. Can the out-wardly radiating movements be more adequately accounted for by changing the scale of analysis to the local level and to short periods of time?

A second puzzle was the remarkable conservatism of Danubian I ceramic design styles. Even though stylistic changes did occur, they were broadly comparable throughout a forested terrain stretching 1,500 kilometers east-west and about 600 kilometers north-south over a 600-year period. How can we account for this ceramic conservatism? These two basic questions provided the problem, the puzzle, that initiated the model-building process.

2. Think of a Process and Make Simplifying Assumptions. What process or processes and simplifying assumptions might initially at least account for

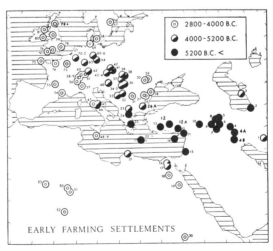

Figure 4.4 The spread of farming into Europe from southwest Asia charted by radiocarbon dates. Source: Clark 1965a:121.

these puzzles? It is generally assumed that the slash-and-burn system of farming that was practiced by Danubian I folk was a causative element in the location of their settlements and that these settlements were probably continually reoccupied over considerable periods of time (Modderman 1971:7–9). One tactic, then, would be to attempt to simplify the extremely complicated movements of slash-and-burn farmers. We could pretend, for example, that the movements are composed of jumps of equal length that take place within equal time intervals. Second, we could pretend that jumps can occur in only one of four directions: east, west, north, or south. Each of these directions is equally probable and will occur at random, although communities cannot move below a southern baseline. This latter restriction is a crucial requirement in this type of model. The structure of this simple model is obviously a crude oversimplification of a complex real-world situation. Nonetheless, it does provide an initial approximation of Danubian I movements, and it does give us something to model. Since we are primarily interested here in accounting for the pattern of Danubian I community movements, we can assume for the moment that it was these movements and relationships that were largely responsible for our second puzzle, the degree of observable ceramic conservatism.

What process or processes could generate these simplified movements? Clarke chose a model belonging to a class of movement models called *random walk models,* who's rationale is the Yule process. In one subclass of random walk models movement occurs throughout a two-dimensional plane containing a lattice of points that are equidistant. Even though Danubian I settlements are located on dispersed loess zones, pretending that they formed a lattice of equidistant points introduces a further simplification. Because of the wide range of simplifying assumptions made, this type of model can be applied to many diverse events, including the outward spread of gas or salt molecules in a container as well as the spread of human communities throughout a region (e.g., Goldstein and Goldstein 1978:327–334). Random walk models exemplify the contemporary trend in many social sciences toward the construction of probabilistic models. This type of model is based on the theory of stochastic (or chance) processes, and incorporates chance mechanisms or probable trends rather than inevitable effects as processes of models.

Random-seeming movements in direction and magnitude from point to point are common in situations where elements, here human communities, are affected by a variety of competing factors. In random walk models the direction and magnitude of a sequence of movements at each transition or move is determined by chance (figure 4.5a). A path of movement through a lattice of points can be produced in many ways, such as the toss of a coin or the drawing of random numbers. Once a method has been chosen to generate movement, the process can be used to produce an indefinitely large number of paths for the units of a model, whether they are molecules or human communities. Again, the process of movement is drastically simpler than what must have happened in the past. But, because it is simpler, the mathematics devised to explain the spread of gas molecules throughout a container or salt molecules in water can be used to predict the pattern of spread of communities.

Although the mathematical details are beyond the scope of this book, one

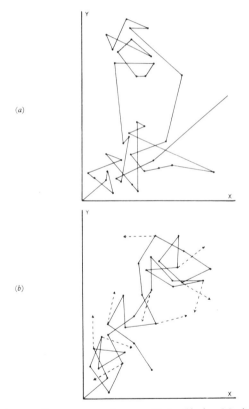

Figure 4.5 Random walk sequences. Source: D. L. Clarke, Models and paradigms in contemporary archaeology, in D. L. Clarke, ed., *Models in Archaeology*, pp. 1–60 (London: Methuen & Co., 1972), figure 1.6.

useful approach involves a Markov process characterized by a set of k states $S = \{S_i\}$, a probability distribution $\{B(t)\}$ over the states at each time, where $B(t) = [b_i(t)]$ and a square matrix $P(t) = [P_{ij}(t)]$. The element $b_i(t)$ is the probability that at a time t an element is in the ith category S_i, while the matrix entry $p_{ij}(t)$ is the probability that an element in state S_i at time $t - 1$ will be in state S_j at time t. In other words, each $p_{ij}(t)$ is a conditional probability. By assuming that all the transition coefficients of $P(t)$ are constant through time, the vector transformations outlined for the Markov process become $B(t = 1) = B(t) \cdot P$, $B(t = 2) = B(t) \cdot P^2$, $B(t = n) = B(t) \cdot P^n$, and $B(t) = B(O)P^t$. This type of stochastic process is called a Markov chain.

3. Develop Interesting Implications and 4. Evaluate the Implications of the Model. A model and its underlying theory become convincing only to the extent that they successfully predict more things than were known at the start. An obvious quantitative result predicted by the application of the formula, that communities spread outward in the loess zones, is too unsurprising to be really convincing: it is an expected outcome of the model. What other quantitative predictions follow from the model? For instance, does this simple model predict *how fast* Danubian I communities spread to the outer edges of their universe? We know that as the size of a container is increased, molecular diffusion increases as the square of the size. In an area twice as large, diffusion takes four times as long; increasing the area by a factor of three increases the time ninefold. Do radiocarbon dates substantiate this pattern of spread for the Danubians?

Notice that we are not trying to predict in detail the path of a single molecule or community, for we assume on the basis of our model that each unit (molecule, community) is in constant chaotic motion, colliding with and rebounding from each other along complex pathways. Instead, our interest is in the pattern of spread that eventually results from this motion, in the *average* behavior of communities that is predicted from probability theory by many tosses of a coin or by other random walk generators. Although community jumps have been simplified for this purpose by assuming that they are of equal length and take place in equal time intervals, the distortion introduced by these assumptions is not as great as it may initially seem. For instance, there must have been an average jump length and time interval. Here we are merely assuming that the uniform jump of our simplified model and the real average are the same. A sensible strategy in archaeology, then, is to search for reasonably similar tendencies and to compare alternative models. This strategy helps minimize the premature rejection of developing models and introduces an element of playful comparison that helps us to be wrong more gracefully.

5. Enrich or Simplify the Model. Let us assume that this simplified model has been positively evaluated. How can it be enriched? Clarke's model was elaborated and brought closer to actual archaeological observations by the assumption that a gradual but steady increase in the size of the human population caused community fissioning at every third move (figure 4.5b). This added assumption has two desired effects. First, it increases "the probability that some derivative settlements of any given ancestral village will remain in the general vicinity of the ancestral site." Second, "the multiplication of settlement units and their constant mutual readjustment [ensures] that over a long period of time the many derivative village units will become widely dispersed in an expanding mass of hunt-and-seek settlement pathways" (Clarke 1972a:22). We already know that random walk models maximize collisions between model components and result in their relatively homogeneous diffusion throughout a container or across a plane. Thus the opportunity for community interaction and homogeneous spread across a loess-rich plain would be enhanced still further by community fission at every third move.

This elaborate model maximizes the *opportunity* for the maintenance of ceramic conservatism. Nonetheless, it still lacks a cultural mechanism that would make ceramic conservatism an expected outcome of colliding communities. Perhaps a search of the ethnographic literature for patterns of social interaction between colliding communities would produce an analogue that would explain ceramic conservatism over large areas. The addition of the analogue would not only elaborate the model still further, it would make it more realistic by injecting a real societal pattern. A search of the ethnographic literature does show a considerable movement of families from one community to another among communities that practice shifting agriculture. This intervillage mobility, like the collision of communities, increases the potential rate of information flow between communities and the opportunity for an interlinked parallel development among communities. If we assume further that the postmarital residence practices of the Danubians were such that they maximized within and between village homogeneity and conservatism, we would have a relatively elaborate model from which we could generate a rich variety of hypotheses. One possible solution is a form of bilocal residence (residence with either the wife's or the husband's family) with 50 percent village endogamy (intracommunity marriage) and 50 percent village exogamy (intervillage marriage), as practiced among the slash-and-burn Iban farmers of Africa. Is this a useful kinship solution for our model? How could this assumption be tested? Are there other fruitful neutral analogies with the Iban? In other words, how can the model be elaborated still further to more precisely answer the two basic questions that initiated the model-building process.

Building a model of Danubian I community movements illustrates several aspects of the model-building process. First, it demonstrates the value of making initial simplifying assumptions and of elaborating this initial model by making additional, more restrictive, assumptions. Second, it exemplifies the fruitfulness of casting models in mathematical terms in at least some phases of the model-building process. Third, it shows the value of analogical thinking, whether the analogy is with the movement of a gas molecule or the residence practices of ethnographically recorded peoples. Fourth, it demonstrates how the scale of a study determines the level of model appropriate for its representation and the processes appropriate for its explanation (Clarke 1972a:23). Finally, it illustrates the role of a model as a source of understanding and a cornucopia from which often startling predictions flow. Although Clarke did not generalize his series of models to include shifting agriculturalists other than the Danubian I, the series could have been generalized by removing proper nouns such as Danubian I and Europe and recasting the elaborated model into a numerical form. Readers interested in Clarke's model should contrast its evaluative qualities with those of other models of the spread of farming whose underlying assumptions are somewhat different (e.g., Ammerman and Cavalli-Sforza 1973; Rowe et al. 1974).

Summary

Chapter 4 introduces the processes involved in building and evaluating operational models, which are important in the cycle of science during the interpretation of sample summaries and empirical generalizations and in the testing of culture histories and scientific theories. Models are meaning providers in their interpretation of objects and spatial distribution in the archaeological record in terms of familiar objects, systems, or processes. A model orders observations and minimizes perceptual confusion by organizing perceptions within a conceptual framework constructed by means of a rationale, or theoretical orientation. It does this by representing observations by concepts, then by ordering the concepts. The resulting structure and relationships of its concepts are the form of a model. An operational model provides a process that makes the form understandable by showing how it behaves. The form provides a systematic set of relationships between concepts, and the process indicates how the relationships work. Form and process give models a predictive capability and can generate anticipated relationships.

Models may be classified from at least five different perspectives emphasizing certain characteristics: material-formal, iconic-analogue-symbolic, a posteriori–a priori, static-dynamic, and real-abstract. A realist-positivist dispute focuses on the question of whether the correspondence between models and reality is one of identity or similarity, with realists favoring identity. However, when human cultures are compared to organic systems, for instance, their structural and processual similarities are referred to rather than an identity in kind.

Building models depends on the skills of abstraction, derivation, and evaluation. With the understanding that there are no guarantees, these steps are recommended for the modeling process: (1) Isolate a well-defined problem to aid the construction of meaningful hypotheses. (2) Think of a process and make simplifying assumptions (to account for observations made on the archaeological record and that might form a basis for the selection of properties for study). (3) Develop interesting implications (by asking what consequences the model has, with consideration of positive, negative, and neutral analogies or correspondences). (4) Evaluate the implications of the model by testing (to determine whether they are supported by empirical observations). (5) Enrich or simplify the model. (Simplify by changing variables to constants, eliminating variables, using linear relations, adding stronger assumptions and restrictions, or suppressing randomness. Elaborate by opposite modifications or by looping in the scientific cycle.) (6) Search for generality to broaden the model (by assigning symbols).

A model may be evaluated for usefulness from the perspectives of fit with reality, fertility, simplicity, ease of enrichment, degree of generality, relatedness, robustness, transparency, testability, or unpredictability, depending on its purpose and degree of maturity. These characteristics may point to potential liabilities of model construction such as excessive formalism, misplaced concreteness, and under-, over-, or misidentification. Finally, a series of stochastic models for social processes proposed by David Clarke is used to illustrate the representational function of models, the process of enrichment and elaboration, and the application of technical symbols in model construction characteristic of most trips around the cycle of science.

Suggested Readings

A number of accounts that provide approaches to model building are:

Caws, P. 1974. Operational, representational, and explanatory models. *American Anthropologist* 76:1–10.

Clarke, D. L., ed. 1972. *Models in Archaeology.* London: Methuen.

—— 1978. *Analytical Archaeology,* 2d ed. New York: Columbia University Press.

Dalton, G. 1981. Anthropological models in archaeological perspective. In I. Hodder, G. Isaac, and N. Hammond, eds., *Pattern of the Past,* pp. 17–48. New York: Cambridge University Press.

Harvey, D. 1969. *Explanation in Geography.* London: Edward Arnold.

Hesse, M. 1966. *Models and Analogies in Science.* Notre Dame, Ind.: University of Notre Dame Press.

Kaplan, A. 1964. *The Conduct of Inquiry: Methodology for Behavioral Science.* Scranton, Pa.: Chandler.

Lave, C. and J. March. 1975. *An Introduction to Models in the Social Sciences.* New York: Harper and Row.

Mihram, G. 1972. The modelling process. *IEEE Transactions on Systems, Man, and Cybernetics* SMC-2:621–629.

Morris, W. 1967. On the art of modeling. *Management Science* 13:707–717.

Prince, H. 1971. Real, imagined and abstract worlds of the past. *Progress in Geography* 3:1–86.

Read, D. 1974. Some comments on the use of mathematical models in anthropology. *American Antiquity* 39:3–16.

Stogdill, R., ed. 1970. *The Process of Model-Building in the Behavioral Sciences.* New York: Norton.

PART TWO

Anthropological Archaeology As Cultural History

In studying the diversity and complexity of human cultures, anthropologists have repeatedly attempted to identify the basic components, the universals or common denominators, of every culture and to classify them in meaningful ways. The identification of common denominators facilitates cross-cultural comparison and the study of the development of an integrated culture. Clark Wissler's *universal culture pattern* (1923), for example, was an early attempt to identify the categories that were necessarily present in every culture. Wissler isolated nine categories:

1. Speech: language, writing systems
2. Material traits: a. food habits; b. shelter; c. transport and travel; d. dress; e. utensils, tools; f. weapons; g. occupations and industries
3. Art: carving, painting, drawing, music
4. Mythology and scientific knowledge
5. Religious practices: a. ritualistic forms; b. treatment of the sick; c. treatment of the dead
6. Family and social systems: a. the forms of marriage; b. methods of reckoning relationship; c. inheritance; d. social control; e. sports and games
7. Property: a. real and personal; b. standards of value and exchange; c. trade
8. Government: a. political forms; b. judicial and legal procedures
9. War

A far more elaborate scheme containing 88 general categories was developed by George Peter Murdock and his associates (1962–1965). Even archaeologists have proposed lists of basic traits (e.g., Childe 1956).

Whether a universal pattern or framework of constants underlies all cultural behavior and, if so, why, is a continuing research focus in anthropology. So far, no one classification of common denominators has found acceptance by all anthropologists, perhaps because no one classification is equally suited to all research programs and problems. Most anthropologists agree, however, on the general categories that should be involved in any classification. These categories are based on universal features of being human, such as (1) our basic structure as animals (for example, we have two eyes, walk upright, have a similar brain structure), (2) our biological needs (for instance, for food, shelter, and psychological comfort), and (3) the problems we share in living together in population aggregates.

A threefold system of common denominators has been chosen here both for its inclusiveness—it includes these general categories—and for its simplicity. These common denominators of every human culture are a *social subsystem,* a *technoeconomic subsystem,* and an *ideological subsystem.* The threefold classification of the social, the technoeconomic, and the ideological follows the current practice in anthropological archaeology of viewing culture as an adaptive system, a system that has been designed to meet the basic problems of human existence. These basic problems are concerned with the inevitable relationships that must form (1) between humans living in groups, (2) between humans and their natural surroundings, and (3) between humans and the unknown or world of symbolic thought. The social subsystem is especially concerned with the dimensions of social organization and interpersonal relations, the technoeconomic subsystem with technological and economic dimensions, and the ideological subsystem with the world of symbolic thought within which knowledge, ideas, beliefs, religion, and other conceptual dimensions of culture build up. Each of these subsystems is objectified in the material remains of its associated behavioral activities and, therefore, provides a material basis for its reconstruction from the archaeological record (Binford 1962); artifacts are to be understood as social documents whose functions or meanings can be defined by their relations to each of these subsystems.

The isolation of common interrelated cultural denominators is also consistent with the systems framework adopted by anthropological archaeologists. For example, if cultures are to be viewed as systems (a methodological principle), archaeologists must strive to understand the structure and behavior of their interrelated parts (a methodological rule). One approach to accomplishing this goal is to conceptualize sociocultural systems as complex networks of interdependent information subsystems, such as the threefold system adopted here. The function and explanation of behavioral activities can then be sought within the web of the adaptive system and its social, technoeconomic, and ideological components. Although anthropological archaeologists usually research the dynamic equilibrium existing within subsystems or between subsystems, one of their ideal goals is the study of behavioral activities within the web of whole adaptive systems and their environment. This holistic approach, which is one of the hallmarks of the anthropological perspective, tends to differentiate anthropological archaeology from other types of archaeology.

Chapters 5 and 6 are concerned with many of the typical questions anthropological archaeologists ask when they analyze the material remains (the *settlement*) of single communities. Although, as we shall see, some questions are more difficult for archaeologists to answer than others, the range of questions that can be asked about single communities is, of course, practically limitless. Among the many questions asked today are What regular activities occurred within the community? Why? Was there a division of labor or status between men and women or between different groups of men and women? Why was this division present and not another? What were the subsistence practices of the community? How large was its population? What was the size of its work force? Did it occupy one geographic location throughout the year? The threefold classification of the social subsystem, the technoeconomic subsystem, and the ideological subsystem is one means of organizing these questions so that the analysis and comparison of sociocultural systems are facilitated. Since these are only general categories and the specifics of each subsystem will vary from one setting to another, one task of the archaeologist is to explicate the similarities and differences between ways of life of communities. Chapter 5 discusses the social and ideological subsystems, while chapter 6 examines the technoeconomic subsystem and biosocial elements of the human population, which is the culture bearer and an important artifact itself of its own culture.

Anthropologists are also interested in social entities larger than communities, such as cultures, groups of related cultures, or transcontinental exchange systems. Which level of analysis is most relevant to a particular anthropologist depends on her or his research interests or problems. For varying theoretical reasons, Chang (1967), for instance, has proposed that the settlement should be the basic unit for reconstructing societies, G. Ernest Wright

(1974) the tell, and Binford (1964) the region. Chapter 7 considers the regional and interregional levels of analysis and interpretation, and chapter 8 introduces the study of sociocultural change through time at several levels. The cross-cultural comparison of sociocultural systems made possible by the identification of common denominators of all cultural systems is introduced in chapter 9 of Part Three.

CHAPTER FIVE

Reconstructing Interpersonal Relationships
and
Symbolic Thought at the Community Level

Can social forms be reconstructed through the archaeological record? Consider the following argument. Since the interactions of members of groups are governed by sets of cultural norms, people should interact in more or less patterned ways. If people's social behavior is patterned, facilities should be constructed and materials discarded or lost in patterned ways, too. Therefore, by identifying pattern in the archaeological record, archaeologists should be able to reconstruct, through a chain of inferential reasoning, a community's social organization and some of the rules of its social structure. Or so it would seem.

Chapter 5 is primarily concerned with the status of this claim, with the questions, How did individuals or groups interact socially from day to day within the community? and How can archaeologists reconstruct these patterns of social interaction? The first section explores the spatial clustering of artifacts and features for clues to the presence of social units; the second section examines a variety of nonspatial approaches to reconstructing family types, residence practices, and other social phenomena; and the third section looks at attempts to reconstruct the political dimension of social subsystems. Finally, the study of the ideological subsystem is introduced in the fourth section.

Identifying Meaningful Units of Spatial Analysis in the Settlement

The analysis and interpretation of social subsystems and their elements generally proceed in two stages in anthropological archaeology. First, the archaeological record is examined for spatial patterning. Second, models of relevant structures, mechanisms, and transformations are proposed to account for the discovered patterns. At the root of this exploratory approach are three working hypotheses: (1) spatial concentrations of artifacts and features in settlements correspond with spatially organized social activities in past communities; (2) spatial patterning of artifacts and features was formed by individuals and groups having cultural models of appropriate and expected patterns of social interaction; and (3) changes in the way space was used in a site universe correlate with past changes in social organization.

Facilities that coexisted at any one time in a community together with other materials, natural features, and their spatial relationships form a *structured space*. This structured space is called a *community structure* or, when studied archaeologically, a *site structure* (Schiffer 1976). The site structure ideally maps or corresponds to the community structure or anatomy of the social unit being studied. Spatial patterning within community structures exists at various levels of analysis, such as individual activity areas, houses, neighborhoods, and administrative centers (Hill 1970b). Just which of these units of social analysis will be available for reconstruction—and most fruitful to reconstruct—will depend on the type and complexity of the communities whose physical remains are being studied. In archaeology the study of the spatial organization of social activities at any level is called *settlement pattern analysis*. When archaeologists pursue settlement pattern studies, they must decide which items coexisted in structured space, how each spatial unit was used, and what changes occurred through time in different but successive structural spaces.

Conjectural reconstructions of social systems through spatial analysis involve the positing of identities. Identities do not provide explanations of the processes that produced various social systems, that maintained them in a state of equilibrium, or that changed them into another set of preferred social relations. Inferring social norms from behavior and its by-products is classification and description. But even proving the existence of norms is difficult. For instance, to take regularities in behavior as evidence of a norm and then to explain the behavior in terms of the norm is obviously redundant (Blake and Davis 1964). Nevertheless, reconstructions of social identities do provide initial insights into the basic forms and building blocks of social systems. Explanations may then be formulated by searching for the processes that affected these forms and building blocks, and their integration through time.

Activity Areas and Tool-Kits

The smallest spatial unit of patterned social behavior in a community is an area where a specific task was carried out by a single individual. In archaeology these spatial units are called *activity areas* and are generally characterized by a set of distinctive features and a scatter of tools and debris (Schiffer 1976). Typical examples of activity areas are the remains of stone chipping stations and food preparation areas. In other instances artifactual analysis may demonstrate that specific artifacts consistently occur together, even though they do not form spatially distinct activity areas. Such associations are called activity sets or tool-kits and are commonly found with burials or in refuse dumps. Tool-kits, like activity areas, are spatial associations of archaeological materials that are assumed, as a working hypothesis, to be meaningfully related to a specific task. Discovering what that task was or determining whether the pattern was only the fanciful conception of a statistician is an objective of archaeological research.

Activity areas and tool-kits are empirically isolated by searching for pattern in the archaeological record. The motivation for this search may be the test of a hypothesis, the construction of an instrument of measurement, a descriptive study, or an exploratory investigation. Among the many quantitative techniques that have been used to isolate patterned spatial associations of artifacts and features in settlements are chi-square, trend surface analysis, and factor analysis.

As an initial step, the search for pattern is often begun by calculating correlation coefficients for pairs of artifacts and feature classes. The matrix formed by the correlation coefficients is then searched for nonrandom pattern with a variety of multivariate statistical techniques (figure 5.1). In some cases, nonrandom spatial distributions have been mapped as a series of contours across a plan view of a site (figure 5.2). In this process of trend mapping areas in which the local density of finds differs either positively or negatively from an average density are highlighted on the map. The contours are then compared with the distribution of postholes, house floors, and other evi-

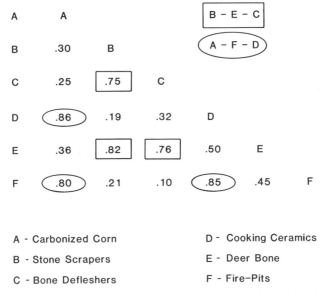

A - Carbonized Corn   D - Cooking Ceramics

B - Stone Scrapers   E - Deer Bone

C - Bone Defleshers   F - Fire–Pits

Figure 5.1   A simplified example of search for pattern in a table of correlation coefficients.

dence for the presence of facilities with potentially interesting associations.

Ideally, activity areas and tool-kits provide important contextual information about the organization of a community's activities. Nonetheless, the presence of sets of consistently co-occurring items in archaeological context may be misleading. Spatial clusters of artifacts and features can result from a wide range of factors besides the localization of behavioral activities. For instance, pseudopatterns may be formed through the localization of discard, periodic cleaning practices, wind and water disturbances, and differential erosion. Some artifacts and features were almost certainly multifunctional, or they may have been used for different purposes in different contexts or during different time periods; task-specific activities may not have been involved. Artifactual patterns produced by a variety of very different behavioral activities may be indistinguishable. Pseudopatterns may be formed by violating the assumptions underlying the application of specific statistical techniques (Cowgill 1968; Speth and Johnson 1976).

It is difficult to distinguish between these different pseudopattern and pattern-generating processes on the basis of spatial patterning alone. What archaeologists discover is discrete localizations of various artifact clusters and

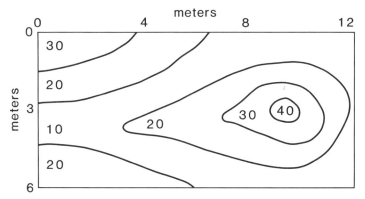

Figure 5.2 A simplified map of the distributional trend of numbers of obsidian flakes per 0.5 m² units in an excavation unit.

associations within a site. These empirical patterns, which are patterns within an archaeological context, must be clearly distinguished from those functionally specific work areas, tool-kits, and other associations that are elements of sociocultural systems and the systemic context. Activity areas and tool-kits are conceptual constructs, identities, that are proposed to make sense of artifact distributions and associations. Like all identities, they must be evaluated for their truth content and fruitfulness within the cycle of science.

Female and Male Work Areas

On a more inclusive level of social integration, activity areas cluster together to form male and female work areas. Houses and other facilities are often divided, at least conceptually, into spaces associated with either females or males. Most of our houses, for example, contain kitchens, workshops, bedrooms for different members of the family, dining rooms, and living rooms. Females and males participate together in common activities in some of these structured spaces, such as the living room and dining room. However, other spaces have been traditionally associated with women's implements and activities or men's implements and male-related activities. While this traditional pattern of the division of labor in American society is slowly changing, its existence vividly illustrates the sexual patterning of space that can occur within a community.

A number of methods have been used in archaeology to suggest the presence and location of male and female work areas and sex-related artifacts. Among these methods are the direct historic approach, ethnographic analogy, the study of artifact associations with skeletons, and the analysis of the spatial associations of artifactual materials with each other. Although none of these approaches is a source of immediate proof, each has been used as evidence to support suggested identities.

An example of the direct historic approach to the identification of female and male work areas is the analysis by Kent Flannery (1976:44–45) and his associates of the contents of House I in the Formative village at Tierras Largas in Mesoamerica. Ethnographically, certain tools in the region have been traditionally associated with the activities of women. These include metates, two-handed manos, pottery charcoal braziers, hammerstones for food preparation, deer-bone cornhuskers, spindle whorls, and sewing needles. Traditional male-related tools include antler tines, pressure flakes, projectile points, a variety of chert bifaces and scrapers, bone-working tools such as fleshers and beamers, celts and other tools for land clearance, weapons, shell-working implements, and a variety of extractive tools. By plotting the spatial distribution of these items, Flannery identified male and female work areas. In House I, male-related chert cores, scrapers, retouched flakes, and at least one biface were in front of or to the left of the door as one entered the house. On the right or "female" half were bone needles, deer-bone cornhuskers, pierced shard discs (probably components of spindle whorls), and a gray ash deposit that was probably the residue of cooking activities. Behavior associated with gender was apparently separated by a midline through the center of the building (figure 5.3).

The Household Cluster

A household cluster is a spatial concentration of house remains, pits, burials, workshops, ovens, and other features and artifacts in an archaeological site. As a working hypothesis, household clusters are assumed to be material manifestations of past households. According to Winter, who coined the phrase, the concept "is useful because it provides a context in which pits, burials, house remains, and other features can be understood not simply as isolated cultural features but as manifestations of a specific segment of society" (1976:25). The concept is intended, therefore, to integrate activity and work areas into a coherent and plausible social whole. Of course, a

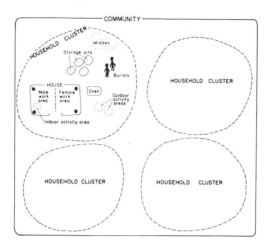

Figure 5.3 A household cluster within its community setting. Source: Flannery 1976, figure 2.18.

meaningful correspondence between households and household clusters must be demonstrated. But once demonstrated, archaeologists have a spatial-social unit by which they are able to compare the activities carried out by household members and the locations of these activities, compare different households, determine which activities were universal and which were confined to only a few families, estimate family sizes, search for role specializations, compare the amount of space occupied by different households, determine the limits of self-sufficiency and the relations between clusters, and so forth. The household cluster is an especially fruitful concept for prehistoric archaeologists, for the spatial structure of this segment of society, the family, is an appropriate unit of analysis in less complex societies.

Two examples will be used to illustrate the value of this concept in settlement pattern studies.

Formative-Period Oaxaca. Formative-period household clusters were studied in a series of sites in the Valley of Oaxaca, Mexico, by Kent Flannery and his student colleagues. These studies, which are becoming research exemplars in anthropological archaeology, are reported in Flannery's *The Early Mesoamerican Village* (1976). Within the sites, houses, bell-shaped storage pits, and graves consistently occurred together. Ovens, midden deposits, and other types of pits were occasionally but not always present. These diverse features were integrated together into a meaningful behavioral unit by the household cluster concept (figure 5.3). The typical cluster "consisted of one house, two to six large storage pits, one to three graves, and various additional features, separated from the nearest contemporary cluster by an open area of 20 to 40 meters; the average size of these clusters was about 300 square meters" (Winter 1976:25). Although this information is significant in itself, it becomes especially valuable when compared with clusters from other time periods.

Iron Age Glastonbury. Another example of the fruitful application of the household cluster concept is found in David Clarke's study (1972b) of the Iron Age settlement at Glastonbury in the west of England. Clarke identified modular units that were repeatedly reproduced on the site (figure 5.4). The iconic symbols in figure 5.4 identify the structural components of these units. A major familial activity area was located in one half of these roughly circular clusters and a minor, largely female and domestic area in the other half. Clarke used these modular units to investigate the social and demographic development of the site through time.

Variability Within the Community

Household, administrative, religious, and other spatial clusters may also be compared to determine the extent of pattern and variability in a community. Sociostructural studies of this type raise many interesting questions. For example, What percent of the community was occupied by households? Which activities were restricted to only one or a few households? Were there universal household activities? Is there evidence for class structure or status differences? Does the size of households vary within the community? Is there evidence for religious, administrative, or craft specialization?

Evidence for universal household activities is found by definition in every reasonably complete household cluster in a settlement. Universal activities in the Formative-period household clusters examined by Flannery and his colleagues included the preparation, procurement, and storage of food and certain kinds of tool preparation. These activities are represented archaeologically by fragments of large storage jars, storage pits, hunting tools such as projectile points, cutting and scraping tools, sewing and basket-making tools, fragments of grinding stones, bones of cottontail rabbit, carbonized kernels or cupule fragments of maize, and fragments of pottery charcoal

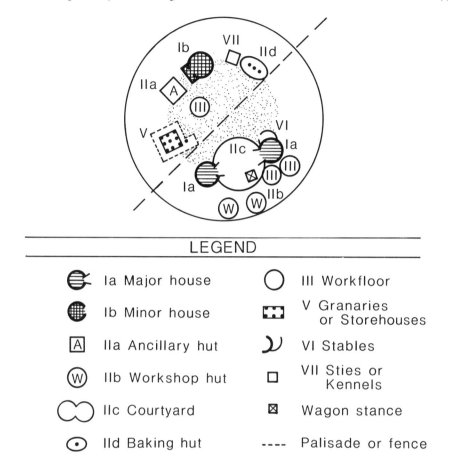

Figure 5.4 A household cluster in a British Iron Age village. Source: D. L. Clarke, A provisional paradigm of an Iron Age society, in D. L. Clarke, ed., *Models in Archaeology*, pp. 801–869 (London: Methuen & Co., 1972), figure 21.1.

braziers. In Glastonbury the major houses were living areas and the focal repositories for tool chests and equipment. A single minor house in each cluster was associated with female activities, such as combing, spinning, querning, leather and fur working, and, archaeologically, with amber, glass and shale beads and bracelets, perforated teeth and boar's tusks, lead and tin spindle whorls, bronze tweezers, and human bones buried in the floor. A consistent community-wide pattern was found in other structures, too.

The presence of universal activities in household clusters in each example suggests that all households carried on at least some largely autonomous economic functions, regardless of any part-time specializations that may have been practiced. In Formative Oaxaca, households apparently did differ in amounts of items, though status differences did not seem to have been a significant factor in their distribution. There does seem to have been a center of wealth and status at Glastonbury, however, for a house in the central area of the settlement contained a hoard that included a bronze mirror, tweezers, two dress pins and cosmetic galena, the only coin and currency bar, a bronze cup, another mirror fragment, a glass-topped pin, amd other valuable items.

Possible regional specializations which involve only one or two households in each village are best considered from a regional perspective (chapter 7). But other activities in both villages seem to have been carried out by specific households. In Formative Oaxaca, concentrations of chert debris, bone fragments, ground stone, and other artifacts and debris in only one or a few household clusters suggest the localization of flint tool manufacture, bone tool manufacture, the production of ground and polished celts, leather working, and other specializations. None of these activities seems to represent the presence of full-time specialists; rather, a form of interhousehold cooperation between primary groups. In Glastonbury, households at different ends of the village seem to have traded and interacted more intensely with different distant centers.

Community Zoning

Communities are usually composed of functionally different zones that group together smaller clusters, such as households and activity areas. Among the many possible zones within a community are cemeteries, higher and lower status residences, plazas, neighborhoods, clan or barrio sections, streets lined with public buildings, marketplaces, administrative and palace complexes, residential wards, and wards of craft specialists, such as potters and carpenters. These zones are organizational units within which relatively independent community activities are carried out by groups larger than the household. Activities at this level of spatial analysis range from the loose integration that results from living together in the same neighborhood to highly organized and systematized behavior in palace or administrative complexes. Even in present-day societies, however, community zones are difficult to recognize at times unless specific group activities such as a craft specialization or a unit-specific ceremony are observed. One of the main problems in identifying social zoning within archaeological sites is the discovery of indicators of social group boundaries above the level of the household cluster.

Zoning within archaeological sites has been most successfully demonstrated by the spatial arrangement of buildings and walls. In the American Southwest, wall abutment analysis has been used to isolate the boundaries of contemporaneous construction units in Puebloan sites. For example, Arthur Rohn (1965, 1971) has emphasized access among restricted spaces to define what other archaeologists have called *local aggregates*, sets of people who cooperatively perform sets of activities in distinct locations (figure 5.5) (also see Reed 1956). Jeffrey Dean (1969, 1970) has used dendrochronol-

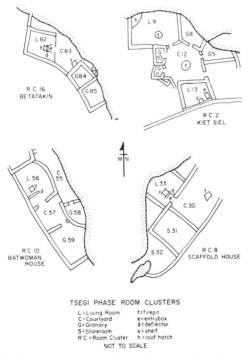

TSEGI PHASE ROOM CLUSTERS

L=Living Room	f=firepit
C=Courtyard	e=entrybox
G=Granary	d=deflector
S=Storeroom	s=shelf
R C =Room Cluster	h=roof hatch
NOT TO SCALE	

Figure 5.5 Tsegi phase room clusters in the American Southwest. Source: J. Dean, Aspects of Tsegi Phase social organization: A trial reconstruction, in W. Longacre, ed., *Reconstructing Prehistoric Pueblo Societies*, pp. 140–174 (Albuquerque: University of New Mexico Press, School of American Research, 1970), figure 12.

ogy to demonstrate the absolute and classificatory contemporaneity of similar site structures.

Some zones existed because communities were socially stratified. One indicator of social inequality in a community is the presence in a settlement of large solid residential houses in one zone and smaller rather flimsy houses in another. Still other zones may indicate the presence of residence divisions (e.g., Longacre 1963, 1964, 1966, 1974), craft wards, or religious or administrative complexes. Many complex communities were even laid out along astronomical lines. Even though spacing principles are still evident in hunter-gatherer camps and villages, their communities tend to be less formally zoned than those of more complex societies. The spatial arrangement of all of these zones, along with roadways and empty spaces, is called the *community plan*. Community plans differ in spacing principles, with some communities having formal zones and others more informal, even haphazard, structural arrangements. Obviously, the empirical identification of settlement zoning is a rich source of hypotheses for archaeologists.

Nonspatial Approaches to Community Social Organization

Anthropologists call the set of norms that structure interpersonal relationships within a community that community's *social structure*. Social structures are systems of ideas and rules within cultures about preferred or accustomed social relations. For a number of reasons, however, people's behavior does not always conform to these ideal sets of rules. For instance, everyone may not share the same understanding of the behavioral implications of the norms; the norms themselves may be ambiguous; people may have selfish reasons for modifying the rules; or, perhaps, some people may be inclined to ignore the rules whenever possible. The resulting patterns of actual social relations formed through this variety of individual decisions and acts is called a community's *social organization*. A community's social organization is the way people actually interact, their patterns of actual, observable behavior. While social structures belong to the cultural realm, to the world of ideas, categories, and rules, social organizations are groups of people, interactions, and events in physical space.

Anthropologists are concerned with how people organize themselves into social groups and networks, with how the elements of social subsystems can be meaningfully distinguished, and with how they may discern the numerous ways in which these elements are integrated together into functioning social wholes. A variety of what have been called nonspatial approaches to community social organization have been developed by anthropological archaeologists. This section reviews several classic examples of these approaches.

Marital Residence Patterns

A newly married couple customarily establishes a new household or moves into the household of a relative, following marital residence rules. Marital residence rules are elements of a society's social structure and, therefore, are guides to proper conduct. To avoid confusion it is helpful to distinguish residence groups (groups of people who live together) from residence rules, and to distinguish both from true descent groups (groups who are related by descent). Even though newly married couples are guided by residence rules, it may be impossible to adhere to these ideal norms in many instances because of overcrowding, scarcity of resources, or other kinship obligations.

The inference of residence patterns from archaeological materials became popular in the United States in the 1960s with the publication of a number of studies that became research exemplars (Longacre 1963, 1964, 1966; Deetz 1965; Hill 1970a, 1970b). Here we are concerned with the part of these studies that concentrated on identifying residence patterns archaeologically; that is, on instrumental-nomological investigations. Underlying these investigations was a set of basic assumptions about the way in which people learn to make tools and other items on the tribal level of social integration. Among these assumptions are (1) many items are made only by women or by men; (2) many people in a community are involved in making items for their family or close kin, for tool making, among other skills, is not a specialized craft; (3) items tend to be discarded in or very near the households where they are made; (4) the more artisans interact the greater will be the stylistic homogeneity of their products. It follows from these assumptions that items made by members of a residence group or other primary group in a tribal society should share many stylistic attributes (figure 5.6). If we have reasons for believing that women were the potters in a specific community, for example, and if the basic set of assumptions is accurate, a high level of stylistic associations on ceramics in spatially related household clusters would serve

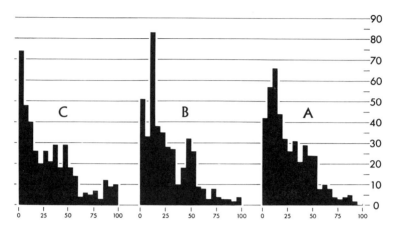

Figure 5.6 Changing attribute patterning in three late Arikara components. The graph shows a breakdown in the number of attribute pairs in a ceramic assemblage (0–90) for different percentage classes (0–100). Component C is the earliest and component A the most recent. Source: Deetz 1966, figure 25-a.

as an indicator of a matrilocal residence pattern, a pattern in which newly married couples move into the household of the wife's family.

Longacre and the Carter Ranch Site. The Carter Ranch site (c. A.D. 1100–1225) is a single, large, U-shaped pueblo of about 40 rooms in eastern Arizona. Several ceremonial structures (kivas) are associated with the block of rooms along with numerous artifacts and a trash mound containing a number of burials. Since the Pueblo Indians practiced matrilocal residence during the early historic period, and since the site was assumed to be a Pueblo settlement, Longacre attempted to demonstrate that the residence pattern at Carter Ranch had also been matricentered. Besides assumptions similar to those mentioned above, it was also assumed that women were the potters, as they were among the Pueblo in the early historic period, and that they passed down preferred design element clusters to their female children and grandchildren, since continuity of residence would have existed in the female line.

Did design elements tend to cluster in localized areas of the site? Longacre (1963, 1964, 1966) defined 175 design elements and element groups in a sample of over 6,000 shards and a number of whole vessels. Statistical analyses of the data demonstrated the presence of two general stylistic clusters. One was associated with a block of rooms on the north end of the pueblo; the other was related to a group of adjacent rooms on the south end. Each of these architectural units was also associated with a ceremonial structure. Additional evidence for the presence of separate residence groups was found in the trash mound. Burials in the mound were separable into three clusters on the basis of orientation and related ceramic design elements. Burials in the north cluster were oriented east-west and were linked with the north set of rooms; those in the south cluster were oriented north-south and were linked with the south set of rooms. There was also a central burial cluster in which the orientation of bodies and the distribution of design elements and element groups were mixed. Most of the ceremonial items included as grave offerings in the trash mound were also associated with this cluster. Presumably, high status individuals from each of the two major residence groups were being buried together in the central locus. Longacre interpreted these data as evidence for the presence of a matrilocal residence pattern. This method of inferring residence practices from the pattern of associations of ceramic design attributes was later refined and expanded in another classic study by James Hill (1970a, 1970b) at Broken K Pueblo (figure 5.7).

Evaluating an Indicator. Inferences to residence patterns from the pattern of association of ceramic design attributes have not gone unchallenged. Stanislawski (1973), for example, has questioned several of the assumptions underlying this approach as it has been applied to the Pueblo region. First, Pueblo women today do not always learn pot making through their female descent line. Second, distributional studies of discarded pots in present day Pueblo villages show that they do not always wind up in the area where they were made. In spite of these and other criticisms, pioneering instrumental-nomological studies such as Longacre's have raised some interesting questions: Is there any relationship between stylistic designs on craft objects and residence patterns? Does stylistic clustering or its absence correlate with particular residence patterns on different levels of sociocultural integration? The give and take of speculation and evaluation have led in this instance to further attempts to prove or improve the validity and reliability of stylistic clustering as an indicator of the presence of specific residence patterns (see the Suggested Readings).

Ember's Cross-Cultural Survey. Other archaeological indicators have been used to infer the presence of particular residence patterns. For instance, Em-

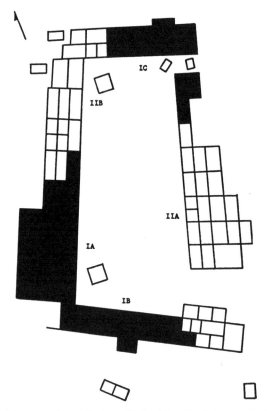

Figure 5.7   Residence units at Broken K Pueblo. Shaded areas indicate residence unit no. 1 and its subunits; the unshaded areas represent residence unit no. 11 and its subunits. Source: Hill 1966, figure 2.

ber (1973) searched a random sample of sixty-three modern societies drawn from the Human Relations Area Files (HRAF) for reliable material culture indicators of residence patterns. Since neolocal societies (in which couples establish independent households) were consistently associated with commercial exchange, especially a money economy, Ember suggested that coins or other standardized currencies are a suitable instrument with which to measure the presence of neolocality. He showed too that bilocality (in which residence was established with either the wife's or husband's family) was the result of depopulation (and, therefore, was probably not present in North America before European contact) and that the size of the living floor area of the average house in a society is a reliable indicator of matrilocal and patrilocal residence in precontact North America. Eighteen of the societies in the sample were patrilocal and had a mean floor area per living house of 326 square feet. Four of the societies were matrilocal and had a mean floor area of 868 square feet. Overlap in floor area size in precontact North American patrilocal and matrilocal societies seems rare. Ember's studies were replicated by Divale (1977), who concluded that one would be right 95 percent of the time in predicting patrilocality when the average house floor area was between 14.5 and 42.7 square meters or matrilocality when the average house floor area was between 79.2 and 270.8 square meters.

Residence Groups and Nonmetrical Cranial Traits. Lane and Sublett (1972) also showed how the analysis of human skeletons may contribute to the identification of prehistoric residence groups. Their basic assumption was that elements of social organizations having biological referents should be objectified in the osteological record. Nonmetrical cranial traits were examined in a series of skulls from cemeteries in the Allegheny (Seneca) reservation that dated from the 1850s to 1930. Their study showed that males but not females tended to cluster in localized geographic regions. This distributional pattern is what one would expect to find among patrilocal residence groups, a residence practice that is ethnographically recorded among the Allegheny even before they shifted to reservation life in the nineteenth century.

Kinship and Descent

Mapping kinship relationships in a society involves determining who thinks they are related to whom. Descent rules affiliate individuals on the basis of a conceptualized recognition of common descent rather than on the basis of strict biological descent. Unilineal descent rules relate members of the father's kin group (patrilineal descent) or the mother's kin group (matrilineal descent), but not both. Nonunilineal descent rules that trace descent through any relative are generally called cognatic. There are several common types of descent groups, including lineages, clans, phratries, and moieties. Descent groups play especially important roles in the organization of economic and political activities in nonindustrialized societies. Therefore, reformulating kinship and descent rules should be of particular interest to most anthropological archaeologists.

A few archaeologists have attempted to infer the existence of specific descent groups from reconstructed residence patterns (e.g., Longacre 1963, 1964, 1966; Deetz 1965). For example, Longacre once suggested that matrilineal descent groups were present at Carter Ranch, although he later discussed the many difficulties involved in inferring descent from archaeological data (1968). Other anthropologists (e.g., Allen and Richardson 1971) have claimed that archaeologists may not be able to infer descent rules from residence patterns or other archaeological data with any accuracy. Descent rules are ideas that people hold. As a result, people related to each other according to one set of rules might not be related by another. How can archaeologists determine, for example, whether a patrilocal descent group related through a virilocal descent rule actually considered themselves to be a patrilineal descent group, too? Since descent rules are conceptual rather than biological relationships, they may or may not be instantiated in the patterning of objects that people make and use.

In spite of these problems, for the purpose of building processual models assumptions can still be made about the type of descent practiced by a past society. If the implications of the model do not match archaeological reality, there is reason to believe that the assumption was inaccurate (e.g., Zimmerman 1977).

Status and Social Stratification

Identifying the major structural elements of a community and determining how they fit together to form a social organization or social structure involve problems of categorization and definition. One categorization of the basic building blocks of social systems is the trilogy of individuals, roles, and groups. Individuals are the people who make up the community. Roles are sets of conventions and expectations, guides to appropriate behavior that exist in the realm of culture. People who adopt or enter a role are expected to adapt to these behavioral expectations and requirements. Roles serve many functions in a community, the most important of which are to promote the integration of the community's members, to help maintain social control, to encourage specialization, and to serve as mechanisms for transmitting expected patterns of social interaction to new members of the community. Social groups are aggregations of individuals who recurrently interact within the context of a set of interconnected roles. Unlike crowds and other aggregations whose interaction is temporary and limited, social groups are aggregations of individuals who function together to satisfy their own needs or the needs of the community over an extended period of time.

Individuals, roles, and groups can be categorized in other ways than on the basis of their functional differences. Each can be ranked in terms of culturally defined standards, such as ease of access to food, wealth, education, and other factors. Their ranking according to these standards defines the *status* they have in a society. The status of a social unit can be defined in two ways: the ease of access of the unit to single commodities like food, gold, and position at the head of the table; or a general index composed of the unit's overall access to a variety of commodities. Status differentiation, the differentiation of people into classes, accompanies the process of functional differentiation as people divide tasks up in a society. The term *class* also has two meanings that parallel the two meanings of status. Class may refer either to people who are in a similar position with respect to some specific resource or to people whose overall status is fairly similar.

Thus the building blocks of social subsystems can be categorized in terms of their vertical rankings—their social statuses—as well as in terms of their horizontal position within a web of functional interdependence. Some human communities have elaborated the number of roles, groups, and classes in their social subsystem through time, while others have maintained relatively undifferentiated social subsystems. It is these changes through time and the reasons for their occurrence that social archaeologists (Redman et al. 1978) are especially interested in understanding.

Grave Wealth as an Indicator of Status. Status was defined as ease of access to single commodities or as a general index of a person, role, or group's ease of access to a variety of commodities. Ease of access to commodities may result from an individual's or group's personal achievements or their birthright. This definition has made it possible for archaeologists to infer the presence of status differences and social stratification in past communities. A common ordinal measure of status equates higher status with more grave wealth. A frequently cited example of this approach to the identification of status and social stratification is Peebles and Kus' study (1977) of burials from Moundsville (figure 5.8). In another study reported by Renfrew (1974:79–81), wealth was not randomly distributed among 490 graves in the cemetery of Chalandriani on the Cycladic island of Syros. There was even a possible touch of snobbery in the Chalandriani cemetery, for very

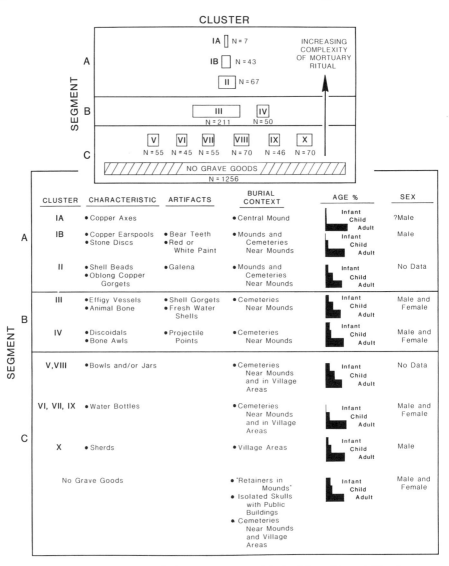

Figure 5.8 Hierarchical social clusters represented in burials at Moundville. Source: Peebles and Kus 1977, figure 3. Reproduced by permission of the Society for American Archaeology from *American Antiquity* 42(3):421–448.

simple pottery forms were absent from the richest graves. Finally, Shennan (1975) attempted to reconstruct elements of the social organization of Early Bronze Age societies in southwestern Slovakia by correlating the estimated value of grave goods with the age and sex of skeletons from cemeteries at Branc (figures 5.9 and 5.10). One of the more interesting recent methods of measuring status and social stratification in this approach is discussed in the next section of this chapter.

Was Stature a Social Status Correlate? Buikstra (1976:37) has explored the possibility that the variable *stature* is a social status correlate. A statistical analysis of the stature of males buried in the Middle Woodland Gibson mound

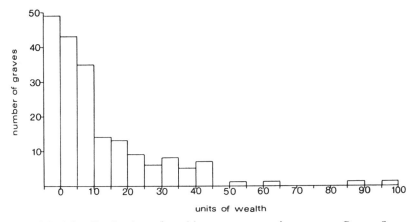

Figure 5.9 The distribution of wealth scores among the graves at Branc. Source: Shennan 1975, figure 3.

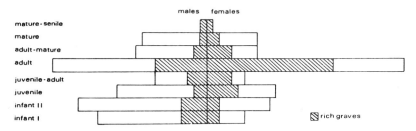

Figure 5.10 The age and sex distribution of skeletons found at Branc; individuals with more than ten units of wealth are distinguished as rich. Source: Shennan 1975, figure 4.

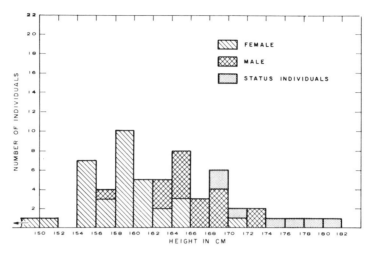

Figure 5.11 Stature estimates for total Gibson adult population. Source: Buikstra 1976, figure 11.

in Illinois showed that stature was not normally distributed (figure 5.11): taller males were associated with high status, as indicated by spatial burial treatment. Did high status individuals have privileged access to food resources? If so, they should have experienced less dietary stress, which would be apparent in fewer Harris lines, less dental hypoplasia, and other indicators. Measurements of the strontium content of the bones of high status individuals failed to demonstrate a higher protein intake than other individuals. Because of the results of this test, the hypothesis was abandoned: high status individuals apparently did not have privileged access to food resources. The hypothesis that seemed to best fit the data posited the existence of distinctive morphological traits that resulted from an ascribed status system and culturally determined marriage customs.

Other indicators of status and social stratification have also been suggested by archaeologists. For example, Binford (1962) has pointed to the appearance of special artifact types among growing populations of hunter-gatherers as possible symbols of achieved status. Assuming that status differences should be reflected in differential access to specific food resources, Brown (1973) attempted to discriminate between high and low status individuals in several archaeological sites in Illinois using the ratio of strontium to calcium. Hoffman (1974) examined the trash disposal practices at

Early Dynastic Hierakonpolis in Upper Egypt for material correlates of status and stratification. As a working hypothesis, Hoffman assumed that the quality of trash in specific activity zones should correlate with the status of the individuals who lived in those zones. Trash from each zone was assigned to one of three nominal socioeconomic groupings: elite, nonelite, industrial. The distribution of each of these groupings was then taken as an indicator of the location of nonelite residential areas, sacred quarters, industrial zones, and elite administrative or residential zones.

Millie's Camp: A Cautionary Tale from Ethnoarchaeology

Communities vary in many characteristics, including the spacing and composition of their household units, the size of their medium-level zones, the complexity of their zoning principles, and their areal extent. Archaeologists assume that this variability has been objectified in the archaeological record and that it is discoverable—that they should be able to make potentially falsifiable statements about past social organizations. But the content and structure of communities on various levels of abstraction are constructs proposed by archaeologists as a means of understanding the archaeological record and the life-ways of past peoples. These constructs are by definition hypothetical. As has been emphasized in earlier chapters, hypothetical constructs or theory must be continually subjected to severe tests.

A number of recent studies in ethnoarchaeology have clearly indicated the probable fallibility of many of our reconstructions of social organizations on the community level. Robson Bonnichsen's illuminating study (1973) of Millie's Camp is a particularly powerful example. Bonnichsen "excavated" a recently deserted Indian camp by carefully recording the spatial distribution of artifacts, litter, and facilities (figure 5.12). The data were interpreted by several archaeological methods. Former residents of the camp were then asked to check the interpretations. How accurate had the archaeologists been? The archaeological data clearly had been misunderstood. Bonnichsen concluded that project archaeologists failed to deduce the reasons behind the behavioral patterns that produced the distribution of material remains at Millie's Camp because they were not familiar with the patterns. Archaeologists' commonsensical, practical approach to interpreting social structure and organization may be misleading, after all, for the normative patterns that ar-

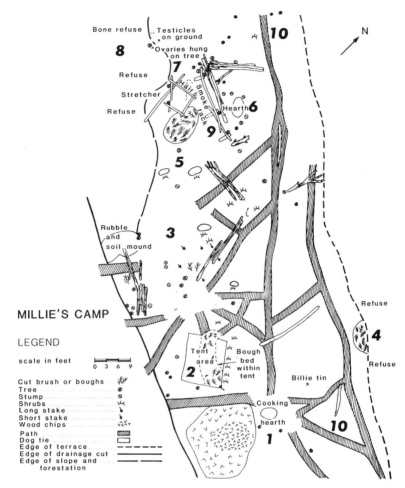

Figure 5.12 Activity areas at Millie's camp. (1) Cooking area, (2) tent area, (3) tent or cache or menstrual retreat area, (4) refuse area, (5) dog-tie area, (6) cooking area, (7) hide-working frame, (8) refuse area, (9) corral area, (10) trails. Source: Bonnichsen 1973, figure 1.

chaeologists are familiar with may be quite different from those of the people whose remains they are studying.

There are many other factors that complicate the reconstruction of elements of social systems besides an unfamiliarity with normative patterns. Inadequate sampling procedures, deterioration of evidence, misinterpretations of data, the ephemerality of some social units, and the failure to view communities in a regional framework all complicate the model-building process. In addition, social differentiation that is not dependent on wealth may be impossible to discern in the archaeological record. Todd (1974:86) gives as an example the Muhtar or head man of a modern central Anatolian village. The Muhtar's house and possessions are not usually differentiated from those of other villagers. Nonetheless, the absence of inequalities in wealth in the village does not mean that they are truly egalitarian in a sociopolitical sense. Since there is a cognitive component in the very concept of social system, a component that may not be explicitly objectified in the archaeological record, as Todd's example suggests, some social anthropologists and archaeologists have regarded attempts by archaeologists to reconstruct social systems as naively optimistic (Leach 1973, 1977; also see M. A. Smith 1955 and Hawkes 1954:162). Archaeologists have responded (e.g., Mellor 1973), and the debate continues.

The Political System

The political system of a society generally performs three basic functions. It helps resolve internal conflicts; it relates one culture to another by warfare, regularized trade, or diplomacy; and it serves as a source of leadership and decision making, which it enforces. In some societies these functions are actually carried out by kinship groups. As societies become more complex, the political system becomes more formal and full-time positions are developed. Political systems have been classified in a number of ways, but one of the most useful for archaeologists is based on this distinction between degree of formality. A *state* has a formal government and is defined as "a culturally organized group of people who share a common territory and are governed by a formally constituted authority" (Knudson 1978:402). In a state-level political organization, the political functions of leadership are performed by full-time officials. *Stateless societies* include those culturally organized groups of people who share a common territory but who do not have a formal governmental structure and full-time officials. In this section we will review several studies that have attempted to reconstruct the political system of stateless societies by analyzing the contents and configurations of their cemeteries.

The Concept of a Burial Program

Anthropologists have suggested that mortuary activity or the mode of burial behavior associated with individuals may provide indirect measures of socially defined roles within a society (e.g., Saxe 1970). This suggestion has been supported by cross-cultural studies that demonstrate a broad correlation between social complexity and the complexity of mortuary activity. Binford (1971), for example, tested a number of propositions concerning burial practices against a sample of forty societies drawn from the Human Relations Area Files. The variable *complexity of status structure* was compared with (1) grave form, orientation, and location, (2) the form, quantity, and quality of grave goods, (3) age and sex, and (4) degree of body preparation, treatment, and disposition. His conclusion was that the proposition "There should be a direct correlation between the structural complexity of mortuary ritual and status systems with socio-cultural systems" was confirmed (Binford 1971:18). Another conclusion drawn from the study was that differential burial should be based on social position among more complex cultures, while age and sex should be more important distinctions among less complex cultures. Thus there appear to be recurrent associations between mortuary activities and socially defined roles within society.

Identifying societal complexity from mortuary site data involves several steps. First, the values of a series of cultural variables, in particular the burial behavior accorded an individual at death, are determined. These values are then correlated with the values of biological variables, such as age, sex, and inherited traits, in an exploratory search for pattern. The reconstructed pattern of mortuary activities is called a *burial program*. Finally, the burial program is compared to ethnographically recorded mortuary practices, and inferences are made to the broader social systems of a society, including the nature and complexity of its political organization.

Identifiable aspects of a burial program include a wide range of culturally defined variables (Brown 1971; Saxe 1970; Buikstra 1976), such as (1) grave locus (in the mound fill, for example, or in a central feature), (2) technical attributes of grave structure (the presence of structural attributes such as logs or limestone slabs, or, perhaps, the amount of energy expended in removing dirt), (3) processing of the corpse (articulated, manipulated, or disarticulated), (4) grave accoutrements (the quantity, quality, and form of grave goods), (5) supralocal items of exchange (such as nonlocal raw materials and other exchange goods), and (6) items of local significance (local raw materials would be an example). The analysis of the associations between culturally defined and biological variables provides answers to such questions as the following: Do structural features within burial sites distinguish certain groups of burials from others? How much energy was expended in mortuary activity? Do subadults and females receive special treatment by a socially defined relationship to a male? Are well-defined retainer classes present? Was age at death significant in determining an individual's final burial locus or the amount of postmortem manipulation that occurred? Did a person's sex limit his or her access to particular burial positions? With whom did conspicuous displays of supralocal artifacts occur? Were they males or females? Old or young? Do cemetery areas occur in clusters in association with specific features of the natural or social environment? Burial programs, which presumably reflect social rules that limit access to specific burial tracts, are then constructed from the information provided by answers to these and other questions.

Since modes of burial treatment are thought to be correlated with and explained by the variable *degree of social complexity,* burial programs are considered particularly appropriate conceptual tools for reconstructing the general outlines of political systems. Fried's evolutionary model (1967) of political organizations has been used by archaeologists for this purpose because of its adaptability to discussions of status and status complexity in terms of material items and the expenditure of energy in burial behavior. Fried's evolutionary model is composed of four levels or stages of social organization: egalitarian, ranked, stratified, and the state. Each level has definable characteristics that archaeologists can compare to traits of prehistoric mortuaries.

In *egalitarian social organizations* age and sex are the major determinants of status; other important determinants are related to subsistence prowess or odd bodily characteristics, such as unusual size or a body deformity. Here the major limitation to high status is a person's ability to cope with expected performances. Burial tracts within egalitarian societies are largely defined by biological traits, and the distribution of individuals within various burial tracts will generally parallel the society's mortality profile (see chapter 6).

In *ranked societies,* access to high status positions is more limited, and the number of high status positions is relatively stable and does not vary with a flux in population size. As a result, fewer individuals occupy high status positions, and the status structure of ranked societies tends to resemble a pyramid. Those at the apex of the pyramid are generally mediators who redistribute wealth. Even though they are not able to accumulate wealth, their day-to-day activities are surrounded by considerable ritual and ceremonial importance. Since the status structure is pyramidal, access to burial tracts should be pyramidal, too. One would expect influence and power to be symbolized by a great expenditure of wealth and energy, and this expenditure to be concentrated in the least accessible burial tracts. Biological characteristics of a familial nature might explain entree into some tracts, but other biological characteristics such as age and sex alone should not.

In *stratified societies,* wealth is concentrated in the hands of a few individuals who represent exploitative authority rather than being agents of redistribution. Since differentiation between social ranks in stratified societies is still greater than in ranked societies, a wider range of social inequality should be represented by a more highly diversified burial program. High-ranking persons should be associated with great wealth and energy-consuming or "expensive" mortuary activities, while low-ranking persons might even lack grave goods and signs of postmortem manipulation; in fact, they may even be excluded from the burial grounds of the upper classes. The presence of metals in their smelted and cast forms is an indicator of early class and state societies, too, as is the presence of money.

These characteristics of stratified societies are even more exaggerated in *state-level societies.* An astonishing example of fabulous grave goods in a state-level society is the imperial bodyguard of 7,500 lifesize soldiers and horses sculpted in clay that were discovered by chance in 1974 near the ancient capital city of Xi'an (Sian) in China (Hearn 1979). The brillantly painted army guarded the mausoleum of the First Emperor of Qin, China's first unifier and the builder of the 1,500-mile-long Great Wall.

The Gibson Burial Program. Buikstra's study (1976) of the Gibson burial program in Hopewellian Illinois is, for several reasons, an interesting example of the use of burial programs as an indicator of degree of political complexity. First, it demonstrates the model-building process in action. Second, it illustrates the fruitful interaction between archaeological data, bioanthropological data, and ideal sociocultural models like Fried's.

There were apparently two tracts in the Gibson burial program, one defined by the presence of an abundance of supralocal items and extensive earth movement and the other by the absence of wealth and conspicuous energy-consumption (table 5.1). Only a few males had access to the first tract. An analysis of the range of individuals interred at Gibson also showed that the

Table 5.1 Supralocal Artifacts in Burial Associations from the Gibson and Klunk Sites

Item	No. of Associations	Subfloor Pit	Original Ground Surface	Within Mound Fill	Central Feature	Ramp	Subadult	Adult M	Adult F
			Locus				With Whom		
Copper:									
Earspools	2	—	—	—	2	—	—	2	—
Panpipe	1	—	—	—	1	—	—	1	—
Beads	2	2	—	—	—	—	2	—	—
Adz	4	—	—	—	4	—	1	2,1*	1*
Conch shell:									
Worked complete shell	2	—	—	—	2	—	2	—	—
Beads	2	1	—	—	1	—	1	1	—
Marginella shell beads	1	—	—	1	—	—	1	—	—
Quartz crystal pendant	1	—	—	—	1	—	—	1	—
Cassis shell, worked	2	—	—	—	2	—	—	2	—
Galena cube	3	1	—	—	2	—	—	2	1
Bear canines, worked	4	1	—	—	3	—	2	2	—
Platform pipes	2	—	—	—	2	—	2*	2*	1*
Mica, cut	1	—	—	—	1	—	1*	1*	—
Roseate spoonbill	1	—	—	—	1	—	1*	1*	—
Shell beads (mussel shell or pearl "slug")	6	2	—	—	4	—	4	2	—

SOURCE: Buikstra 1976, table 15.
*Multiple burial association.

cemetery was not reserved for the privileged: all had access to the cemetery when they died. In Fried's terminology, limited access to valuable goods and prestigious burial treatment are signs of a ranked or stratified society, and the association of supralocal items and extensive earth movement with only a few individuals is a sign of a stratified society. Was Gibson society stratified, then? The presence of a total community population in a mortuary site is, however, not generally associated with a stratified society but with ranked and egalitarian societies. In politically more complex societies, few people, especially the very young, are included in burial groups with high-ranking people. Buikstra concluded that the best model of Middle Woodland social organization at Gibson was a ranked society. The absence both of multiple well-defined retainer classes and of conspicuous displays of wealth also indicates a less than stratified society. As this example shows, the gradation between Fried's four political levels may be more continuous than the ideal model suggests.

Here it is useful to ask, Do all "basic patterns of social relationships have an equal coherence and relative stability" (Murdock 1959:134)? Can we expect all patterns to be equally visible in the archaeological record if they do not have equal coherence and relative stability? How fruitful is it to borrow ideal sociopolitical models developed by sociocultural anthropologists with very different aims and subject matter in mind (e.g., Renfrew 1974:69–70)? For instance, Fried's classificatory system is an evolutionary model that uses broad catchall categories that may have meaning only in a restricted economic sense. The illuminating discussion of the concept *chiefdom* by Todd (1974), Renfrew (1974), and others in Moore (1974) illustrates many of the problems of applying ideal catchall sociopolitical categories to archaeological data. If Fried's classificatory system continues to be adopted by archaeologists, further refinements will clearly be necessary to satisfy a broader range of research objectives.

Problems with Inferences from Single Communities

In spite of the stimulating suggestions that have been made in these and other studies, single communities often tell us very little on their own about social and political organization. For instance, evidence for social stratification should be more readily apparent at a large settlement in a stratified or state-level society than at special extractive sites or small villages, and a single cemetery may be aberrant in a culture. Evidence for social organization must ultimately be considered within a regional perspective, for the pattern of location and the contents of sites themselves may be evidence of centralized authority. For instance, the emergence of a hierarchical settlement system is one of the clearest indicators of the increasing interdependence of separate residential groups, and hence of the evolution of more complex social organizations. Locational analysis and other approaches to identifying social systems at the regional level are discussed in chapter 7.

The World of Symbolic Thought: The Ideological Subsystem

Since questions concerning people/land relationships have seemed the easiest to answer with archaeological data, anthropological archaeologists have traditionally concentrated their research efforts on reconstructing community subsistence systems. This research focus has often fostered the uncritical assumption that, at least in less complex societies, factors of the physical environment cause change in human societies. In recent years, conjectures about seemingly more elusive aspects of the life-way of past communities, such as status systems, rules for postmarital residence, and political systems, are becoming almost commonplace, as we have seen, as anthropological archaeologists have become interested in the way kinship and descent, age, sex, and inequality structure social life. Like other anthropologists, they have become interested in the reasons *why* societies became organized in particular ways.

This growing emphasis reflects an increasing awareness by archaeologists of the importance in change and stability of people/people relationships, an importance that V. Gordon Childe (1958) grasped many years ago. It is also the result of the recent adoption of the methodological principle that most if not all of the components of past sociocultural systems are objectified in some manner in the archaeological record. If this assumption is reasonably correct, there is no theoretical justification for believing that ecological and economic data are any more direct or immediate in the archaeological record than data of past social systems. The task of archaeologists is to discover how this objectification occurs, what pathways it follows, and what form it takes in the archaeological record. This section looks at a seemingly more elusive subsystem, the ideological subsystem.

All known human societies have stories that explain the world and make it intelligible. These stories are expressions of philosophies and religious beliefs, world views, sets of ethical principles, myths, and other features of ideological subsystems. Ideological subsystems also contain ideas concerning the regularity of nature or the seasons, the behavior of animals, number systems, and other bits of knowledge. Together these stories and bits of knowledge help human societies cope with their social and natural environments within the limitations of their technology and other cultural equipment. Ideological factors influence people's actions and other cultural components through a process of psychological conditioning, the impact of ideas on human behavior. Some anthropologists maintain that this impact plays a crucial role in maintaining cultural systems and in promoting their change. Nonetheless, the importance of ideological factors (as compared to environmental factors, for example) in the direct promotion and inhibition of cultural change is still a controversial issue in the social sciences, an issue that is examined in greater detail in chapter 11.

Attempts to demonstrate the causal impact of ideological factors on sociocultural systems have nearly always been elusive and controversial in archaeology, for ideological factors are elements in subjective conceptual systems that may be fuzzy to begin with and that are differentially grasped and participated in by members of societies: they are not easily observable empirical phenomena like volcanic eruptions, droughts, and wars. Because individual behavior motivated by ideological factors may not be tightly patterned, archaeologists must examine the archaeological results of fuzzy, overlapping, behavioral activities that are personal interpretations of partially shared symbolic systems. In addition, as societies become increasingly complex in class structure, racial composition, ethnic diversity, shared knowledge systems, and religious beliefs, it becomes increasingly difficult to reconstruct ideological subsystems, for they become too diverse and complex to be profitably studied as conceptual wholes. While recognizable ideologically related facilities such as temples, burial mounds, and churches become increasingly visible archaeologically as social complexity increases, it becomes correspondingly more difficult to reconstruct features of the ideological realm without greatly oversimplifying and distorting complex systems.

For these and other reasons, archaeologists have tended to shun or to look askance at reconstructions of ideological subsystems. This has been particularly true of archaeologists committed to thing-oriented or to positivist schools of archaeology, for knowledge of physical behavior has seemed easier to falsify than knowledge of conceptual or symbolic systems. Nonetheless, archaeologists have also come to realize that by definition the concept *human behavior* contains an essential conceptual component and, therefore, that all subsystems have a conceptual component. There is no a priori reason why archaeologists should be able to reconstruct the conceptual codes within other subsystems but not within the ideological subsystem. Whether one's interest is social structure, economic institutions, or religious beliefs, the procedures for testing hypotheses remain the same. Delimiting ideological elements does not introduce methodological problems in interpretation and empirical falsification that differ in archaeology from those that are present in the reconstruction of any other conceptual system. The content of all of these systems must be inferred from the archaeological record; empirical referents must be identified; and, as an explicitly adopted methodological rule, hypotheses must in principle be falsifiable. This realization in part has lead in recent years to an increasing interest in the ideological systems of prehistoric peoples, a legitimate interest now acknowledged by the term *cognitive archaeology*.

Cognitive Archaeology

Robert L. Hall (1976, 1977), in a series of studies, demonstrated how cognitive archaeology might supplement economic and political interpretations of sociocultural systems. In fact, Hall takes modern archaeologists to task for placing undue emphasis on technoenvironmental factors and for not attempting in America to think in Indian categories. For example, the peace pipe or calumet is a familiar ceremonial item in the early historic period in the eastern United States. Violence within and between tribal groups was absolutely forbidden when the sacred tribal pipe was present. Similar appearing pipes are present in the archaeological record in the eastern United States for at least several thousand years. Can the form and context of these pipes tell us anything about the rituals of prehistoric peoples and about the possible functions of these rituals?

Historic peace pipes were nearly always in the form of a weapon. Among the Pawnee, for instance, the pipe had the form of an arrow; the Osage word for calumet even means "arrowshaft" (Hall 1977:503). Hall argues that "the weaponlike appearance is the result of a specific ceremonial custom: the peace pipe was a ritual weapon." Did earlier platform pipes have a similar function and a parallel form? Among the Middle Woodland Hopewell the common weapon was the spear thrower or atlatl. According to Hall, Hopewell platform pipes may be symbolic manifestations of flat atlatls with effigy spurs (figure 5.13). Similarities between atlatls and platform pipes include the curvature of their shafts and the location of the effigy spur in the same area as the atlatl spur. A Hopewell platform pipe could represent "the archaeologically visible part of a transformed ritual atlatl, a symbolic weapon which in Middle Woodland times probably had some of the same functions as the calumet of historic times, itself a ritual arrow" (Hall 1977:504–505). Besides being an item of exchange between groups, more importantly, Hall suggests, it may have been "part of the very mechanism of exchange," a mechanism that on analogy with peace pipe ceremonialism among historic American Indians tended to reduce intergroup conflict and to ease communication and exchange over a large region of central North America. Although this identity needs further corroboration, Hall's study is a stimulating attempt to grapple with the cognitive component of a prehistoric artifact form.

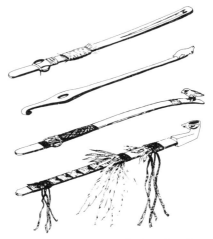

Figure 5.13 Flat atlatls from aboriginal North America. Source: Hall 1977, figure 2. Reproduced by permission of the Society for American Archaeology from *American Antiquity* 42(4):499–518.

The Importance of World View

A world view is the way a people see themselves in relation to the universe and the things that they think are within it. The study of world views is concerned with underlying implicit assumptions about such things as causality, the self, space, time, or human nature (Kearney 1975, 1976). Clues to a people's world view are sometimes obtainable through a study of their sacred geography (Vogt 1974), art (Fischer 1961), architecture, ceramics, and gravestones. As culturally organized systems of knowledge or culturally specific cognitions, world views structure the way people come to know about the world and, therefore, their behavior.

Deetz's cognitive historical model (1974, 1977) for early Anglo-America is an interesting and highly readable study of the implications for analyses and interpretations of the archaeological record of the concept of world view. In this model, early Anglo-America is divided into three periods: an initial English (A.D. 1620–1660), an Anglo-American (A.D. 1660–1760), and a Georgian (A.D. 1760–1835). Each of these periods was, according to Deetz, associated with a different world view or mind-set: the initial English with a medieval world view that was organic, heterogeneous, corporate, and asymmetrical; the Anglo-American with a typical strongly conservative folk culture that was resistant to change and that resulted in strong, locally oriented political units; and the Georgian with a progressive and innovative structure, homogeneity in material culture, the individual, and an insistence on order and balance.

A brief description of the Georgian world view shows how these world views permeated all aspects of life, from ceramics and gravestones to architecture, the decorative arts, and the organization of space. In contrast to the earlier medieval world view, the Georgian stressed order, symmetry, balance, and homogeneity. These themes appear in architecture, for example, in rigidly symmetrical and bilateral house plans. The classical Georgian house had "a central doorway flanked by paired evenly spaced windows and a central second-floor window directly over the door" and "a central hall that separates two sets of two rooms each" (Deetz 1977:111). This plan emphasized spatial specialization and the isolation of family members within the house (figure 5.14). A Georgian world view is also apparent in matched individual sets of china, for even patterns of food consumption changed. Food was eaten in communally used wooden trenchers in earlier New England,

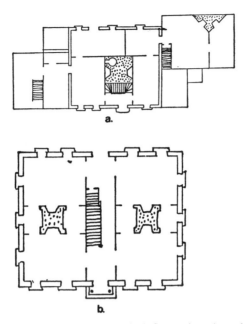

Figure 5.14 Symmetrical and asymmetrical floor plans in colonial America. a. Fairbanks house, Dedham, Massachusetts. b. Typical Georgian house plan. Source: James Deetz, *In Small Things Forgotten: The Archaeology of Early American Life*. Drawings by Charles Cann. Copyright © 1977 by James Deetz. Reprinted by permission of Doubleday & Company, Inc.

while individual place-settings characterize the Georgian period. As a last example, the Georgian emphasis on the individual is present in burial practices. Single stones often marked the resting place of a family during earlier periods, but Georgians were buried in individualized graves with their own markers.

Deetz's study suggests that a utilitarian or materialist interpretation of human activities may be highly misleading, for architecture, patterns of food consumption, and many other social and technoeconomic institutions are forms of self-expression molded by a world view. However, Deetz (1974:21) also suggests that the cognitive dimension of material culture assemblages becomes more visible and more explicit as one moves up the scale of sociocultural complexity, for less complex sociocultural systems tend to be dominated by more urgent subsistence requirements than do more complex systems.

Summary

Chapter 5 is concerned with some of the typical questions anthropological archaeologists ask when they analyze the material remains of single communities in order to identify social and ideological subsystems. Useful in settlement pattern analysis are the concepts of activity areas and tool-kits, such as those found in burials or refuse dumps, and chi-square, trend surface, and factor analysis techniques. Methods used to find male and female work areas and sex-related artifacts include the direct historical approach, ethnographic analogy, the study of artifact associations with skeletons, and analysis of spatial associations. Patterns could, however, be caused by other than social factors, so identities must be examined within the cycle of science.

The search for universal activities in household, administrative, religious, and other spatial clusters may also be compared to determine pattern and variability in a community. The spatial arrangement of buildings and walls used in the study of community zoning to designate activities carried out by larger-than-household groups helps arrange socially stratified communities into a community plan.

Nonspatial approaches to community social organization include the study of marital residence patterns through instrumental-nomological investigations. Studies by Longacre at the Carter Ranch site inferring that Pueblo Indians practiced matrilocal residence have been challenged, however. Other studies have looked to commercial exchange, depopulations, size of living floor area, and analysis of skeletons to identify residence patterns and groups. Studies of kinship and descent (who thinks they are related to whom) have been attempted from reconstructed residence patterns, but many believe that such groups cannot be inferred with accuracy—people related by one set of rules may not be related by another.

The differentiation of rank (status and social stratification) involves the process of functional differentiation in vertical rankings and horizontal positions within a web of functional interdependence. In this context, social *groups* are aggregations of *individuals* who recurrently interact within the context of a set of interconnected *roles*. Studies show that status (ease of access to commodities) may be indicated by grave wealth, but apparently not by physical stature. The Bonnichsen study of a recently deserted Indian camp followed by interviews of former residents indicated that studies of trash disposal data clearly had been misunderstood in some instances, probably because archaeologists were not familiar with the patterns of the groups they were studying. Inadequate sampling procedures, deterioration of evidence, misinterpretations of data, ephemerality of social units, and lack of a regional perspective as well as the fact that social differentiations not dependent on wealth may be impossible to discern in the archaeological record all complicate these studies.

Political systems serve to resolve internal conflicts, relate one culture to another, and provide leadership and decision making. Mortuary site studies indicate that differential burial was based on social position in complex cultures while age and sex were more important among less complex political structures. Identities such as locus, technical attributes, corpse processing, and accoutrements are useful in classifying political systems as egalitarian, ranked, stratified, and states. Studies of burial programs in Hopewellian Illinois demonstrate the modeling process and illustrate interaction between archaeological and bioanthropological data, and ideal sociocultural models. Anthropological archaeologists have concentrated on reconstructing community subsistence systems, but have become more interested in the whys of social organization and in the ideological subsystems that help people cope with their environments. Although such factors are not easily observable, cognitive archaeology (the study of ideological systems) is a legitimate way to deal with cognitive components in prehistoric artifacts. The Deetz study of early Anglo-America, for instance, categorized groups according to their world views and suggested that evidence of world view becomes more visible as systems become more complex.

SUGGESTED READINGS

There is a large body of literature that discusses the possibilities and problems of reconstructing social organizations from archaeological materials. A few of these accounts are:

Adams, E. C. 1983. The architectural analogue to Hopi social organization and room use, and implications for prehistoric northern Southwestern culture. *American Antiquity* 48(1):44–61.

Allen, W. L. and J. B. Richardson III. 1971. The reconstruction of kinship from archaeological data: The concepts, the methods, and the feasibility. *American Antiquity* 36:41–53.

Brockington, D. 1976. Archaeology as anthropology: Reconstruction of residence and descent patterns. *The Kansas Working Papers in Anthropology and Linguistics*, pp. 143–161. Lawrence: University of Kansas.

Crumley, C. 1976. Toward a locational definition of state systems of settlement. *American Anthropologist* 78:59–73.

Dickens, R., Jr. and J. Chapman. 1979. Ceramic patterning and social structure at two late historic Upper Creek sites in Alabama. *American Antiquity* 43:390–398.

Longacre, W., ed. 1970. *Reconstructing Prehistoric Pueblo Societies*. Albuquerque: University of New Mexico Press.

Renfrew, C. 1974. Beyond a subsistence economy: The evolution of social organization in prehistoric Europe. In C. Moore, ed., *Reconstructing Complex Societies*, pp. 69–96. Supplement to the Bulletin of the American Schools of Oriental Research, No. 20. Cambridge, Mass.: American Schools of Oriental Research.

Tainter, J. and R. Cordy. 1977. An archaeological analysis of social ranking and residence groups in prehistoric Hawaii. *World Archaeology* 9:95–112.

Upham, S. 1982. *Polities and Power*. New York: Academic Press.

The social dimensions of mortuary practices are discussed in:

Brown, J. A., ed. 1971. *Approaches to the Social Dimensions of Mortuary Practices*. Memoirs of the Society for American Archaeology, No. 25. Washington, D.C.: Society for American Archaeology.

Chapman, R. W. 1977. Burial practices: An area of mutual interst. In M. Spriggs, ed., *Archaeology and Anthropology: Areas of Mutual Interest*, pp. 19–33. British Archaeological Reports, 5.19. London: BAR Publications.

Rathje, W. 1970. Socio-political implications of lowland Maya burials: Methodology and tentative hypotheses. *World Archaeology* 1:359–374.

Rothschild, N. 1979. Mortuary behavior and social organization at Indian Knoll and Dickson Mounds. *American Antiquity* 44:658–675.

Tainter, J. 1978. Mortuary practices and the study of prehistoric social systems. In M. Schiffer, ed., *Advances in Archaeological Method and Theory*, Vol. 1, pp. 105–141. New York: Academic Press.

Several accounts of the implications of ethnography for archaeology are:

David, N. 1971. The Fulani compound and the archaeologist. *World Archaeology* 3:111–131.

Donnan, C. and C. Clewlow, Jr., eds. 1974. *Ethnoarchaeology*. Monograph 4. Los Angeles: Institute of Archaeglogy, University of California.

Gould, R., ed. 1978. *Explorations in Ethnoarchaeology*. Albuquerque: University of New Mexico Press.

Kramer, C., ed. 1979. *Ethnoarchaeology: Implications of Ethnography for Archaeology*. New York: Columbia University Press.

Problems in archaeology of identifying regional boundaries are discussed in:

Englebrecht, W. 1974. The Iroquois: Archaeological patterning on the tribal level. *World Archaeology* 6:52–65.

Friedrich, M. 1970. Design structure and social interaction: Archaeological implications of an ethnographic analysis. *American Antiquity* 35:332–343.

Hodder, I., ed. 1978. *The Spatial Organisation of Culture*. Pittsburgh, Pa.: University of Pittsburgh Press.

Several comprehensive studies of spatial analysis in archaeglogy are:

Clarke, D. L., ed. 1977. *Spatial Archaeology*. London, New York: Academic Press.

Hodder, I., ed. 1978. *The Spatial Organisation of Culture*. Pittsburgh, Pa.: Univeristy of Pittsburgh Press.

Hodder, I. and C. Orton. 1976. *Spatial Analysis in Archaeology*. New York: Cambridge University Press.

Upham, S., ed. 1979. *Computer Graphics in Archaeology*. Anthropological Research Papers, No. 15. Tempe: Arizona State University.

A number of interesting attempts to reconstruct ideological and symbol systems are:

Deetz, J. 1977. *In Small Things Forgotten: The Archaeology of Early American Life*. New York: Anchor Press/Doubleday.

Flannery, K. V. and J. Marcus. 1976. Formative Oaxaca and the Zapotec cosmos. *American Scientist* 64:374–383.

Fritz, J. 1978. Paleopsychology today: Ideational systems and human adaptation in prehistory. In C. Redman et al., eds., *Social Archaeology*, pp. 37–59. New York: Academic Press.

Grieder, T. 1975. The interpretation of ancient symbols. *American Anthropologist* 77:849–855.

A recent review of studies of the biocultural interface is:

Hassan, F. 1981. *Demographic Archaeology*. New York: Academic Press.

CHAPTER SIX

Coping with the Natural Environment on the Community Level: The Technoeconomic Subsystem

Technoeconomic systems mediate between humans and their natural surroundings. More specifically, at the community level the technoeconomic system is a buffer between the human population, the rest of a community's sociocultural subsystems, and the natural setting. The main elements of technoeconomic systems are modes of subsistence and production, tools and machines, procedures for allocating goods and services, rules for regulating economic activities, and the knowledge that makes all of these activities possible. *Technology* refers to the material equipment and technical knowledge components of a technoeconomic system. The remaining components make up the *socioeconomic system* proper, the social arrangements employed in applying the technological components—the material equipment and technical knowledge—to the production, distribution, and consumption of goods and services. A community's technoeconomic system or economy is, therefore, "the way in which resources, technology, and work are combined to satisfy the material requirements of human beings and of social groups" (Bohannan 1963:211). According to this definition, these material requirements involve the satisfaction of kinship, prestige, and other social obligations as much as they do such biological needs as food, shelter, and clothing.

The cultural materialist research program assumes that determinants of the technoeconomic subsystem dominate and shape the structural organization of societies. While technology and the natural habitat may play the dominant role in less complex societies, and the social arrangements employed in the application of technology may be more determinant in more complex societies, the major determinants of the configurations of sociocultural systems are, nonetheless, thought to be technoeconomic. As a methodological rule priority in research is given to the technoeconomic subsystem. Archaeologists have been especially receptive to this research program, for information about the technoeconomic subsystem has seemed most self-evident and accessible in the archaeological record. As a result, some of the most striking advances in archaeology in recent years have come in people-land studies and in the application of the ecological approach.

Whether the major determinants of sociocultural systems are technoeconomic or not is a broad, overriding, empirical question in the social sciences that can only be answered by actually examining the role of the technoeconomic subsystem in specific sociocultural contexts through time. Regardless of the ultimate importance of the technoeconomic subsystem, the collection of techno-economic-ecological data remains a basic task of the archaeologist for several more mundane reasons. First, it is essential for reconstructing the technoeconomic subsystem. Second, given the close interaction between sociocultural subsystems and the reliance of archaeologists on indirect measures, techno-economic-ecological data have proven essential in many instances in modeling social and political organizations, settlement interactions, exchange networks, and patterns of sociocultural change. For instance, identifying the presence of particular social elements and political organizations may depend on the recognition of craft specialization, the redistribution of goods, the subsistence emphasis, wealth, and other technoeconomic traits.

In approaching the reconstruction of a technoeconomic system, archaeologists ask questions like the following: What was available for exploitation? What modes of production were present? Was there a division of labor based on age, sex, or special abilities? Were there cycles of economic activity that corresponded to seasonal environmental changes? What were the nature and amount of goods produced? How was land used? Was production energy-efficient? Was group labor systematically organized? Did individuals have personal possessions? Did everyone have equal rights to and an equal share of land and resources? Was the family or community the primary unit of production and consumption? Were there trading arrangements with other families or communities? Was commerce formally organized? Were there regular marketplaces? How did a community perceive its environment? Showing how archaeologists answer questions like these would fill many volumes. In this chapter only two aspects of the technoeconomic system are considered: the meaning of the term *environment* and the resources that were exploited. Additional information that can be derived from the human population as an artifact of its own culture is considered in the third section.

Different Meanings of the Term *Environment*

Every human community exists within a physical environment that is a source of materials and energy. The nature and amount of these resources, along with annual rainfall, animal biomass, and other environmental variables, present limitations within which sociocultural systems must adjust. Knowing what was available for exploitation is a prerequisite for understanding why certain economic decisions were made rather than others. Environmental reconstructions serve as a base for examining patterns of species and raw material exploitation, of seasonal scheduling in the food quest, of seasonality in site occupation, and of diet. They help account for artifacts and features by suggesting what may have been harvested or processed, hunted and butchered, preserved and stored. And they help identify which building materials and minerals were used and which were not. Botanists, palynologists, mammalogists, and other specialists in the natural sciences examine these remains and aid in their interpretation (Brothwell and Higgs 1969). In fact, the most extensive and active interdisciplinary cooperation within archaeology has involved the reconstruction of past environments and the identification of animal and plant remains from archaeological sites (MacNeish 1967).

It is easy to assume from nearly all of these studies that environment means soil types, the composition of animal and plant populations, the presence of water or natural routes, and other natural phenomena. However, when we think of our own physical surroundings, we tend to think of buildings, roads, fields, shops, and the distribution and location of neighboring towns and cites. Our use of the term shows that the land in people/land interactions is not natural but has been altered and built to varying degrees by people themselves. Communities adapt to built rather than to natural environments. The greater the level of technological complexity of a society, the more likely the environment will be manipulated and built. If environment is to provide at least partial explanations of cultural activity, it must be more broadly defined to include those "man"-made features that are the result of people/land interactions, for humans as "actors" live in a partly man-made, partly natural environment. Perceiving the physical landscape in this sense produces more realistic models, for climate, soil, drainage, topography, *and* the distribution and location of villages, fields, routes, and other built features of the landscape influence the patterning of human activity.

A still more fundamental distinction can be made between an *objective* and a *subjective* sense of environment. If we think about it, we soon realize that things are not always what they seem. People's actions are conditioned by what they believe exists, by their set of cutural expectations; that is, by a cognitive element. A very real difference exists between an objective and a subjective sense of environment. For example, the objective linear distance between two places is commonly measured in miles or kilometers. The same distance in a subjective sense is measured in terms of cost, time, perceived ease of access, and desire. People act in an environment made up of subjectively located destinations. Therefore, maps, environmental data, and other raw information do not always provide the key to human movement and behavior. What is significant in an environment varies with the subjective perceptions of human groups and cannot be determined a priori. For these reasons, the subjective rather than the objective environment has increasingly become the more interesting of the two in most social sciences concerned with explaining human behavior. The reconstruction of elements of the natural environment has now entered the ambit of environmental possibilism: environmental reconstructions provide settings within which personal decisions, chance, cultural preferences, technological capability, and other factors play a determinant role.

The importance of perceptual filters in decision making raises new and difficult problems for archaeologists. What was the *effective* environment, for instance? Is *carrying capacity* a culture-free concept? In addition, since communities react to subjective rather than objective environments, the parameters of the environment become much more flexible. Even though the model-building process becomes less straightforward, modeling subjective environments also leads to more realistic models.

The Problem of Determining Which Resources Were Exploited

How do archaeologists determine which resources were exploited? This section looks at a number of attempts to measure the range and abundance of specific exploited resources and at some of the problems that have been encountered in interpreting these measures.

Measuring the Abundance of Vertebrate Archaeofaunas

Some of the many problems involved in reconstructing community subsistence practices can be illustrated by examining several methods of measuring the abundance of vertebrate archaeofaunas. Ideally, these methods should provide valid and reliable measures of the actual contribution of each taxon to the diet of a community. Archaeologists would then be able to determine precisely how important one taxon was compared to another; they would also be able to chart changing patterns of exploitation through time. But do valid and reliable measures of the abundance of vertebrate archaeofaunas exist? If not, what is the nature of the measures that have been used? The three measures of abundance that have received the greatest analytic attention in recent years are the number of identified specimens, the minimum number of individuals, and the amount of meat represented (Casteel 1976; Chaplin 1971; Grayson 1979; Payne 1972; Uerpmann 1973; Ziegler 1973).

Number of Identified Specimens as an Abundance Measure. One of the earliest methods of measuring the relative importance of animal species in the diet simply involved counting the individual bones of each species identified in a sample. The number of identified specimens per taxon (NISP) method becomes suspect as soon as one realizes that 100 bones from an animal species could represent anywhere from 1 to 100 different animals and that the number of identifiable specimens varies from species to species. If any one bone is not necessarily independent (statistically) of any other bone, then simple counts and percentages are not truly representative of the sampled population, and statistical methods such as chi-square, which assume item independence, are clearly inappropriate. These and other problems of the measure are discussed in Binford and Bertram (1977), Bőkőnyi (1970), Casteel (1971, 1972), Chaplin (1971), Daly (1969), Grayson (1973, 1979), Payne (1972), Perkins (1973), Reed (1963), Thomas (1969), Uerpmann (1973), and Watson (1972).

Minimum Numbers of Individuals as an Abundance Measure. The minimum number of individuals per taxon (MNI) measure avoids the problem of interdependence. Here the most abundant element of an animal species (left femur, right humerus, and so on) is taken as an indicator of the minimum number of individuals of the species present in a sample. This minimum number is then multiplied by the average weight of an adult of that species to obtain, it is hoped, figures that reflect the relative dependence of the community on each of the species (table 6.1) (White 1953; Chaplin 1971). However, this method too is based on debatable assumptions (e.g., Grayson 1979:203–224). The highest number of skeletal elements in a sample—right femurs, let us say—may not be a reliable indicator of the absolute importance of an animal in the diet of a prehistoric people because of the differential deterioration rates of various bones (e.g., Binford and Bertram 1977; Casteel 1971), butchering practices, intercommunity ex-

Table 6.1 Minimum Numbers of Individuals as an Abundance Measure

Species	Number of Bones	Percentage	Minimum Number of Individuals	Estimated Pounds of Meat	Percentage
Odocoileus virginianus (White-tailed deer)	299	49.9	9	765.0	34.3
Ursus americanus (Black bear)	4	0.7	1	210.0	9.4
Bison bison (Bison)	24	4.0	2	800.0	35.9
Castor canadensis (Beaver)	176	29.4	8	252.0	11.3
Taxidea taxus (Badger)	2	0.3	1	13.0	0.6
Procyon lotor (Raccoon)	24	4.0	7	122.0	5.5
Lutra canadensis (River otter)	4	0.7	1	13.0	0.6
Ondatra zibethica (Muskrat)	12	2.0	3	6.0	0.3
Geomys bursarius * (Pocket gopher)	10	1.7	2	—	—
Tamias striatus * (Eastern chipmunk)	5	0.8	2	—	—
Martes or *Mustela* sp. (Fisher or weasel)	1	0.2	1	3.5	0.1
Carnivore (Probably domestic dog)	36	6.0	3	45.0	2.0
Mouse *	2	0.3	1	—	—
Total	599	100	41	2,229.5	100

NOTE: Only mammals are listed in the table.
* Species not considered a food item.

change, unrepresentative samples, garbage disposal practices, and the failure to attempt to match left and right elements. A minimum number of individuals is, after all, only a minimum number. Further difficulties arise when a faunal sample is not treated as a homogeneous analytic unit but is subdivided among strata and features. Differences in the number and extent of analytic units in a site—the aggregation problem—will obviously have an important effect on the minimum numbers of individuals counted (Grayson 1973, 1979:203–224; Casteel 1977). For instance, if a small faunal collection is aggregated by natural stratum, the minimum number of individuals could vary widely if five rather than three strata were defined. As a result, minimum numbers provide only nominal measures of taxonomic abundance in some instances.

Amount of Meat per Taxon as an Abundance Measure. Since a cow and a pig produce different amounts of usable meat, the abundance of taxon alone is not a valid measure of the dietary importance of an animal species to a community. In the MNI measure, this problem is solved by multiplying the minimum number by the average weight of usable meat per adult animal. An underlying assumption of the measure is that all of the usable meat of an average adult animal was eaten. The weight-of-bone approach to measuring the amount of meat per taxon is based on the assumption that (minimally) only the usable meat associated with bone found in the sample was eaten (Grayson 1979:224–227; Uerpmann 1973). Here the amount of meat actually represented in the sample is estimated by comparing the actual weight of bone for each taxon with prepared tables that list the weight of bone ratio to the weight of usable meat per species. Additional inferences can then be made from this minimal figure by examining the potential effects on the total of butchering practices, differential preservation, chances of recovery, the differentiation of "natural" from "cultural" bone (Thomas 1971), and other intervening variables. Still, the simple linear relationship between bone weight and meat weight assumed in this measure is inadequate, for experiments have shown that meat weight is related curvilinearly rather than linearly to bone weight (Casteel 1978). For example, bone weight can vary from 82 percent to 2 percent of meat weight, as the weight of bone varies from 100 to a million grams. As a result, the measure is invalid. For these reasons, Grayson (1979:227) has concluded that "an appropriate way of measuring relative taxonomic abundance in terms of meat weight does not seem to be available."

The examples in this section raise interesting measurement problems in archaeology: mainly, what is the nature of the variable that archaeologists are trying to measure (Grayson 1979:227–229)? For instance, if we are trying to measure the abundance of different taxa in the environment at some point in the past in order to reconstruct a paleoenvironment, the taxa in the environment must be inferred from the bones in archaeological sites. At best these counts provide ordinal-level information. However, if we are trying to measure the abundance of taxa used or the amount of meat consumed by a community, as we are here, the variable of interest is the abundance of vertebrate taxa within a site. In this case a ratio scale measure of taxonomic abundance may be required, and ratio scale measures must be sought to accomplish this goal. As we have seen, present approaches to measuring the abundance of vertebrate archaeofauna only provide nominal or ordinal measures at best.

An Ordinal Measure of Degree of Reliance on Cultigens

Several measures have been proposed for assessing the degree of reliance of past human populations on plant foods. One of the simplest involves counting the numbers of plant fragments recovered during excavation. However, an accurate assessment of the relative importance of plant species in a diet is hampered by differential deterioration rates, inadequate recovery techniques, and other intervening variables. This unwelcome outcome of floral analysis in archaeology has left many critical problems unresolved. For example, the spectacular Hopewell culture complex in the Eastern Woodlands of North America is associated with immense burial mounds containing lavish grave goods. Can hunting-gathering societies build remains like these? Most archaeologists have argued that they cannot, at least in an Eastern Woodlands environment: Hopewell populations must have had an agricultural base. Bender, Baerreis, and Steventon (1981) tested this hypothesis by measuring the relative dependence of Hopewell and non-Hopewell peoples on maize.

Plant groups follow a number of photosynthetic pathways (e.g., Bender 1971; Smith and Epstein 1971). C_4 plants such as maize, sorghum, millet, and some canes show less discrimination against ^{13}C and a higher (less negative) $^{13}C/^{12}C$ ratio than plants in the C_3 photosynthetic pathway. To simplify a complex set of symbols, terrestrial C_4 plants have a range of values for the isotope ^{13}C between -8 and -14, while the range for terrestrial C_3 plants is -23 to -30. Since organic carbon is preserved without deterioration in the collagen of fossil bone, measurements of the isotope values of collagen in human skeletons should reflect the degree of reliance of human populations on C_4 or C_3 plants. Since maize was one of the few C_4 plants in the Eastern Woodlands in the prehistoric period, these values should also serve as measures of the degree of reliance of prehistoric populations on domesticated plants.

Bender, Baerreis, and Steventon (1981) determined the ^{13}C-^{12}C ratios of skeletal samples from three separate time periods: early Archaic hunter-gatherers, the Hopewell, and later Mississippian and Woodland agriculturalists. Table 6.2 lists the values for the ^{13}C isotope in the three samples. Archaic populations (6000–1000 B.C.) are generally regarded as hunter-gatherers; the values in table 6.2 confirm their status as nonmaize consumers. The recorded values are also compatible with values attained for other Archaic populations in New York and Illinois (Vogel and van der Merwe 1977; van der Merwe and Vogel 1978). Mississippian and Late Woodland populations (A.D. 800 to the historic period) are generally regarded as agriculturalists, for hoes and carbonized grains are found in their sites. The values in table 6.2 confirm their status as maize consumers, although an extremely wide range in maize consumption is apparent. Still, there is no overlap with Archaic values. Given these two base lines, one early and the other late, were the Hopewell maize consumers or not? The values for Hopewell skeletal samples from Wisconsin, Illinois, and Ohio clearly show that maize was not an important item in the Hopewell diet. The highest values that occur in the most southern of the sites (Gibson) may indicate some maize consumption, but the statistical error involved makes even this conclusion uncertain. The hypothesis is rejected: the Hopewell did not have an agricultural base.

Table 6.2 raises other interesting questions. The distribution of values seems to be associated with status or sex at several Mississippian and Late Woodland sites. For example, low status individuals at Aztalan (numbers 29–32 in table 6.2) apparently consumed more maize as a group than did high status individuals (numbers 25–27). At Cahokia this association is reversed: higher status individuals (number 33) ate more maize than people with a lower status (numbers 34–36). At Ledders, a terminal Late Woodland burial mound in Illinois, males (numbers 42–44) consumed slightly more maize than females (numbers 39–41). And at Rock Island in Wisconsin, maize consumption seems to have been minimal for this late time horizon. Al-

Table 6.2 Isotope Values of ^{13}C from Burials in the Eastern Woodlands

Site	Sex Archaic	^{13}C o/oo	Site	Sex Mississippian	^{13}C o/oo
1. Reigh (W)	F?	−21.4			
2. "	−	−21.7	25. Aztalan (W)	−	−17.0
3. "	M	−22.1	26. "	−	−19.2
4. "	−	−23.1	27. "	−	−17.1
5. "	−	−21.8	28. "	F	−12.0
	Hopewell		29. "	−	−18.5
			30. "	−	−16.4
6. Millville (W)	F	−22.6	31. "	−	−14.5
7. "	F	−22.5	32. "	−	−14.4
8. "	F	−22.7	33. Cahokia (I)	M	−16.5
9. Trempealeau (W)	−	−21.5	34. "	−	−18.7
10. "	−	−22.7	35. "	F	−20.0
11. Gibson (I)	M	−20.6	36. "	F	−15.0
12. "	M	−21.0	37. "	−	−15.9
13. "	M	−21.3	38. "	−	−15.2
14. "	M	−21.6		*Late*	
15. "	M	−20.7		*Woodland*	
16. "	M	−20.7			
17. Edwin Harness (O)	F	−24.1	39. Ledders (I)	F	−19.8
18. "	F	−22.7	40. "	F	−17.5
19. "	F	−21.2	41. "	F	−17.0
20. Seip (O)	M	−21.1	42. "	M	−16.5
21. "	F	−21.0	43. "	M	−15.0
22. "	M	−23.4	44. "	M	−14.7
23. "	M	−22.7	45. Rock Island (W)	−	−19.4
24. "	M	−22.1	46. "	−	−19.9

SOURCE: Bender, Baerreis, and Steventon 1981. Reproduced by permission of the Society for American Archaeology from *American Antiquity* 46(2):346–353.
NOTE: W = Wisconsin, I = Illinois, O = Ohio.

though the values in each of these measures is along a ratio scale, intervening variables (such as the presence of other C_4 plants) effectively make these values only ordinal measures.

Identifying and Measuring System Strain

Archaeologists have usually assumed that environmental stress plays a prominent role in promoting variability in human behavior and cultures through time. Drought, shortened growing seasons, and other changes in the natural environment may sufficiently upset the steady-state equilibrium

conditions of sociocultural systems that some often drastic adaptive response is necessary to return the systems to a near steady state. It has also
been assumed that system strain can be identified by merely identifying the
appearance of stress-inducing factors in the natural environment. As a result, many archaeological field projects have concentrated time and effort on
the reconstruction of the natural environment and its change through time.
But our earlier distinction between objective and subjective environments
should cause us to pause and ask whether stress is system-specific. Does stress
always produce a strain? By definition, stress is a constraining force or influence. We should not expect stress to exist independent of a specific sociocultural system and its threshold for coping with environmental change: the
same environmental changes that disrupt the stability of one system may have
little or no effect on another. The appearance of stress-inducing factors in
the natural environment, then, are invalid indicators of sociocultural stress,
for environmental change must produce a strain on a system before stress is
present. This line of argument has led Reid to suggest that "any method of
identifying stress must first consider the identification of behavior indicating
strain" (1978:197).

How can strain in sociocultural systems be identified and measured? Reid
(1978) has approached this problem by adopting hypotheses presented by
Hill and Plog (1970) and Hanson (1975) that relate subsistence-lack stress
to experimentation and diversification in behavior. Diversity promotes stability by increasing the number of homeostatic feedback loops, thereby
spreading and cushioning the risk of system strain. Watt has couched this
(methodological) principle in terms of a lawlike statement that applies to
subsistence stability: "The greater the variety of foods the human population has available for harvesting, hunting, or fishing, the less the likelihood
of human catastrophe due to a disaster befalling a particular food species
(1972:75–76). More generally, Reid has assumed that "the greater the diversity, the greater will be the stability of a cultural-behavioral system and
thus its capacity to withstand stress" (1978:199).

An implication of these hypotheses, principles, and lawlike statements is
the notion that diversity is a measurable indicator of strain. Reid has proposed that system strain can be identified and measured by isolating behavioral diversity in the archaeological record. For example, if subsistence-lack
stress is creating strain on the subsistence system, it should be represented
in a relative increase in the diversity of subsistence-related tools, facilities,
and behavior. By isolating behaviors exhibiting diversity, one can identify

the system under strain as well as, by extension, the source of environmental stress. The rationale underlying this approach is summarized by Reid:

> By focusing on behavior under stress we are not only nearer that which we seek to explain, but we also allow for the possibility that all critical environmental factors cannot be examined. If strain can be isolated, then it may be possible to estimate the environmental factor responsible when that factor cannot be measured and examined directly. In many cases it may be sufficient to know only that strain was present regardless of the specific stress factor producing that strain. (1978:201)

Reid (1978:199–200) used the following measure of diversity (which was derived from information theory) to identify the locus of strain and to monitor stress: $DI = (N/N1! \ N2! \ . \ . \ . \ N_n!)1/N$, where DI represents the diversity index, N the sum of all units within the set (that are being used to indicate diversity), N1, N2, . . . N_n represents the sum of all units within the subsets N1, N2, . . . N_n, so that $N = N1 + N2 + \ . \ . \ . \ N_n$, and N! (N factorial) equals $N \times (N-1) \times (N-2) \times \ . \ . \ . \ 3 \times 2 \times 1$. The following assumptions underlie the application of this index (p. 200):

1. Diversity is a manifestation of strain.
2. A relative measure of diversity provides a relative measure of strain.
3. The diversity index actually measures diversity in the archaeological record.
   a. The partial sets measured in the archaeological context actually represent the total sets in the systemic context.
   b. The partial sets measured actually reflect strain in the system.
4. Variations in diversity reflect variations in system strain. Only stress-induced strains cause an increase in diversity.

The diversity index has been used to test a hypothesis that had been proposed to account for the growth and abandonment of the Grasshopper ruin in east central Arizona (Reid 1978:201–211). Grasshopper is a large pueblo of about 500 rooms that was occupied between circa A.D. 1275 and 1400. The pueblo grew rapidly during this period and was then abandoned. Were the processes of population aggregation or abandonment responses to stress? If they were, stress should be represented in strain and diversity during the period of aggregation or abandonment. The hypothesis tested was: At Grasshopper, aggregation occurred in response to local conditions of environmental stress. Underlying the test was the basic assumption that "under conditions of subsistence stress, stability of a cultural-behavioral system is restored by an increase in diversity of subsistence related procurement and processing tools, and behavior" (p. 202). Reid systematically related the hypothesis, the basic assumption, acceptance-rejection criteria, definitions of terms, test implications, subsidiary assumptions, actual tests, and the evaluation of measures and assumptions within a formal research design. Space does not permit an extended discussion of the research design, but a listing of the test implications will illustrate at least the nature of the Ns used in the diversity index: during periods of subsistence strain "an increase is expected in (1) the diversity of animals procured for food, (2) the diversity of plants procured for food, (3) the use of normally unused domestic animals as food resources, (4) the use of food of 'scrubby' animals, those with a lower ratio of usable meat to total biomass, and (5) the diversity of implements and facilities used in food procurement and processing" (p. 203). Analytic units were operationalized, and the diversity index was used to measure the degree of strain in each category of the test implications. Reid concluded that the combined measures did not adequately support the hypothesis that aggregation occurred in response to local conditions of environmental stress. Therefore, the hypothesis was not retained.

What Does Pattern in the Archaeological Record Mean?

Both measures of stress and of the relative abundance of animal species in a past diet rely on numbers of items found in archaeological sites. But are the absolute or even relative numbers of items in a site representative of the numbers of items actually exploited or used by a past community? If they are not, the interpretation of archaeological data becomes still more difficult.

The most obvious approach to identifying structure and pattern in the activities of community life from the archaeological record is to search maps of artifact and facility distributions for some order or structure. As I mentioned in chapter 5, many mathematical techniques have been applied to distinguish nonrandom clusters of artifacts and facilities. Pattern, however, only implies some degree of regularity within a limited frame of reference— here, items within the excavated units of a site. Pattern in the spatial distribution and associations of one or more artifact types is a property of a site matrix. When archaeologists assign functional names such as flint-chipping area to localizations of artifact clusters, they are making a sociocultural interpretation, an identity, because activity areas, like tool-kits, are properties of sociocultural systems. Each interpretation is a hypothesis or construct that should be confronted by a series of tests.

A sensible question to raise here, is What processes produce nonrandom patterns in archaeological sites? As mentioned in chapter 3, archaeologists have assumed until recently that spatial patterns of archaeological remains "reflect the spatial patterning of past activities" (Schiffer 1972:156; also see Hodder 1978). Of course many material items that once existed are no longer available for study, for they have been destroyed by time and the elements. Enough material items usually survive, however, to enable archaeologists to search out patterns that can be instrumental in testing hypotheses or building models. In fact, the more subtle and difficult patterns are to detect, the more readily archaeologists believe that they are the instantiations of real behavioral patterns. But we must be aware of distortions of original patterns in the archaeological record caused by natural processes or even by human behavior. Before we can test hypotheses about past behavior, the possibility must be evaluated that pattern in the archaeological record does not reflect human behavioral patterns at all or that it does so only in very subtle ways.

This line of argument introduces a question that archaeologists cannot ignore: How does the archaeological record originate? A little thought will convince you that it is a very complicated process. For example, archaeologists must take into account the durability of tools, the number of times that they may have been used, the number of tools of one type that may have been used, and so on. Ammerman and Feldman (1974) have proposed that the number of times an activity is performed per year, the likelihood that a particular tool type will be used in an activity, and the "dropping rate" are all likely to influence deposition rates—and thus archaeological analyses. Schiffer (1976) has called these processes C transforms and has illustrated their depositional effects with flow diagrams (figure 6.1) (also see O'Shea 1978; Stier 1975; White and Modjeska 1978). In Schiffer's terminology, once items have been deposited in the archaeological record, they are likely to experience N-transforms, that is, disruption by natural processes such as rodent activity, oxidation, and earthworm movement (Wood and Johnson 1978). All of these processes are involved in the formation of the archaeological record as the archaeologist finds it.

Other distortions of systemic context pattern occur through the activities of the excavators themselves. For example, as soil is removed from a site it

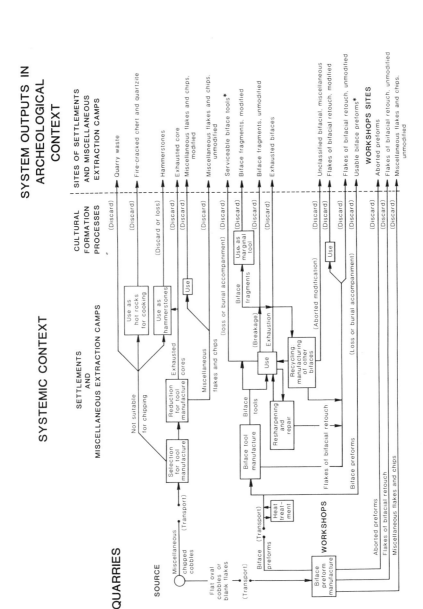

Figure 6.1 A flow model of systemic context outputs into the archaeological record. Source: House 1975 as reproduced in Schiffer 1976, figure 4.3.

is generally passed through screens that trap artifacts and ecofacts. Experiments have demonstrated that the larger the mesh size of the screen, the greater the loss of information. Seeds, grain fragments, fish-bone, and other small items easily slip through a quarter-inch mesh, for instance. The use of wet-sieving has revolutionized the recovery of many small items such as these. In fact, wet-sieving has created a new problem for the archaeologist—an overabundance of material to be analyzed. Still other improvements in the on-site conservation of fragile objects and the recognition of facilities have increased retrieval efficiency during site excavation.

Even if C-transforms and N-transforms were clearly understood and every item in excavated units recovered, the relative and absolute abundance of food species in a past diet may be distorted by sampling effects. Figure 6.2 dramatically illustrates the problem. Each stratum contains the same number of similar objects. However, sampling decisions—where and what one excavates—have produced erroneous trends. Open circles seem to increase through time, Xs appear more abundant in lower strata, and Hs peter out in the middle strata. Are there sampling strategies that avoid these distortions?

Short of total site excavation, no sampling strategy can guarantee a representative sample. But some strategies produce more representative samples than others. Several archaeologists have evaluated sampling strategies at the regional level (e.g., Redman 1974; Mueller 1975; Plog 1976a). A similar study was carried out by Ammerman and his colleagues at the community level (Ammerman, Gifford, and Voorips 1978). Since it is difficult to

Excavated Portion

H	X	H	O	O	O	X	H	X
X	H	H	O	O	X	O	X	H
X	H	X	X	O	H	O	H	O
X	O	H	X	X	H	H	O	O
O	O	H	X	X	H	H	X	H

Figure 6.2 Sampling distortions in excavation. Even though the frequency of artifact types is the same in each level, there appears to be a trend from Xs to Os in the excavated portion of the site. Hs, Xs, and Os are abstract symbols that represent any particular artifact type, such as different styles of projectile points.

evaluate the effectiveness of sampling strategies without knowing the composition of the sampling universe, they "excavated" a small historic Masai
pastoralist settlement in Kenya. The site enclosed an area about 80 by 60
meters (4,000 m²). The site was encircled by a post and thorn brush fence
and contained several small pens (figure 6.3); a few single-family dwellings
were located along the internal perimeter of the fence. Since the contents of
the site were known, the site could be repeatedly "sampled" with different
sampling strategies. The sampling strategies could then be evaluated by
comparing the inferred parameters of each sample to the parameters of the
known universe. To simplify the experiment, estimates of only four animal
taxa were compared: (1) *Bos taurus,* (2) bovid (a general category), (3) ca-
prini (sheep and goats), (4) mammal (fragments of mammal bone that could
not be assigned to one of the other categories). The sampling strategies that
were evaluated were random cluster sampling, central trenching, and prior
knowledge (usually based on the density of surface debris). Ten to twenty
different simulation runs were recorded for each strategy and for different
excavation unit sizes where appropriate. New units were added in each run
in a stepwise manner to assess the impact of sample size on the reliability of
parameter estimates. In this experiment the specific questions that were being
asked were, How much of a site has to be excavated to obtain reliable estimates? Does the size of the sampling unit have an appreciable effect on the
estimates? Does central trenching, a more traditional nonprobabilistic sampling strategy, produce a better or worse estimate? Does prior information—material concentrations on the site surface, for instance—produce better
or worse estimations? Clearly, questions such as these must be taken into
consideration when one is reconstructing community subsistence practices.

Although Ammerman and his colleagues (1978) are cautious in generalizing their findings to other kinds of sites, their simulation study suggests
that (1) reliable estimates of population parameters can begin to be made
with a 3 to 10 percent sample in all strategies; (2) smaller excavation units
produce more reliable estimates than larger units in random cluster sampling; (3) the gain in estimation is quite modest beyond about a 15 to 20
percent site sample; (4) central trenching does not seem to produce better
or worse estimates than random cluster sampling when 5-by-5-meter squares
are used in both strategies; (5) prior knowledge produces biased estimates
in the short run but reasonably accurate estimates in the long run. However, the lessons to be drawn from this experiment depend too on the goals
of an excavation. For instance, random cluster sampling techniques and most

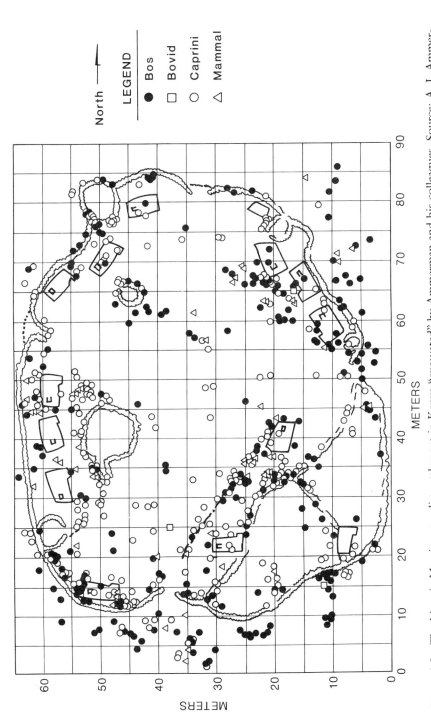

Figure 6.3 The historic Masai pastoralist settlement in Kenya "excavated" by Ammerman, D. P. Gifford, and A. Voorips, Towards an evaluation of sampling strategies: Simulated excavations of a Kenyan pastoralist site, in I. Hodder, ed., *Simulation Studies in Archaeology*, pp. 123–132 (N.Y.: Cambridge University Press, 1978), figure 1.

judgment sampling strategies do not produce especially reliable estimates of population parameters when there is a wide diversity in numbers of elements per group in sampling units or of estimates in units. This range of diversity is not a problem when the excavation goal is the recognition of spatial patterns and activity areas.

Estimating the abundance of food species exploited by a past community is not a simple, straightforward process. Transformation processes, techniques of retrieval, and sampling strategies are among the intervening variables that make the reconstruction of past economies a puzzling challenge for archaeologists. Among the common strategies adopted to cope with this situation is the building of simplified models that at least initially ignore many of these factors. Another strategy is the reconstruction of potential land use patterns before excavation.

Land Use Patterns: Modeling a Community's Catchment Area

Models of land use patterns can be built from a diverse source of information. We have already discussed how archaeologists use the contents of sites to reconstruct paleoenvironments. Another common approach is *site catchment analysis,* a method adapted to the problems of archaeological research by Vita-Finzi and Higgs (1970) from a model of agricultural activity originally proposed by von Thünen in 1876. A basic assumption of the method is that people's economic behavior is rational, and that, as a corollary, rational people would not normally be expected to pursue energy-expensive economic activities. Several conclusions follow from this assumption and corollary that have been influential in modeling land use patterns in archaeology. First, the distance an area is from a settlement should correlate with its intensity of exploitation: in general, the closer an area is to a settlement, the more intense will be its exploitation. Analytically, at least, it should be possible to define the optimum zone or catchment area around a settlement within which most resource exploitation activities occur. The most effective strategy for archaeologists is to concentrate on this optimum zone, for the frequency and extent of activities quickly attentuate beyond this zone. As a methodological rule, broad environmental zones are inappropriate units of analysis for constructing potential land use patterns: they are too broad to indicate which resources were most likely exploited; analyses of subsistence activities should concentrate on the localized optimum zone.

In the von Thünen model, places were circumscribed by concentric rings of land use, with the most intensely exploited and profitable land nearest the center. By assuming that the place was situated on a relatively flat plain, the catchment area could be circumscribed by a circle with a 5-kilometer radius. Case studies in the ethnographic and agricultural literature indicate that the radius should more appropriately be about 10 kilometers for hunter-gatherers and 1 kilometer for simple agriculturalists. Since few villages and towns occur in flat, featureless plains, the models have been made more realistic by having the boundaries of the catchment areas conform to the time-effort expenditure involved in moving outward in several directions from the edge of the settlement (figure 6.4). Studies of Kalahari Bushmen and European peasant agriculturalists indicate that a two-hour walk from the edge of a site is an appropriate distance for hunter-gatherers and a one-hour walk for agriculturalists. The size and shape of the catchment area will now depend on factors such as uneven topography, water barriers, and neighboring communities that impede straight-line movement. Once the boundaries of a catchment area have been established, the percentage of land useful for various economic activities can be calculated. The distribution of soil types is generally used for this purpose, with specific soils labeled "arable," "grazing," "marsh," and "dune," for example. These percentages serve as the basis for inferences to land use patterns. As an example, communities surrounded by high percentages of arable land are assumed to have been intensive producers of vegetable and grain products.

Site catchment analysis is a suggestive method. However, many intervening variables probably distort actual land use patterns. Level of sociocultural complexity is one such variable. In complex societies, villages and towns are often located in specific areas for reasons other than local resource exploitation: a settlement may be a node within a formal trade network, for example, or the settlement may be an administrative center that receives its food through import. In each of these cases the settlement cannot be treated as a closed system. The method works best for relatively self-sufficient communities of hunter-gatherers and simple agriculturalists. Even here the determination of the size of exploitation territories and potential land use practices depends on information that is generally difficult to obtain in archaeology. For example, the amount of arable land necessary to support a population of farmers depends on the size of the population, the productivity of the land, the crops actually planted, crop yield, and the degree of closure of the settlement system. All of these variables must be estimated and

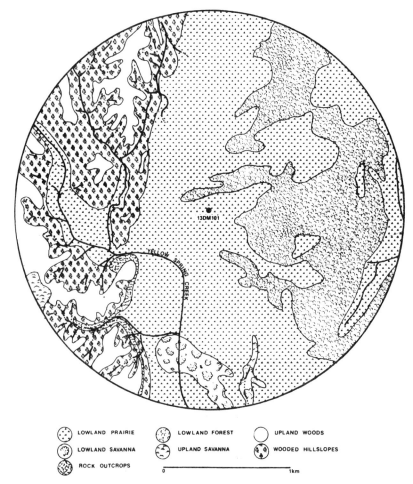

Figure 6.4 A site catchment. Shown is the Schmeiser site catchment in Iowa, showing vegetative, mineralogical, and hydrological resources. Source: Tiffany 1983, figure 2.

then tested with independent data. Field boundaries, plant remains, and tool-kits are sources of information, as is ethnographic analogy (e.g., Flannery 1976).

There are still other problems with site catchment analysis: (1) more study is needed to show that the one- and two-hour boundary limits are not ar-bitrary; (2) because of disease, conflict, level of technological complexity, or labor force size, a community may not have been able to rationally exploit a catchment area; (3) settlements are often occupied only seasonally by hunter-gatherers and some agriculturalists; (4) other locational factors, such as trade, defense, and solitude, are not taken into consideration; (5) even settled farmers will travel great distances due to laws of inheritance, kinship obligations, and so on; and (6) the vagaries of decision making are not taken into consideration—communities that collectively made poor decisions probably would not have survived (Roper 1979). For these reasons, other land use approaches have been suggested or seem more appropriate, such as the simulation of the movement of sites into an area to demonstrate particular economic preferences (Hodder 1978:25) or the simulation of the interaction between communities in different microenvironments and the effect of this interaction on site location. In spite of these problems, site catchment analysis has been a fruitful approach in archaeology, for it has focused research on the microenvironment rather than on the macroenvironment. Perhaps its greatest use is yet to come, for the method provides a unit of analysis within which the interrelationships between numerous variables can be simulated.

The Farmer's Dilemma: A Game Theoretical Model

Site catchment studies reconstruct optimal diets given a least-cost assumption and certain knowledge about transportation costs and crop yields. But all of us have read about farmers who have made wrong decisions in exploiting their resources. As a result, they have fallen heavily into debt or have had to sell their farm. Farmers are forced to make many decisions every year that affect their profit margin. One of the most important is whether to take a chance with high-yield, weather-sensitive crops or to play it safe by planting lower-yield, more weather-tolerant crops too. If they are too cautious, they will never make a substantial profit; if they take too many chances, they may lose their farm. This is the farmer's dilemma.

Game theory is a decision-making mechanism for dealing with situations such as the farmer's dilemma (Tidswell and Barker 1971:17). Unlike site catchment analysis, it does not assume complete rationality and perfect knowledge. However, it does require considerable knowledge about soil fertility, length of fallow periods, average crop yields per acre, and so forth. The basic principle of game theory can be illustrated with a simple example. Let us assume that we can plant three crops that have varying yields under different weather conditions. In any given year we can expect the following yields for equal units of land:

	very dry and hot	*moderate*	*very wet and cold*
Crop A	45	60	55
Crop B	0	200	0
Crop C	20	70	60

If we knew for sure that it was going to be a mild (moderate) summer, we would be foolish not to plant crop B in as many fields as possible. But we live in an area with unpredictable weather. We would be ruined if the summer weather was actually very dry and hot or very wet and cold. What combination of crops should we plant to maximize our profits and minimize our losses in this uncertain environment? Although there is a "mini-max" solution to this problem, many of us would be tempted to take an occasional risk to increase our profit margin. Let us find out how successful we would be.

Imagine that you have an opportunity to manage a farm for six years (someone overheard you talking about rationality, least-cost assumptions, and so on). By accumulating a larger profit margin than your neighbors, you will prove that you are a better farmer than they are. Your farming venture will be made simpler but no less instructive by assuming that (1) all "competing" farmers have the same number of equally fertile fields; (2) every farmer has fields of the same size as his or her neighbors; and (3) the only variable that affects crop yield is summer weather. Every farmer has eight crops, two of which (1 and 2 in table 6.3) must be planted every year to restore soil fertility. The other six crops can be grown in any field, although none of the eight crops can be grown in any one field for more than two years in a row. You must plant at least six of the crops (including the two constants) every year to maintain your own nutritional needs. And every crop must be planted at least once during the six years or the seed will rot. The productivity of each crop per acre is listed for six possible weather conditions in table 6.3. Table 6.4 lists the fields and their acreage. If you prefer, you can assign the crops appropriate names, such as wheat, beans, and alfalfa.

Although you can play the game by yourself, it is more instructive to compete against others and to observe the effects of different decision-making strategies. The game is started by distributing crops among the ten fields

Table 6.3 Crop Yields Per Acre Under Different Summer Weather Conditions

	1	2	3	4	5	6
					Dry-Cool with	Wet-Warm with a
Crop	Wet-Warm	Dry-Warm	Wet-Cool	Dry-Cool	Late May Frost	Very Dry Harvest
1	20	8	6	15	2	3
2	6	10	5	5	5	8
3	3	5	5	4	15	20
4	20	12	6	22	3	4
5	6	4	18	4	8	9
6	8	20	7	5	9	15
7	6	7	8	7	12	18
8	6	4	20	4	5	6
Total Yield	75	70	75	66	59	83

for the first year according to the rules stated above (as in the example for year one in table 6.4). Use a work-sheet like the one in table 6.4. Once the crops have been distributed for the first year, roll a single die to determine the weather conditions for that summer. Now calculate the income for each field and enter it below the crop number as in the example. For instance, if crop 6 is grown in field 5 and the weather is wet and cool (a 3 on the die), the yield for the year will be 7 (profit per acre) × 15 (the size of the field) = 105. Add the profits for each field together and enter the total at the bottom of the first-year column. Now repeat the procedure for the next five

Table 6.4 Work-Sheet for the Farmer's Dilemma

Field No.	Area in Acres	Yearly Yield (Crop/Income)						Total Profit
		1	2	3	4	5	6	
1	30	4/120	/	/	/	/	/	
2	8	8/48	/	/	/	/	/	
3	20	1/60	/	/	/	/	/	
4	25	6/375	/	/	/	/	/	
5	15	6/225	/	/	/	/	/	
6	25	4/100	/	/.	/	/	/	
7	35	2/280	/	/	/	/	/	
8	12	2/96	/	/	/	/	/	
9	10	5/90	/	/	/	/	/	
10	35	4/140	/	/	/	/	/	
	Totals	1,534						

NOTE: Income for the first year is calculated for wet-warm weather and a very dry harvest (conditon from table 6.3.)

years. If your profit for any one year falls below 1,300, remove yourself from the game: you do not have enough calories to continue. If your total profit for the six years falls below 11,500, you lose too: you are bankrupt. To determine how good a farmer you are, compare your total profit with that of other players. What strategy seemed most successful?

Even this simple game gives us important insights into the interplay between luck and planning in the technoeconomic subsystem. It also forcefully illustrates one of the limitations of site catchment analysis and demonstrates that site catchment analysis would be a more realistic approach if the indeterminancy that underlies game theoretic models were incorporated into the method.

The Biocultural Interface: The Human Population

Physical anthropologists are bioanthropologists who among other interests examine the skeletons found in archaeological sites for evidence of age at death, sex, disease, diet, and other physical characteristics. Information provided by these studies has been used to both enrich and test the models of community life proposed by archaeologists. It is probably fair to conclude that recent advances in the study of the skeletal populations of past communities are among the most interesting and potentially informative recent advances in anthropological archaeology (Hassan 1981:xi).

This section is a brief introduction to the study of the physical remains of past human populations from a biosocial perspective. It concentrates on health, nutrition, and population dynamics.

Reconstructing the Health of Earlier Populations

Bioanthropologists are now considering a wide range of questions about the health of people living in earlier communities. For instance, How long did they live? How many babies died and of what sex? How many adolescents died and of what sex? How resistant were they to diseases? Which diseases were they subject to? Why? Were specific endemic diseases such as measles or chickenpox present at a constant rate in the population? Were there epidemic diseases? What injuries occurred? What was the most common cause of death? Can the causes of death be broken down by age, sex, status, or some other category? Is there evidence of trauma and violent injury? Did social stress exist (that is, did every individual have equal access to proper foods and living conditions)? Were they experiencing environmental stress? What kind?

These questions can be answered through *epidemiological research* (the study of epidemics) and other specialities in bioanthropology. For instance, the study of ancient diseases is called *paleopathology*. Paleopathologists are able to study ancient bodily diseases because many diseases mark or distort human bone tissue in identifiable patterns. Among the diseases that leave characteristic signs on bones are arthritis, bone tumors, leprosy, osteomyelitis, syphilis, tooth abscesses, tuberculosis, and yaws. Caries, severe attrition of the teeth, and the effects of periodontal diseases are also conspicuous in human skeletal material. However, many other diseases do not affect bone at all and remain unrecognized among earlier populations. That they may have been present is suggested by the presence of lice and other pests on mummies. An example of one of the many approaches developed by paleopathologists will illustrate the potential value to archaeologists of the study of the health of earlier populations.

An interesting and relatively new approach to assigning work activities to one sex or the other through stress indicators and other biocultural instruments is *osteobiography,* the reconstruction of the life histories of individuals through the analysis of their skeletons (Saul 1972, 1976). The comparative frequencies of stress indicators provide archaeologists with stimulating and unexpected clues to the daily life of the inhabitants of past communities. Specific body movements and activity patterns result in particular patterns of stress on the knees, the arms, the back, and the head. The identification of these patterns in earlier populations provides archaeologists with plausible body movements and activity patterns that can be tested by moving through the cycle of science. Many varieties of cultural behavior are recorded in the human skeleton. For instance, there seems to be a correlation between age- and sex-specific role behavior and patterns of longevity, pathology, dental disease and attrition, population structure, and other biological variables. Changes in these patterns suggest shifts in age- and sex-specific role behavior (Angel 1947, 1972; Hoyme and Bass 1962).

Are there patterns of functionally produced biological traits that show what a body regularly did during its lifetime? How can age- and sex-specific role behavior be inferred from human skeletal remains? In one osteobiographic study, Edynak (1976) examined a series of skeletons from four small Yugoslavian burial mounds that dated from the Iron Age through the medieval period, a recent enough time to effectively use the direct historic approach to suggest common adult roles. Each of the skeletons was inspected for evidence of chronic stress. Physical stress on the skeleton is most directly reflected in degenerative arthritis of the joints. Specific patterns of degenerative arthritis are best understood in terms of functional anatomy and best interpreted by analogy with modern occupational behavior, such as bending and lifting heavy objects. Since these patterns only occur under physical stress induced by persistent patterned behavior, osteobiography is generally restricted to adult skeletons.

Edynak was able to functionally differentiate females from young and mature males, and young from middle-aged women. The lifestyle of women generally resulted in chronic back stress, stress in the shoulders, and severe dental attrition. Chronic back stress is evident in the compression of the joints of the spine, and degenerative arthritis occurs in the shoulder area. This pattern suggests the repeated bending and lifting of heavy objects and such activities as hoeing. Males exhibited a pattern of more direct stress on all joints, and pelvic-lumbar degenerative arthritis related to the absorption of shock from below. Frequent fractures apparently related to violent activities also occur in male skeletons. These functional patterns in both women and men correlate well with ethnohistoric inferences. Women hoed household garden plots and repaired stone fences. They also probably prepared hides by chewing them, and they may have chewed more grit by eating more vegetables prepared by stone grinding than men. The men were cattle-herders, horseback riders, and soldiers. All of these activities together reasonably explain the patterns of arthritis and fractures in male skeletons. However, ethnographic parallels do not always exist for patterns of degenerative arthritis. Recent studies of Neanderthal skeletons show massive skeletal stress in both males and females and even in adolescents; nonetheless, age- and sex-specific role behavior has remained difficult to reconstruct (Trinkaus 1978). Still, the patterns of degenerative arthritis are new data that suggest interesting model-building possibilities.

The Nutrition of Early Communities

Earlier sections in this chapter reviewed some of the many ways in which archaeologists reconstruct the subsistence strategies of early communities. Bioanthropologists are also able to provide additional nutritional information through skeletal analysis, for the diet of a community is mirrored in the general health of skeletal populations and in the mineral content of bone.

The nutritional health of earlier populations can generally be determined from the state of their skeletons. Skeletal pathologies, dental diseases, and changing average stature from one generation to another or from one area to another point to the presence of nutritional stress. Skeletal pathologies resulting from nutritional stress include malformations such as rickets, caused by vitamin deficiencies, and congenital developmental aberrations. Numbers of dental caries and degree of tooth attrition are direct measures of the dietary practices of earlier populations, as are the growth patterns of children and adolescents as recorded by their skeletal size.

One promising approach to studying the dietary practices of earlier populations is trace element analysis, a method for determining the level or amount of specific trace elements absorbed into the bony tissues. Trace elements are minerals that are present in less than 0.01 percent of the human body mass. Although these minerals by definition are present in the body in very small amounts, many are essential to the proper growth and health of the human body throughout the life cycle. Among the essential dietary elements, copper, iron, iodine, manganese, strontium, and zinc are trace elements. Once these elements have been ingested into the body as part of food and water, they must be absorbed into the skeletal system to be useful in trace element analysis. Among the techniques now being used to trace mineral levels throughout the skeletal structure are neutron activation, atomic absorption spectroscopy, emission spectroscopy, and electron microprobe. These techniques vary in their ease of application and the degree to which they destroy bone during analysis.

It has been claimed that trace element analysis potentially can contribute to studies of diet, dietary stress, the growth and development of individuals, sex and age statuses, and disease states (Wing and Brown 1979). In addition, the approach is suited to tracing the spread and adoption of various cultigens, especially when plant remains are absent or have not been retrieved during excavation. An interesting example of this particular approach is Gilbert's analysis (1975) of the zinc, copper, manganese, and strontium content of a prehistoric North American skeletal population. A probable dietary shift from hunting and gathering to maize (corn) cultivation was demonstrated in the study. The study of the long-term effects of all of these factors on cultural practices and human populations is uniquely suited to the diachronic perspective of anthropological archaeology.

Population Dynamics

In a sense human skeletons are artifacts, for they have been shaped in part by cultural practices. Determining the age at death, the sex, the stature, and the health and nutritional status of individuals from their skeletal remains provides anthropological archaeologists with important information about these practices. However, this information is only a base from which broader inferences about the structure of past populations and the processes that shaped them can be made. The study of the structure of a population and of the processes (the dynamics) that molded that structure is the study of population dynamics. In this section, two characteristics of human populations, biological distance and demography, are examined.

Estimating Biological Distance Between Populations. Biological distance is a measure of the morphological affinities between two or more individuals or populations. The method is based on the common sense assumption that individuals having many traits in common are more closely related than those with fewer shared traits. Although biological distance measures measure morphological traits, they are generally considered indirect measures of the degree of genetic relationship that exists or once existed between compared individuals or groups. Studies of biological distance have proliferated in the last two decades with the development of new statistical techniques of analysis and more efficient computers.

There are both metric and nonmetric techniques for measuring biological distance. The use of metric traits as indirect measures of the genetic variability between and within populations is often unreliable for a number of reasons. First, cranial measures are limited in value because of the intentional or unintentional deformation of the cranium that results from binding, confinement to a cradleboard, or even simple cultural differences in the length of time children are made to sleep on their back, side, or front. Second, environmental and nutritional factors severely affect the size and morphology of the postcranial skeleton. Third, the teeth can be severely altered by attrition, especially in prehistoric populations. The ideal traits for measuring biological distance are nonmetric traits that are not age- or sex-related and that can be recognized on a fragment of bone. These traits include multiple mental foramina, supraorbital foramina, and ossicles at lambda. Taken together, they produce mean measures of association between individuals or populations that permit inferences about their genetic relationships. As a general rule, however, when one is selecting either metric or nonmetric traits, one examines those variable traits that can be scored for the largest number of skeletons in all populations.

Biological distance measures are useful in generating and evaluating a wide range of questions. For instance, Was there biological continuity between one population and another? Was the spread of cultural complexes the product of migration or of the diffusion of ideas? Were populations genetically homogeneous or was there a constant influx of new individuals? Are there family resemblances among individuals in the same burial mound or with the same status items? Building models of biological variability, of the dynamics of human populations, helps suggest and test questions like these. A necessary key word in the analysis of biological distance, however, is caution, for the characteristics of the gene pools of small populations can change relatively rapidly.

Two examples will illustrate the contribution that measures of biological distance have made to studies of prehistoric sociocultural systems. Both of these examples demonstrates the test of a hypothesis derived from the study of archaeological materials.

Who Were the Prehistoric Redbird? The Redbird Focus is a late prehistoric archaeological culture located in the upper Plains area of the central United States. Archaeologists had demonstrated a close similarity in material culture between the Redbird Focus and another focus in this area, the Lower Loup Focus. Since the Pawnee were considered historic descendents of the Lower Loup Focus, the Redbird Focus was also considered to be prehistoric Pawnee. However, W. Raymond Wood (1965) suggested an alternative interpretation. Wood maintained that only a small number of pottery shards really linked the two foci: most of the other artifacts were not diagnostic. These shards may have been fragments of vessels that were imported or made by captured women. He concluded the Redbird Focus was prehistoric Ponca.

Jantz (1974) tested these conflicting identities by using multivariate statistical techniques to compare measurements taken on the skull of skeletal samples representing Arikara, Ponca, Pawnee, and Omaha populations. The statistical tests demonstrated the probable presence of several distinct patterns. First, males were clustered by language group (figure 6.5). The Dhegiha Siouan-speaking Omaha and Ponca were clearly separable from the Caddoan-speaking Pawnee and Arikara. Second, Arikara and Omaha fe-

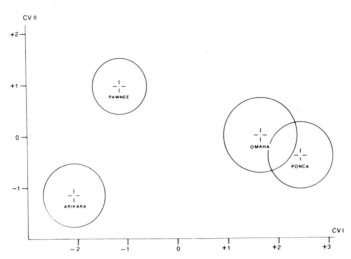

Figure 6.5 Biological distance between four groups of northern Plains Indian men. Source: Jantz 1974, figure 1. Published with the permission of the *Plains Anthropologist*.

males also were clustered according to language group. But the Ponca and Pawnee were not; they were in fact very similar to each other (Figure 6.6). Jantz then compared the crania associated with the Redbird Focus with samples of both Omaha (Siouan) and Arikara (Caddoan) skulls. The results of the test tended to support Wood's hypothesis, for the Redbird Focus skulls clearly fell within the Omaha range of variation. Besides critically testing alternative identities, Jantz's study also raised new research problems. For instance, Ponca and Pawnee women apparently moved more frequently than males and other females between tribal groups. What specific cultural practices would account for this pattern of movement? And so the cycle of science continues.

Hopewell Stability. Jane Buikstra (1976) recently tested a number of hypotheses suggested by archaeologists about the Hopewell people who inhabited the central Illinois River Valley between about 150 B.C. and A.D. 400. Two of these hypotheses will be examined here. First, archaeologists had suggested that the Hopewell occupation of the valley was both long-term and relatively sedentary. If this proposition is true, the inhabitants of the villages in the valley should have become genetically more distant from each other with the passage of time. If genetic traits are mirrored in mor-

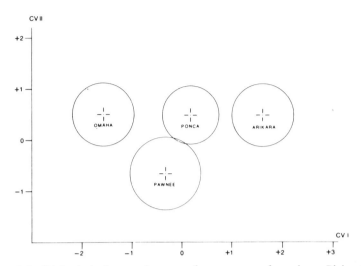

Figure 6.6 Biological distance between four groups of northern Plains Indian women. Source: Jantz 1974, figure 2. Published with the permission of the *Plains Anthropologist*.

phological (epigenetic) traits (a methodological assumption), increasing genetic isolation among contemporary communities should be observable in their diverging morphological characteristics. Since the communities would be breeding isolates, skeletons within contemporary mortuaries should be relatively homogeneous. These test implications can be corroborated or falsified by examining the range of morphological variability that is present in the mortuary populations in the study. Since each mortuary group was composed of burial mounds containing multiple individuals, if the variability between mounds was low, the hypothesis would have some support, it would be corroborated. On the other hand, if there was marked variability, the possibility of individual or group mobility would have to be considered. Buikstra's comparison of the skeletal characteristics of populations from the Gibson and Klunk mound groups tended to corroborate the proposition that the Hopewell occupation of the valley was both long term and relatively sedentary (figure 6.7).

Archaeologists had also suggested that a ruling class (perhaps an intrusive group) occupied high status positions in Hopewell villages. The morphological variability of individuals situated in high status positions in mound clusters was compared with that of individuals in low status positions. Were the individuals located in the high status positions part of an interbreeding

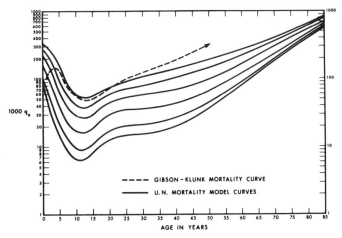

Figure 6.7 Mortality curves for Gibson-Klunk and a U.N. model. Source: Buikstra 1976, figure 8.

subgroup of privileged families who acquired their status through birthright? Or did all the individuals in the mound group come from the same breeding isolate? Buikstra's comparison of morphological traits supported the second alternative, which suggests that status was probably achieved by each individual on the basis of personal skills.

Demography. Demographic parameters are values of variables such as population size, age-sex profile, or population density, and vital statistics such as the probable death rate in a community, the length of time individuals of certain ages and sexes can expect to live, or the proportion of people in various age, sex, and social classes who die each year. The reconstruction of demographic parameters such as these provides a data base that may be useful in testing hypotheses or in interpreting the functions of past communities and their changing population composition. Since the number and size differences of communities within a region, their density and age-sex profile, and other demographic parameters are empirical instantiations of cultural systems, their study also provides clues to the structure of the social, technoeconomic, and ideological subsystems of these more elusive systems. The study of population parameters is called *demography*.

Estimating Prehistoric Population Sizes. The size of archaeological populations within communities can be estimated with a variety of techniques.

For example, Kidder (1958), Naroll (1962), and Leblanc (1971) have suggested methods of determining population size from the amount of living space or the number of houses in a community. Each of these techniques depends on the ability of archaeologists to accurately delimit contemporary living space or house boundaries. Ascher (1959) has suggested that the amount of midden debris can serve as an indicator of population size, while Wiessner (1974) has proposed a formula based on ethnographic data, and Renfrew (1974:77) has used the productivity of the total amount of arable land as an indirect measure of the variable. All of these measures are based upon archaeological materials.

Bioanthropologists also use mortuary site burial series to estimate population sizes. Every individual in a mortuary site series is placed in these approaches in a category according to age at death and to sex. These categories are usually arranged according to five-year periods (table 6.5), and the numbers and percentages in them serve as basic data for further calculations. Three demographic parameters that are often determined from these data and that are used in estimating population size are mortality curves, crude mortality rates, and survivorship curves. *Mortality curves* are simply plots of

Table 6.5 Life Table Reconstructed from Skeletons in a Maryland Ossuary

Age Interval (x)	No. of Deaths (Dx)	% of Deaths (dx)	Survivors Entering (lx)	Probability of Death (qx)	Total Years Lived Between X and X–5 (Lx)	Total Years Lived After Lifetime (Tx)	Life Expectancy (e°x)
0	56	29.79	100.00	.2979	425.525	2297.900	22.98
5	12	6.38	70.21	.0909	335.100	1872.375	26.67
10	7	3.72	63.83	.0583	309.850	1537.275	24.08
15	14	7.45	60.11	.1239	281.925	1227.425	20.42
20	9	4.79	52.66	.0910	251.325	945.500	17.95
25	12	6.38	47.87	.1333	223.400	694.400	14.50
30	21	11.17	41.49	.2692	179.525	470.775	11.35
35	20	10.64	30.32	.3509	125.000	291.250	9.61
40	13	6.91	19.68	.3511	81.125	166.250	8.45
45	11	5.85	12.77	.4581	49.225	85.125	6.67
50	8	4.26	6.92	.6156	23.950	35.900	5.19
55	4	2.13	2.66	.8008	7.975	11.950	4.49
60	0	0.00	0.53	.0000	2.650	3.975	7.50
65	1	0.53	0.53	1.0000	1.325	1.325	2.50
70	0	0.00	0.00	.0000	0.000	0.000	0.00

SOURCE: Ubelaker 1978, table 13.

the percentages of individuals in each age category: they provide a basic demographic profile of a population (figure 6.8). *Crude mortality rates* are estimates of the average number of people per thousand who die each year. The rates are determined by the formula $M = 1000/e^{o}x$, where M is the crude mortality rate and $e^{o}x$ is life expectancy at birth. Sharp differences in crude mortality rates point to disease, nutritional stress, and other cultural and environmental variables that merit investigation. *Survivorship curves* are estimates of the percentage of individuals in subgroups (usually age and sex categories) of a theoretical population of one hundred people that will still be alive at the end of a five-year period. Survivorship curves are especially suited for demonstrating differential mortality within subgroups of a population (McKinley 1971). Very young children, for example, may have less of a chance of survival than a person who has already managed to survive into adolescence. In addition, a temporal sequence of survivorship curves may vividly illustrate an acceleration of the mortality rate due to disease, an increase in conflict, and so on (figure 6.9). For instance, Robbins (1977:22) was able to report incidences of infanticide and intentional abortion among the Late Woodland peoples in Ohio at the Fort Ancient Incinerator site by compar-

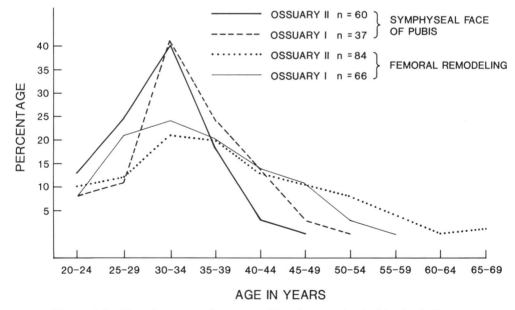

Figure 6.8 Mortality curves for two prehistoric ossuaries in Maryland. Source: Ubelaker 1978, figure 116.

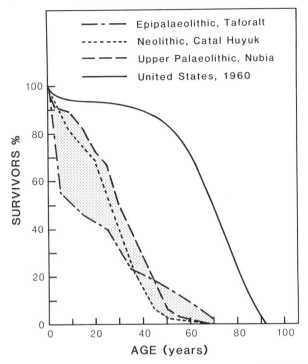

Figure 6.9 Survivorship curves of Upper Paleolithic, Epipaleolithic, Neolithic, and United States populations. Source: Hassan 1981, figure 7.8.

ing age and sex distributions. Problems during childbirth become apparent in age and sex profiles by higher than normal numbers of infant burials and burials of women in their early reproductive years.

By using information in mortality and survivorship curves and in crude mortality rates, bioanthropologists are able to estimate minimum sizes of populations. First, certain assumptions about the representativeness and stability of a mortuary series have to be satisfied. Then *life tables* based on contemporary United Nations model mortality rates can be used to estimate the size of an ancient population. Life tables provide typical profiles of the expected distribution of individuals in common types of cemeteries by age and sex (Acsadi et al. 1974; Weiss 1973; Hassan 1981:103–117). A typical cemetery profile generally is a variation on the theme of high infant mortality, lower mortality during childhood and middle age, and gradually increasing mortality in later adult life. In some cases it will become obvious from comparing percentages of individuals in age categories with life tables that a mortuary series does not contain a representative cross-section of a population. Perhaps the cemetery was only for individuals who had achieved status, in which case the very young would be excluded. If the mortuary series does contain a representative sample of the population, life tables can be used to estimate the probable size of the population at that time period by comparing the community with modern communities with similar profiles.

Cumulative mortality profiles also provide reasonable estimates of population size from skeletal material (Howells 1960). The profile is calculated by subtracting the number of people who died in a time period (expressed in percent) from the number of people alive at the beginning of the period (again expressed in percent). This of course is the population size by definition. Here, however, crude mortality rates and survivorship curves are being calculated to determine the percentages. If a stable population is assumed, an arbitrary birth-death rate may also be chosen from comparative data. For example, if there were ten births and ten deaths per year in the Middle Woodland Gibson community in Illinois, the death rate would be about 3.3 percent per year (Buikstra 1976:26). This seems a reasonable rate, since Clark Wissler (1936) once estimated the death rate per year for living American Indian groups from the Plains as ranging between 2.1 and 6.7 percent.

Buikstra (1976) used these figures to estimate the population size during the Hopewell period of the Kampsville Valley, in which these mounds were built. Her estimate of 50 to 100 people provides anthropological archaeologists with a working guide when modeling the Hopewell sociocultural system in this region. They might be interested, for instance, in how many people would constitute the work force (in the middle-to-young age range) in a typical Hopewell community in the valley. In this case a working figure of about 26 people or 65 percent of a typical Middle Woodland population of 40 people can be calculated from the mortality rate and other available measures.

By making a series of assumptions, one can make population estimates even for very large regions. It has to be assumed, for instance, that the geographic boundaries of a breeding population have been accurately established and that the number of burial mounds and the average number of individuals in a mound within a region are known. Buikstra (1976) has estimated the population density of the lower Illinois River Valley during the Middle Woodland period using the formula $P = S \times N \times A/m^2 \times t$, which is based on similar assumptions. In this formula P is population density per square mile, S is the minimum number of skeletons per totally excavated mortuary units, N is the estimated number of Middle Woodland mounds in the region, A is average age at death, m^2 is the number of square miles in the research universe, and t is the length of the temporal unit. For the lower Illinois River Valley, a density of 0.46 people per square mile was obtained with this formula: $0.46 = 30 \times 840 \times 28/2800 \times 550$. Although this is a very tentative estimate of a regional population, similar densities for historic Indian tribes were recorded in the United States by Alfred Kroeber in *Cultural and Natural Areas of Native North America* (1939).

Summary

Chapter 6 examines technoeconomic subsystems and biosocial elements of past human populations, which are the culture-bearers and important artifacts of their own cultures. Environmental reconstructions serve as a base for understanding why certain economic decisions were made, provided environment is defined broadly to include built as well as natural features. Further, subjective rather than objective definitions of environment lead to more realistic if less straightforward models. Anthropological archaeologists have used several methods to determine which resources were exploited. The counting of identified specimens, minimum numbers of individuals, and amount of meat per taxon provide only nominal or ordinal measures. Means of determining degree of reliance on plant foods include counting plant fragments and isotope values of collagen in human skeletons, which also provide only ordinal measures. A diversity index developed to measure system strain did not support the hypothesis that at Grasshopper aggregation occurred in response to local conditions of environmental stress.

Transformation processes, techniques of retrieval, and the vagaries of sampling strategies are among intervening variables that make the reconstruction of past economies a puzzling challenge. Strategies for coping with this situation include building models that initially ignore many factors and reconstructions of potential land use patterns using site catchment analysis, particularly for relatively self-sufficient communities. Other land use approaches include simulation of movement of sites into an area and of interaction between communities in different microenvironments and the effect of such interaction on site location. An example of game theory (the farmer's dilemma about what to plant in a given year) demonstrates variability of decision-making strategies and illustrates the limitations of site catchment analysis.

The study of diseases (epidemiological research or paleopathology), stress, osteobiography, and reconstruction of life histories of individuals through degenerative arthritis patterns provide interesting model-building possibilities for the health and habits of prehistoric groups. Skeletal analysis of trace elements and of the spread of various cultigens mirror dietary shifts and nutrition habits. Human skeletons also provide information about biological distance (between populations) through the study of genetic, preferably nonmetric traits such as multiple mental foramina, supraorbital foramina, and ossicles at lambda. Redbird Focus and Hopewell stability studies illustrate the contributions that measures of biological distance have made to studies of prehistoric sociocultural systems. Demographic parameter studies help interpret functions of past communities and their changing population compositions by estimating prehistoric populations from the amount of living space, the number of houses in a community, and mortuary site burial series (mortality curves, crude mortality rates, and survivorship curves). Life tables and cumulative mortality profiles also help in estimating population size. Such methods have been used to estimate the population density of the lower Illinois River Valley during the Middle Woodland period with the formula $P = S \times N \times A/m^2 \times t$.

Suggested Readings

There are numerous studies in archaeology of the complex relationships between subsistence systems and the environment. A variety of approaches are presented in:

Begler, E. and R. Keatinge. 1979. Theoretical goals and methodological realities: Problems in the reconstruction of prehistoric subsistence economies. *World Archaeology* 11:208–226.

Butzer, K. 1971. *Environment and Archaeology: An Ecological Approach to Prehistory*, 2d ed. Chicago: Aldine-Atherton.

Earle, T. and A. Christenson, eds. 1980. *Modeling Change in Prehistoric Subsistence Economies*. New York: Academic Press.

Findlow, F. and J. Ericson, eds. 1980. *Catchment Analysis: Essays on Prehistoric Resource Space*. Anthropology UCLA, Vol. 10, Nos. 1–2. Los Angeles: Dept. of Anthropology, University of California.

Flannery, K. V., ed. 1976. *The Early Mesoamerican Village*. New York: Academic Press. (See especially pages 103–117.)

Higgs, E., ed. 1972. *Papers in Economic Prehistory*. Cambridge: Cambridge University Press.

——, ed. 1975. *Paleoeconomy*. Cambridge: Cambridge University Press.

Jarman, M., C. Vita-Finzi, and E. Higgs. 1972. Site catchment analysis in archaeology. In P. Ucko, R. Tringham, and G. Dimbleby, eds., *Man, Settlement, and Urbanism*, pp. 61–66. London: Duckworth.

Roe, D., ed. 1971. Subsistence. *World Archaeology* 2(3).

Roper, D. 1979. The method and theory of site catchment analysis: A review. In M. Schiffer, ed., *Advances in Archaeological Method and Theory*, Vol. 2, pp. 119–40. New York: Academic Press.

Zubrow, E. 1972. Environment, subsistence, and society: The changing archaeological perspective. In B. Siegel, ed., *Annual Review of Anthropology*, Vol. 1, pp. 179–206. Palo Alto, Calif.: Annual Reviews.

Two reviews of the concept of environment as perceived are:

Brookfield, H. 1969. On the environment as perceived. *Progress in Geography* 1:51–80.

Prince, H. 1971. Real, imagined and abstract worlds of the past. *Progress in Geography* 3:1–86.

CHAPTER SEVEN

Analysis and Interpretation at the Regional and Interregional Levels

Communities are usually components of larger economic, social, religious, and political systems. To use Arthur Koestler's concept (1967), they are *holons,* systems that are elements within ever more inclusive larger systems yet are themselves composed of tiers of systems of decreasing size. Facing outward, they are members of regional, hemispheric, and global systems; facing inward, they are tiers of neighborhoods, households, and other systems of decreasing size. Distorted interpretations of ancient communities may occur when they are studied as if they were hermetically sealed and no reference is made to extracommunity influences and relationships. Imagine trying to understand London or New York without taking into consideration their social, economic, and ideological ties with other areas of Europe or the United States and with the world at large. Communities are usually intricately and tightly interrelated with each other through regional and interregional institutions.

Since cultures contain unifying themes that thread their way throughout the fabric of entire societies, how should multicommunity societies be studied? Are communities always the most effective units of analysis? Experience has demonstrated that in large and complex societies, societywide institutions, such as pansociety art, literature, and ideology, and mechanisms of societal communication and exchange are generally more effective units of analysis than single communities. Even in smaller and less complex societies, communities move through regions following traditional seasonal schedules and interact with each other for mutual defense or the exchange of goods and ideas. Looking at broader areas makes apparent patterns that would be missed if one focused only on isolated communities and makes the characteristics of communities more meaningful within the context of regional and interregional patterns.

Chapter 7 focuses on archaeological attempts to understand human interaction within regional and interregional space. Some models for generating settlement patterns are developed in the first section; the second section examines models of the rate of interaction between communities; and the third section reviews problems of reconstructing technoeconomic systems at the regional and interregional levels.

Some Models for Settlement Patterns

At the regional level of analysis, settlement interrelationships can be examined either synchronically or diachronically. In a synchronic study, interrelationships between settlements are reconstructed and analyzed at a moment in time. This is the approach taken in this chapter. Diachronic studies examine the development of intercommunity relationships through time. Diachronic approaches to regional studies in anthropological archaeology are discussed in chapter 8.

Problems in Identifying Settlement Patterns

Anthropological archaeologists generally assume the methodological principle that the adaptive strategy developed or adopted by a people creates a complex web of interaction and interdependency which binds communities together into a functioning, systemic whole. A people's *settlement system* is defined by the functional role and pattern of integration of each of their communities within this overall adaptive strategy (Flannery 1976:162). To reconstruct a settlement system, the amount and rate of flow of energy, information, and people between communities during an annual cycle must be measured and the seasonality of occupation of each community and its functional role within the complex adaptive system established. Reconstructing a people's *settlement pattern* involves the much less difficult task of establishing the number, size, and spatial distribution of the entire range of sites that they occupied. But even reconstructing the settlement pattern of a prehistoric group of people presents archaeologists with problems. Several of these sources of error are mentioned here, for the reliability of regional settlement pattern studies depends in part on the quality of data on which they are based.

Establishing Contemporaneity. Settlement system studies assume that there is a relationship between the way in which spatial behavior is organized, the size, number, composition, and location of settlements, and the cultural and environmental constraints that are at work. To analyze the past settlement system in structural terms, the formative processes that constrain the use of space must be identified and the contemporaneity of the components of the dynamic system firmly established.

The basic data of regional settlement pattern studies in archaeology are maps showing the distribution of sites or artifacts (figure 7.1). But it is usually problematic whether sites mapped together actually represent contemporaneous communities. Even though the building of regional chronologies has been a long-term traditional endeavor of archaeology, radiocarbon determinations are still not precise enough to establish the contemporaneity of components separated by less than several hundred years. Still, it is obviously essential to know whether small compact hamlets were the outlying

Figure 7.1   The distribution of the Fox Lake archaeological culture in Minnesota. Source: Anfinson 1979, figure 36.

wards of a nearby town or its temporal precursors. Since fine-scale dating remains impossible for the great majority of sites, the plausibility of site contemporaneity must be demonstrated through stratigraphic analysis and through the comparison of the formal and stylistic content of their components (Marquardt 1978). These methods leave considerable room for error.

Although missing information cannot be supplied by speculation alone, systematic procedures can be adopted that mitigate the effects of its absence. For instance, the intensity of survey in an area and the corresponding number of sites located can be weighed and the likelihood of sites occurring in unsurveyed or now destroyed localities assessed (Hodder and Orton 1976:19). Another interesting approach is the use of Monte Carlo models, which simulate the effects on settlement patterns of site losses of particular magnitudes (Clarke 1972a:24–26).

Establishing Meaningful Regional Boundaries. Although it may not seem problematic, the procedure of establishing the boundaries of regions by plotting on maps the distributions of formal and stylistic attributes of artifacts is a particularly troublesome source of error for archaeologists in settlement pattern studies (Hodder 1978). A sociocultural system is an instantiation of a cultural system. But the sociocultural expressions of cultural systems may vary widely from one community to another in their degree of shared, observable traits. For example, in highly complex societies the material and stylistic differences between farming hamlets and administrative centers may be very pronounced. In fact, it may be impossible to demonstrate that they are units of the same sociocultural system even when they share common ceramic styles, for culturally distinct communities may "buy" ceramics from the same professional potters. In less complex societies, subsistence tasks are generally allocated by season in different locations. Since the core tasks are different, the tool assemblages may be so different that it is difficult to demonstrate whether components of sites express functional, temporal, or cultural variation. In more inclusive sociocultural systems, such as regional exchange systems, political systems, or religious networks, the archaeological delineation of sociocultural boundaries may be even more difficult to establish, for membership in these systems is not always reflected in such familiar mediums as pottery or stone (Engelbrecht 1974). A number of different strategies have been adopted to deal with this problem. Some archaeologists have simply side-stepped the issue and demarcated the boundaries of regions on the basis of convenient geographic units such as valleys (Flannery 1976). Others have used sophisticated simulation studies for the same purpose (Wobst 1974).

The problem of establishing meaningful regional boundaries is compounded by the practical difficulty of defining such units as tribe or society even historically or ethnographically (Naroll 1964). Bishop and Smith (1975), for example, point out that ethnic groups like the Cree and Ojibwa in early historic northwestern Ontario merged into one another. Their names are useful abstractions rather than designators of clear-cut and readily definable ethnic units. This situation arises most frequently among band-level and simple horticultural groups where membership is fluid and variable; the nucleation of families in these groups often results from political pressure or environmental opportunism and not because of intimate economic or social interaction within a defined territory. For instance, in band-level societies food was generally collected noncooperatively by individuals or families for their own household, and any surplus was distributed through giftgiving to neighbors and members of other communities (Sahlins 1972). This practice was an efficient mechanism for adjusting to food shortages, internal conflicts, or demographic shifts, for individuals and families could move during periods of hardship to other communities in which they had established giftgiving relationships. For all of these reasons, archaeologists cannot assume that straightforward correlations between the material culture of two or more communities necessarily means a commonality of language or similar ethnic or tribal affiliations (Hodder 1978:3–24). By so doing they may be committing the fallacy of misplaced concreteness and positing the existence of cultures or other ethnic units that do not exist.

In spite of recent advances in theory and technique, the establishment of meaningful regional boundaries in archaeology remains a difficult and uncertain enterprise that is encumbered still further with major conceptual problems with the regional approach itself. For instance, we cannot always assume, as mentioned in chapter 1, that the system and its environment of parameters can be closed within the same spatial boundary, that the degree of interaction is related to spatial proximity, or even that the interactions that are relevant to any given problem are spatially discrete.

The success of settlement studies in anthropological archaeology depends from the very start on the satisfaction of the assumptions of the regional approach and on the resolution of the problems of site contemporaneity, incomplete information, and the establishment of meaningful boundaries. Assuming for the moment that these problems have been adequately controlled, how are settlement distribution patterns recognized and how can these patterns be accounted for?

Settlement Distribution Patterns

As mentioned in chapter 5, the study of the location and spatial arrangements of artifacts, facilities, and sites is called settlement pattern analysis (or, from geography, *locational analysis*). Since artifacts, facilities, and sites must be located somewhere, settlement pattern or locational analysis has become the keystone of entire research efforts (Gumerman 1971). Locational studies of settlement patterning focus on many different levels of analysis. Three of these levels have been considered basic in archaeology: the shape of individual dwellings or structures, the plan of communities, and the spatial relationship of communities to one another. On the regional level of analysis, the complex interplay between social distance, subsistence needs and the geometry of location has made locational studies one of the most challenging and interesting research frontiers in archaeology today.

Identifying Distributional Patterns. A fundamental quest in the search for rational pattern in the landscape is precise, objective, and accurate data. Locational studies of settlement distributions begin by measuring or determining the relationship of sites to each other, to features of the natural environment, or to both. These measurements are often compared with ideal random, regular, or clustered distributions for further insights into the nature of a regional pattern. A random distribution is one in which there is no structured patterning between contemporaneous communities. In other words, the settlement pattern has no discernible order (figure 7.2B). In regular patterns, settlements are uniformly spaced throughout a region; ideally each settlement should be equidistant from its nearest neighbors (figure 7.2C). In clustered patterns, settlements are grouped around a valuable natural or social resource (figure 7.2A). These terms are generally given more precise connotations to facilitate regional and comparative analyses.

A quantitative and systematic expression of the pattern of settlement distribution can be obtained by several methods. In archaeology a popular method is the descriptive statistic *nearest neighbor analysis* (Clark and Evans 1954). In nearest neighbor analysis, the distance to the nearest neighboring community is measured for each settlement, and a coefficient or index of

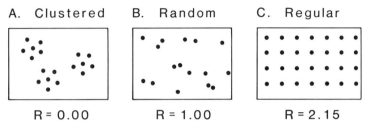

Figure 7.2 Hypothetical settlement patterns.

clustering (R) is calculated. If settlements are absolutely clustered the value of the coefficient is 0.0 (figure 7.2A). If they are completely randomly distributed the value is 1.00. If they are entirely dispersed the value is 2.15. Nearest neighbor analysis provides a measure of the agglomerative tendencies of settlements in a region by determining the extent of deviation from randomness of the settlement pattern. Table 7.1 and figure 7.3 provide an example and the procedure for this statistical approach.

Establishing a measure of settlement pattern dispersion is only a basic step in settlement pattern studies. The more important question in anthropological archaeology is, What processes generated the pattern?

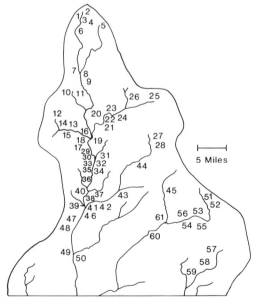

Figure 7.3 Distribution of archaeological sites in the upper Rock River drainage, Minnesota.

Table 7.1 A Procedure for Nearest Neighbor Analysis

The following procedures are to be used with the map in figure 7.3.

(1) Number the sites as shown in figure 7.3. Now choose which sites are to be compared. A minimum of 30 sites are necessary if the results of the analysis are to have any real validity. There are 60 sites in figure 7.3; 59 of these sites are compared in the test.

(2) Sites on the boundaries of a region cannot be used as bases of measurement if their nearest neighbor could lie outside the region. However, distances to them can be measured. A useful procedure is to join these peripheral sites to form a buffer zone. In figure 7.3 the edges of the drainage system form an effective boundary; only the bottom right site may have a nearest neighbor lying outside the region (distances to this site can be measured, but it cannot be used for comparison).

(3) Number the sites on the map and from each in turn measure and record the distance to its nearest neighbor. Record all of the measurements in a table that has the following format: Point 1—distance to nearest neighbor in the unit of measurement (in this case miles); Point 2—distance to nearest neighbor; and so on.

(4) Add all of the distances and divide by the number of measurements taken to obtain the mean. This is known as the *observed mean;* in the worked example it is $68.5/59 = 1.16$.

(5) Determine the density of points in the area by the formula

$$\text{Density} = \frac{\text{no. of points in study area}}{\text{area in study area}}; \text{ for the worked example the}$$

$$\text{density is } \frac{60 \text{ (total no. of points)}}{558 \text{ (area in sq. miles)}} = 0.11.$$

(6) Calculate the expected mean in a random distribution by the formula

$$\text{Expected mean} = \frac{1}{2\sqrt{\text{Density}}} = \frac{1}{2\sqrt{0.11}} = \frac{1}{0.66} = 1.5.$$

(7) Finally, determine the random scale value by the formula

$$\text{Degree of randomness} = \frac{\text{observed mean}}{\text{expected mean in a}}, \text{ which in the}$$
$$\text{random distribution}$$

$$\text{example is } R_n = \frac{1.16}{1.50} = 0.77.$$

Subjectively one would judge the distribution of sites in the map to be clustered along the river. However, the R_n value of 0.77 approaches a random distribution. In this case the denticulate shape of the drainage might have produced a false random pattern.

Processes That Generate Random Distributions. A random distribution of settlements within a region may result from several processes. First, the aggregate pattern of site locations at any one time may truly be random: decisions about where to locate sites may have resulted in an aggregate random pattern. Here the number of independent influences operating in the pattern-generating process are many and small, so that in aggregate they emulate the effect normally obtained from a random process, in which elements of chance play a large role. Second, a random pattern may be the misleading result of site destruction and uneven survey. Third, the plotting together of functionally different sites, such as burial mounds and hunting camps, and the accidental inclusion of sites from different time periods may also produce by chance a random pattern.

Random distributions of sites are rare in settlement pattern analyses. One approach to checking the plausibility of an apparently random settlement pattern is a simulation of the effects of various sources of error.

Processes That Generate Uniform Distributions. The presence of uniform patterning in settlement distributions is often an indicator of competition between communities. The nature and extent of this competition is something to be examined and explained. A basic rationale in locational studies of settlement distributions is the principle of least cost, the same principle underlying site catchment analysis. According to this principle, settlements are located to minimize the effort expended in dealing with the environment. For instance, hunter-gatherer settlements may be uniformly dispersed to minimize competition over homogeneously distributed food resources. In the majority of instances, however, the location of settlements is a compromise between the minimization of competition for natural resources and accessibility to centers of scarce natural and social resources. Even in less complex societies there is a demand for services and products such as obsidian or rare metals that cannot be easily supplied by individual communities within the society. In more complex societies, service and economic centers exist for the procurement and circulation of a wide variety of resources. These centers may be the focus of administrative, military, or religious services, or a central place such as a market from which food, craft items, and other specialized products are dispersed.

The Spatial Impact of Exchange. Pattern within uniform settlement distributions can be examined both horizontally and hierarchically. For these analyses, site size must be determined in addition to site location. The key question now becomes, Is there any order or pattern in site spacing *and* size? When one is building models of settlement systems, variation in both site spacing and size is important, for a number of hypotheses relate these two variables. For instance, "As settlements increase in size so they become fewer in number," and "As settlements increase in size so the distance separating them also increases."

Although we are primarily interested in the processes that generate these relationships, let us pause to inquire into the processes that form the shape of a settlement area. Uniformity in horizontal relationships between settlements maximizes efficiency by minimizing the effort expended when traveling through a catchment area surrounding a community. Effort is also minimized by agglomerating scarcer products and services in centers, as mentioned earlier. The most efficient shape of the area surrounding a settlement would be a circle, for the average person living in the circle could reach the center with the least effort if the circle were a flat, featureless plain. However, when circles are packed together, they become compressed, and hexagonal areas now provide the minimal average effort necessary for moving from anywhere within the area to the center (figure 7.4). Chapter 10 provides a sketch of a theory that explains these shifting settlement configurations.

Hexagon size seems to depend on a settlement's relative importance and

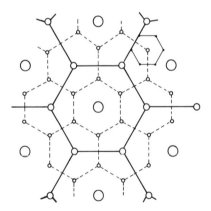

○ nth order center and trade area

○ ——— n-1 order center and trade area

∘ ------- n-k order center and trade area

· ——— smallest order center shown

Figure 7.4 Systems of hexagonal trade areas.

on its principal mode of transportation. For instance, comparative studies demonstrate interesting regularities in the size of hexagonal areas. These regularities are presumably a result of the principle of least cost in action. Since movement minimization is an important factor in traveling to a market center on foot or by cart, there is usually a maximum preferred distance that people are willing to travel. In these studies this distance is usually in the range of 3 to 7 kilometers. Above this distance, the effort expended in travel outweighs the advantages gained in actually going to market. Below this distance, markets tend to become too crowded to ensure the survival of each market. This distance range seems to be the most efficient for one mode of transport, for movement is minimized and simple market economics are observed. The result is a regularity in spacing between settlements and market centers. This simple spatial model provides a rationale and processes that account for the uniform distribution of settlements in "packed" regions.

In areas of uneven terrain the processes that produce uniformity in spacing across a flat, featureless terrain may be operating even though they seemingly do not produce uniform settlement distributions. This can be demonstrated by nearest neighbor analysis and other techniques based on the measurement of simple straight-line distances between settlements. In these cases, settlement areas may be delineated by a number of methods besides the drawing of hexagons. Constructing Thiessen polygons is one such method. A *Thiessen polygon* is drawn by connecting the midpoints between a site and its surrounding neighbors, and taking the smallest enclosed space (figure 7.5). The resulting polygon is considered to bound the areas that would have been most efficiently served by settlements, for every point within the polygon is closer to its central place than to any other. This method also takes into consideration the presence of rugged topography, rivers, lakes, and other disruptions of a natural flat plain. In addition, the procedure defines for every place the number and location of first-order neighbors, places with contiguous polygons. Some interesting tendencies have been discovered in the spatial relations of first-order neighbors. For example, simpler settlement patterns tend to have a smaller average number of contiguous polygons, and the mean distance between first-order neighbors tends to decrease with increasing societal complexity (Chadwick 1978:48–49).

Processes That Generate Hierarchical Relationships. Hierarchical relationships between contemporaneous settlements come into existence when activities or services are not in sufficient demand to support their presence

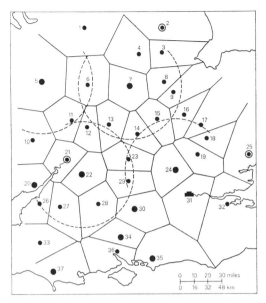

Figure 7.5 Thiessen polygons drawn around Romano-British walled towns. Source: I. Hodder and C. Orton, *Spatial Analysis in Archaeology* (N.Y.: Cambridge University Press, 1976), figure 4.4.

at lower levels. As a result, specialist centers tend to be spaced further apart than are villages and other small habitation settlements. Centers like these perform all of the functions of lower-order centers plus a group of central functions that differentiate them from lower-order settlements. These insights into the important influences that central functions have on settlement patterning in complex societies has led in geography to the development of *central place theory*, a theory that explains the size and spacing of settlements (central places) packed together in a region. This theory was originally formulated by Christaller and later refined by Lösch and more recent geographers (e.g., Haggett 1965; Berry 1967). Since the relationship between central places and their hinterlands is a worldwide phenomena, central place theory provides a framework within which settlement systems from any time and place that satisfy the initial conditions of the theory can be analyzed and interpreted. Central place theory is an example of a social science theory that has been borrowed by cultural historians to interpret specific regional settlement configurations.

Although central place theory is developed more thoroughly in chapter

10, its basic assumptions are briefly mentioned here to show how it approaches the explanation of uniform settlement distributions. Central place theory has three basic assumptions. The first is the principle of least cost. Since the inhabitants of a region attempt to maximize the efficiency of available resource exploitation, settlements in a packed homogeneous plain tend to be arranged in a hexagonal lattice distribution. The second is that larger settlements have larger hinterlands than smaller settlements because they provide a larger number of services. Each successively larger community serves an increasingly larger number of surrounding communities (figure 7.4). The most efficient location of communities from the smallest to the largest will be in the center of hexagons, following the principle of least cost. Successively higher communities will be in the center of increasingly larger hexagons, with settlements of increasing size at the six points of the hexagon. Whether a hierarchy in size distribution is present or not is calculated by measuring the modal size of communities and their spatial distributions. According to the theory, if a hierarchy in size distributions is present, it is accounted for by those settlement determinants that underlie the theory. Third, it is assumed that service hinterlands for settlements of equal size do not overlap. Subsidiary assumptions are that (1) the distribution of population and purchasing power should be uniform, (2) physical characteristics and resources should be uniform, and (3) transport facilities in all directions should be equal.

The spatial arrangements of settlements at different levels in a central place hierarchy can assume a number of forms, depending on whether the critical settlement system variables are transport, market, or administratively oriented (figure 7.6). Archaeologists have modeled the theoretical optimum

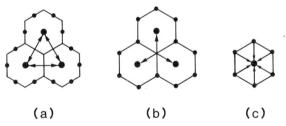

(a)   (b)   (c)

Figure 7.6   Idealized variants of central place settlement models. In each model every large center has direct access to six smaller settlements, but each smaller settlement relates to only three larger centers in (a) the marketing model, to two larger centers in (b) the transport model, and to one larger center in (c) the administrative model.

distribution of settlements within a region by reconstructing what these critical settlement variables may have been. Even deviations from the theoretically optimum distribution of villages and towns may provide valuable data, for they may indicate the possible influence of other variables, such as topography, limitations on transport, the presence of localized natural resources, external political or trade ties, and so forth. This modeling process has served too as a source of hypothesis in inferring the functions of prehistoric settlements (Hodder 1972). For instance, the role of presumed service centers has been established by examining the types of activities that occurred within the centers but not within smaller surrounding communities, and the roles of settlements within hexagons have frequently been inferred from regional plots of artifact types.

Other settlement models have been used in archaeology besides the classic central place model. Each of these alternative models is based on a different set of assumptions. For example, not all settlement models assume that a particular range of services is provided to tributary areas of constant size regardless of the hierarchical rank of a service center. Instead they assume that the size of the tributary area varies with the size of the service center (Clarke 1972a). As a result, these models imply different spatial constraints and different expectations in actual settlement distributions. For instance, smaller centers would not be expected to develop as close to large centers as they would to one another. Some of these models actually seem to correspond better to existing empirical evidence than does a central place model.

The Rank-Size Rule. Since variation in the size of settlements is assumed to be the result of economic, political, and other variables, anthropological archaeologists, like geographers, are interested in discovering what these differences might mean in their own regions of study. A simple hypothesis that can be applied in any region is the rank-size rule, which is based on the assumption that there is a relationship between the sizes of settlements and their importance in rank within a region (Zipf 1949). The rank-size rule states that for any given region there will be a largest settlement and all other settlement sizes will be predictably related to that of the largest settlement. This relationship is expressed by the formula $P_n = P_i(N)^{-1}$, where P_n is the population size of the nth ranked settlement and P_i is the population of the largest settlement. Simply stated, the formula means that the second largest settlement should be half the size of the first, the third one-third of its size, and so on. For example, if the largest settlement contains 100,000 people, the fourth-ranked settlement should contain $P_4 = 100,000 \times (\frac{1}{4}) = 25,000$ people. The rank-size hypothesis can be tested in any region by measuring the size of contemporaneous populations and by comparing the resulting rank-size distributions with those predicted by the formula. Substantiation of the rank-size rule in geography has lent some support to central place theory and has further emphasized the fundamental relationship between the size, number, and spacing of communities.

In the rank-size hypothesis the Ps represent population figures. However, measures of population figures still have low validity in archaeology. As a result, the spatial extent of settlements (S_n) has been employed as an indirect measure of population size, and $S_n = S_i(N)^{-1}$ has been substituted for $P_n = P_i(N)^{-1}$ (Hodder 1979:118). Here the underlying idea that the *n*th ranked settlement is some function of the $(N-1)$th settlement is retained, although S and P are not consistently equivalent in magnitude.

Brown, Bell, and Wyckoff (1978) applied the rank-size rule to a series of Caddoan sites in the Arkansas River drainage of eastern Oklahoma. In the study they categorized sites and mound group enclosures into a number of hierarchical levels and then rank-ordered selected sites and enclosures within one level according to size (figure 7.7). The lower plot in figure 7.7 illustrates the fit between ideal and actual rank-size ratios for mound group enclosures. Although the fit of the rank-order of the largest three enclosures is very close to the ideal, the actual rank-order distribution as a whole has a strongly concave slope. The nature of deviations from the ideal is, however, a source of hypothesis (Johnson 1977). In this case the concave slope may indicate the existence of missing enclosures that would conform to centers below the third ideal order or the operation of a single underlying factor, such as strongly centralized political control. The upper plot in figure 7.7 shows the relationship of ideal and actual rank-size ratios for total site size data. In this case the deviation from the ideal has formed a convex curve. Convex curves result from the operation of a heterogeneous set of factors or from the mixing of sites from different time periods or settlement systems. Despite these deviations, the Caddoan data support the rank-size hypothesis.

Central place theory has made archaeologists aware of a series of interesting questions. For instance, Is there a hierarchical or a network relationship between settlements within a region? Did larger settlements serve areas in proportion to their size in an interlocking spatial pattern or were tributary

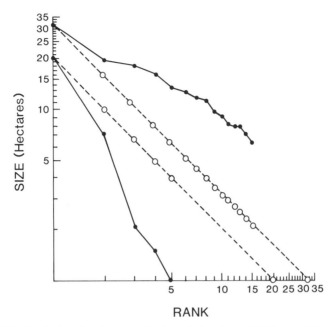

Figure 7.7 Rank-size distribution of selected sites from Oklahoma. Upper pair of curves represent orderings by total site size (actual order is a continuous line, ideal is a broken line). Lower pair of curves represent orderings by size of mound enclosures. Source: Brown, Bell, and Wyckoff 1978.

areas of constant size? Are size differences between settlements correlated with environmental variables rather than with a patterned distribution of neighboring settlements? Are size differences between settlements primarily the result of social, political, or economic factors? If the determining variables were economic, were they rooted in reciprocal or redistributive patterns of exchange?

Ethnographic comparisons indicate that the probable answers to questions like these will depend in part on the complexity of the societies being studied. In less complex societies relatively small numbers of goods and services are produced or acquired. As a result, economic relationships tend to be tied more closely to the local area, while political, religious, and kinship relationships are networked over larger areas. In more complex societies with developed economic systems and centralized political authorities, socioeconomic transactions tend to occur throughout larger networks as well as within and between local communities. Here new types of transactions, such as tribute for military protection, tightly network settlements within regions. Besides these lessons from ethnographic comparisons, prehistoric archaeologists in particular can never accept without question the conclusion that the processes that produced historic settlement distributions necessarily produced similar appearing patterns in the archaeological record. In the prehistoric period, population sizes of settlements were generally smaller than in the historic period, most prehistoric settlements were uninfluenced by state-level societies, and few regions were packed with large populations.

Processes That Generate Clustered Distributions. Clustered settlement distributions are the most frequently encountered settlement patterns in prehistoric archaeology. This should not be an unanticipated conclusion, for settlement patterns reflect the subsistence practices of a society. An intensive agricultural base permits greater concentrations of populations, the establishment of larger, more permanent settlements, and the founding of settlements in less favorable environmental areas. The hunter-gatherers and simple agriculturalists that prehistoric archaeologists usually study have settlement patterns geared to the seasonal availability of food resources within their regions. Thus settlement is less permanent as groups of people move back and forth from villages to hunting, fishing, and gathering camps during the seasonal cycle. As a result, processes such as site agglomeration around villages, the exploitation of localized rather than dispersed resources, and the gradual outward spread of villages from a parent settlement during population growth tend to produce clustered settlement patterns. Since multiple sites may be occupied throughout the year, a simple count of sites would be a misleading measure of population size or site interrelationships within a central place settlement lattice. Similar distortions would occur in regions where shifting cultivators moved their villages from one area to another every few years or among complex societies where farmers lived in agricultural villages for part of a year and in cities during the remaining months.

In less complex societies, then, settlements are more likely to aggregate around social and environmental variables, such as religious centers, soil or vegetation types, altitudinal zones, or distance from nearest water. A description of these associations and the identification of important variables for the modeling process can be obtained through simple tests of association. In these tests, distribution maps are made of soil type, water supply, vegetation cover, slope, and other environmental variables. Land types are then developed from the overlapping distribution of these variables. Finally, the number of contemporaneous settlements on each land type is calculated and measures of association are calculated to determine whether settlements are significantly associated with specific land types or not (Zarky 1976). Green's examination (1973) of the association of Mayan sites in northern Belize with the distribution of soils, vegetation cover, water supply, and other environmental variables is one example of this approach.

Simulation Models and the Location of Sites. Descriptive settlement patterns like these can be made systemic by employing game theory and other simulation procedures, procedures that model the decisions that were made in locating sites in specific areas. The rationale of these models is generally the least-cost assumption that the decisions that must be made throughout the seasonal cycle were made to optimize the exploitation of the resources in a region at the least possible cost. Large numbers of variables are often manipulated in these simulations. Among these are soil quality, wind direction, amount of sunshine in a particular season, rainfall patterns, vegetation cover, slope, grass competition, nutritional value of plant and animal resources, transportation costs, and severity of pests. Computer printout maps are then generated that indicate the most likely settlement distributions given criteria derived from the study of actual site locations in a study area. By continually comparing theoretically expected settlement distributions generated by the model with observed site distributions, a best-fit systemic model is gradually arrived at. A classic example of this approach is Thomas' model (1972) of Great Basin socioeconomic patterns for seasonal relationships between sites (figure 7.8).

An appreciation of some of the underlying determinants of site location and of the dynamics of simulation models can be provided by a simple example. Imagine that we have randomly sampled a small portion of a river drainage system. Imagine, further, that among the sites we found were the remains of horticulturalists who moved into the region during a 100-year period some time in the past. What data would we require to make a rational assessment of why the sites of the horticulturalists are located where they are? What determinants of settlement location must we (minimally at least) take into consideration? By attempting to work the simple simulation exercise that follows, the reader should begin to understand (1) how settlement patterns can be predicted by simulation, (2) the likelihood of these patterns being correct, (3) the effect of data limitations, (4) how people make decisions on the basis of imperfect knowledge, and (5) how chance elements may affect location decisions.

Among the factors that may have determined whether specific locations

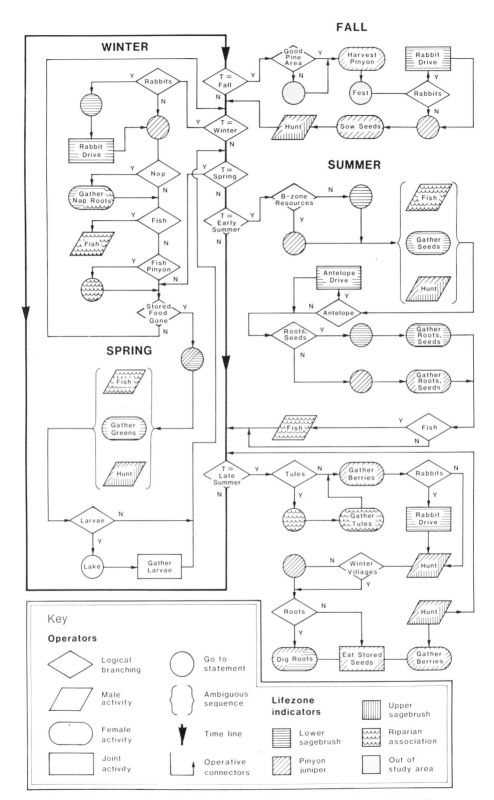

Figure 7.8 An outline of the Shoshonean subsistence system. Source: D. H. Thomas, A computer simulation model of Great Basin Shoshonean subsistence and settlement patterns, in D. Clarke, ed., *Models in Archaeology* (London: Methuen & Co., pp. 671–704).

were satisfactory or not were the availability of (1) water, (2) wild plant and animal food, (3) firewood, and (4) arable land. In this model the factors provide a structural framework within which settlement decisions must be made. The level of prosperity of the communities in the model depends on whether these decisions are disastrous, merely satisfactory, or cleverly opportune. As we can imagine, group decisions in these circumstances are compromises between strong cultural and personal preferences, the closeness of enemies, the personality traits of decision makers, the extent of knowledge of the new environment, and so forth. This cultural and personal element is taken into account in the simulation model by a strong chance factor (that is, by the toss of the die). As in Clarke's simulation mentioned in chapter 4, the nondeterministic nature and personal elements of human behavior are modeled by stochastic processes. Although individual and short-term behavior cannot be accurately reconstructed by this method, the stochastic rationale permits the prediction of group behavior in the long run.

The data provided in map form in figure 7.9 consist of a river drainage system and the distribution of some of its resources. The player of the simulation can allocate the following maximum number of points for each of

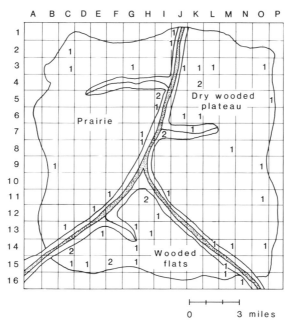

Figure 7.9 A simulation map for predicting site locations.

the four resources: water 10, arable land 8, firewood 5, wild animal and plant food 4. The total number of points possible for any grid is 27. If you are doing this exercise as a group project, discuss the weighing of these factors with other members of your group to see if you agree with these weighings or wish to change them. (The exercise is open-ended in that you are able to make major decisions like this. Nonetheless, you must always make it clear why you are altering a suggested parameter.) Now award points for each of the four sets of factors according to your judgment for each grid, placing the four subtotals in the corner of the grid squares as follows: water, top left-hand corner; firewood, top right-hand corner; wild animal and plant food, bottom left-hand corner; and arable land, bottom right-hand corner. The total number of points for the grid square should be placed in the center of the grid. For example, suppose a square is located in the river valley. Here the allocation may well be $^{10}_4$ 2 7 $^5_8$.

The next step is to translate the total allocated to each square into a running total by adding the points serially, beginning with the upper left-hand square and moving to the right. For instance, (add 1) 1, (add 1) 2, (add 1) 3, (add 1) 4, (add 26) 5–30, and so on in figure 7.10. Since the squares containing the greatest range in their running total have the greatest chance of being selected, the weighing allocated to the various factors remains im-

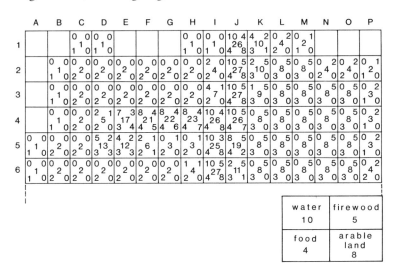

Figure 7.10 An example of allocation of points in the simulation exercise. (Only the upper portion of the grid is shown.)

portant in deciding the location of future sites, despite the chance element in the selection process. The higher the total number of points in a square, the greater its chance of being selected. (Strictly speaking, the numbers should be modified to add up to one, since probabilities must always sum to one.)

Now, using a random numbers table, pull numbers until fifty sites have been selected. For example, if 0080 is pulled, the square containing 80 within its range is awarded a site (in this case J2 in figure 7.10). A settlement pattern generated by this procedure is shown in figure 7.9.

Compare your results with others if possible. If there is a marked zoning within a particular area, it may be caused by similar interpretations of the broader processes at work. These processes create unequally attractive resource zones. Nevertheless, specific site locations within these zones depend on chance, just as they depended in the past on opportunities often presented by chance to migrating horticulturalists.

The crude data and simple methods employed in this exercise only illustrate the idea of a simulation. Still, the reader should have gained some appreciation of the role that simulation models can play in the cycle of science. Similar simulation exercises can be made more realistic by superimposing a grid of hexagons over original land-surveyor maps or other maps of reconstructed environments for areas and time periods that interest you. The use of the hexagon allows the addition of two more settlement variables, like ease of transportation and access to raw materials. The reader can also vary the variables that he or she thinks are important in determining settlement locations. For example, *access to fish* may be more important than the more general *access to wild animal and plant food* and *access to water transport* more important than *access to chert sources*. Finally, the type of incoming population can be altered. For instance, the incoming populations may be hunter-gatherers. In this simulation the availability of arable land would diminish in importance as a determining factor in the location of settlements. The hypothetical distributions obtained in either simulation can now be compared with actual site distributions for goodness of fit and the model corrected or elaborated.

Modeling the Rate of Interaction Between Communities

The distribution of archaeological materials is often a fertile source of ideas for modeling the relationships that may have existed between settlements within a region, the location of the boundaries of the region, the configuration of exchange systems, and other sociocultural parameters. Regional studies of the distributions of artifacts frequently begin with the search for trends in the distribution of percentages of artifacts or amounts of raw materials in total assemblages. In these searches either the percentages of a single artifact or raw material may be compared assemblage by asemblage, or the relationship between two or more variables, such as amounts of obsidian and a pottery type, can be examined as they vary throughout a region. Models are then built to interpret and reproduce the empirically produced spatial trends in the data. In the evaluation of the models, spatial processes are compared to determine the probability that different processes could have produced similar appearing spatial trends or that the same processes could have generated trends that appear dissimilar.

The Gravity Model

As we have seen, archaeologists have borrowed a variety of models from geography to interpret and model spatial trends. The borrowed models have been used to analyze trade and exchange patterns, to establish the contemporaneity of sites, to verify catchment areas, and for many other purposes. The gravity model is one of these borrowed models. The gravity model is based on the rationale that larger centers tend to attract interaction from larger areas than smaller centers. The source of the model is obviously Newtonian physics of matter. This is a very useful yet simple model that seeks to predict the amount of human interaction of one kind or another that will occur or has occurred between two places. The gravity model of interaction is based on two common-sense assumptions. First, people are more likely to journey to a distant settlement in direct relation to the amount of activity occurring at that place. Second, people are more likely to travel to the nearer of two equally attractive places when they are at unequal distances.

In the social sciences, the gravity concept of interaction generally states that an attracting force of interaction between two places of human activity is created by the population masses of the two places, and that a friction against interaction is created by the intervening space over which the interaction must take place. In other words, the amount of interaction between two centers of population concentration varies directly with some function of the distance between them. This relationship can be expressed mathematically by $I_{ij} = f(P_i P_j)/f(D_{ij})$, where I_{ij} is the amount of interaction between center i and center j, P_i and P_j are the populations of areas i and j, and D_{ij} equals the distance between centers i and j. Among the simplifying assumptions of the model are (1) all individuals generate the same degree of interaction; (2) all individuals are capable of interacting either directly or indirectly with one another; (3) the amount of interaction a person has at a given location is inversely proportional to the difficulty of communicating with or traveling to that location; and (4) the friction against interaction is directly proportional to the intervening physical distance between two centers.

Archaeologists have measured population size in the gravity formula by determining the density of sites within the boundaries of a cluster of settlements or by measuring the area components cover (Hodder and Orton 1976). Probable patterns of contact between settlements can then be predicted and the empirical implications of the predictions tested like any hypothesis against the frequencies or percentages of raw materials, artifacts, or shared stylistic designs in site assemblages (figure 7.11).

Like all simple models, the gravity model is not without its weaknesses,

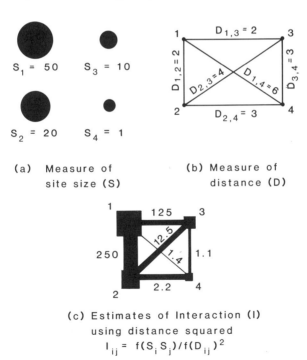

Figure 7.11   A simple example of the Gravity model.

especially when applied in archaeology. For instance, the effectiveness of the model is weakened in archaeology by the crudity (low level of validity) of the operational definitions generally employed. Site size is an unreliable measure of population size. Compare the size and population densities of New York City and Oklahoma City, for example. Furthermore, an index of economic activity is a better measure of attractiveness than either population size or site size, and travel effort is a better measure of distance than the linear distance between two sites. Finally, regardless of the goodness of fit of a model, archaeologists still face the problem of equifinality, for different spatial processes may produce the same pattern of artifact and trait distribution.

The Distance-Decay Model

The amount of interaction between communities can also be modeled by measuring the "decay" of artifact or style frequencies or percentages over space (figure 7.12). Distance-decay models deal with the decreasing occurrence of objects and events with increasing distance from their source. Among the typical objects and events whose decay has been traced are raw materials, innovations, and neighborhood effects. The rationale of this class of models—the gravity depletion effect—also underlies contagious disease models, models of declining degrees of optimality, and many spatial diffusion models.

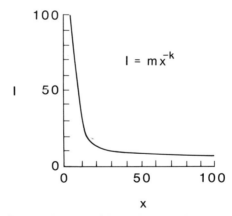

Figure 7.12   The distance-decay model. Both interaction (I) and distance (x) are on a linear scale in this model.

In distance-decay studies the statistical technique commonly applied is regression analysis, where $Y = a - bX + e$. Here X is the distance between two objects, Y is a measure of their similarity, and a, b, and e are constants. Besides plotting the decay of single artifact types over space, regression analysis has been used to measure the decay in the similarity between artifact types over space, as the interpretation of the symbols in the last sentence indicates. Hodder and Orton (1976) have investigated the likelihood that different forms of falloff curves will be produced by specific spatial processes. If one form of regression relationship is produced by a single spatial process, archaeologists will be able to determine the spatial processes at work by identifying the falloff curve. However, if a variety of different spatial processes produce similar regression relationships, the interpretation of spatial pattern in archaeology will obviously be less straightforward. Several applications of the distance-decay model are examined in the last section in this chapter.

The outcome of these and other interaction studies depends of course on the quality of available data and on the minimization of error in research designs. Archaeologists must be alert to factors that make the seemingly simple task of interpreting the distribution of artifacts complex and difficult. These include inadequate sampling procedures, inconsistent typologies, the inappropriate grouping together of different depositional units, postdepositional artifact movements, and other factors that influence the numbers of artifacts that are categorized as similar for one reason or another. The identification of pattern in the distribution of artifacts and the eventual construction of models may also be affected by the scale of analysis of a research project. For instance, the inconsistent association of an artifact type with a specific burial type may be masked if the region studied is so small that it contains only one cemetery.

Reconstructing Technoeconomic Systems

Both ideas and material items flow through community, regional, and interregional exchange systems. The form that these systems take depends on many factors, including scale (local, long-distant, or both), items exchanged (finished products, nonperishable raw materials, perishable foods, or personal services), sociopolitical complexity (band, tribe, chiefdom, or state), mode of transportation (foot, horseback, boat, or truck), and population density. Exchange occurs because resources are rarely distributed evenly throughout geographic spaces: most are made, grown, or naturally present as raw materials in local concentrations. Since people desire or need these resources, trade and exchange systems gradually form. Archaeologically, it is easier to document the exchange of nonperishable remains such as pottery, obsidian, or copper. But ethnographically recorded socioeconomic systems demonstrate that food, wood, wine, salt, and other perishable materials were major items of exchange in many systems as well. Once reconstructed, the form of exchange systems often serves as a valid indicator of the nature of societal complexity, status differences, group relationships, patterns of information dissemination, and many other sociocultural variables.

In complex societies, exchange occurs in formal market centers, money is the medium of exchange, and the professional roles of buyer, processor, and seller are recognized. Models of exchange for these societies are usually built around different types of marketing mechanisms. The distributions of artifacts, style elements, and raw materials then provide a test of the presence of one or another marketing mechanism. For instance, if the main marketing of products was concentrated within a market town, the distribution of the manufactured products should show a concentration within the town locale and along the main roads radiating out from it. As mentioned earlier in this chapter, central place theory is a fertile source of interpretive explanations for spatial distributions and interrelationships like these.

In less complex societies, reciprocity and nonmarket redistribution mechanisms are more common forms of exchange. Hodder and Orton (1976:146), Winter and Pires-Ferreira (1976), and Pires-Ferreira (1976) provide archaeological examples of redistributive exchange in which material items were brought into a central place and then redistributed by nonmarket mechanisms. Struever and Houart (1972) have reconstructed a similar system among a hierarchy of Middle Woodland Hopewell sites in Illinois. In their study the distribution of material items showed that status objects flowed through the regional exchange system while utilitarian items were confined to local areas. Since high-status objects were concentrated in the bigger and more complex mound groups, the authors suggested that these particular archaeological sites may once have functioned as regional transaction centers (figure 7.13).

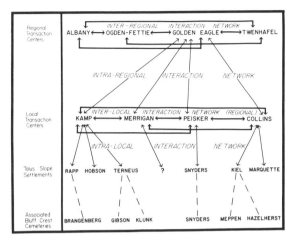

Figure 7.13   A hierarchy of interaction networks among Illinois Middle Woodland sites. Source: Struever and Houart 1972.

Testing Models of Regional Exchange

A Test of a Model of Exchange Among the Maya. Like all models, models of regional exchange must be evaluated against independent data. Tortellot and Sabloff (1972), for example, tested a model of exchange among the Maya by subjecting one of its principal hypotheses to a test. The hypothesis tested was that items involved in local trade would be primarily utilitarian, while the items more likely traded long distances would probably be nonutilitarian prestige items. Two questions were raised: Were the distributions of utilitarian and luxury goods similar throughout the exchange system? If they were not, what was the sociopolitical significance of these distributions for intracommunity and intercommunity contact and exchange? A three-level model of Maya exchange was developed and the spatial distribution of items exchanged at each level was mapped (figure 7.14). The three levels were (1) local exchange of utilitarian goods (particularly foodstuffs), (2) regional exchange of raw materials needed to make utilitarian articles, and (3) highland-lowland exchange of exotic materials destined for prestige contexts. The distribution of items supported the hypothesis. Tortellot and Sabloff concluded that ancient Maya communities were connected only at the elite level and were never linked by any kind of trade-induced mutual symbiosis.

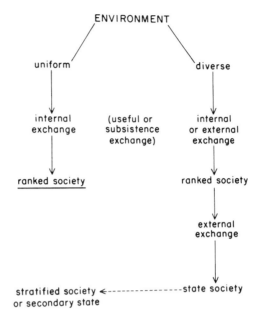

Figure 7.14   A model for the relationship between environment, exchange, and sociopolitical organization. Source: Tortellot and Sabloff 1972, figure 2. Reproduced by permission of the Society for American Archaeology from *American Antiquity* 37(1):126–134.

A Test of a Basic Assumption. In another study, Stephen Plog (1976b) tested a basic assumption on which many models of community exchange are based. This assumption is that the degree to which designs are shared by social segments or communities is directly proportional to the amount of interaction between units. In the previous section the gravity model was used to measure the intensity of interaction between contemporaneous communities in the past. Interaction is a broader, more abstract concept than exchange, but measures of interaction may be rough, indirect measures of intensity of exchange. The basic assumptions underlying methods of measuring the relationships between past communities from the archaeological record have rarely been tested, and many basic questions about this approach in archaeology have been left unanswered. For instance, Is it always the case that two settlements that share many design styles or other items are more closely related (that is, interact more) than either is with a third settlement with fewer shared similarities? Does the nature of the contact between communities influence the degree to which they share design styles or other attributes? Would as many traits be shared if communities were engaged in intense conflict rather than peaceful but sluggish trade? Does the gravity model or similar models accurately predict the amount of interaction that took place between communities within a region? Arguing from shared traits to interaction to shared traits is circular.

Plog tested this basic assumption with data from a series of sites in the American Southwest and Mesoamerica. As a first step, it was given the following empirical interpretation: If design similarities do measure community interaction, the similarity coefficients (in tests) should vary directly with the population of the communities and inversely with the distance between them. At least 75 to 100 stylistic elements were chosen for study on artifacts to which every individual in a society would most likely have had equal access. Tests of the assumption failed to show a consistent statistically significant positive correlation between population or community size and the degree of similarity of stylistic attributes (table 7.2). Plog's study is particularly interesting, for it points out the difficulties involved in controlling the initial conditions of tests of assumptions like this.

Table 7.2 Predicted Interaction Intensity Compared with Similarity Coefficients on Design Elements for Five Oaxacan Villages

Site Pair	Rank by Distance	Predicted Interaction Intensity	Brainerd–Robinson	Pearson's *r*
Fábrica San José–San José Mogote	10	1	1	2
San José Mogote–Tierras Largas	9	2	2	4
Fábrica San José–Tierras Largas	8	5	4	6
San José Mogote–Huitzo	7	3	7	8
Fábrica San José–Huitzo	6	6	3	7
Tierras Largas–Abasolo	5	7	8	5
Huitzo–Tierras Largas	4	8	9	10
Fábrica San José–Abasolo	3	9	6	3
San José Mogote–Abasolo	2	4	5	1
Huitzo–Abasolo	1	10	10	9

SOURCE: Plog 1976, table 9.3.
NOTE: Column one ranks the site pairs by distance in miles; column two ranks them by intensity of interaction predicted by the gravity model. Columns three and four rank the site pairs in terms of shared designs on Atoyac yellow-white pottery as measured by Brainerd–Robinson and Pearson's *r* coefficients.

Transport Networks and Graph Theory

In analyzing spatial distributions and spatial relationships, an obviously fundamental variable that must be taken into consideration is distance. Among other things, the success of an activity is conditioned by its relative location and ease of access to information and desired items. If spatial distributions and spatial relationships do become more efficient in stable settlement systems as they develop (as we would anticipate if the principle of least effort is valid), transportation networks should become more connected and less dispersed through time. This anticipation raises several interesting questions. For example, What is the influence of a transportation network on activities? How can important characteristics of transportation networks be measured? Here we are interested in the second of these questions.

Among the independent variables contributing to the pattern of a transportation network are relief, shape, size, population density, and degree of economic development. Each of these factors is a variable because its value may vary with available technology and time. Each of these five variables can also be measured. For instance, relief can be measured by running a number of transects across a region to obtain verticle cross-sections. An index can then be constructed by comparing straight-line distances with these convoluted distances. In this measure the effects on transportation of water barriers, forests, lack of water, and other factors can also be added. The lower the index, the easier transportation across a region should become. The shape of a region can be measured with the simple formula Index of Shape = L/l, where L is the length of the longest axis and l the length of the perpendicular to the boundaries midway along the long axis. This measure indicates the degree of compactness of a region, that is, whether it is elongated or round. Measures of the other variables are relatively straightforward, involving square kilometers, the average number of people or sites per square kilometer, or the speed of transport. Other measures of the network as a whole include degree of connectivity (the proportion of transportation routes to settlements or places), the degree of dispersion (the average distance between places), and diameter. Measures relating to individual places within a network include degree of accessibility and distance to furthest place in the region. Together these measures provide a more objective overview of the character of a transportation network and of the fundamental distance relationships among the places within it.

Many of these measures have been made precise by borrowing notions

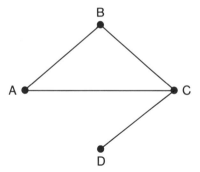

Figure 7.15 A simple graph with four points (A, B, C, D) and four lines (AB, AC, BC, CD).

from graph theory (figure 7.15). For example, the water system in figure 7.16 can be treated as if it is an ordinary graph with X edges terminating in Y vertices. The graph is called a network, the edges routes, and the vertices places. In the network in figure 7.16, places are marked P_1, P_2, . . ., P_n, and routes L(12), L(23), and so on, with the parenthetical numbers representing the linear distance of routes. Among the properties that define ordinary graphs and, thus, networks treated as ordinary graphs are (1) graphs have a finite number of places, (2) every route is a set consisting of two places and the shortest path between them, (3) every route joins two different places, (4) at most, only one route may join a pair of places, and (5) routes are two-way (no distinction is made between initial and terminal places on routes). On planar graphs such as figure 7.16, places are defined as a settlement, the juncture of two or more routes (whether the juncture is occupied or not), or the end of a route. As a region develops and the network fills in, more junctures are created. This has the effect of introducing new places with strategic locations in the exchange network and of shifting the relative location of already existing locations.

Various measures of the relative cohesiveness of networks such as the water system in figure 7.16 can be made. For instance, (1) the *associated number* of a place is its longest distance to any other place (255 for P_1 and 240 for P_2 in the figure) and, therefore, an indication of how accessible it is within the network; (2) the *central place* of a network is that place whose associated number is a minimum; (3) the *diameter* is the maximum associated number; (4) the *dispersion* of a network X, D(X), is the sum of the distances between each place and each other place; and (5) the *accessibility* of a network to a place is the sum of the distances between that place and each other place.

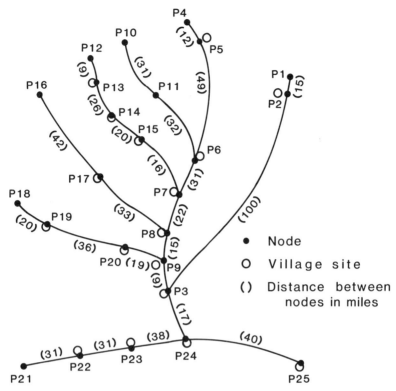

Figure 7.16 Examining settlement networks through graph theory.

Another measure, *degree of connectivity*, is L*/observed number of routes, where L*, the maximum possible number of routes in the network, is equal to m(m−1)/2 and m is the total number of places in the network.

These measures are useful in analyzing a region as a whole, the position of particular places within the region, details of the region, or in comparing regions. As a descriptive exercise of a network as a whole, the water system in figure 7.16 has 25 places and 24 routes, the maximum connectivity is L*=25(25−1)/2=300 and the degree of connectivity is L*/L=300/24=12.5, the diameter of the network is 257, and there is one central place (P_9) (the place with the lowest associated number).

Descriptive approaches to transportation networks via modern graph theory are attractive because of the relative simplicity of the theory and the opportunity it provides anthropological archaeologists for viewing places in terms of wholes and for viewing networks as wholes. However, these approaches have drawbacks, too. How, for instance, can archaeologists meaningfully identify the boundaries and relevant places of the settlement systems they are trying to describe? Which places and routes should be included? Are all places and routes known? Can subjective distances be ignored? Although these decisions are usually made by definition and by arguments of relevance, their degree of accuracy obviously affects the results of any analysis.

Indicators of Reciprocal and Redistributive Exchange

Karl Polanyi (1957, 1959) has argued that there are three major modes of exchange in human societies: reciprocity, redistribution, and market exchange. Market exchange is the system that we are familiar with in which goods and services are exchanged at prices set by supply and demand. In a system based on redistribution, goods are collected in an administrative center and then reallotted downward to consumers. Reciprocity is most simply defined as the system of exchange that involves neither markets nor administrative hierarchies. Since commodities that flow through reciprocal economies are not pooled for redistribution as in redistributive economies, several indicators exist for distinguishing these two modes of exchange in the archaeological record. Winter (1972) has proposed that in reciprocal economies, households should vary from one another in two key variables: proportions of obsidian (or other goods) from various sources and sources used. In a redistributive economy, less variation from one household to another would be expected in each of the variables than in a reciprocal economy. Because individual households negotiate for their own commodities in reciprocal exchange systems, the commodities associated with each household should be varied in terms of sources represented and proportions from each source within a village. Both the sources and the proportions of commodities from each source should be less varied in redistributive systems where the commodities are controlled and pooled by an elite for later redistribution (figure 7.17b).

Since the exchange of obsidian in the Early and Middle Formative in Mesoamerica was thought to have been by reciprocal exchange, these indicators of the presence of the two mechanisms of exchange permit a test of this interpretation. Winter and Pires-Ferreira (1976) tested the interpretation (an identity) with archaeological data from household clusters in two village sites

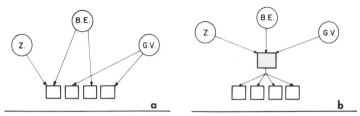

Figure 7.17 Models of exchange systems in Formative Oaxaca. a. Reciprocal. b. Redistributive. Z, B.E., and G.V. represent separate obsidian sources. Source: Flannery 1976, figure 10.9.

in Oaxaca. Three types of information were recorded for Early and Middle Formative household clusters in these sites. First, the percentage of obsidian compared to chert was calculated in each cluster. Second, the relative contribution of each obsidian source to a cluster was calculated for each time period. Finally, the variation between household clusters in source usage was calculated for villages at various time periods. The first calculation provided a measure of relative access to obsidian, the second a measure of source diversity, and the third a measure of change in source diversity through time.

The results of the analysis supported the proposition that obsidian was being obtained through negotiations by individual households in Early Formative components at Tierras Largas, a small village. No single family seems to have had privileged access to obsidian, for it is distributed more or less evenly between households. This is the distribution that one would also expect if obsidian was a utilitarian rather than a luxury item. A variety of sources were also being used differentially by various households. These data support the presence of a reciprocal exchange system at least in these households: it seems that each household cluster was negotiating separately with "trade partners" (figure 7.17a). However, evidence of pooling increases through later household clusters at Tierras Largas and is present in a sample of obsidian from eleven late Early Formative houses at San José Mogote, a large village. The proposition is false, then, and evidence for the unexpectedly early appearance of a redistributive economy has possibly been discovered.

Both of these indicators require further testing under controlled conditions. However, the study is an excellent example of a carefully thought out instrumental-nomological investigation.

Modeling Interregional Exchange

Modal interregional exchange networks have been reconstructed in archaeology by a variety of approaches. In general these approaches have concentrated on such items as obsidian, exotic ores, distinctive cherts, and sea shells which occur in abundance in archaeological sites, that do not easily deteriorate, and whose source can be confidently determined. Three of these studies are examined here.

Obsidian Flow in the Near East. One of the most frequently studied prehistoric exchange items is obsidian, for it occurred in abundance in exchange systems in a number of regions of the prehistoric world, it is practically indestructible, and its source can usually be determined through its trace elements. Obsidian exchange routes have been traced in the eastern Mediterranean, on the northwestern Great Plains in North America, in Mesoamerica, and in other areas. These studies have generally proceeded by incorporating the volume of obsidian and its pathways of movement into processual models of exchange that are designed to account for the raw data.

A classic example of this approach is Renfrew, Dixon, and Cann's (1966; also see Dixon, Cann, and Renfrew 1968) study of the distribution of obsidian in Neolithic villages in the Near East. Optical spectroscopic analysis identified obsidian from the Ciftlik flow in central Turkey with twelve sites. The linear distance of each of these sites to Ciftlik was recorded, and the percentages of imported obsidian versus local flints and cherts were calculated for each assemblage. A linear regression analysis of the relationship between these two variables produced the regression lines in figure 7.18. Except for a "supply zone" 100 to 300 kilometers around the obsidian source, the lines demonstrate an exponential decrease in percentages of obsidian from Ciftlik. The percentages of obsidian in assemblages in the supply zone were at least 80 percent. At Tabbat al-Hammam, 400 kilometers away in Syria, the percentage was 5 percent. And 900 kilometers away at Beidha in southern Jordan it had dipped to 0.1 percent. The authors suggested that the distribution of obsidian in their study area could be accounted for by a chainlike pattern of exchange in which half the obsidian flowing down from the north was kept by each village in the chain.

Simulation of a Linear Exchange System Under Equilibrium Conditions. In reciprocal exchange systems, direct exchanges take place between individ-

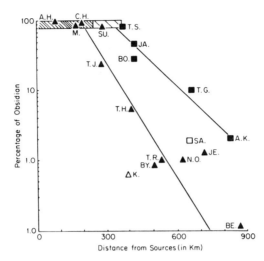

Figure 7.18 Regression analysis of obsidian flow in Neolithic villages in the Near East. Source: Renfrew, Dixon, and Cann 1968, p. 328.

uals or local groups on a reciprocal or complementary basis. Material goods are passed from one group to another and from one area to another as if they were links in a chainlike structure. Since people in prestate-level societies generally prefer trade with relatives, imaginary kin ties are often established to create trade partnerships that smooth exchange between links. The links in the chain frequently become so extended, however, that distant consumers have only a vague notion of the ultimate source of their traded goods. This distance factor is especially critical in chainlike reciprocal exchange systems through which utilitarian goods are flowing.

The possible disruptive effects of this factor have been discussed by Rappaport (1968) for the Maring. Maring villagers produce salt or stone axes for exchange, depending on their distance from the sources of these items. Both are utilitarian goods that are traded for each other and for goods from other tribes to the north and south. Some items that reach the Maring from the north, such as sea shells, are kept and the remainder are passed on with salt to the south. The same is true of stone axes, bird-of-paradise plumes, and fur that reach the Maring from the south. What if people in one link of the chain decided that they no longer wanted to participate in the network? What if, for example, their population declined drastically or grew dramatically so that they no longer needed large numbers of axes or needed all that they could get? The result would be a disruption of the flow of goods.

Rappaport (1968:106) has suggested that this weakness is counterbalanced by the exchange of "exotic" items that serve as systemic regulators, that is, as a mechanism that ensures the perpetuation of the exchange system and the flow of utilitarian goods. The demand for these items, according to Rappaport, ensures the flow of other material goods throughout the system.

These features of reciprocal exchange systems generate several patterns of association between material goods that should be observable in the archaeological record. As we saw in the last section, since exchange is through individual trading partners, there should be a wide range of variation in the amounts and sources of exchanged materials from one household to another in the same settlement. Evidence for the long-distance exchange of exotic "regulatory" items should also be present in many households. Pires-Ferreira and Flannery (1976:290) suggest that such exotic materials as Pacific Coast pearl oyster shell, macaw plumes, and lumps of magnetite ore served this function in Formative Mesoamerica in their flow north from Oaxaca in the chainlike route that moved obsidian southward.

Wright and Zeder (1977) constructed a series of simulation models of linear exchange systems that incorporated Rappaport's insights. Their objective was to build a model of a reciprocal exchange system that was capable of maintaining equilibrium in the face of fluctuating population sizes and resource demands. The model that eventually proved successful was controlled by two hierarchically arranged regulatory devices that were dependent on information carried by systemic regulators. Their successful model had the following features (from Wright and Zeder 1977:235–237):

1. There is a universe of eight linearly arranged villages with production occurring only in the first and eighth, which are assumed to have limitless resources. Communities exchange as units and exchange is possible only between adjacent communities.
2. There are two classes of commodities: demographically dependent commodities that are used in fixed ratio to population and demographically nondependent commodities that are not. These are henceforth termed vital and symbolic commodities. Each producer makes one of each class of commodity in some ratio to its own population.
3. In each iterative "year" in the model, each community first takes what it needs of the vital commodity and passes on the rest to the next community. Second, each takes a set fraction, the same for all

communities, of the symbolic commodity and passes on the remainder.

4. Each year the population of the component communities changes, so that the production of all commodities and the consumption of vital commodities will change. The model contains two hierarchically arranged regulatory mechanisms.

a. Every year each producer corrects the production of its vital product by increasing or decreasing its production as a direct function of the increase or decrease in the received symbolic commodity over the amount received in the previous year divided by the local production of its own symbolic commodity. Since the difference in receipts is always small relative to local production, this is a minimal correction.

b. In years in which a producer fails to receive any vital commodities, it corrects the production of its own vital commodity by changing it as a direct function of the increase or decrease in the received symbolic commodity over the amount received in the previous year.

Like most models, this one is based on a number of simplifying assumptions. For example, (1) whole communities rather than many sets of partners, as is generally the case, are assumed to exchange goods; (2) only two commodities are exchanged rather than the usual large number; (3) it is assumed that there are only two producers when in actuality every community in a network often participates in the production of at least one commodity; (4) commodities are assumed to be either demographically or nondemographically dependent when commodities are rarely purely one or the other; and (5) knowledge of the received goods is assumed to affect local production (Wright and Zeder 1977:237). Several steps are suggested for elaborating the model to make it conform better with real-exchange networks (p. 239).

Despite these oversimplifications, the model has interesting implications for the interpretation of archaeological data (figure 7.19). For example, it provides a plausible argument for the suggestion that the mechanism for the movement of marine shell through the Late Archaic communities in the Lower Tennessee Valley was a network of trading partners that linked the coast to the interior (Wright and Zeder 1977:238). Winters (1968) had rejected this possibility because it presumably implied a steady flow of goods. The archaeological record showed that the relative quantities of marine shell did fluctuate even though the size of local populations rose and declined grad-

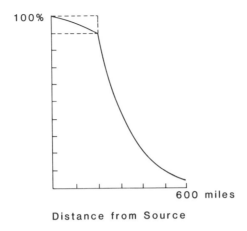

100%

600 miles

Distance from Source

Figure 7.19 A simple diagram of down-the-line exchange.

ually over a much longer time period. Furthermore, there were few goods that could have been exchanged southward from the valley, and the amount of copper entering the system from the north was apparently too small to maintain the system in relation to the large quantities of marine shell that were present.

These apparent inconsistencies, however, are actually anticipated by the model. For instance, commodity supply is a function of changes in producer populations rather than the population of intermediate links; therefore, correlations between supply and producer population fluctuations should be sought in the archaeological record. Also, according to the simulation model, regulatory symbolic commodities need not be contributed by communities in the middle of the chain. Finally, one would anticipate smaller amounts of copper relative to marine shell, for the Lower Tennessee Valley is much closer to the sources of shell; archaeologically, then, geographic gradients of marine shell and copper should be discovered that are analogous to the falloff pattern of obsidian in the Near East described by Renfrew, Dixon, and Cann (1968). Conversely, one would expect to find systemic regulators in the Near East that perpetuated the flow of obsidian.

Wright and Zeder's simulation model of a linear exchange system fulfills the basic functions of an operational model in that it (1) identifies a mechanism that generates an observable form, (2) accounts for an array of observations, (3) produces unanticipated answers and questions, and (4) suggests new avenues of research. For a critique of the model see Ammerman, Matessi, and Cavalli-Sforza (1978).

Neolithic Axe Dispersal in Britain. The simulation of exchange processes by Ammerman, Matessi, and Cavalli-Sforza (1978) and Wright and Zeder (1977) assumes that settlements are arranged in a linear pattern along which resources flow in ever decreasing amounts. Even though both projects have produced interesting results, both were acknowledged to be unrealistic by their authors. Primitive exchange between communities is rarely restricted to nearest neighbors. Nor does exchange generally flow down linear arrangements of communities. Finally, communities are rarely altruistic enough to take only what they need from a large volume of material and then pass on the rest to their next nearest neighbor.

A second somewhat more realistic approach to the simulation of exchange processes allows the resources being exchanged to move randomly among all points on a map. Hodder and Orton (1976), for example, simulated the random walk of one type of artifact from a single source to determine whether different dispersal processes would produce different falloff curves. As in the random walk model discussed in chapter 4, the dispersal followed a set of specific rules governing the number of steps allowed a walk, the length of each step, and so on. Falloff curves were calculated by plotting the frequency of artifacts that ended in ten distance bands around the source. Several conclusions were reached. First, the pattern of spread of less valuable artifacts (those that moved only a few short steps and, therefore, had less of an energy investment) could be differentiated from the pattern of spread of more valuable artifacts (those that moved many steps and, therefore, had more of an energy investment). Second, the same falloff curves could often be produced by remarkably different dispersal procedures (Hodder and Orton 1976; also see Hodder 1974).

The simulation of Neolithic axe dispersal in later fourth- and third-millennium B.C. Britain by Elliot, Ellman, and Hodder (1978) is another example of the second of these two approaches to the simulation of exchange processes. Petrological analyses had associated a large number of Neolithic axes (818 in all) with at least three partly contemporaneous sources in northern Wales and western England. On the assumption that these axes were produced approximately contemporaneously, the reproduction of their spatial distribution in the modeling process is a goal for simulation studies.

Since different hypothetical processes could have produced the distribution, different simulation models are possible. Even though individual exchanges of axes were presumably not random, Elliot and his colleagues chose a random walk process to generate distributions of axes, for "the overall exchange patterns can be compared with a random process" (Elliot, Ellman, and Hodder 1978:81). The entire study area was divided into an 11×11 grid system of 121 cells composed of squares 50 kilometers on a side. A finite number of axes was started from two sources in each run, which lasted until the axes from both sources were exhausted by traveling a predetermined number of steps. The concept of competition between sources was introduced into the model by assuming "that the more axes in a particular area, the less the probability of another axe being required in the area" (p. 82). The concept was operationalized by controlling the maximum number of axes allowed in any one cell. Three separate simulations were generally run for each set of controlling variables. Both means and standard deviations were then obtained for the simulated data, and the differences between the simulated and actual statistics were calculated for each cell. Figure 7.20 represents the outcome of one of these runs. The emerging pattern of axe dispersal suggested to the authors that the exchange of axes in Neolithic Britain was probably comparable to the ceremonial gift exchange of axes in Australasia discussed by Clark (1965b).

The random walk model briefly summarized here represents an early stage in model building. A set of rules was found that generated the known distributional pattern of axes. In addition, the model contained interesting implications for further research. Among the many ways in which the model could be elaborated and made more realistic would be the consideration of the effect on distributional patterns of (1) higher population densities and great localized wealth, (2) grid systems of different sizes and locations (the ecological fallacy discussed in chapter 9), (3) axe dispersal from all contemporaneous sources rather than from just pairs of sources, (4) varying the period of output of different sources (instead of assuming that each source produced the same volume of material over the same time period as every other source), and (5) allowing axes to avoid one another during a walk rather than at the end of a walk (Elliot, Ellman, and Hodder 1978:85). Besides these internal elaborations, the basic underlying assumption of the model (that exchange was based on a system of reciprocity) could be examined. Was the dispersal of axes really the result of localized, reciprocal exchange? Or were other dispersal mechanisms such as redistribution or special-purpose long-distance trips to sources actually more significant in the move-

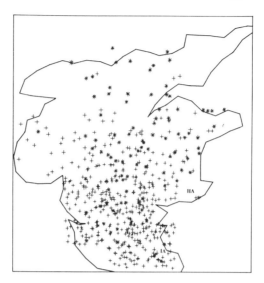

Figure 7.20   A simulation run of axe dispersal in Neolithic Britain. Symbols represent axes from two different sources. Source: K. Elliott, D. Ellman, and I. Hodder, The simulation of neolithic axe dispersal in Britain, in I. Hodder, ed., *Simulation Studies in Archaeology,* pp. 79–87 (N.Y.: Cambridge University Press, 1978), figure 4.

ment of materials in Neolithic Britain? These questions and suggested research directions point to the fertility of this class of model.

Summary

Chapter 7 considers the regional and interregional levels of analysis and interpretation, presenting models for the study of synchronic (at one moment in time) interrelationships of settlements. Settlement pattern, or location, analysis focuses on the shape of individual structures, the plan of communities, and spatial relationships of communities. Such studies begin by measuring the relationships of sites to one another and to features of the natural environment, using methods such as nearest-neighbor analysis. Some problems in identifying settlement patterns include establishing contemporaneity, establishing meaningful regional boundaries, and using incomplete information. Random distributions include many small, independent influences while uniform patterning probably results from a combination of competition and accessibility to centers of trade. Uniform spacing between settlements maximized travel efficiency while size depended on a settlement's relative importance and principal mode of transportation. Systems of hexagonal trade areas are shown graphically by a Thiessen polygon indicating topography, rivers, lakes, and other disruptions. Simple patterns tend to have a smaller average number of contiguous polygons, and mean distance between first-order neighbors tends to decrease with increasing societal complexity.

Central place theory is a useful spatial model that operates on the principles of least cost and larger number of services. The rank-size rule states that for any given region there will be a largest settlement and all other sizes will be predictably related to that of the largest settlement, lending support to central place theory and emphasizing the fundamental relationships between the size, number, and spacing of communities. Economic relationships tend to be tied more closely to local areas, while political, religious, and kinship relationships are networked over larger areas. Descriptive settlement patterns can be made systemic by employing game theory or other simulations to find a best fit with past reality.

Included among models for community interaction are the gravity model, stating that the amount of interaction between two centers varies directly with some function of the distance between them, and the distance-decay model, which deals with the decreasing occurrence of objects and events with increasing distance from their sources. These studies commonly use the technique of regression analysis.

Reconstruction of technoeconomic systems includes factors of scale, items exchanged, sociopolitical complexity, mode of transportation, and population density. Spatial distributions supported the hypothesis in a model of exchange among the Maya that items involved in local trade would be primarily utilitarian while those traded over long distance would be nonutilitarian prestige items. A model of sites in the American Southwest and Mesoamerica failed to show a consistent statistically significant positive correlation between community size and the degree of similarity of stylistic attributes. Among transportation network variables are relief, shape, size, population, density, and degree of economic development, measures made more precise through graph theory. Studies of Early and Middle Formative Mesoamerica exchanges of obsidian supported the proposition that obsidian was obtained through negotiations by individual households (reciprocal economy). How-ever, later evidence of pooling indicated that an unexpected early appear-ance of a redistributive economy was possible.

Modal interregional exchange networks have concentrated on items that occur in abundance, that do not easily deteriorate, and whose source can be determined. Studies of obsidian flow in the Near East used optical spectro-scopic and linear regression analysis to show a chain of exchange. A linear exchange system made under equilibrium conditions suggested that exotic items served as systemic regulators. A study of neolithic axe dispersal in Britain used a more realistic approach by allowing resources being exchanged to move randomly and indicated that the pattern of spread of less valuable ar-tifacts could be differentiated from that of more valuable ones. The authors' suggestions for further research directions point to the fertility of this class of model.

SUGGESTED READINGS

A number of informative studies of settlement archaeology are:

Chang, K., ed. 1968. *Settlement Archaeology*. Palo Alto, Calif.: National Press.
—— 1972. *Settlement Patterns in Archaeology*. Addison-Wesley Modules in Anthropology, No. 24. Reading, Mass.: Addison-Wesley.
Clarke, D. L., ed. 1977. *Spatial Archaeology*. London, New York: Academic Press.
Cunliffe, B., ed. 1978. Landscape archaeology. *World Archaeology* 9(3).
Evans, S. 1980. Spatial analysis of Basin of Mexico settlement: Problems with the use of the central place model. *American Antiquity* 45:866–875.
Fitting, J. and C. Cleland. 1969. Late prehistoric settlement patterns in the Upper Great Lakes. *Ethnohistory* 16:289–302.
Flannery, K. V. 1972. The origins of the village as a settlement type in Mesoamerica and the Near East: A comparative study. In P. Ucko, R. Tringham, and G. Dimbleby, eds., *Man, Settlement and Urbanism*, pp. 23–54. London: Duckworth.
Gregory, D. 1975. Defining variability in prehistoric settlement morphology. Chapters in the Prehistory of Eastern Arizona, IV. *Fieldiana: Anthropology*, Vol. 65, pp. 40–46. Chicago: Field Museum of Natural History.
Gumerman, G., ed. 1971. *The Distribution of Prehistoric Population Aggregates*. Prescott, Ariz.: Prescott College Press.
Johnson, G. A. 1977. Aspects of regional analysis in archaeology. In B. Siegel, ed., *Annual Review of Anthropology*, Vol. 6, pp. 479–508. Palo Alto, Calif.: Annual Reviews.
Marcus, J. 1973. Territorial organization of the lowland classic Maya. *Science* 180:911–916.
Parsons, J. 1972. Archaeological settlement patterns. In B. Siegel, ed., *Annual Review of Anthropology*, Vol. 1, pp. 127–150. Palo Alto, Calif.: Annual Reviews.
Smith, B., ed. 1978. *Mississippian Settlement Patterns*. New York: Academic Press.
Ucko, P., R. Tringham, and G. Dimbleby, eds. 1972. *Man, Settlement and Urbanism*. London: Duckworth.

Among the many studies of interaction between communities are:

Adams, Robert M. 1974. Anthropological perspectives on ancient trade. *Current Anthropology* 15:239–258.

Bradley, R. 1971. Trade competition and artifact distribution. *World Archaeology* 2:347–352.

Bray, W., ed. 1973. Trade. *World Archaeology* 8(2).

Crumley, C. 1979. Three locational models: An epistemological assessment for anthropology and archaeology. In M. Schiffer, ed., *Advances in Archaeological Method and Theory*, Vol. 2, pp. 141–173. New York: Academic Press.

Earle, T. and J. Ericson, eds. 1977. *Exchange Systems in Prehistory*. New York: Academic Press.

Hodder, I. 1974. Regression analysis of some trade and marketing patterns. *World Archaeology* 6:172–189.

Hodder, I. and C. Orton. 1976. *Spatial Analysis in Archaeology*. New York: Cambridge University Press.

Plog, S. 1980. *Stylistic Variation in Prehistoric Ceramics*. New York: Cambridge University Press.

Smith, C. 1976. *Regional Analysis in Archaeology*. 2 vols. New York: Academic Press.

Wilmsen, E., ed. 1972. *Social Exchange and Interaction*. Anthropological Papers, Museum of Anthropology, University of Michigan, No. 46. Ann Arbor: University of Michigan Press.

CHAPTER EIGHT

Processes That Promote Sociocultural Change

Anthropological archaeologists are interested not only in how societal systems work and why, they are interested in answering questions that ask how societies came to be the way they were in the past. For example, What is sociocultural change? When does a sociocultural system cease being one kind of system and become another? What about change should be studied? Diachronic studies have always been regarded as a potential strong suit of archaeology, for more than anything else, archaeology adds a temporal dimension to the study of human beings in social groups. Long-term studies of change help us understand the impact on economic and other social behavior of new technologies, new subsistence crops, the effects of weed growth or deforestation, long-term vegetation successions, and other factors. The explanation of cultural change is a fundamental research goal of anthropological archaeology.

Chapter 8 explores the modeling of sociocultural change. The first section asks, How should change be studied? The second through fourth sections review problems of modeling, change in sociocultural subsystems, colonization and the expansion of settlement, and the growth of settlement hierarchies. The fifth section introduces total society simulation.

How Should Change Be Studied?

All archaeological materials are contemporary: they do not exhibit sociocultural change. Archaeologists must impose categories upon their subject matter, arrange them into abstract chronological frameworks, and account for what appear to be changes in the contents of these categories through time. These decisions are made within the intellectual climate of particular research programs for studying sociocultural change. Theoretical and metaphysical judgments come into play in answering such questions as What are useful ways of studying change? and What is change? The two research programs that have dominated the study of sociocultural change in anthropological archaeology are *cultural historical reconstruction* and the *cultural processual approach*. Each of these research programs has different general aims, methods, and periods of popularity within anthropological archaeology.

Cultural historical reconstruction dominated archaeological research in North America during the first half of the twentieth century. It was succeeded as a general research strategy by processual studies, which have grown in importance since the early 1960s. A cultural historical approach has been identified with a normative view of culture, an inductive methodology, the ordering of archaeological data into chronological and spatial frameworks, and the descriptive chronicle of what happened in the past (Sharer and Ashmore 1979:477–504). The primary goal of the cultural historian is the reconstruction and interpretation of the flow of past sociocultural events. A cultural processual approach has been identified with a systematic-ecological-evolutionary concept of culture, a deductive methodology, and the goal of explaining rather than "merely describing" what happened in the past (Sharer and Ashmore 1979:507–535). In recent years the emergence of systems, cultural ecological, and multilinear cultural evolutionary models have been associated with the cultural processual approach. Since the cultural processual approach has been discussed in Part One, only the implications of this approach for the study of sociocultural change in the past are reviewed here.

A primary goal of the processual approach is the explanation of change through the discovery of processes that have generated change. Archaeologists approaching the study of change through this perspective have generally adopted in principle the other methodological principles and rules that characterize the processual research program in anthropological archaeology: a culture is a system with interacting parts; instances of cultural stability and change can be understood by discovering processes that work to hold systems together or that result in their change; since the parts of a sociocultural system are interrelated and interdependent, the ramifications of changes in cultural variables, such as intensity of trade or population size, can be traced throughout the system; study the dynamics of changing systems rather than isolated material objects. The methodological principles that underlie the theoretical foundations of contemporary anthropological archaeology exhort archaeologists to view sociocultural systems as unique wholes and to approach behavioral changes in the past *as if* they had taken place within the complex web of these adaptive wholes.

Like all research programs, the cultural processual approach rests on many assumptions that cannot be refuted empirically. They are methodological or metaphysical principles that must be evaluated on the basis of their research fruitfulness and the depth of insight they bring to a subject. From this perspective, neither the cultural historical approach nor the cultural processual approach is right or wrong; each must be evaluated on how well it has fulfilled a research objective. Recent reviews of the goals and methods of cultural historians have tended to caricature the approach in a manner consistent with research or paradigm shifts in other disciplines (Kuhn 1970). Nonetheless, like many other new research programs, many of the goals, methods, and concepts of the processual approach remain problematic. For instance, according to some archaeologists a main goal of the processual approach is the discovery of the causes of changes that have occurred in past sociocultural systems. What is meant by *cause*, however, has usually remained ambiguous, for cause can refer either to a regular sequence of events or to underlying necessary connections. Is the reconstruction of a pattern or the evoking of mystical connections an adequate causal explanation? What is the connection between cause and explanation? Similarly, the familiar distinction between cultural history and "mere chronicle" is possibly based on a confusion underlying assumptions that we might not want to accept. A chronicler in this sense lists events in a time order, while the cultural historian links the events by means of a causal explanation. But what if more than one possible causal chain exists? Since sociocultural systems and their subsystems are not closed systems, the logic of their change may be upset by totally extraneous events. The implication is that more than one possible causal chain nearly always exists. This is one reason why historians insist on the importance of narrative, on the description of the facts. In archaeology, the cultural historian has first of all to establish, by critical study of the evidence, that something she or he believes to be the case really is the case. Clearly, then, mere chronicle plays an indispensable role in the cycle of science, and a chronicler is not any less a scientist than a "mere theoretician" in the cycle.

Even if we adopt the causal explanation of sociocultural change through time as a goal, there remain unresolved and perhaps unresolvable clashes between different conceptual models of what it means to be human, where the locus of change is, or what form that change may take. For example, until recently, anthropological archaeologists generally assumed that sociocultural systems change gradually rather than by sudden internal shifts or catastrophic jumps. Is this assumption supported by contemporary models of change and the archaeological record (see Renfrew 1979)? What is the relationship between human beings as biological animals and their culture? Can the relationship be treated as a psychological constant? Can biological determinants explain at least in part the observable differences between Neanderthal and more recent archaeological sites? Is it particularly fruitful to use the possession of an integrated culture as the criterion of human status? Would it not be logically circular to project this pattern back to very early human forms without demonstrating the presence of pattern first? In studying earlier human forms, it may be more fruitful to concentrate on the behavioral evolutionary aspects that made cultural adaptation possible rather than on the analysis of the holistic integration of culture traits. Similarly, how can an abstract generic concept like *culture,* which is derived from empirical observations of a very concrete nature, be applied in any meaningful analysis of the developmental aspects of human evolution and adaptation? As we have seen, Wissler adopted a reductionist solution to this problem and simply assumed the phenomenal unity of what he called a universal pattern of culture. Is this legitimate?

This line of reasoning raises other interesting questions about the locus of sociocultural change. For example, if human beings share a psychobiological constant and if the stimuli for change are internal (that is, biologically coded), one would expect all societies to share the same structure and content. But cultural systems obviously exhibit great variability in both of these variables. Therefore, it seems more reasonable to conclude that external sources provide the primary stimuli for sociocultural change. This conclusion has been regarded as the best evidence for a sociocultural rather than a psychobiological explanation of dissimilarities between human social groups. If these arguments are accepted, a number of methodological principles and rules can be formulated. For instance: (1) change is never initiated or caused by factors internal to a given system; (2) there is a causal feedback relationship between cultural systems and their environments; and (3) examine those mechanisms and other factors lying outside human social groups to learn why they differ in their beliefs, behavior, or other characteristics (search for external environmental perturbations!). But cannot the "logic" of a cultural system foment internal change (Braybrooke 1970)? And does not the reliance on external explanations assume that culture is in peoples' heads rather than having in a sense an ontological existence of its own? These are questions to ponder.

Modeling Change in Sociocultural Subsystems

The actual focus of most studies of sociocultural change in anthropological archaeology is not the sociocultural whole but one or more properties of a subsystem: the growth and demise of exchange systems, the emergence and collapse of class structures, the spread of religions, or other subsystem transformations. This section looks at three of these studies.

An Environmental Stress–Cognitive Inconsistency Model of the Olmec Collapse

Robert Drennan (1976) has interpreted Olmec art through rituals of sanctification. According to this model, the Olmec art style diffused rapidly throughout Mesoamerica in the Early Formative as a mechanism "sanctifying" the establishment of high-ranking individuals and administrative authority. The three major centers where the Olmec style was most elaborately developed along the southern Gulf Coast were San Lorenzo, La Venta, and Tres Zapotes. Olmec development seems to have reached its peak at San Lorenzo between 1150 and 900 B.C. and then to have collapsed suddenly. That the collapse was also violent is evident in defaced monuments and other signs of internal conflict. What changes in society occurred at this time and why did they occur?

Drennan has proposed an environmental stress–cognitive inconsistency model as a plausible and testable interpretation of this collapse. To briefly summarize the salient points of the model: the increasing population requirements and rituals of sanctification required by the growing system led to large population concentrations around San Lorenzo and other centers. This proved to be a maladaptive demographic shift, for the available integrative mechanisms, especially the control hierarchy for regulating social, economic, and ecological variables, were unable to buffer the population against stochastic fluctuations of the environment. The result was a social catastrophe with massive desanctification bringing about "the sudden and violent end to the manufacture of ritual artifacts and structures" (Drennan 1976:364). The model shows how this fatal spiral might be predestined by the logic of the system under certain conditions by interrelating social, economic, demographic, and environmental variables (figure 8.1).

From a functional perspective, systems of ritual ensure that social conventions and important messages from the elite will be accepted by the general populace. But the cost of systems of ritual can spiral upward dramatically. In Formative Mesoamerica the cost involved the exchange and processing of exotic materials, the construction and maintenance of specialized structures, the support of ritual specialists, and other obligatory expenses. As systems of ritual grow, the expense involved in their maintenance can become so great that stress is created on local resources. The result in technologically limited systems that cannot dramatically improve production is a fatal spiral in the intensification of productivity and ritual. The growth of the ritual system and its facilities leads to a demand for greater production; this exhortation is expressed in an increased flow of sanctified messages and in greater pressure on the social conventions that surround production; and unless human motivation is dramatically changed, the entire system of sanctification becomes severely strained when production finally cannot meet demand. The fatal spiral moves through the intensifying cycle of increased

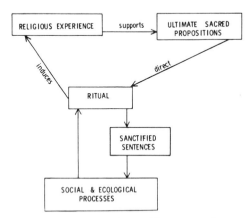

Figure 8.1   The circular relationship linking ultimate sacred propositions, ritual, and religious experience. Source: Drennan 1976, figure 11.8.

production requirements to increased ritual expenses to further requirements—and so on.

According to the model, the agricultural system at San Lorenzo and La Venta was unable to respond to these repeated demands, for the system had production limits. On the one hand the massive labor requirements of the centers pulled in population. On the other the agricultural needs of the centers depended at least in part on tropical forest agricultural systems in the huge surrounding hinterland zones. The centrifugal tendencies of tropical forest agricultural systems would have diverted people and food resources from the centers. As a result, control hierarchies and their rituals of sanctification may not have been able to regulate the very social, economic, and environmental variables they were designed to once their burgeoning populations were exposed to periodic severe environmental fluctuations.

How did severe environmental fluctuations bring about the collapse of the system? Drennan argues within the framework of his model that environmental stress prevented "the carrying out of certain ritual activities, the prescriptions for which were drived from the ultimate sacred propositions" (Drennan 1976:362). The result would have been behavior inconsistent with a person's beliefs and the rise of cognitive inconsistency. Cognitive consistency theories stress the need to "maintain an unequivocal behavioral orientation" (Gerard 1968:456). The substantial discomfiture introduced by inconsistent behavior can be reduced by (1) changing the cognitive elements associated with behavior, (2) adding new cognitive elements that account for inconsistent behavior, or (3) changing the inconsistent beliefs. Drennan (1976:362) suggests that the inconsistent beliefs were changed in this instance and that this change led to the collapse of the complex belief system of which Olmec art was an integral element. With the collapse of the belief system, the socioeconomic system may have collapsed as well. To completely eliminate cognitive inconsistency, the major remaining elements of the belief system—the monuments and symbols—would have to be destroyed too. In fact, "the destruction of these monuments would, in itself, be a ritual act communicating the final demise of the belief system upon which their existence was contingent" (p. 363). Drennan completes his formulation of the environmental stress–cognitive inconsistency model by showing that it is consistent with existing archaeological data, that it makes a range of predictions that could be tested with new data, and that it is supported by ethnographic examples of similar collapses.

The Emergence of the Self: Indicators of Self-Awareness

Robert Drennan's use of the concept of cognitive inconsistency is an example of a psychological theory applied to a model of change in the prehistoric past. A. Irving Hallowell (1959), in a classic paper, proposed that anthropologists study the psychological dimension of evolution, the evolution of mental capabilities. His premise is that the processes of evolution were almost certainly not confined to the biological realm alone. If we accept this premise, a legitimate question is whether or not there has been a significant correlation between the growth of human psychological capabilities and the capacity of humans to assimilate complex cultures. Was cultural growth, initially at least, dependent on psychobiological growth?

In the introduction to Part Two, the reductionist concept of a universal pattern of culture was introduced. The subdivisions of this hypothetical pattern are widely used within anthropology as organizational categories, and they have been used for this purpose throughout this book. Among the basic categories of some univeral patterns are speech, tool making, and other capacities that make a cultural mode of adaptation possible. But even though the Australopiths made simple tools, it is doubtful whether they had a cultural mode of adaptation in this sense. They may not have had tools to make tools or a system of communication equivalent to contemporary human speech. If a universal pattern of culture does not apply to all the Hominidae, when did a cultural mode of adaptation appear in human evolution and how can archaeologists identify or measure its presence? What are the evolutionary roots of the cultural mode of adaptation? This is the problem that Hallowell set out to explore.

Hallowell began by asking a basic question: What capacity is necessary for the emergence of a cultural mode of adaptation, for a truly human lifeway? Some capacities, such as speech, are probably necessary. Of these, one of the most essential is self-awareness or the capacity for self-objectification. Hallowell thought that societies functioned as moral orders. Within this interpretation of fully human societies self-objectification plays an essential role: "The functioning of a social system as a moral order implies a capacity for self objectification, self identification, and appraisal of one's conduct, as well as that of others, with reference to socially recognized and sanctioned standards of behavior" (Hallowell 1959:50). The appearance of self-objectification as an integrative mechanism in human evolution made possible larger and more varied social groups having a greater diversity of roles than previously possible. How can this transformation in psychological structure be recognized in the archaeological record? What should archaeologists look for? This is a fundamental problem in anthropology and archaeology, for this psychological restructuring made a cultural mode of adaptation, cultural readaptation, and cultural change possible.

Hallowell (1959:54) suggested that self-objectification is "contingent upon the capacity for the symbolic projection of experience in socially meaningful terms, i.e., in a mode that is intelligible interindividually." Intrinsic symbolic processes are functionally integrated with and expressed by external symbolization in a material media. These externally expressed symbolizations transmit shared meanings within systems of social action. Neither intrinsic symbolic processes nor externally expressed symbolization are confined to culture-bearing humans. Studies have shown, for instance, that intrinsic symbolic processes occur in subhominid primates as well as in some lower species. Chimpanzees have been taught gestures that may be considered a primitive form of extrinsic symbolization. Intrinsic symbolic processes and externally expressed symbolization, however, are most highly developed in and characteristic of human beings. Since the communication of meanings embodied in extrinsic symbolization must be expressed through a material medium, archaeologists can look for material objects that express symbols. Speech acts are an important material expression of intrinsic symbolic processes, for "the use of personal pronouns, personal names and kinship terms, made it possible for an individual symbolically to represent and thus to objectify himself in systems of social action" (Hallowell 1959:57). Speech acts, of course, are not objectified in the archaeological record: stone, bone, paint, and similar materials are. Extrinsic symbolic systems expressed through visual modes like these help human beings living in groups share a common world of meaning. They also help the archaeologist identify the symbolization process, if Hallowell is correct in his argument.

What is the earliest evidence for extrinsic symbolization expressed in a visual mode in the archaeological record? Does it appear suddenly and in abundance or does it gradually accumulate through time (figure 8.2)? The appearance of ochre and other red pigments on Neanderthal burials in the Middle Paleolithic has been interpreted as an example of ritual symbolizing blood and warmth and possibly a belief in an afterlife. Other evidence indicates too that it was in association with Neanderthals that extrinsic symbolization first appears in relative quantity in the archaeological record. A cultural mode of adaptation may have first appeared among some Neander-

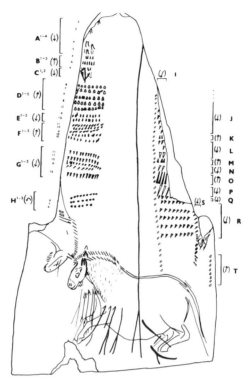

Figure 8.2 Notations on the Upper Paleolithic La Marche bone. Source: Page 822 of A. Marshack, Upper Paleolithic notation and symbol, *Science* 178:817–827. Copyright © 1972 by A. Marshack. Reproduced with permission of the author.

thal societies, then, although the evidence for human speech is equivocal. Of course, this interpretation is based on our ability to recognize symbolic representations as such. Even everyday tools, facilities, and food can gain a special symbolic meaning in certain situations, such as burials. Once identified as a symbolic representation, the meaning of the representation must be inferred; this has generally been accomplished in prehistoric archaeology through ethnographic analogy, the direct historic approach, and other model-building techniques.

Is Population Pressure the Prime Mover in Sociocultural Change?
A Test of a Hypothesis

Do human populations grow until they reach the productive limits of their subsistence systems? If they do, do new, more productive subsistence systems and new, more complex sociopolitical systems emerge when these limits are reached? More baldly, are the origins of complex sociopolitical systems such as the state rooted in or caused by population growth (Grigg 1976; Harner 1970; Boserup 1965; Dumond 1965; Smith 1972, 1976; Spooner 1972)?

Elizabeth Brumfield (1976) tested the population pressure hypothesis with data from Formative sites in the eastern Valley of Mexico. Population pressure is present, according to her theoretical definition, whenever "the total needs of a population approach the maximum output that its subsistence system will produce" (p. 236). Two variables are involved in this definition: needs of a population and productivity of the resources a population possesses; population pressure is defined by a specified relation between these variables. The values of both variables will vary from community to community, depending in part on the cultural system of which they are components. The system of production limits the maximum productivity of the environment (e.g., Boserup 1965). Fertilizers, tractors, and high-yield plants produce more per acre now in a year, for instance, than that acre was likely to produce per year in the prehistoric period. The needs of a population are not an absolute either, for levels of consumption vary between communities and perceived needs are usually difficult to measure.

Brumfield tested the population pressure hypothesis by first making a number of assumptions and then by specifying the empirical implications of these assumptions. The first assumption was that there should be a high positive correlation between the needs of communities under population pressure and their productive capabilities. In very productive subsistence systems, community needs should be numerous. The second basic assumption was that needs would vary only in proportion to the size of community population and in relation to the amounts and fertility of available resources when communities shared a uniform culture. Cultural variables, such as level of consumption and subsistence technology, would be controlled in these situations. A third assumption was that all communities within the study area shared a uniform culture. Given these assumptions, population pressure would be "expressed in a simple correlation between the relative number of inhabitants at each village and the relative potential of agricultural land available to each village" (Brumfield 1976:237). Should these two variables not covary through time, there would be grounds for concluding that population pressure was not an important factor in sociocultural change in this region. The identification of a falsifying instance would also cast doubt on the population hypothesis and on theories that incorporated this hypothesis as an axiom.

To test the covariance of the two variables, Blumfield gave each variable an empirical interpretation. The size of residential site area was used as an indicator of population size (Blumfield 1976:236–237). For example, the assumption was made that a site with twice the residential area of another had twice the population. The productive potential of a village was empirically defined as the amount of agricultural land available to the occupants of each site times the relative fertility of that land. Site catchment analysis was used to estimate in hectares the amount of land within a 5-kilometer radius of each village that was suitable for digging-stick cultivation. Available agricultural land would then be a function of three variables: site size, density of site packing, and catchment topography. The relative fertility of arable land was estimated from recent agricultural censuses, and fertility ratios were developed according to whether or not land was irrigated, fertilized, and so on. The ratios produced relative measures of productivity that could be used in comparing sites (table 8.1). A linear regression analysis was then used to measure the relationship between the size of each site and the productive potential of its catchment area (figure 8.3). In a linear regression, if the behavior of one variable, X, is a perfect predictor of the behavior of another variable, Y, it is concluded that the two variables are perfectly correlated and that X explains 100 percent of the variance in Y (p. 240). When the prediction of one variable by the other is less than perfect, as is usually the case, linear regression analysis provides a measure of the strength of the existing correlation. A search for pattern among the measures revealed four clusters: a positive correlation for Late Formative sites over 50 hectares in size; no correlation for Late Formative sites smaller than 50 hectares; and a positive correlation for all Terminal Formative sites (even though two separate clusters were present, one for sites over 80 hectares and one for smaller sites). This pattern suggests that population pressure was localized in the Late Formative, only affecting sites larger than 50 hectares. Population pressure

Table 8.1 Relationships Between Size and Productive Potential of Prehistoric Settlements During the Late and Terminal Formative

Site	(1) Size (ha)	(2) Log_{10} of Site Size	(3) Arable Land (km²)	(4) Relative Fertility	(5) Productive Potential (3×4)	(6) Ratio of Population to Productive Resources $(1 : 5)$
Late Formative sites						
Tx-9	33	1.52	72.5	.84	60.8	.54 : 1
Tx-12	86	1.93	61.2	.84	51.4	1.84 : 1
Tx-22	45	1.65	73.3	1.10	80.6	.56 : 1
Ix-2	37	1.57	17.6	.85	15.0	2.46 : 1
Ix-6	65	1.81	17.9	.73	13.1	4.96 : 1
Ix-7	30	1.48	39.1	.73	28.5	1.05 : 1
Ch-2	60	1.78	35.4	.96	33.8	1.76 : 1
Ch-3	67	1.83	29.0	.96	27.8	2.41 : 1
Ch-4	35	1.54	31.8	.96	30.4	1.14 : 1
Ch-7	86	1.93	21.6	1.92	41.5	2.07 : 1
Ch-8	130	2.11	34.8	1.92	66.9	1.94 : 1
Ch-12	43	1.63	66.8	.82	54.8	.78 : 1
MEANS	60	1.78	41.8	1.05	42.0	1.79 : 1
Terminal Formative sites						
Tx-1	74	1.87	89.9	.90	80.9	.92 : 1
Tx-17	118	2.07	54.2	.84	45.5	2.62 : 1
Tx-30	50	1.70	50.8	.84	42.6	1.17 : 1
Tx-50	52	1.72	51.0	1.10	56.1	.93 : 1
Ix-4	37	1.57	21.4	.85	18.2	2.03 : 1
Ix-5	32	1.50	19.6	.73	14.1	2.27 : 1
Ix-10	32	1.50	34.0	.73	28.9	1.11 : 1
Ch-5	54	1.73	54.7	.96	52.3	1.04 : 1
Ch-14	75	1.88	29.4	1.92	56.4	1.33 : 1
Ch-18	38	1.58	24.8	.96	23.7	1.62 : 1
Ch-25	35	1.54	6.0	1.92	11.5	3.06 : 1
Ch-26	90	1.95	12.7	1.92	24.4	3.71 : 1
Ch-27	129	2.11	26.4	1.92	50.7	2.54 : 1
Ch-29	43	1.63	51.4	.82	42.1	1.02 : 1
MEANS	61	1.78	37.6	1.17	39.1	1.81 : 1

SOURCE: Brumfield 1976, table 8.3.

was a general condition of all Terminal Formative sites greater than about 30 hectares.

What factors were responsible for the more universal condition of population pressure in the Terminal Formative? Why were there two tiers of population pressure? Blumfield suggests three factors that could account for

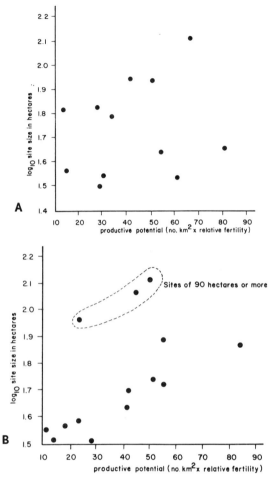

Figure 8.3 Plots of productive potential versus size for Formative sites in Mesoamerica. A. Late Formative (550–250 B.C.). B. Terminal Formative (250B.C.–A.D. 100). Source: Brumfield 1976, figures 8.12 and 8.13.

this change: (1) population growth, (2) decreases in subsistence system productivity resulting from environmental deterioration, and (3) increases in level of consumption. Both continued population growth and environmental deterioration were considered insufficient to account for the observed changes on the basis of available information. Sociopolitical factors reflected in the two-tier nature of population pressure during the Terminal Formative are thought to provide a better explanation. Large regional centers seem to have been able to draw produce or "payments" from smaller settlements on a systematic basis. A new pattern of production and consumption like this one normally accompanies the inception of a statelike political organization. The presence in the Terminal Formative of a strongly developed state organization is demonstrated by the regular spacing of large sites around regularly spaced administrative centers. This pattern suggests the planned resettlement of at least a portion of the population.

Did population growth cause the emergence of a complex sociopolitical system in the eastern Valley of Mexico? Blumfield (1976:247) concludes that population pressure in the Terminal Formative seems more an effect of the evolution of the state than a cause. In the Late Formative some settlements for whatever reason expanded to the maximum size allowed by their productive systems. Pressures generated by the problems involved in maintaining these large nucleated populations resulted in the establishment of tribute relationships with smaller sites and in the emergence of regional centers. Overpopulation or population pressure as such was probably never a general feature of the Formative period in this region. At least in this instance the population pressure hypothesis seems to have been falsified.

Colonization and the Expansion of Settlement

Various models have been developed to account for the pattern of spread of settlement of particular types into a region. Nearly all of these models assume that distance exerts a "friction" on migration. The rate and volume of migration are assumed to be inversely related to distance. On a map this would mean that larger proportions of migrant communities should appear closer to rather than farther from the source of migration. This hypothesis could be tested by repeated runs of a simulation model with the formula $M = K/D^a$. Here, M could stand for magnitude of migration, K for a constant to be determined, D for distance, and a for a modifier of physical distance that would simulate the effects of barriers that increase travel effort, such as major rivers, rugged topography, or dense forests. David Clarke's random walk model, elaborated as an example of the model-building process in chapter 4, is one instance. Other common models include wave-of-advance and least-cost rationales. In this section the use of both of these rationales is illustrated with a model of agricultural spread across Mesolithic

Europe and a model of the spread of agricultural settlements into Scandinavia.

Building a Colonization Model: The Wave-of-Advance Model

The wave-of-advance model applies to situations in which both population growth and diffusion are taking place at the same time. The model itself specifies the set of quantitative relationships that hypothetically hold between three variables: rate of population growth, local migratory activity, and velocity of population expansion outward. Following a formulation by Skellam (1951), the velocity of the advance of the wave front p is given by $\varphi\surd(2\alpha)$, where φ is the standard deviation of the local migratory activity and α is the growth rate in the exponential treatment of population growth. According to the model, population growth and local migratory activity produce a diffusionary process "which takes the form of a population wave expanding outward at a steady radial rate" (Ammerman and Cavalli-Sforza 1979:275). The diffusionary process not only provides an explanation of settlement patterning through time under certain conditions, it has predictive implications that can be tested against substantive settlement data. Ammerman and Cavalli-Sforza (1971, 1973, 1979) have applied the wave-of-advance model to the spread of early farming in Europe. Initially, they concentrated their research on measuring the rate of spread of early farming with the thought in mind that rate measurements might provide a clue to the processes involved in the spread. An early analysis of fifty dated sites using regression techniques indicated that the farming population had gradually expanded outward at an average rate of about 1 kilometer per year (table 8.2; Ammerman and Cavalli-Sforza 1971). A later, more refined study based on eighty dated sites resulted in the computer production of maps on which isochrons representing equivalent times were drawn (Cavalli-Sforza 1974:88). Having established a fairly regular pattern of agricultural advance in Europe, several explanations of how this spread could have occurred were explored (Ammerman and Cavalli-Sforza 1979). The model finally selected for study, the wave-of-advance model, is a demic diffusion model, in which the spread of the new economy is linked with population movements of some kind, in contrast to a stimulus diffusion model, in which items and ideas are passed from one group to another without population movement.

The two components that determine the rate of spread of the wave front

Table 8.2 Regional Rates of Neolithic
Diffusion in Europe

Sites	Diffusion Rate
Mediterranean	1.52 km per year
Western Mediterranean	2.08
Balkans	0.70
Bandkeramik	5.59
All of Europe	1.08

SOURCE: Ammerman and Cavalli-Sforza 1971, table 2. Reproduced by permission of the Royal Anthropological Institute of Great Britain and Ireland.

in the model are population growth and local migratory activity. The fruitfulness of wave-of-advance simulations depends on the feasibility of establishing meaningful theoretical definitions and valid measures for each of these concepts, for each can be conceived of from several different perspectives. Population growth, for example, can be conceived of as accelerating exponentially or as having the pattern of a logistic curve. According to the first conception, population N would steadily accelerate over time t, while in the second, pace of growth would be relatively high at the start and then become progressively slower as population size reached a saturation level in terms of local carrying capacity (figure 8.4). Ecological studies indicate that the latter conception is generally the more realistic of the two. The migration component can also be conceived of from various perspectives. One def-

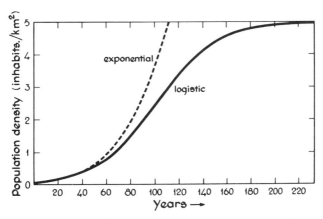

Figure 8.4 Exponential and logistic population growth curves. Source: Ammerman and Cavalli-Sforza 1979, figure 12.2.

inition of migration distribution for a population is the frequency distribution of the distances between settlements in which a population has lived at different times in its lifetime. Different models of migratory behavior, such as a random process model, can then be compared with these frequency distributions. The model adopted by Ammerman and Cavalli-Sforza assumes a continuous random diffusion in time and space. By interpreting α in terms of the logistic conception of population growth, the formula $p = \sigma \sqrt{(2\alpha)}$ can then be assigned the following values: $p = 1$ km/year, $\sigma = 18$ km per generation, $\alpha = .039$. Ammerman and Cavalli-Sforza's procedure for obtaining these values are beyond the scope of this book.

A number of simplifying assumptions have been incorporated into the mathematical formulation of the wave-of-advance model as presented here. For instance, (1) movement is assumed to be taking place continuously in time and space even though discontinuous population movement is more realistic; (2) the plane of movement is assumed to be a featureless landscape without inhibiting barriers, such as mountain ranges; (3) statistical independence among individual movements is assumed even though the directions of sequences of moves are nearly always interrelated; (4) all points in the plane are assumed to be equally attractive when in reality some may be more attractive than others (Ammerman and Cavalli-Sforza 1979:286–287). However, as repeatedly stated in earlier chapters, oversimplifications such as these are normal characteristics of exploratory mathematical models. As the model is tested and elaborated, its assumptions are made increasingly more realistic whenever it is mathematically feasible. In this case the wave-of-advance model has proven rigorous enough to serve as the basis for simulation studies.

The BANDK 2 simulation model of Bandkeramik settlement patterns formulated by Ammerman and Cavalli-Sforza (1979:289–290) assumes that the shifting swidden type of farming system was adopted by Bandkeramik farmers, that this farming system affected their settlement pattern, and that the settlement pattern consisted of a linear sequence of sites with side branches at intervals to the main linear network. It is helpful to think of this network as a river with stream branches. Several constraining rules were built into the simulation program: (1) each run could only be initiated when a few locations at one end of the network were occupied and all other locations were open for occupation; (2) population growth within each "village" (location) could only expand along a logistic curve; (3) a new village was split off an existing village whenever a certain population size was reached; (4)

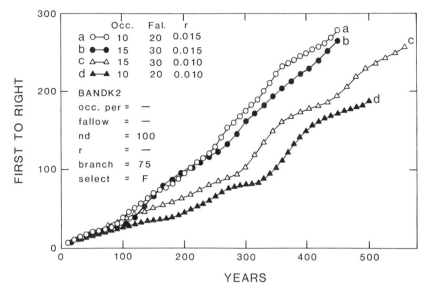

Figure 8.5 Simulation runs of wave-of-advance model. Source: Ammerman and Cavalli-Sforza 1979, figure 12.7.

every location could only be occupied for a specific period of time before it passed into a fallow period; (5) fallow periods were of a specific length; and (6) villages had to relocate to new territories at the end of each period of occupation (in other words they could not disappear).

Site locations within the network were allowed to take one of three states: occupied by a small village; unoccupied but available for settlement; and unoccupied and unavailable for settlement (in a fallow state). By allowing the two main variables of the model, growth rate and length of occupation-fallow period, to vary, distinctive patterns of advance were generated (Figure 8.5). These patterns provided additional insight into the general model. In addition, the model demonstrated how an outward spread of people and material culture could be set up and maintained through the processes of local population growth and migratory activity. These processes and the wave-of-advance model provide one possible explanation of the pattern of movement of farming into prehistoric Europe.

Enriching a General Model: A Least-Cost Model of the
Colonization Process

A least-cost rationale can also be used in building migration models. An
example is Stanton Green's decision-making model (1980) for low-density
agricultural populations in temperate forests. In Green's model, interactions
between settlement, demographic, and environmental variables are examined from a least-cost perspective to determine how they affect a fourth
variable, the flow of food resources into a sociocultural system, the subsistence system. In agricultural societies, soil fertility, distribution of suitable
farming soils, drainage, length of growing season, and many other variables
of the natural environment clearly affect the subsistence potential of a society. But the choice of a subsistence strategy is also affected by social organizational, economic, technological, and settlement system factors. For example, a society's settlement system affects the use of land resources by
defining land tenure and inheritance practices, property rights, and the size
and structure of the habitat that is exploited. Demographic variables such
as producer-consumer ratio, sex structure, and household size and composition affect agricultural strategies by directly influencing the organization of
labor and the composition of social roles within the society. It is advantageous in modeling the dynamics of a subsistence system to consider the interaction effects of all of these variables.

Green's least-cost model of the colonization process is an attempt to model
agricultural expansion as a form of subsistence change as expanding populations adjust to new physical and social environments. The theoretical focus
of the study is the identification of a web of processes that would account
for the characteristics of expanding agricultural systems and their interrelationships with their social and natural environments. To oversimplify an involved discussion, the "costs" of an agricultural system can be viewed as a
function of land and labor-capital investment costs. Varying proportions of
these two factors produce an array of production outputs for the system, as
illustrated by the substitution function in figure 8.6. The least-cost strategy
for a particular agricultural system is determined in the model by stipulating
that the less expensive factor in land and labor-capital investment costs will
be maximized and the more expensive factor minimized whenever possible.
Since a variety of information sources indicate that land is considered less
expensive than labor in nonmarket farming systems, the relative costs of the
two factors can be represented by the nonsymmetrical steep line x–y in fig-

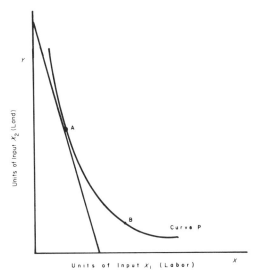

Figure 8.6 An agricultural substitution function in a least-cost model of colonization. Alternative inputs X_1 (labor) and X_2 (land) can be substituted for each other to produce a given amount of output represented by curve P. Point A represents an extensive land-use strategy, point B an intensive land-use strategy. Line x-y represents an isocost line, and its tangent at point A is the least-cost combination of land and labor. Source: Green 1980, figure 7.1.

ure 8.6, where y units of land cost are equivalent to x units of labor cost. The best least-cost solution for a system is graphically determined by moving the x–y line until it touches the substitution function. However, not all strategies are feasible, for the net value of a piece of land decreases to zero as the transportation costs to and from an area approach the productivity of the land. Therefore, a land constraint must be built into the graph to indicate when this point is reached; any point above the line will then represent an overextension of land and an expensive strategy. This line is graphed as m–n in figures 8.7 and 8.8.

Given this constraint, strategies can be assessed as either optimal or expensive. For example, strategy A in figure 8.7 is expensive, since the distance between the resource and the place of its use will incur prohibitive costs. The situation can be optimized by adopting one of several alternatives. First, as in C in figure 8.7, the population can fission into two separate communities and expand the exploited habitat. Or, as in D in figure 8.8, the land-use system can be intensified by decreasing the land input to

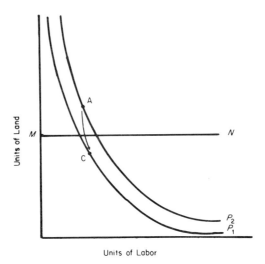

Units of Labor

Figure 8.7 An extensive strategy within a least-cost model of colonization. If increased production needs call for expansion beyond the marginal limits (represented by land constraint line m-n), the settlement can maintain a least-cost extensive strategy by decreasing its production needs through fissioning. Production needs then decrease from P_2 to P_1 and the least-cost land-use strategy from A to C. Source: Green 1980, figure 7.2.

within marginal limits while increasing the proportion of labor-capital-investment input. Both of these strategies would lower the land-labor-capital investment input below the m–n line as illustrated in figures 8.7 and 8.8. In nonmarket, low-density situations where new land is available for colonization, an extensive colonization strategy (figure 8.7) would be the optimal solution given the least-cost rationale of the model.

The model as developed so far has testable implications for settlement location, size, and longevity in any expanding agricultural system in a nonmarket, low-density situation. For example, frontier settlements should be located in areas where a demonstrable full extension of land is possible. Furthermore, in situations where new land is available, colonization should follow one of two usually consecutive patterns of settlement movement and land extension once production demands exceed agricultural output on a regular basis. In the first, settlements would move back and forth from one catchment area to another in a cyclical pattern of expansion as fields become exhausted and eventually reusable again. In the second, settlements would be pushed directionally outward to alleviate production demands as regional

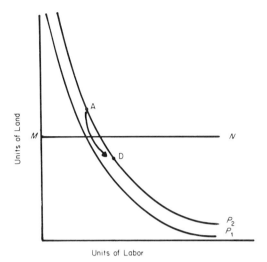

Figure 8.8 An intensified land-use system within a least-cost model of colonization. If production needs increase and land extension is not possible, land-use intensification will occur. This is represented by sliding down the production curve (P_2) from strategy A to D, thereby increasing the labor to land ratio and coalescing the lands being cultivated to within the marginal limits defined by land constraint m-n. Source: Green 1980, figure 7.3.

population density increased or environmental biodegradation began to occur. In cases where agricultural intensification rather than extension occurs, one would expect settlements to increase in size and perhaps to become more nucleated to meet the labor demands of intensified agriculture; regional population density would be expected to increase, too.

Following a discussion of the ecological features of temperate forest habitats, Green (1980:225–226) also summarizes more specific expectations for the colonization of temperate forests:

1. Agricultural colonization of temperate forest habitats will be characterized by extensive agricultural strategies.
2. The ecological response to this exploitative pattern will be an initial period of large increases in agricultural and natural net productivity, followed by a relatively long period (60–85 years) of low agricultural yield (under extensive strategies). If no irreparable destruction has occurred in the abiotic environment (e.g., erosion or degradation), the ecosystem would be expected to succeed to a mature secondary forest.

3. The long-term cultural adjustment to this culture-ecological situation will be to exploit the initial period of high productivity and, with the option of land extension, to allow the forest to regenerate before reexploiting it.

4. In the case of serial colonization, successive groups would be expected to use more intensive farming techniques to manage the simplified temperate ecosystems. The occupation of intensive farmers would result, in turn, in limiting the cycling of the initial colonizers and requiring their directional habitat expansion.

Green's least-cost model of the colonization process is an interesting example of the enrichment of a general model. Least-cost models are generally expressed as a relationship between procurement strategies and resource availability. This model has been enriched by including sociocultural and ecological variables. In the latter section of Green's study the fit of the model with real-world situations is evaluated with ethnohistorical data for the agricultural colonization of northern Savo in Finland and prehistoric data from the Neolithic in Denmark. Both comparisons lend support to the model and indicate areas where further adjustments would result in an even more realistic model of agricultural colonization in temperate forest habitats.

The Growth of Settlement Hierarchies

Anthropological archaeologists have borrowed a variety of models that help account for the development of regional service centers and the emergence of hierarchies of settlements. In accounting for these settlement developments, it is obvious that population growth may "fill in" a region through the processes of village fissioning, increased competition for land, and the resulting movement toward a more uniform distribution of settlements in space. But how do service centers develop and how can we account for the pattern or form of settlement hierarchies? This section examines several possible answers to these questions.

Central Place Models

Regional centers emerge for a variety of reasons. For instance, processes internal to a sociocultural system may lead to population growth, increasing division of labor and specialization, and the emergence of social stratification. One possible result of this scenario is the promotion of interregional trade and the formation of a service center for the exchange of materials and services. Alternatively, external contact and trade may stimulate regional specialization and the emergence of a center. Whether centers develop as a result of internal or external stimuli, where they develop depends in part on the existing degree of complexity of a settlement hierarchy. For example, when only small communities are present, centers are more likely to emerge near major resources, between ecological boundaries, or at the hub of potential transportation routes. When competition between large centers is already present, secondary centers generally emerge along the boundaries of the service areas of the larger centers in order to satisfy the demands of people living in the hinterland zones. The result of either of these processes is the growth of a center or market place in which exchange is not primarily controlled by institutional kinship obligations. In actual situations all of these processes may occur together, with the intensity of particular processes varying from one instance to another.

The body of theory that has developed around the study of the emergence of central places is called *central place theory* and the models that emerged from this theory are called *central place models*. In archaeology the pattern of distribution of sites in space has been compared with the ideal spatial distributions of the settlements in these models. When a reasonable fit is found, it is assumed, as a working hypothesis, that the primary functions and relationships of the sites are the same as those of the settlements in the model. Independent evidence is then gathered to test the correspondence of the model with archaeological reality. Of course the actual location and functions of settlements are generally the complex product of many interacting variables. As a result, a close correspondence between the ideal model and archaeological reality will frequently not exist. Whether distributional studies like these will lead to an understanding of the processes of center development will depend, therefore, on the complexity of the situation and the extent to which alternative settlement models predict distinct spatial expressions.

What processes are involved in the generation of settlement patterns through time? On a macrolevel, geographer Peter Haggett (1965:97) has distinguished between *deterministic* and *probabilistic* rationales in the modeling of settlement development through time. In deterministic models, settlements develop configurations "determined" by guidelines built into the logic of the settlement system. For instance, in figure 8.9 settlements mul-

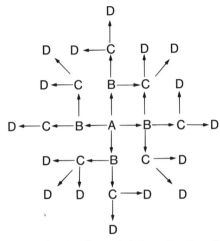

Figure 8.9   Idealized growth of a deterministic regional settlement pattern. A = origin, B = first stage, C = second stage, D = third stage.

tiply outward from a centrally located parent village through three systematic and ordered stages. In this deterministic model, expansion proceeds at the same rate and is symmetrical in all directions. The result is a uniform settlement pattern with a primary center surrounded by tiers of regularly spaced associated villages. In probabilistic models the form of settlement patterns results from random processes that are only restricted by certain "rules" of settlement location, such as the availability of water. If figure 8.9 represented a probabilistic model, site locations could occur at random in each of the growth phases, even though constraining variables would influence the spacing and function of individual settlements.

In interpreting settlement growth in particular regions, archaeologists typically play with several central place models to determine which has the closest fit with archaeological reality. For example, a deterministic model of settlement growth along a linear river and its tributaries implies a symmetrical pattern in which settlement expansion proceeds at first outward along the main river and major tributaries in a symmetrical manner; only later in the evolution of the system do as many villages appear on the tributaries as along the main river. By contrast, villages would be located at random throughout the riverine network in a probabilistic model, although constraining variables would keep the pattern from being completely random. In choosing between these and other competing models, archaeologists must explicitly state their rationales and the details of their models so that the testable result of each model is clear. As an illustration, Flannery (1976:173–180) suggested that the following set of deterministic rules may have generated the initial regular linear spacing between six villages in the Etla region of the Valley of Oaxaca during the Late San José phase (1000–850 B.C.) of the Formative (figure 8.10):

1. The first settlement in the region will locate near a good ford on the river near the center of the valley.
2. Expansion of settlement will be symmetrical upstream and downstream.
3. The first stage of expansion will take the form of spinoff communities along the river, midway between the original community and the limits of the valley; the second stage will involve new villages

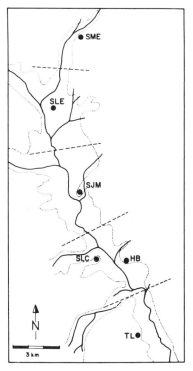

Figure 8.10 Linear pattern of site distribution along the Atoyac River during the Late San José phase in Mesoamerica. Source: Flannery 1976, figure 6.9.

spaced midway between the previously founded spinoff communities; and so on.

4. The pattern will continue to fill in until some socially determined spacing is reached (in the Etla case, about 5 kilometers).
5. Given that spacing, however, villages will have a latitude of perhaps 0.5 kilometers upstream or downstream to select a suitable place for settlement.
6. Other factors being equal, villages will locate on that side of the river which affords them the best catchment area for mountain hunting lands, piedmont wild plant collecting areas, and special resources such as salt, flint, or pottery clay.
7. As the pattern begins to fill in, some villages may place outlying *barrios* at or near some of these special resources.
8. Through time, some of those outlying *barrios* may grow to be villages in their own right.

Flannery's deterministic model explains how the regularly spaced linear series of villages evolved along the river. Now a well-planned test of the implications of this model with independent data can be carried out to determine the fit of the model with the dates of occupation of the villages, their specialized functions, and so on.

Generating Rank-Size Relationships By Stochastic Processes

What pattern of rank-size relationships between settlements in a hierarchy should be expected if stochastic processes were at work in the past? How should deviations from this pattern be interpreted? Studies by geographers (see Curry 1964, Thomas 1967, and Chapman 1970) suggest that rank-size relationships generated by stochastic processes will produce an exponential continuum of settlement sizes that are related to each other by a fixed ratio. Curry (1964), for example, used an entropy model to consider the total number of ways in which a population would be distributed among a fixed number of settlements if every settlement had an equal chance of attracting individuals within the population. The most probable state of the settlement-population system when entropy was maximized produced a rank-size relationship in which the population of the nth settlement in size was a constant ratio of the largest settlement's population. According to this analysis, the rank-size rule discussed in chapter 7 is an anticipated outcome of this "most probable" relationship (figure 8.11).

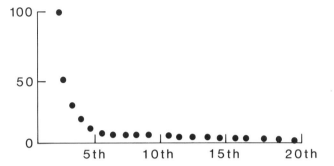

Figure 8.11 The rank-size rule. A graph with arithmetic axes showing hypothetical relations between site size and rank.

Thomas (1967) examined the effect of stochastic processes on rank-size relationships with the aid of a model that contained the rule: The number of people already in a settlement influences the number of people that will be attracted to the settlement in the future. Beginning with a set of normally distributed settlement sizes and the additional assumption that settlement size and population changes are determined by a very large number of independent variables that produce in aggregate a random effect, he demonstrated that larger centers will attract more people than smaller centers even though population growth was stochastically independent from one period to the next. Thomas' study also showed that the results of such a stochastic process would be a log-normal frequency distribution of population or settlement sizes. Ideally the rank-size line formed by plotting rank against size should produce a relatively flat curve with a smooth gradient, a curve reflecting an exponential continuum of settlement sizes.

In spite of these "ideal" conclusions, studies of actual settlement size distributions demonstrate obvious departures from an exponential continuum in size distributions. For instance, when a high degree of order and lower entropy are present, curves tend to be steep and have sharp gradients. Berry (1961) has named the two extremes of rank-size relationships the *rank-size* and the *primate*. The rank-size relationship is the ideal case discussed above, which has an exponential continuum of settlement sizes. By contrast, one or more very large settlements dominate a number of much smaller settlements in primate relationships. A stepped hierarchy among settlements with fixed sizes as predicted by classical central place theory would be an intermediate form. Beckman (1958) and others have suggested that if random variation is allowed to operate on a clearly stepped hierarchy, that is, on a situation resembling the ideal primate relationship, a blurring of steps will occur and a continuum of settlement sizes will eventually appear.

Berry (1961) has suggested that the movement from a primate to a rank-size relationship is related to a number of variables, including the length of time the urbanization process has been in effect and the complexity of economic and political systems. In earlier and simpler urban societies, fewer forces will be acting on the rank-size pattern. The result will be a primate situation with gaps in size in the settlement continuum. As the urbanization process continues and societies become larger and more complex, the number of forces acting on the rank-size pattern will increase. As a result, gaps in the continuum will close and the rank-size exponential curve will appear. Crumley (1976) has applied the theoretical insights in Berry's study to the growth of early states.

The most thorough examination of patterns of rank-size relationships among archaeological sites and their implications for the growth of hierarchies has been conducted by Hodder (1979). A range of stochastic processes was examined that could have produced rank-size relationships among twelve data sets, including Neolithic earthen long burrows, Early Dynastic sites from Iraq, Romano-British walled towns, and other settlement size distributions. A graph was constructed to illustrate the shape of the rank-size curve for each of the twelve data sets (see figure 8.12 for an example).

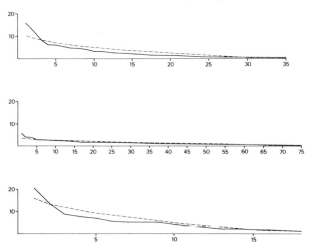

Figure 8.12 Rank-size curves. Actual (solid line) relationships between rank (horizontal axis) and size (vertical axis) for Early Dynastic sites from Iraq (i) to two sets of Late Helladic sites (j–k) compared with curves (dashed line) predicted by allocating sizes from the normal distribution. Source: Hodder 1979, figure 5.2.

Five growth processes were then used to simulate ideal curves obtained with the data sets. The analysis of the two sets of curves demonstrated that a variety of processes were probably responsible for the distribution of actual data. Only two of these processes will be discussed here.

The first process involved the random selection of imaginary sites from a normal distribution having the same mean and standard deviation in site sizes as the actual data. After every run of the simulation model, sites were ranked by size in descending order. After twenty runs for each data set, the average size values for each rank were calculated and plotted (figure 8.13). The best fit between actual and ideal curves occurred with information collected from Roman Fenlands sites. Both curves had little concavity, suggesting that there were few marked constraints on settlement formation and size in that particular settlement system. The fifth process modeled site size distributions according to central place theory, in which a clear, stepped hierarchy in both numbers and sizes of settlements is assumed. In this simulation the best fit between actual and ideal curves was obtained for Iron Age multivallate hillforts. The simulation suggests a contagious growth process within a constrained, nonrandom, settlement hierarchy.

Hodder introduced independent evidence to show that the rank-size curves obtained in both cases were the ones to be expected. Many of the more unreliable data sets did approach the ideal curve, in which entropy is maximized, even though in certain cases strongly centralized control and author-

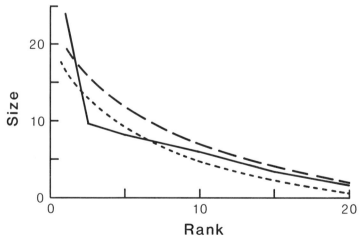

Figure 8.13 Simulation predictions (broken lines) for some Late Helladic Province sites (continuous line). Source: Hodder 1979, figure 5.3.

ity (as with the Early Dynastic data set) should have been expressed in a rank-size relationship closer to the primate pattern. However, a number of studies (e.g., Chapman 1970) have suggested that the random blurring of rank-size relationships will tend to increase entropy in a pattern and, therefore, obscure order. In archaeology, random blurring may occur, for example, when the size of settlements is incorrectly estimated or when noncontemporaneous settlements are included in a study.

The rank-size rule by itself is simply an empirical finding that lacks a theoretical basis. Hodder's theoretical investigation shows how deviations from the rank-size rule may occur, how they may be detected, and how they may be initially interpreted within the model-building process.

Total Society Simulation

A characteristic methodological principle of anthropological archaeology is the doctrine of functionalism, which states that sociocultural systems are composed of interdependent parts that cannot be fully understood apart from the whole. Total society simulations treat a variety of cultural subsystems together and provide, therefore, a test of the feasibility of actually reconstructing sociocultural wholes. Most total society simulations in archaeology focus primarily on settlement and subsistence systems, for the process of modeling these systems and comparing their system states to archaeological data has always seemed, as mentioned earlier, relatively straightforward in archaeology. Total society simulation should be distinguished from catastrophe theory. While both examine sociocultural systems such as cultures or societies as wholes, catastrophe theory does not reduce systems to subsystems in order to model the complex whole. Instead, societies, cultures, and other sociocultural units are viewed as dynamic systems having a global qualitative behavior of their own that evolves with time and that can be studied as a whole without examining their complex internal interactions (Renfrew 1979).

A classic example of total society simulation is Larry J. Zimmerman's computer simulation (1977, 1978) of settlement change in the Glenwood locality of western Iowa. Between A.D. 900 and 1400, the Glenwood locality was occupied by Central Plains tradition horticulturalists who located their lodges either in loose clusters on stream terraces or in straggling lines along ridges. Anderson and Zimmerman (1976) suggested the following algorithm to account for this settlement variability:

1. Populations culturally similar to those labeled Central Plains tradition began occupying the Glenwood locality between A.D. 800 and 900.
2. These people selected locations for their earthlodges on ridgelines, usually at some distance from their nearest neighbors.
3. Locations were probably in or near forested zones, where wild foodstuffs were hunted and gathered. Slash-and-burn horticulture was minimally practiced in gardens near the lodge.
4. Nuclear family structure was the predominant residence grouping, with matrilineal descent and proximal matrilocal residence.
5. This pattern remained stable until about A.D. 1200, when climatic change occurred.
6. Increasingly dry westerly winds brought decreased rainfall. The forested zones decreased in extent, especially on the ridges, causing a decrease in available resources.
7. Stress occurred on the subsistence base, giving rise to intensification of horticulture.
8. With horticulture as the primary subsistence base and the ridgelines too dry for such practices, subsistence activity focused on the stream floodplains and on low nearby hillslopes where the water sources were more consistent.
9. Lodge building locations shifted to these areas.
10. In an effort to save valuable garden lands, houses were built in small clusters and were larger in size to house extended families (from Zimmerman 1977:42).

While accounting for archaeological materials in the Glenwood locality, the algorithm as proposed by Anderson and Zimmerman is untestable, for operational definitions of terms and explicit statements of relationships between its major components are missing. Zimmerman (1977, 1978) attempted to provide the algorithm with a more detailed, conceptually dynamic form in a subsequent study.

Modeling Glenwood settlement variability began with the identification of salient components (natural environment, population, social organization, subsistence, the system's behavioral mechanism, and locational rules) and the integration of these components within a simple open-ended flowchart (figure 8.14). The procedures for computer flowcharting enable human locational decisions to be visualized as a dynamic process having im-

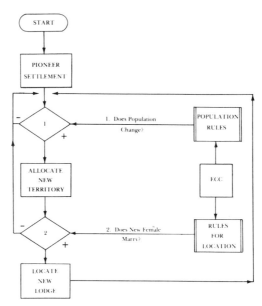

Figure 8.14 Simplified flowchart for simulation of settlement subsistence systems. Source: Zimmerman 1977, figure 2.

plications for settlement location through time. A simulation of Glenwood locality settlement-subsistence systems was then initiated by introducing one or more lodges into the flowchart, a process that could be replicated while the values of the components were being systematically changed. The resulting locations of the lodges were determined by the number of lodges introduced and the values assigned each component of the model.

Since the components of the settlement-subsistence system had to be made operational, the constituent elements and rules governing each component had to be conceived in very specific and logical ways. For example, (1) population size was controlled by rules for birth, death, and mating based on a neo-Malthusian model for population growth. As the number of people occupying a lodge increased, additional territory near the lodge was allocated. When a new family was started, both new territory and a new lodge were allocated according to the set of locational rules incorporated into the model. (2) The environmental component was divided into five resource-zone types after an examination of the varying potential of flora and fauna for the Glenwood population. The values of these zones as preferred habitat locations were altered too to simulate a climatic change, erosional processes, or change in the availability of natural resources. (3) The elements and rules that govern social organization were established by a careful examination of available ethnographic and archaeological evidence for the region. A matricentric social organization was assumed, whose characteristic features changed after the initiation of climatic stress around A.D. 1200. The predominant features of preclimatic stress social organization were nuclear or small extended family kinship groupings; family-owned hunting, gathering, and horticultural territories; locality exogamy; matrilineal descent; and proximal matrilocality, while climatic stress and postclimatic stress social organization was characterized by larger extended families; clan-owned exploitative territories; locality exogamy; matrilineal descent; and full matrilocality (Zimmerman 1977:75–76). The elements and governing rules of the other major components of the model were delimited in a similar manner. In each case the elements and governing rules were assumed to be hypotheses whose fruitfulness would be evaluated by the fit between the archaeological record in the Glenwood locality and the predictions that flowed from simulation runs.

A number of inferences about locational behavior in the Glenwood locality were made at the end of seven simulation runs: (1) the occupation of the locality by Central Plains tradition people was far shorter than suspected (based on the fit between actual and predicted numbers of lodges for different lengths of time); (2) climatic change, if it did occur, had little influence on settlement strategy (since the population density was too low to produce stress on the carrying capacity of the environment); (3) the known distribution of lodges could simply have been the result of preferred postmarital residence patterns rather than alterations in locational rules due to decreased availability of resources; and (4) locality population levels were far smaller than suspected (Zimmerman 1977:122–127; 1978:36).

The results of the simulation are not a source of proof about any particular event in the prehistory of the Glenwood locality. Nevertheless, they do demonstrate that, given specific assumptions and conditions, either certain ideas are feasible or they are not. For example, the model supports the idea that a satisfying rather than a maximizing process is sufficient to produce an approximation of known settlement variability in the Glenwood locality. People were apparently making locational decisions that would satisfy their biological needs and culturally defined desires rather than provide optimal solutions. Furthermore, the model generates a variety of testable predictions regarding the contemporaneity of lodges, their general sequence of occupation, the time span of the Central Plains tradition occupation of the locality, and so on.

The simulation model of locational processes in the Glenwood locality is not a very realistic model in its present form, for it incorporates very general and oversimplistic conceptions of a number of salient components, such as population and natural environment (Zimmerman 1977:128–133). However, these components can be made more specific and realistic as the model is elaborated and tested. Despite these almost inevitable drawbacks of exploratory total society models, the simulation has shifted the focus of investigations from artifacts and features toward their behavioral correlates within systemic contexts.

Summary

Chapter 8 introduces the study of sociocultural change through time at several levels. Archaeological materials do not exhibit change in themselves but must be arranged into chronological frameworks within particular research programs, such as cultural historical reconstruction or the cultural processual approach. Both approaches must be evaluated on the basis of how well they fulfill particular research objectives, but since cultural systems exhibit variability in structure and content, a sociocultural rather than a psychobiological approach to dissimilarities seems most reasonable.

In practice, most anthropological archaeology studies of sociocultural change focus not on the whole but on one or more properties of a subsystem. Dreenan's proposal of an environmental stress–cognitive inconsistency model for the collapse of the development of Olmec art was consistent with existing archaeological data, made testable predictions, and was supported by ethnographic examples of similar collapses. Hallowell has investigated the question of evolutionary roots of the cultural mode of adaptation. Assuming that self-awareness is essential for the emergence of a cultural mode of adaptation, he asked how it might be recognized in the archaeological record and concluded that it could be found in material objects that express symbols. Once these symbols are identified, the meaning would have to be inferred through ethnographic analogy, direct historic approach, and other modeling techniques. Brumfield tested the population pressure hypothesis with data from Formative sites in the Valley of Mexico. She concluded that both continued population growth and environmental deterioration were insufficient to account for changes and that sociopolitical factors provide a better explanation.

Most models accounting for patterns of settlement assume that distance exerts friction on migration. Other common models include wave-of-advance and least-cost rationale. Ammerman and Cavalli-Sforza's wave-of-advance model of Bandkeramik settlement patterns demonstrated how an outward spread of people and material culture could be set up and maintained through the process of local population growth and migratory activity, one explanation of the pattern of movement of farming into Mesolithic Europe. Green's decision-making model for low density agricultural populations in temperate forests examined interactions between settlement, demographic, and environmental variables from a least-cost perspective to determine how they affected a fourth variable, the flow of food resources into a system. This model was expanded to include sociocultural and ecological variables in the comparison of ethnohistorical data for agricultural colonization of northern Savo in Finland with prehistoric data from the Neolithic in Denmark.

Anthropological archaeologists typically play with several central place models for the development of regional service centers and emergence of hierarchies to determine best fit. Flannery suggested that a deterministic model generated the initial regular linear spacing between six villages in the Valley of Oaxaca during the Late San José phase of the Formative. Studies by geographers suggest that rank-size relationships generated by stochastic processes will produce an exponential continuum of settlement sites related to each other by a fixed ratio. But this is an extreme, and Hodder's study showed how deviations may occur from the rank-size rule, how they may be tested, and how they may be initially interpreted in the modeling process.

Total society simulations treat a variety of cultural subsystems together, focusing on settlement and subsistence systems. Zimmerman's computer simulation identified salient components and integrated them in a simple open-ended flowchart, supporting the idea that a satisfying rather than a maximizing process is sufficient to produce an approximation of known settlement variables in the Glenwood locality of western Iowa. Despite drawbacks, total society simulation has shifted the focus of investigation from artifacts and features toward their behavioral correlates within systemic contexts.

Suggested Readings

Among the many studies of sociocultural change in archaeology are the following interesting accounts:

Deetz, J. 1965. *The Dynamics of Stylistic Change in Arikara Ceramics*. Illinois Studies in Anthropology, No. 4. Urbana: University of Illinois Press.

Earle, T. and A. Christenson, eds. 1980. *Modeling Change in Prehistoric Subsistence Economies*. New York: Academic Press.

Eighmy, J. 1981. The use of material culture in diachronic anthropology. In R. Gould and M. Schiffer, eds., *Modern Material Culture*, pp. 31–49. New York: Academic Press.

Friedman, J. and M. Rowlands, eds. 1978. *The Evolution of Social Systems*. Pittsburgh, Pa.: University of Pittsburgh Press.

Hasler, F., J. Sabloff, and D. Runge. 1978. Simulation model development, a case study of the classic Maya collapse. In N. Hammond, ed., *Social Process in Maya Prehistory*, pp. 553–590. New York: Academic Press.

Hill, J., ed. 1977. *Explanation of Prehistoric Change*. Albuquerque: University of New Mexico Press.

Plog, F. 1974. *The Study of Prehistoric Change*. New York: Academic Press.

Renfrew, C. and K. Cooke, eds. 1979. *Transformations: Mathematical Approaches to Culture Change*. New York: Academic Press.

Tainter, J. 1977. Modelling change in prehistoric social systems. In L. R. Binford, ed., *For Theory Building in Archaeology*, pp. 327–351. New York: Academic Press.

Thomas, D. H. 1972. A computer simulation model of Great Basic Shoshonean subsistence and settlement patterns. In D. L. Clarke, ed., *Models in Archaeology*, pp. 671–704. London: Methuen.

Tilley, C. 1981. Conceptual frameworks for the explanation of sociocultural change. In I. Hodder, G. Isaac, and N. Hammond, eds., *Pattern of the Past*, pp. 363–386. New York: Cambridge University Press.

The growth of settlement hierarchies in archaeology is discussed by:

Chadwick, A. 1977. Computer simulation of settlement development in Bronze Age Messenia. In J. Bintliff, ed., *Mycenaean Geography: Proceedings of the Cambridge Colloquium, September 1976*, pp. 88–93. Cambridge, Eng.: Cambridge University Press.

Flannery, K. V. 1972. The cultural evolution of civilizations. *Annual Review of Ecology and Systematics* 3:399–426.

Hammond, N. 1975. Maya settlement hierarchy in northern Belize. *Contributions of the University of California Archaeological Research Facility* 27:40–55.

Hodder, I. and C. Orton. 1976. *Spatial Analysis in Archaeology.* New York: Cambridge University Press.

Renfrew, C. and K. Cooke. 1979. Holistic behavior and catastrophe theory. In C. Renfrew and K. Cooke, eds., *Transformations: Mathematical Approaches to Culture Change*, pp. 419–423. New York: Academic Press.

The debate over the relationship between population growth and social change can be found in:

Cowgill, G. 1975a. Population pressure as a non-explanation. In A. Swedlund, ed., Population studies in archaeology and biological anthropology. *American Antiquity* 40:127–131. Memoir 30.

—— 1975b. On the causes and consequences of ancient and modern population changes. *American Anthropologist* 77:505–525.

Dumond, D. 1965. Population growth and cultural change. *Southwestern Journal of Anthropology* 21:302–324.

Harner, M. 1970. Population pressure and the social evolution of agriculturalists. *Southwestern Journal of Anthropology* 26:67–86.

King, T. 1974. The evolution of status ascription around San Francisco Bay. *Ballena Press Anthropological Papers* 2:35–53.

Smith, P. E. L. 1972. Changes in population pressure in archaeological explanation. *World Archaeology* 4:5–18.

Spooner, B., ed. 1972. *Population Growth: Anthropological Implications.* Cambridge, Mass.: MIT Press.

PART THREE

Anthropological Archaeology As
Social Science

Anthropological archaeology is generally associated with the types of studies that have been reviewed in Part Two. However, there is another, though
still muted, trend in anthropological archaeology toward the acquisition of
general knowledge: knowledge about culture rather than about particular
cultures. A primary goal of the social sciences is the discovery of general
knowledge, knowledge that applies to all human societies or to all societies
of a specific type whenever and wherever they might occur. In chapters 2
and 3 this goal was identified with science *sensu stricto*. Part Three is concerned with the status of the claim that anthropological archaeology is or
can be a social science whose fundamental goal is the discovery of general
statements as well as scientific theory and knowledge. Can anthropological
archaeologists discover validated general statements and participate in the
social sciences in this sense? If not, is this due to the nature of the subject
matter (the archaeological record), to the inability of archaeologists to develop appropriate methodological tools, or to a confusion between the concepts of history and natural science?

It is frequently claimed that anthropological archaeology has made giant
strides toward becoming a true, exact science in the last three decades. This
claim has been made for a number of reasons: (1) specialized research projects have accumulated rapidly; (2) new theories, methods, and techniques
have been borrowed from other fields; (3) theorizing has become more
prevalent; (4) a new conception of science (logical empiricism or positivism) has been adopted; and (5) it is precisely with the natural science themes

of careful measurement, the search for laws, theory building, prediction, and experimentation that anthropological archaeology has been most concerned in recent years. But the writings of the more abstract theorists often have had little to contribute to theory and are not theoretical at all, at least as the term theory is understood by most philosophers of science. What is now called archaeological theory consists for the most part of general orientations toward data, such as the systems approach, the ecological approach, the spatial approach, or the cultural historical approach. Instead of suggesting clear, verifiable statements of relationships between specified variables, these theoretical discussions suggest types of variables that need somehow to be taken into account. Rather than being theoretical, they are methodological in that they are about the appropriateness of specific assumptions, methods, and techniques.

A related, basic problem is whether the sort of data described in site reports are sufficient for the advancement of scientific archaeology. Anthropological archaeology has clearly developed through time in the sense that observations in the field are more extensive. But has it led to cumulative scientific knowledge in that the pieces of knowledge gained fit together theoretically and empirically? Consider the following argument. Scientific theories are generally assumed to be composed of universal conditional statements about sets of phenomena, such as the rise of state-level societies or the intensification of agricultural practices. If this is so, theory is rarely the end product of archaeological research, for the typical results of site excavations are inductive inferences to the parameters of specific populations of artifacts and features. Thus neither comparisons between projects nor predictions to other cases can be easily made. As a result, individual projects rarely lead to cumulative scientific knowledge.

If a science of archaeology is possible, what would the structure of such a science be like? Although a range of possibilities exists, it would presumably consist of systems of interrelated general propositions of the type "Whenever or wherever A then B." Precise data and places could then be fitted into these causal or functional correlations. Chapters 9 and 10, which concern the formulation of propositions like these, are truly exploratory, since most research in anthropological archaeology is noncomparative and nontheoretical in a formal sense. Chapter 9 considers the potential of the comparative method in archaeology. Cross-cultural comparisons are important for a variety of reasons: (1) comparison is a means of discovering more general statements about cultural phenomena; (2) in the absence of the experimental method, comparison is the only means of testing general statements; (3) comparison is the primary source of the laws needed in the covering-law model of explanation; (4) unless comparison is made explicit there can be no theory in archaeology; and (5) to describe any sociocultural system or archaeological site, categories, terms, and concepts that transcend individual cases must be used. Since this list implies that comparison is inevitable, it should be done as explicitly and systematically as possible. Cross-cultural comparisons are approached in chapter 9 by reviewing general problems of the comparative method, examples of cross-cultural comparison, and evolutionary theory as a more extended example of the application of the comparative approach within anthropological archaeology.

Chapter 10 introduces the process of formal theory building. This process has always remained an ideal in science, a set of standards against which theories can be judged to assess their adequacy. An attempt is made to ascertain what formal theories in anthropological archaeology would look like. Since a wide variety of approaches to the formulation of theories has been proposed, the approach adopted is necessarily restricted and not a review of the range of available possibilities. In the chapter, the structure of formal theories is discussed, steps to building at least a rudimentary theory are laid out, and two sketches of the formalization process are provided.

Finally, is labeling anthropological archaeology a science just an effort to make it respectable by identifying it with the natural sciences? Is it a passing fancy, a sign of the times, or, more severely, a pretense? If it is a pretense, will it hinder the development of archaeology? Since generalization entails the loss of uniqueness and variegation, is this sacrifice worth the price? Will "it lead to a systematic neglect of the historical dimension in the explanation of human behavior, and does it set up ideals of explanation and goals whose pursuit can only lead to sterility, frustration and even intellectual corruption" (Dixon 1973:viii)? Philosophers of social science have debated these issues and the extent to which those sciences devoted to the study of human beings as conscious, social animals can adopt or adapt the proven methods of the physical sciences. Chapter 11 considers a few of the arguments in this debate by concentrating on differing conceptions of science, the concept of a scientific law, and possible barriers to the formulation of laws in the social sciences.

CHAPTER NINE

Cross-Cultural Comparisons

Comparative archaeology can be broadly defined as the systematic and explicit comparison of archaeological data from two or more sociocultural systems. Although the cross-cultural approach is rooted in the study of individual sociocultural systems, comparative archaeology is about the scope of application and the truth content of general statements and scientific theories. Comparativists try to discover or propose what is common to all past sociocultural systems, to only certain types of these systems, or to individual past sociocultural systems. Since generalizations to classes of sociocultural systems cannot be based on simple, unique cases, generalizations of this type in archaeology cannot be formulated without cross-cultural comparison (e.g., Renfrew 1974:93). Comparative archaeology is central to the task of universalizing archaeological theory and to the continual reassessment of general statements. If a science of human beings is possible, it might be argued, the route to its realization in archaeology is through comparative studies.

Cross-cultural comparisons are undertaken for a number of reasons, for instance the following: (1) They are the main means of testing statements that posit general functional relationships among elements within past and present cultures. Examples of general hypotheses are: "As technology evolves, the way of life of peoples improves"; "Higher levels of productivity will yield surpluses, which, in turn, generate higher levels of sociopolitical complexity"; "Sociopolitical organization varies with the natural habitat and the technoeconomic means of exploiting that habitat." Cross-cultural research tests general hypotheses like these by comparing their proposed relationships within a sample of cultures. (2) Cross-cultural comparative studies are also prominent conceptual tools in formulating generalizations, that is, in exploratory research. Social science is concerned with the general rather than the particular, but what is general is clearly difficult to determine a priori. Exploratory studies establish relationships among cultural and environmental variables and determine the universes within which they are applicable. The goal of exploratory research in comparative studies is to find out what is universal and just what universe the general statements apply to. Typical universes in archaeology include a particular community, a site, a culture area, all Neolithic societies, and all human (*Homo sapiens sapiens* or even *Homo*) societies. Comparative investigations are potentially a source of the concise lawlike statements that are essential to the construction of scientific theories and the deductive model of explanation and prediction. (3) Comparative studies are also an essential methodological tool in the construction of universal grammars of sociocultural behavior. Among the elements of these grammars are sociocultural types, developmental stages, levels of sociocultural integration, and similar processes, units of analysis, and other phenomena. (4) Finally, comparative macroarchaeology is a fundamental approach in constructing inferential histories of complex interacting networks of societies, culture areas, or countries. Cross-cultural statements are part of the constant interplay between theories, hypotheses, and observational data.

The statements that comparativists formulate express regularities among the association of cultural elements in forms such as "Where A, there B." But how can meaningful statements like these be made when we know that no two objects or events in either archaeological or systemic context are exactly alike? How can legitimate cross-cultural comparisons be made? The usual answers to these questions are based on a number of often implicit methodological presuppositions that underlie the comparative research program or approach. First, we all know that our everyday experiences seem to repeat themselves: we all participate in at least some recurring patterns of behavior. It seems reasonable to assume that other parallel patterns exist in many parts of the world and that similar patterns occurred in the past. Cross-cultural comparisons become possible when we concentrate on what is shared in these situations rather than on what is unique.

Second, the universe of social phenomena is assumed to be ordered rather than chaotic. Comparativists describe causal relations that actually exist in a deterministic universe; they do not impose order on a factually chaotic universe where order does not exist. Third, regularities among the association of cultural elements are assumed to be discoverable. Fourth, social phenomena are assumed to be ordered because of common problems that humans share in adapting to their natural surroundings, in living in groups, and in coming to grips with the unknown. All human communities must procure food to survive, procreate, and maintain social order. Cultures as complex adaptive systems are independent solutions to these common problems of human existence. Fifth, if general statements are variable, it is assumed that they will vary in predictable ways for clusters of communities sharing adaptively similar solutions in an ordered social universe. Sixth, it is assumed that the psychobiology of human groups has been a constant for at least the last 40,000 years.

The comparative method—the method of controlled comparison—is the poor cousin in most social sciences of the controlled experiment in the physical sciences. Comparative methodology, however, is the best available approach at the present time for controlling cross-cultural inferences. Archaeological studies should be an integral ingredient in this approach, for most cross-cultural surveys are synchronic or deal with very short periods of time within recorded history. They examine information from the ethnographic record and from societies in the world today. Archaeology adds the dimension of great time depth to cross-cultural comparisons and a sample of cultures uninfluenced by industrialization and modern colonial expansion. Until they are checked against prehistoric cultures and their universes of applicability established, cross-cultural generalizations of many kinds must remain suspect.

Problems of Cross-Cultural Comparison

Cross-cultural comparison can be instructively introduced by reviewing five of the many complex problems that comparativists must resolve. These five problems are: (1) Which units of analysis should be compared? (2) What properties should be studied? (3) What kinds of statement should be proposed or tested? (4) How should units of analysis be selected? (5) On what theoretical bases should comparisons be made? These questions incorporate the three basic questions that are asked of all comparative methods: What is compared, why, and how? Answers to these problems are best regarded as attempts to control systematic error or bias in comparative studies. Each of these five general questions is examined below.

Which Units of Analysis Should Be Compared?

Cross-cultural studies associate properties of sociocultural systems and their subsystems. Properties such as population size, degree of reliance on produced foods, and per capita energy consumption are examples. However, the value of a cross-cultural comparison depends to a significant extent on the degree of comparability of the units of analysis that make up a sample. Fairly precise theoretical and operational definitions of units of analysis are a necessary first step in ensuring comparability. The demand for explicit definitions in comparative studies forces archaeologists to define what they mean by and how they measure such terms as *tribe, intensive agriculture,* and *a culture.* Not only must these definitions be fairly explicit, they must be applicable cross-culturally. When anthropological archaeology is approached as a social science, the basic problem of the comparability of units of analysis magnifies the importance of precise and explicit concept definitions and measurements.

A characteristic approach to the identification of appropriate units of analysis in comparative studies involves the construction of a taxonomy of valid structural types. Comparisons are then made within these types and between one type and another. Examples of structural types include the band, the composite household, the segmentary lineage, the peasant community, the nuclear family, and the theocratic state. Just which of these types will be the most appropriate unit of analysis in a research project depends on the goals of the project; no one type is equally appropriate for all projects.

The possibility of employing structural types in comparative studies in archaeology that are comparable to units of analysis studied by other social scientists can be illustrated by the concept *society,* a unit of analysis frequently compared by sociologists. A society has been defined by Marsh (1967), a sociologist, as a group of interacting individuals that share at least four characteristics: (1) a definable territory; (2) a system of recruitment based largely on sexual reproduction; (3) a shared culture; (4) a high degree of political independence. Although the term *archaeological culture* has a notoriously wide range of definitions, an archaeological culture is roughly comparable to a society in this sense. Marsh's four characteristics of a society can be operationally defined in archaeology through measurements of artifacts, site distributions, and human skeletal populations. Although the validity of some of these measures may be low, archaeological cultures defined by these criteria can be included in large-scale cross-cultural comparisons that contain contemporary societies as defined at least by Marsh. Besides societies and their subsystems, even larger structural units, such as interregional exchange networks or religious institutions, can be used as units of analysis, too.

In each of these cases a judgment has to be made that the units of analysis in a sample are of the same kind. The comparison of unlike units, such as a small community of hunter-gatherers with a settled community of peasants enmeshed in a state-level sociopolitical system, unless justified, can produce misleading results. Hunter-gatherer communities are generally low on a scale of interdependence, while peasant communities are constrained and supported by economic, political, and religious ties. Even comparisons between similar structural types can produce misleading results if the scale of comparison is not similar, for the degree of association between two or more variables may depend on the scale of analysis used. A familiar example is the shifting association between houses and trails as the scale of analysis is changed. Their association may be practically nonexistent within a small area of a settlement. As the level of analysis is increased to the community and regional levels, the association becomes increasingly stronger. This is often called the *ecological fallacy,* the mental error committed by assuming that properties strongly (or weakly) associated at one level of analysis will be as strongly (or weakly) associated at other levels. Whether the association remains constant or varies is an empirical question (Harvey 1968).

In many cross-cultural studies, comparisons are made between subsystems or properties of communities from different levels of sociocultural integration. Examples are comparisons between modern industrialized societies and subsistence horticulturalists or among economic, educational, kinship, religious, political, recreational, or other social institutions. In these cases, cross-cultural comparisons may lead to uncertain results, for the range in variation of complexity of communities or institutions that are high on a scale of integration is greater than that of communities or institutions that are lower on the scale.

What Properties Should Be Studied?

A property may be a material or a nonmaterial feature of a culture or even a feature of the biological population, such as some aspect of the reproductive cycle, of basic nutritional requirements, of childbirth frequencies, and so on. A material manifestation (the curve of a pot), a set of rules (for post-marital residence), a relationship (between individuals of different status), and an institution (a religious ceremony) may all be properties in cross-cultural comparisons. Cross-cultural studies compare properties of sociocultural systems such as these, but which properties should be studied, how should they be defined or expressed, and how can they be isolated? Should properties of things or processes be compared?

In general, comparative research compares subsystems or particular aspects of the subsystems of sociocultural systems: the economic, demographic, and religious subsystems are examples. The properties that are compared in these studies are *universal* rather than *culture-bound* terms. *Synders*, a particular projectile point type in the American Midwest, and *Oneota*, an archaeological culture group, are culture-bound terms: they are specific to an archaeological culture or culture group that is delimited in space and time. *Sharp point* and *horticulturalist* are universally applicable terms: they are *culture-free* concepts that could have meaning in any social system. Here abstractions such as society, cultural pattern, structure, process, and house form prove useful, for generalization requires repeatable, identifiable units that tend to have a limited number of forms (Renfrew 1974:93).

A related issue in comparative research in anthropology is whether emic or etic concepts should be used when making comparisons. Emic concepts are definitional categories of a people whose culture or cultural remains are being studied; emic concepts are elements of their culture. Etic concepts are definitional categories that are imposed on the cultural practices or remains of a people from the outside; they are elements of the observer's culture. Prehistoric archaeologists obviously must impose concepts on the material they study. In so doing they run the risk of imposing their own culturally biased definitions of concepts, such as cannibalism or money, on the materials they study. The significance of the etic-emic issue for archaeological research is amplified in chapter 11.

The data of comparative archaeology are measures ideally made on universally applicable scales. When these scales are not available, their development becomes a fundamental goal of research. The nominal scale can be used to compare the presence or absence of one or more properties cross-culturally. One such scale is hunter-gatherer, food-producer, and industrial nation. But universalization is ideally achieved by expressing properties of social systems or material objects in terms of ordinal, interval, or ratio scales. Although measurements on interval and ratio scales, such as the metric system or an analogue scale of shapes, are preferred because of their greater statistical power and theoretical value, most comparative measures in the social sciences are still expressed in terms of ordinal scales, in terms of small, medium, and large, for example, rather than 1, 10, and 50 acres. Still, a valid ordinal scale is more powerful and valuable than a nominal scale measure. For instance, frequency of warfare, extent of political authority, and intensity of food-production are more suitable for comparative analyses than warfare, political authority, and food-production. However, the goal remains of measuring these variables along interval or ratio scales, for variation along these scales provides greater precision of comparison and resolves the problem of borderline cases where, for example, hunter-gatherers plant some crops.

Determining how to measure the presence or degree of a property of a prehistoric sociocultural system and how to make this measure universally applicable are formidable problems in comparative archaeology. Of course measures of theoretical variables are constrained by limitations of the archaeological record. But the most important limiting factor in comparative archaeology today is the lack of explicit theoretical and (especially) operational definitions for many common terms, such as *food producer* or *hunter*. Since these terms are used with many different theoretical meanings and measurements in mind, it is seldom apparent what is being compared. This is not a problem unique to archaeology, however, for the problem of precise, explicit, concept definition plagues comparative studies in all of the social sciences.

Many universally applicable variables can be measured with relative ease in archaeology. Examples are the acreage of settlements, the length of houses, and the capacity of ceramic containers. Furthermore, most of these variables can be measured with standard interval and ratio scales, such as the metric system. Other more abstract properties, such as population size, degree of reliance on produced foods, and social complexity may also be measured and compared, even though archaeologists usually have to invent appropriate scales themselves. Scales for concepts like these have been developed in many instances a number of times. In these cases it is not clear whether each scale measures a different variable or not. For example, the variable *population size of a community* has been measured by equating population size with the total roofed dwelling area in square meters divided by 10 m^2 (Leblanc 1971:210) and with the formula, site area $= (0.23 \pm 0.68) \times$ population^b, where b $= 1.96$ (figure 9.1; Wiessner 1974:343).

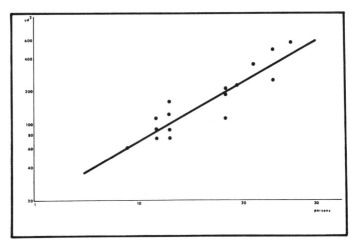

Figure 9.1   Relationship between settlement area (y-axis) and population (x-axis) of Bushmen camps. Area = a × population[b] plotted on double logarithmic paper, where a = −0.23 ± 0.68 and b = 1.96; r = .91. Source: Wiessner 1974, figure 4. Reproduced by permission of the Society for American Archaeology from *American Antiquity* 39(2):343–350.

The concept *social complexity* has been measured by Naroll's Social Complexity Index and by Freeman's Folk-Urban Scale. Naroll's index equates social complexity with the weighted average score on the variables settlement size, number of team types, and number of craft specialities (which he operationally defines), while Freeman's scale is based on eleven traits, including the presence or absence of trade with other societies and the presence or absence of a complex, unambiguous written language (Naroll 1956; Tatje and Naroll 1973; Freeman 1957). Definitions of both concepts use different sets of variables in their theoretical and operational definitions. Are the measures compatible? Are the same underlying theoretical abstractions—population size and social complexity—being measured? Are the concepts equally valid measures? The development of universal operational measures for archaeology's more abstract terms is an exciting research frontier in which success is essential to the further development of comparative archaeology.

What Kinds of Statement Should Be Proposed or Tested?

Cross-cultural studies search for or test general statements that are hypotheses varying in form, scope, and degree of integration within a body of theory. Some hypotheses state that an event or object has a particular property. Typical logical forms for these hypotheses are "All A's are B's" and "Where A, there B, there C. . . ." "All Neolithic societies are food-producing societies" is an example. But this form of univariate, deterministic relationship often states a tautology (as in this case), for property B or C may be contained within the definition of A. As a result, the hypothesis is true or false according to the definition of A that has been used. Part of the definition of a Neolithic society is food production, for instance. This difficulty may be avoided by concentrating on the relationships between two or more variable properties. Hypotheses of this type have forms such as "The greater the A, the greater the B" and "The less the A, the greater the B." These statements may concern the functional relationships between two, three, or a whole series of properties of social phenomena. As mentioned in the last section, greater precision is introduced when the compared properties are expressed as quantitative variables.

Most hypotheses formulated by archaeologists are about specific archaeological cultures or culture groups. They pertain to subsets of societies rather than to societies at a particular level of integration (all hunter-gatherers, for instance) or to all societies. Although hypotheses like these are at the very heart of cultural historical research, they limit comparison and the formulation of ever more general theories by introducing proper names (nominal terms) and traits rooted in specific cultural-historical contexts. This problem is similar to that of culture-bound properties. The scope of the hypotheses can be universalized by generalizing their terms and freeing their boundary conditions from specific spatial-temporal contexts.

A more fundamental problem arises when traits or regularities are viewed as conditioned by their cultural historic context—as if their meaning is dependent on the total sociocultural context in which they occur and they are inseparable elements within this context. These assumptions form the basis of the *functional argument* against cross-cultural studies. Cross-cultural comparisons are usually synchronic in that they compare systems at points of time or they deal with very short periods of time. In either case, systemic contexts are reconstructed and a functional or causal nexus between empirical regularities and aspects of these contexts are searched for or tested. Empirical regularities lose their meaning, according to the functional argument, when they are lifted out of their systemic contexts. As a result, comparison itself becomes meaningless. A methodological principle hidden in this argument states, "Every culture is a unique configuration"; the methodological rule that follows is "Every culture must be examined as a totality and only in terms of itself." This relativist position assumes that no two cultures are alike, that it is analytically indefensible to abstract parts from wholes, and that meaning is distorted if elements are abstracted for purposes of comparison.

The question of the inviolability of cultural wholes is an ideological issue that has been heatedly debated in anthropology. Comparativists agree with the obvious statement that no two cultures are alike just as no two atoms or masses are alike. But they insist that the comparativist's research program is methodologically legitimate, heuristically suggestive, and scientifically fruitful. If correlations between properties are persistently low across a sample, they are more likely to argue that the results are due to the existence of coincidence, intervening variables, functional equivalents, multiple or parallel causality, or any combination of these factors rather than abandon the core principles of their program.

The functional argument may be answered in various ways. For instance, all parts of a culture may be functionally related in some manner, but some parts may be more functionally independent than others. Harsanyi (1960), for example, has argued that the economic subsystem has a higher degree of autonomy than other subsystems. Furthermore, one might maintain that whether or not a structure of invariant empirical relations exists in a class of systems is a question whose answer cannot be determined by an a priori dictum, for it is an empirical question. All social sciences (and indeed all sciences) grapple with the problem of what can be left out and what must be included from the context of a phenomenon when it is isolated for study. If none of these arguments is convincing, ideal structural types such as a mythical ideal hunter-gatherer society may be proposed. In this approach, ideal social and environmental conditions are imaginatively constructed and hypotheses generated within the context of these conditions, even though they may never occur in reality. Bridging arguments that connect the model with actual cultures are then constructed to test the implications of the ideal type.

Hypotheses, besides varying in form and scope, may occur either in isolation or as a logically deducible statement of a theory. However, the strong statistical support of an isolated hypothesis may be the result of accidental association within a sample. Observed regularities are not in themselves evidence of a causal nexus; there is no necessary connection between experimental uniformities, or statistical correlations, and their antecedent events. As the next chapter will indicate, one of the purposes of a theory is to provide explanations or a contextual position for hypotheses. Since a hypothesis has a contextual position within a theory, the probability of its strong confirmation being in error is greatly reduced, especially if there is strong support for other hypotheses within the theory too. A goal of science, then, for this reason and others, is the integration of hypotheses within the framework of theories.

In summary, a goal of cross-cultural studies is to search for or test hypotheses that relate two or more variables, that are universal in scope, and that are deducible from a systematic and consistent body of theory.

How Should Units of Analysis Be Selected?

G. P. Murdock once estimated that as many as 5,000 human societies have existed since the emergence of our species, *Homo sapiens*. Ideally, a complete enumeration of this universe would be desirable so that random samples could be drawn, for only worldwide samples extending far back into the past will yield universal rather than culturally specific comparisons for the concepts *society* and *culture*. Sampling remains a major problem in comparative archaeology, however. If the standard statistical measures of association are to have any meaning, samples must be representative and randomly selected. Nevertheless, many archaeological data are inaccessible: sites have been destroyed, reports have never been written, the contents of extant sites remain unknown. There are undoubtedly errors in published reports, too. Even if personal bias, accidental loss, and other sources of error were eliminated, the problem of obtaining statistically valid samples would still loom large in comparative archaeology.

The crux of cross-cultural sampling was pointed out by Sir Francis Galton in 1889 in a now famous exchange with Sir Edward Tylor following Tylor's pioneering paper before the Royal Anthropological Institute on the cross-cultural survey method (Tylor 1889:272). The problem, which is now known as *Galton's problem* or the *Tylor-Galton problem,* involves the requirement of independence in statistical testing. In statistical testing, the theory of probability provides the theoretical bases for evaluating chance as a factor in the origination of seemingly significant relationships. However, a criterion for the use of the theory of probability is that all units in selected samples must be uninfluenced by each other. If this criterion is violated, the results of tests of association may be spurious. A basic research problem is distinguishing between those regularities in tests that are the result of functional relationships within cultures, for example, from those that are the result of historic connections between cultures. How do we know whether every society (or other structural type) in our samples represents an independent way of life? Are we discovering functional associations (*adhesions,* in Tylor's graphic term) independently arrived at or the effects of cultural diffusion? This is Galton's problem, a problem that must be solved in all comparative studies in the social sciences.

A number of attempts have been made to solve Galton's problem. Only a few are mentioned here (see Naroll, Michik, and Naroll 1974 for a summary of solutions). To understand more clearly what is required in a solution to Galton's problem, let us restate the problem in stastistical terms. Rigorous tests of theories or general statements involve statistical tests of the significance of measures of association. These tests establish the probability that chance alone could have caused the levels of association found. Since the samples in such tests must be randomly selected, (1) all items in the samples must have an equal or known probability of being included in a sample and (2) all items must be independent; the selection of one item must in no way influence the selection of any other in a sample. Both of these conditions can be met and the problem solved by enumerating the population of interest and numbering it and then drawing the sample from a table of random numbers. In anthropology, however, it is usually impossible to enumerate all human sociocultural systems in a universe, for not all of these ways of life in communities have been described or are known. In addition, the term *sociocultural system* has not yet been precisely enough defined for comparative studies.

Let us assume, for the sake of argument, that the unit of analysis has been adequately defined and that the sample population is representative of the universe from which it was drawn. The problem that remains to be solved is Galton's problem—the statistical requirement for sampling: it is necessary to demonstrate that the traits in a study are independent of each other and did not diffuse as a unit. Once independence has been established, we can argue that significant associations between traits are the result of recurring functional relationships that arise in response to similar human conditions. One solution is to perform a linked-pair test in which the geographically closest units in a sample are compared for possession of the trait or traits being tested. In this solution it is assumed that high positive or negative occurrences in adjacent pairs as measured by an association coefficient and evaluated by means of a chi-square test indicate that the trait or traits were diffused in the sample. When both traits in a partial association are affected, the lack of independence may be removed by the use of measures of partial association (Naroll, Michik, and Naroll 1974:128). A simpler solution is to apply the three-degree rule, in which all units in the sample must be at least three degrees of latitude or longitude from each other. This rule helps ensure that variations of the same society or culture are not included in the same sample. In general, comparativists regard tests for Galton's problem as effective and the resulting samples as remarkably representative.

Some writers have discounted Galton's problem. (e.g., Ember 1971; Schaefer 1974). For example, Schaefer et al. (1971) found no statistically significant difference between samples chosen by a stratified method to eliminate diffusion bias and those chosen randomly. These results seem to apply to both correlations of traits and frequency distributions. If these arguments are accepted, either the totality of available units or units selected by random sampling can be used with equal effectiveness. This may be the result, however, of the small size of most cross-cultural sample populations and the tendency of the units in the populations to be widely separated from each other in space and (to a lesser degree) in time.

A more common and alternative sampling strategy within anthropology is the intensive small-scale comparison of societies or other units within a geographical region called a culture area. A *culture area* is a geographical region within which a fairly large number of historically and ecologically related societies exist or have existed. Each of the societies or other structural types within a culture area is likely to differ in some cultural traits but, for these reasons, to share some traits as well. Generalizations are made by studying the pattern of this intraregional variety and asking such questions as, What factors led to the emergence of this societal type in this particular cultural-historical setting? or Were social structural or technoeconomic factors most important within this culture area? A classic study of this type is Symmes' study (1962) of emerging Plains Indian societies.

Making comparisons within delimited culture areas rather than worldwide samples is preferred by many comparativists for several reasons. First, constants are naturally present. Since each unit of analysis has presumably been affected by similar environmental and historical influences, controls exist within the culture area itself. By definition, too, a culture area is more likely to contain similar cultures and other structural types. Regional comparisons provide a quasiexperimental situation in which some variables are held constant while others are being studied. Second, the regional approach to comparative studies facilitates actual field work when new data are being collected since the units of study are close together. Third, the universe of societies is likely to be better known in well-worked culture areas than it is for worldwide comparisons where data are often unavailable.

Comparative studies within regional and worldwide universes are not incompatible. Hypotheses formulated within the framework of a well-known culture area are a source of research questions that can be extended to ever more inclusive universes by gradually generalizing the hypotheses. By extending regional hypotheses, culture historians learn whether the processes at work within their culture areas are unique or whether certain institutional or trait configurations have arisen independently more than once. The study of the similarities and differences among sets of historically related archaeological cultures is a legitimate research goal in archaeology, too. Since the comparative scope of universes in archaeology is wider, the extension of general hypotheses formulated in archaeology has intriguing possibilities for the development of anthropological theory.

A variety of sampling techniques has been used in selecting units for comparison. In general, stratified sampling has been found to be more appropriate than simple random sampling for most types of comparative analyses. The most commonly selected criteria for stratifying universes have been geographic or cultural areas or levels of sociocultural integration. Even the availability of information in a library has been used to stratify some universes.

On What Theoretical Bases Should Comparisons Be Made?

Ideally, cross-cultural comparison should be a process guided by theoretical presuppositions rather than simply a matter of exploratory fishing with statistical tests of association and independence. What theoretical positions underlie taxonomies of structural types in anthropology? Are there coherent bodies of theory in archaeology from which hypotheses can be derived for comparative testing and to which empirical comparative studies can be related? Although general theories are few and far between in archaeology, testable general statements have been generated by processual archaeology, neoevolutionism, nineteenth-century unilinear social evolution, and other research programs. Still other, isolated, general statements that lack a systematic and explicit theoretical basis can easily be found by paging through culture histories and site reports. These statements are generally employed to explain phenomena in archaeological and systemic contexts as if they were established covering laws. Examples are: "Generally speaking, the more sedentary the society, the larger and more permanent the structures it builds" and "Hunting and gathering tribes are usually well fed and unobsessed by food."

Some Cross-Cultural Comparisons

What are cross-cultural comparisons like? How are they made? What kinds of results do they provide? This section and the next provide typical examples of cross-cultural comparisons and discuss the implications of these studies for archaeological research. As we will see, most cross-cultural statements are tendency statements (Whenever A, then B a significant number of times) that only apply to most cultures, at most times, and in most places.

Societal Characteristics: Frequencies and Percentages

Many comparativists have been interested in the extent to which societal types correlate significantly with specific cultural traits. Can we expect to find patterned differences among societal types by geographical region or do the idiosyncracies of the natural and social environment of a society have little influence on the configuration of its cultural traits? Archaeologists have paid little direct attention to this question in their own analyses of the archaeological record, although they have borrowed the conclusions of comparative studies by other social scientists as principles underlying their models.

A vast amount of systematic information on human societies on a worldwide basis has been coded in the Human Relations Area Files (HRAF). Information from the files has been published in the *Ethnographic Atlas* (Murdock 1967a, 1967b), in the journal *Ethnology* (founded by George Peter Murdock), and in various other sources (e.g., Bourguignon and Greenbaum 1973). Categories of information on hundreds of societies from all parts of the world are included in the HRAF data banks. Most of this information was gathered from ethnographic reports, the records of explorers and missionaries, and the reconstructions of historians. The sample of human societies, which is considered a sample of world societies, includes information on over 900 societies, ranging in time from the early historic to A.D. 1960. Although about 93 percent of these societies date to periods since 1850 (and most of these to the twentieth century), the Icelanders of the eleventh century A.D. are included, as are three ancient societies (Ancient Egypt in 1400 B.C.; Babylonia in 2000 B.C.; the Hebrews in 800 B.C.). As might be expected from the diversity of sources, the quality of information in the HRAF is uneven. Still, the files remain the best available sample of human societies, and significant insights have been derived from looking at cultural phenomena on a worldwide basis.

The coded information for the sample in the HRAF has been broken down into categories, such as population size, craft specialization, beliefs about God, and presence of class systems. One of the most frequent uses of this large mass of information has been the exploratory search for significant correlations. Usually, these correlations have been sought between societal types and cultural traits. These studies provide archaeologists with a rich source of insight that can be incorporated into the research process during the model-building phase. Examples are Jochim's set of models (1976) of hunter-gatherer subsistence and settlement, Wilmsen's mathematical model (1973) of the spacing of hunting bands, and Tuggle's investigations (1970) of exogamy. Several studies are reviewed here to demonstrate the potential of the approach. In these studies no attempt at correlation is made and all distributions are in the form of totals and percentages. Since only one archaeological study using a whole-world sample has been attempted (Schaefer 1977), examples will be taken from cultural anthropology and sociology.

Correlates of Societal Types

One approach to studying the distributions of cultural phenomena is to distribute societies among basic societal types and then to search for significant associations between societal characteristics and individual societal types. In a study by the Lenskis (1974), for example, 694 societies from all parts of the world were distributed among six basic societal types: hunting and gathering (151), simple horticultural (76), advanced horticultural (267), agrarian (both simple and advanced) (96), fishing (44), and herding (both simple and advanced) (60). Tables 9.1 to 9.3 show the correlations between

Table 9.1 Median-Size Communities and Societies by Societal Type

Type of Society	Median Size of Communities	Median Size of Societies	Number of Societies *
Hunting and gathering †	40	40	93–62
Simple horticultural	95	95	48–45
Advanced horticultural	280	5,800	107–84
Agrarian	‡	over 100,000	58–48
Fishing	60	60	20–22
Herding	55	2,000	17–22

SOURCE: Lenski and Lenski 1974, table 5.2.
* Since data are seldom available for all 915 societies in the files, this column indicates the number of societies for which data were available and on which the statistics are based. The first of the two figures indicates the number of cases on which the median size of communities is based, the second, the number for the median size of societies.
† In this table and in the following two tables, all the hunting and gathering societies referred to are *advanced* ones.
‡ Murdock's method of coding community sizes does not permit one to give a precise figure for the median size of communities in agrarian societies.

Table 9.2 Beliefs About God by Societal Type (in Percentages)

Type of Society	Beliefs * A	B	C	D	Total	Number of Societies
Hunting and gathering	60	29	8	2	99	85
Simple horticultural	60	35	2	2	99	43
Advanced horticultural	21	51	12	16	100	131
Agrarian	23	6	5	67	101	66
Fishing	69	14	7	10	100	29
Herding	4	10	6	80	100	50

SOURCE: Lenski and Lenski 1974, table 5.4.
* A = no conception of Supreme Creator; B = belief in a Supreme Creator who is inactive or not concerned with human affairs; C = belief in a Supreme Creator who is active in human affairs but does not offer positive support to human morality; D = belief in a Supreme Creator who is active and supports human morality.

Table 9.3 Presence of Slavery in Societies by Societal Type (in Percentages)

Type of Society	Percentage Having Slavery	Number of Societies
Hunting and gathering	10	142
Simple horticultural	14	66
Advanced horticultural	83	243
Agrarian	54	84
Fishing	51	43
Herding	84	50

SOURCE: Lenski and Lenski 1974, table 5.5.

these societal types and the dimensions of population size, religious beliefs, and social inequality.

Correlates of Geographical Regions

The Lenskis' study involved a sample of world societies distributed among basic societal types. Information from studies like this provide archaeologists with expected associations among cultural traits and societal types, and, importantly, with basic criteria for defining societal types in prehistory. Correlates of societal types distributed throughout the world can also mask, however, the patterns that are peculiar to particular ethnographic areas. Are there interesting and significant regional variations among societies?

Bourguignon and Greenbaum (1973) surveyed societal characteristics by distributing 863 societies into six major ethnographic regions of the world on the basis of the geographic location of the societies. The six regions were sub-Saharan Africa, the Circum-Mediterranean, East Eurasia, Insular Pacific, North America, and South America. In this study, statistical data on a variety of societal characteristics were summarized for each region. Tables 9.4 to 9.6 show the relative importance of dependence on hunting, types and intensity of agriculture, and settlement patterns. In Bourguignon and Greenbaum's study, a characteristic profile of cultural traits began to emerge for the various world regions that is useful in distinguishing one major world area from another. The fact that characteristic patterns peculiar to particular ethnographic areas emerged lends support to the integrity and potential value

Table 9.4 Degree of Dependence on Hunting

Code	Percentage of Dependence	Total No.	Total %	Sub-Saharan Africa No.	Sub-Saharan Africa %	Circum-Mediterranean No.	Circum-Mediterranean %	East Eurasia No.	East Eurasia %	Insular Pacific No.	Insular Pacific %	North America No.	North America %	South America No.	South America %
1	0–25%	662	77	229	96	96	100	85	90	117	92	73	33	62	70
2	26%–45%	151	18	7	3	–	–	8	9	9	7	108	49	19	21
3	46%–75%	38	4	2	1	–	–	1	1	1	1	26	12	8	9
4	76%–100%	12	1	–	–	–	–	–	–	–	–	12	6	–	–
	Total	863	100	238	100	96	100	94	100	127	100	219	100	89	100

SOURCE: E. Bourguignon and L. S. Greenbaum, *Diversity and Homogeneity in World Societies* (New Haven: HRAF Press, 1973), table 2.

NOTE: 1 = hunting and gathering; 2 = simple horticultural; 3 = advanced horticultural; 4 = agrarian.

Table 9.5 Type and Intensity of Agriculture

Code	Type	Total		Sub-Saharan Africa		Circum-Mediterranean		East Eurasia		Insular Pacific		North America		South America	
		No.	%	No.	%	No.	%	No.	%	No.	%	No.	%	No.	%
1	Casual agriculture	29	3	–	–	5	5	6	6	1	1	9	4	8	9
2	Shifting agriculture	328	38	170	71	13	14	28	30	22	17	33	15	62	70
3	Horticulture	84	10	–	–	–	–	1	1	80	63	–	–	3	3
4	Intensive agriculture	236	27	60	25	75	78	47	50	16	13	32	15	6	7
5	Complete absence of agriculture	186	22	8	3	3	3	12	13	8	6	145	66	10	11
	Total	863	100	238	100	96	100	94	100	127	100	219	100	89	100

SOURCE: E. Bourguignon and L. S. Greenbaum, *Diversity and Homogeneity in World Societies* (New Haven: HRAF Press, 1973), table 8.
NOTE: Code the same as in table 9.4.

Table 9.6 Settlement Pattern

Code	Type of Settlement	Total No.	Total %	Sub-Saharan Africa No.	Sub-Saharan Africa %	Circum-Mediterranean No.	Circum-Mediterranean %	East Eurasia No.	East Eurasia %	Insular Pacific No.	Insular Pacific %	North America No.	North America %	South America No.	South America %
1	Migratory bands	61	7	8	3	10	10	6	6	10	8	16	7	11	12
2	Scattered neighborhoods	176	20	91	38	22	23	12	13	34	27	7	3	10	11
3	Seminomadic or semi-sedentary communities	208	24	11	5	11	12	19	20	3	2	147	67	17	19
4	Compact, permanent towns or villages, or complex towns with outlying settlements	405	47	124	52	53	55	52	55	79	62	49	22	48	54
5	Compact, impermanent villages shifting locations every few years	13	2	4	2	–	–	5	5	1	1	–	–	3	3
	Total	863	100	238	100	96	100	94	100	127	100	219	100	89	100

SOURCE: E. Bourguignon and L. S. Greenbaum, *Diversity and Homogeneity in World Societies* (New Haven: HRAF Press, 1973), table 18.
NOTE: Code the same as in table 9.4.

of large-scale, cross-cultural studies. However, in contrast to world societies as in Murdock's sample (1967a), the information derived from this study is applicable only to the known cultural universe.

Associations Between Floor Plan and Cultural Features

The large-scale, cross-cultural studies that we have reviewed have been designed by social scientists as exploratory tools within the framework of their own research projects. They have not been particularly sensitive to problems of archaeological research or especially directed toward the study of material culture. A few frequency-and-percentage studies have been carried out, however, by archaeologists or by other social scientists interested in the interpretation of the archaeological record. As in other cross-cultural studies, these studies first attempt to define significant cross-cultural regularities between material culture and social systems in the world sample or within specific geographic regions. The regularities discovered are then used in the reconstruction and interpretation of prehistoric social patterns (e.g., Chang 1958, 1962).

Comparison has focused in many of these studies on the association between floor plan or size and other cultural features. Ember's study (1973) of floor area sizes as indicators of matrilocal and patrilocal residence in precontact North America has already been mentioned in an earlier chapter. In another study, Whiting and Ayres (1968) treated floor plan as an independent variable from which other cultural features could be predicted. A series of hypotheses associating the independent variable with a variety of dependent variables was then tested in a sample of 136 societies distributed throughout six ethnographic regions in the following frequencies: Africa (10), Circum-Mediterranean (16), East Eurasia (25), Insular Pacific (22), North America (38), South America (25). Predictions were then made from each of these summary associations. For instance, Given a society with large and/or multiple-roomed rectilinear houses, one can be fairly certain of finding either status distinctions, extended families, or both; Given a rectilinear house of any size or type, one can be reasonably certain that the society is sedentary; Where curvilinear floor plans are present, the chances are three to one that the society practices a polygynous form of marriage. Tables 9.7 to 9.10 show the relationships between shape of dwelling and a variety of cultural features.

Table 9.7 Relationship Between Shape of Floor Plan
and Number of Rooms

Number of Rooms	Primary House Type	
	Rectilinear	*Curvilinear*
One	31	23
Two	12	1
Three	3	0
Four	4	0
Five	6	0
More	1	0

SOURCE: Whiting and Ayres 1968, table 7.
NOTE: Relationship between rectilinearity and multiple rooms, $p = < .001$.

Table 9.8 Relationship Between Number of Rooms in Dwellings, Family
Organization, and Status Distinctions

	No Social Class or Wealth Distinction		Social Class or Wealth Distinctions	
	Independent Families	*Extended Families*	*Independent Families*	*Extended Families*
More than one room	2	7	9	17
One room only	19	10	7	13

SOURCE: Whiting and Ayres 1968, table 8.

Table 9.9 Relationship Between Type of Settlement and
House Type

Type of Settlement	Primary and Secondary House Types		
	Rectilinear	*Both*	*Curvilinear*
Nomadic	8	0	7
Seminomadic	7	15	12
Sedentary	59	4	10

SOURCE: Whiting and Ayres 1968, table 9.
NOTE: Difference between nomadic and sedentary societies, for rectilinear vs. curvilinear houses only, $p = < .005$.

Table 9.10   Relationship Between Shape of Dwelling and Form
                  of Marriage

| | Primary House Type | | |
Form of Marriage	*Curvilinear*	*Both*	*Rectilinear*
Monogamous	6	2	27
Polygynous	19	12	40

SOURCE: Whiting and Ayres 1968, table 13.
NOTE: Difference between monogamous and polygynous societies, in terms of presence
or absence of curvilinear houses, p = .025.

Several approaches to establishing population size from floor area size were
mentioned in earlier chapters. As another example, Cook and Heizer (1968)
estimated the relationships among size of houses, settlement areas, and population size for thirty regions in aboriginal California. Their study demonstrated a close logarithmic association between village area and number of
inhabitants within these regions. The association was logarithmic rather than
linear because of the pattern of floor space increase above a minimum average of six persons per individual house. In the calculation of the floor space
per individual house, 20 square feet were allotted to a minimum average of
six persons; "additional persons involved an increase of 100 square feet each,
such that as the mean number of occupants increased, the floor space per
person approached a limit of 100 square feet" (Cook and Heizer 1968:114–

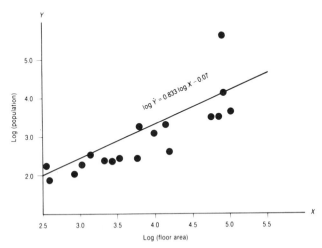

Figure 9.2   Log-log relationship between population size and floor area. Source:
Thomas 1976:435.

115). Raoul Naroll (1962) also demonstrated a logarithmic relationship between human population and the floor area they inhabited. A log-log transformation of Naroll's data by Thomas (1976:434–435) produced an allometric line of regression given by $\log Y = 0.833 \log X - 0.07$ (see figure 9.2).

Correlations and Tests of Hypotheses

Cross-cultural information can also be used to test hypotheses, as indicated by Whiting and Ayres' study. Each of the examples in this section is a small-scale regional study that was designed to test specific hypotheses. The first example examines a hypothesis widely accepted among archaeologists: "Females are responsible for the pottery in archaeological sites." This hypothesis has been a basic assumption underlying a number of attempts to correlate ceramic design elements and patterns of postmarital residence, as was mentioned in an earlier chapter. Were women really the potters? Thomas (1976:327–329) drew a random sample of twenty pottery-making societies within aboriginal North America. A tabulation of the results of the survey (table 9.11) indicate that sixteen of the twenty societies did have female potters. Is this lopsided distribution a result of mere chance association or did females really tend to be the potters in aboriginal North America? Thomas used the *sign test*, a nonparametric ordinal statistic, to determine the probability that such an extreme distribution could have happened by chance alone.

Table 9.11   Twenty Randomly Selected North American Societies

Society	Potters	Society	Potters
Nunivak	+	Zapotec	−
Baffinland	−	Cochiti	+
Yokuts	+	Ponca	+
S. Ute	+	Klamath	−
Shivwits	+	Sanpoil	+
Kaibab	−	White Knife	+
Walapai	+	Chemehuevi	+
Oto	+	Arikara	+
Hano	+	Hidatsa	+
Tewa	+	Mixe	+

SOURCE: *Ethnographic Atlas*, Murdock 1967, in Thomas 1976:328.
NOTE: + means all or most potters are female; − means all or most potters are male.

The resulting probability of 0.0071 was well within the limits necessary for rejecting the null hypothesis that no differences existed in the prevalence of female and male potters in aboriginal North America. Females do tend to be the potters (at least at the 0.01 level of significance). Still, the hypothesis is not a universal statement, for 20 percent of the societies sampled did have male potters. As Thomas concludes, "The analogy remains probabilistic" (1976:329).

Thomas (1976:318–319) has also provided another interesting example of a small-scale, cross-cultural study. This example is confined to a single culture area, the American Southwest. In a now classic study, Julian Steward (1937) suggested that the presence of matrilineal clans within aboriginal societies in the Southwest in the historic period was most likely the result of cultural adjustments to changing ecological pressures in the prehistoric period. Increasing population pressure, one of the dominant ecological variables, eventually led to the expansion of small villages. As populations expanded, localized exogamous lineages became increasingly crowded together within large multilineage communities. Clans eventually evolved, according to Steward, as ceremonies, totems, and other integrating devices were adopted to maintain group solidarity and corporate identities. This apparent trend should be visible in the archaeological record in the changing ratio of habitation rooms and kivas, with the number of habitation rooms presumably increasing through time in relation to ceremonial kivas. Steward's hypothesis was tested by Thomas, who compared the changing room:kiva ratio in a number of Pueblo villages dating between Pueblo IV (A.D. 1300–1700) and the historic period. An ordinal scale nonparametric statistic, the Wilcoxen two-sample test, was used to test the hypothesis (table 9.12). A nonparametric statistical technique was employed in this case because the actual ratios of kiva to habitation room in each village were difficult to determine. The null hypothesis of *no* significant increase in the room:kiva ratio was *not* rejected for this sample. At least for these data, Steward's ecological hypothesis was not supported.

Small-scale regional comparisons of archaeological data can also be performed to discover the possible existence of more than one sociocultural system, or temporal and functional differences within a system. For instance, archaeologist James Fitting (1965, table 1; see Thomas 1967:287) tested the distribution of measurements on 256 fluted projectile points for normality. If the measurements were normally distributed, the plausible argument could be made that the points were being manufactured by mem-

Table 9.12 House:Kiva Growth Rates in the American Southwest

Period	Site	House:Kiva Ratio
Pueblo IV	Tshirege, Rio Grande	60:1
PIV	Tsankawi, Rio Grande	30:1
PIV	Otowi, Rio Grande	90:1 (?)
PIV	Yapashi, Rio Grande	92:1 (?)
PIV	Kotyiti, Rio Grande	240:1 (?)
Pueblo V	Oraibi, Hopi	35.4:1
PV	Walpi, Hopi	34.2:1
PV	Sichumovi, Hopi	36:1
PV	Shipaulovi, Hopi	33.3:1
PV	Mishongnovi, Hopi	31.8:1
PV	Hano, Hopi	52.5:1
PV	Zuni	95.4:1
PV	Zuni	289.8:1

SOURCE: Steward 1955:165–167; information adapted from Thomas 1976:318–319.

NOTE: $p = 0.0823$, the result is not significant and the null hypothesis is not rejected for $\alpha < 0.0823$.

bers of a single sociocultural system, perhaps a band of wandering hunters. If the measurements were not normally distributed, the presence of two or more populations of fluted points must be explained. The hypothesis that the points were drawn from a normally distributed population was tested with chi-square, a nominal-scale nonparametric statistic. The calculated chi-square value ($X^2 = 28.8$, where $X^2_{0.05} = 12.6$) was sufficiently large to reject the hypothesis: the points were most likely *not* drawn from a normally distributed population. In this case the nonnormal distribution could represent either cultural, functional, or temporal differences within the sample. More information is required in this example to decide between competing hypotheses. Still, the probable existence of functional or temporal differences within the universe, or of more than one sociocultural universe, rasies interesting research questions that must be investigated further.

Evolutionary Theory and Comparative Archaeology

Comparative studies have been closely associated with evolutionary theories throughout the history of anthropology. In fact, the comparative method and evolutionist anthropology were so closely linked at one time that they

were considered equivalents. Today a general evolutionary orientation or research program still structures research and categorization in many areas of
archaeology and anthropology.

An evolutionary perspective raises many interesting and complex questions for archaeologists. For example, Are there clearly recognizable sociocultural types in the prehistoric record? Were the earliest sociocultural systems of a less or a more complex type than more recent sociocultural systems?
Can these sociocultural types be grouped into directional stages through which
human technology, social organization, and ideology have progressively
passed? If there are such stages, how can we understand the transitions from
one stage to the next? Why did some sociocultural systems transform from
one stage to another while others did not? Since the archaeological record
is weak in direct evidence of transitions in social structure, archaeologists
have often turned to virulent forms of technological or ecological determin-
ism in seeking answers to some of these questions. However, most social
scientists have tackled questions like these through comparative studies. The
results of several of these studies are reviewed below.

To comprehend the challenging questions that evolutionary theory poses
for comparative archaeology, it is helpful to have some understanding of
their interrelated growth. Nineteenth-century evolutionary theory emerged
in opposition to explanations of culture change couched in terms of supernatural influences or "causeless spontaneity." Although there was a paucity
of reliable data at the time, evolutionists were intent upon establishing an
empirically based scientific discipline of anthropology. Among the methodological dicta they adopted in their emerging research program were the following: (1) study cultural phenomena in a naturalistic manner rather than
in, for instance, a supernatural; (2) explain cultural differences in terms of
sociocultural experiences rather than in terms of the psychobiological basis
of human groups (called the biopsychological constant and the psychic unity
of mankind theses); and (3) use the comparative method as a social studies
substitute for the controlled experimental and laboratory techniques of the
physical sciences.

By the second half of the nineteenth century, social inquiry in Europe was
clearly dominated by an evolutionary or at least developmental orientation
(e.g., Tylor 1871; Morgan 1877). After searching for pattern among the
data from known contemporary aboriginal societies, the *classical evolutionists*
proposed a sequence of stages that was assumed to be universal, unilineal,
and characterized by progress (figure 9.3). One function of the sequences

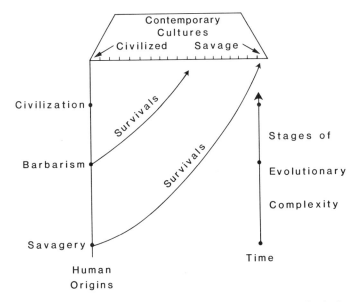

Figure 9.3 Stages of evolutionary complexity according to the classical evolutionists.

of stages proposed was explanatory (in the sense of a pattern explanation): institutional similarities and differences were explained by pointing to the position of cultures along a continuum of development from simple to complex. The pattern had predictive relevance for archaeology, too, for, by knowing the stage of development of a prehistoric culture, other institutions, artifacts, and activities could, supposedly, be predicted as once present.

Evolutionary approaches to the study of human societies were essentially eclipsed throughout most of the first half of the twentieth century for a number of reasons. One of the most influential reasons was the Social Darwinist and racist implications of some earlier evolutionary writings. There were other, more academic, reasons. Much of the information available to classical evolutionists was based on highly unreliable and biased accounts of distant societies by explorers, missionaries, and other travelers. As the magnitude of these errors became increasingly apparent, a reaction grew against armchair speculation. The nineteenth-century evolutionists' concentration on stages or levels and their unilineal connotations also deflected the interest of anthropologists away from the study of particular cultures and their social systems. It soon became apparent that certain aspects of the world's cultures were not understood very well at all. The result was the emergence of cultural relativism, historical particularism, functionalism, and a greatly increased emphasis on field work in both anthropology and archaeology. New and more reliable data were collected. The emphasis in anthropology shifted away from comparative studies to the systematic description of the structure and functioning of specific cultures.

Developmental and evolutionary issues were revived after World War II by V. Gordon Childe, Julian Steward, Leslie A. White, Elman Service, and others for a diversity of reasons. For instance, "backward" areas of the third world were becoming rapidly modernized and "developed." According to some scholars, at least, these transformations exhibited directional tendencies. Many contemporary evolutionists, or *neoevolutionists,* as they were called, such as Steward and White, strongly argued that the main goal of anthropology should be the elaboration of scientific knowledge rather than the writing of contemporary histories. Anthropologists should concentrate on the discovery of cross-cultural regularities through time and their explanation in cause-and-effect terms rather than the description of individual societies. They argued in addition that the antievolutionary movement was counterproductive to the development of a genuine science of sociocultural phenomena. By emphasizing the organizational peculiarities of particular cultures, the cultural relativists were detracting from the study of cross-cultural regularities and the development of a science of humankind.

Many neoevolutionists provided evolutionary sequences of stages and typologies of societies. However, their research strategies varied widely. For instance, Childe (1951a, 1951b, 1954) used the archaeological record to demonstrate progressive and evolutionary advances in the history of humankind. Impressive innovations, such as food production, metallurgy, the wheel, and other, mainly technoeconomic, advances, led, according to Childe, to revolutionary changes in human societies. All sociocultural subsystems, the technoeconomic, the social, and the ideological, were dramatically affected by these innovations. The result was the emergence of successive stages as human societies evolved from mobile Paleolithic hunters and gatherers to sedentary farmers to civilized dwellers in classical urban centers.

White and Steward emphasized different strategies in their own evolutionary studies (e.g., Sahlins 1960). Steward (1949, 1955) concentrated on the study of *specific evolution,* that is, the parallel adaptive changes of cultures in somewhat similar structural-ecological niches. The goal of Steward's methodology was the formulation of middle-range theories based on the positing of similar mechanisms that produced similarities in structure in parallel niches. White (1959), on the other hand, emphasized the study of *general evolution,* the formulation of grand theory about culture and the cumulative, collective experience of humankind. The goal of White's methodology was the classification of types of social organization in terms of an ideal, unilineal scheme of general social development that was concerned with progress, the rise of higher forms, and the mechanisms responsible for progression. Although every society in the world clearly has neither gone through the stages sequentially nor evolved at the same rate, the stages do characterize, according to White, the evolution of human societies writ large, of culture rather than of cultures. Each of these two research strategies has proven relevant in anthropology to different types of problems. In the remainder of this section we will concentrate on general evolution and on some of the comparative studies that have formulated or tested universal stages of development.

Two key questions that classical and contemporary evolutionists have both asked are, Are there really stages or steps through which human sociocultural systems have passed? If there are, how can the superiority of one system over another be measured? To answer these questions, an evolutionary theory must do at least three things (e.g., Marsh 1967). First, it must provide a typology of societies organized within the framework of an evolutionary scheme of stages. Here a difference between cultural growth and cultural development or evolution must be taken into consideration. Growth is only an additive process, a change within a cultural type. In contrast, cultural evolution is a transformation of structure, a change from one type to another. An evolutionary approach involves, therefore, the construction of structural types and the organization of these types into some logical sequence of increasing complexity. Second, an evolutionary theory must provide criteria for determining evolutionary direction. This is why terms such as *more complex* and *less complex,* which can be evaluated objectively by referring to degrees of differentiation or specialization, are used for stages of evolution rather than such terms as *higher* or *lower.* For White, more evolved societies have greater energy-harnessing potential than less evolved societies. These criteria are an essential ingredient in any evolutionary theory, for evolution is minimally defined by directional change as compared to random change or cyclical change. Finally the framework of stages has to be fruitful in comprehending the transition of actual societies from one stage to another. Only the first two of these three criteria will concern us here.

Measuring Evolutionary Complexity

How can we measure evolutionary complexity? How can we form types of cultures? A widely adopted strategy has been to measure complexity by some absolute criterion, such as the complex variable *societal differentiation* (defined as "the number of structurally distinct and functionally specialized units in a society"). The resulting culture types are then grouped into a rough continuum of broad progressive stages often called *levels of sociocultural integration* in anthropology. The definition of these levels has been a principle objective of some anthropologists for many years. Like all typologies, the resulting methodological frameworks are constructs created within the context of a specific network of issues and problems. Steward (1955), for example, insisted that his levels of sociocultural integration were heuristic devices for ordering data and dealing with problems of transformation and not actual empirical sequences. Different sequences may be as variable, then, as the issues and problems themselves. Service (1962) and Sahlins (1968) proposed a sequence (band-tribe-chiefdom-state) based on the largest autonomous sociopolitical unit engaged in collective action. An alternative sequence (egalitarian-ranked-stratified-state) based on organizational structure was proposed by Fried (1967). Childe (1956) organized his sequence around archaeologically observable technological criteria. Each of these sequences has its own heuristic value, for it focuses on different complexes of traits. For example, Fried's sequence of stages focuses on basic similarities in organizational structure among groups of societies that otherwise vary widely in the details of their cultural content.

Other social scientists have tried to provide measures for the concept *level of societal complexity*. Their work has concentrated on formulating valid and reliable indicators at different levels of measurement. Some have proposed single dimension measures such as societal differentiation, mentioned earlier (Marsh 1967). In other cases a complex of sociocultural traits has been used to create a variety of indicators, which is then combined to form a single index vlaue. Naroll (1956), for instance, proposed a ratio-scale three-trait index of social development using the traits *occupational specialization, organizational ramification,* and *population of the largest settlement.* Each of these traits was found to have a high log-log correlation with the others. Multivariate nominal-scale measures of level of societal complexity include Freeman's nine-item Guttman scale (1957) of societal complexity, Carneiro and Tobias' fifty-item Guttman scale (1963), and Charles McNett's five-level sequence (1973) of stages of settlement pattern. In spite of their different foundations, all of these indices seem to be measuring the same underlying variable—societal complexity or level of civilization,—for they correlate well with one another. Each is also relevant to different kinds of problems. For instance, Naroll's index is involved most directly with evolutionary theory, Carneiro and Tobias' is the most elaborate and contains the most general information, and McNett's is operationally the most directly applicable to the archaeological record.

Two of these complexity measures, Freeman's scale of societal complexity and Naroll's social development index, will be used to illustrate the construction of evolutionary scales. Freeman's study (1957) was designed as an empirical test of Robert Redfield's folk-urban typology. Redfield (1947, 1953) had originally proposed a folk-urban dichotomy. In a later work he suggested that there may be an evolutionary continuum between the two extremes of the dichotomy toward ever greater functional complexity. Freeman redefined the traits Redfield had used in his dichotomy and devised twelve general, culture-free categories that could be applied to any sociocultural system. The statistical technique used in the test was the Guttman scale, a nominal scale. In a Guttman scale a trait is either present or absent. Thus, in Freeman's scale of societal complexity, traits in the twelve categories were either present (which would indicate greater complexity and urbanism) or absent (which would indicate less complexity and more folk).

The primary characteristic of the Guttman scale is unidimensionality or cumulativeness. It assumes that the set of examined traits, the twelve categories in this case, forms a continuum in which the addition of each trait constitutes a step in a regular sequence. Culture types are defined as those societies having the same number of scale items. Of course, the number of societies in a sample, their range in complexity, the number of categories used, and other factors determine the number and definition of culture types that will be discovered. Once a scale or scalogram is constructed, inferences may then be made about the evolutionary sequence in which traits appear (from bottom to top in table 9.13) and about the relative complexity of the societies in the sample (from left to right in table 9.13). For example, according to table 9.13, trade developed with other societies before subsistence economies based primarily on agriculture or pastoralism appeared in the evolutionary record.

Traits in the twelve categories were scored present or absent for fifty-two societies representing at least fifty different culture areas. Eleven of the traits

Table 9.13　An Example of the Use of the Guttman Scale

Society	Scale Items									Scale Steps
	1	*2*	*3*	*4*	*5*	*6*	*7*	*8*	*9*	
Dutch	X	X	X	X	X	X	X	X	X	9
Aztec	X	X	X	X	X	X	X	X		8
Iroquois	X	X	X	X	X	X	X			7
Ila	X	X	X	X	X	X				6
Tallensi	X	X	X	X	X					5
Mosquito	X	X	X	X						4
Chukchee	X	X	X							3
Apayao	X	X								2
Copper Eskimo	X									1

NOTE: 1 = Presence or absence of trade with other societies; 2 = Presence or absence of a subsistence economy based primarily on agriculture or pastoralism; 3 = Presence or absence of social stratification or slavery; 4 = Presence or absence of full-time governmental specialists; 5 = Presence or absence of full-time religious or magical specialists; 6 = Presence or absence of full-time craft specialists; 7 = Presence or absence of a state of at least 10,000 population; 8 = Presence or absence of a standard medium of exchange with a value fixed at some worth other than its commodity value; 9 = Presence or absence of a complex, unambiguous written language.

　　In this scale of societal complexity it is assumed that greater complexity equates with the addition of new scale items.

formed an almost perfect Guttman scale of development (coefficient of reproducibility =0.96). A twelfth trait, social integration, was dropped when it was found to vary independently from the eleven other traits. Freeman's cross-cultural study produced a number of positive results. It defined and provided empirical support for the folk-urban continuum; it provided twelve distinct scale types for measuring societal complexity; and it supported a unilineal concept of the evolutionary process of cultural development from less complex to more complex societies.

　　Naroll's index of social development (1956) proposed an allometric relationship between degree of social evolution and extent of urbanization. Tatje and Naroll defined allometric growth as "growth of one part relative to another part, or relative to the whole, at such a rate that there is a linear regression of the logarithms of the dimensions" (1973:769–770; also see Naroll and von Bertalanffy 1956). The index of social development is based on relationships between (1) degree of occupational specialization, (2) degree of organizational ramification, and (3) size of settlement. The first two variables were considered measures of degree of social evolution, while the third was regarded as an indicator of degree of urbanization. Every society has an index value, which is a composite of its individual scores for all three indicators. Each of the indicators (craft specialization, organizational rami-

Table 9.14 Calculated Indices of Social Development for Thirty Peoples

Ethnic Unit	Raw Scores			Weighted Scores			
	P	*T*	*C*	*P*	*T*	*C*	Index
1. Yahgan	Nbhd	3	2	—	11	12	12
2. Naron	80	3	2	19	11	12	14
3. Yagua	50	3	4	17	11	24	17
4. Ainu	207	6	2	23	29	12	21
5. Ona	500	3	4	27	11	24	21
6. Inland Forest	75	5	4	19	24	24	22
7. Egedesminde	279	4	5	24	18	28	23
8. Moken	280	4	5	24	18	28	23
9. Kiwai	400	4	6	26	18	31	25
10. Lesu	232	5	5	24	24	28	25
11. Ramkokamekra	298	7	3	25	33	19	26
12. Lafofa Nuba	Nbhd	6	4	—	29	24	27
13. Hupa	200	6	5	23	29	28	27
14. Bella Coola	400	8	3	26	36	19	27
15. Flathead	800	6	4	29	29	24	27
16. Ulithi	142	7	5	22	33	28	28
17. Toda	Nbhd	6	5	—	29	28	29
18. Nama	2,500	8	4	34	36	24	31
19. Lepcha	Nbhd	8	5	—	36	28	32
20. Crow	1,600	7	6	32	33	31	32
21. Nuer	500	7	8	27	33	36	32
22. Hopi	1,350	8	10	31	36	40	36
23. Tikopia	440	10	11	26	42	42	37
24. Cuna	1,800	9	9	33	39	38	37
25. Samoa	500	14	9	27	51	38	39
26. Zululand	15,000	14	10	42	51	40	44
27. Dahomey	11,093	21	10	40	61	40	47
28. Nupe	29,848	14	16	45	51	48	48
29. Inca	200,000	22	17	53	62	49	55
30. Aztec	350,000	17	35	55	56	62	58

SOURCE: Naroll 1956, table 3. Reproduced by permission of the American Anthropological Association from *American Anthropologist* 58(4):687–715.
NOTE: P = population of settlement; T = team types; C = craft specialization; Nbhd = neighborhood, defined as a population distribution pattern in which no settlement is larger than an extended family.

fication, settlement size) was defined so as to be useful in archaeological research.

Naroll's three indicators were applied to a nonrandomly selected sample of thirty non-Western societies and, in a later restudy, to two stratified probability samples (Tatje and Naroll 1973). Composite indices were cal-

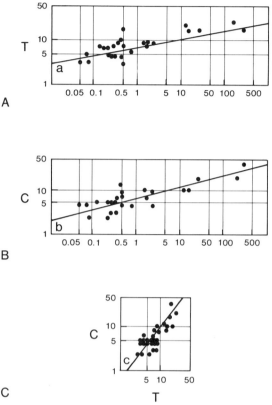

Figure 9.4 Correlates of social development shown by linear regression of logarithms of three traits. A. Number of team types (T) and settlement population (P). Line a shows the regression formula $P = (T/2)^6$. B. Number of craft specialties (C) and settlement population (P). Line b shows the regression formula $P = C^4$. C. Number of craft specialties (C) and number of team types (T). Line c shows the regression formula $C^4 = (T/2)^6$. Source: Naroll 1956, figure 2. Reproduced by permission of the American Anthropological Association from *American Anthropologist* 58(4):687–715.

culated for all of these societies, with the scores ranging from a high of 58 for the Aztec to a low of 12 for the Yahgan (table 9.14). Naroll's cross-cultural study produced several interesting results. First, an allometric relationship was demonstrated to exist between the three variables in both instances. Each variable was shown to have a very high coefficient of correlation with the others and a linear regression of their logarithms (figure 9.4).

Second, the index scores provided a convenient measure of the relative complexity of each society in the sample. Third, the study demonstrated a general pattern of allometric growth for human social and cultural evolution not unlike that known for biological evolution (Naroll and Von Bertalanffy 1956). Finally, if the allometric relationship between population of a settlement and total floor area under roof in a settlement was accurate, a rough estimate of minimum societal complexity could be made by estimating settlement size from the floor area of the largest known site in an archaeological culture.

Why Measure Societal Complexity?

Defining structural types, levels of integration, and measures of societal development is not an end in itself. Each plays important roles in hypothesis testing, the delineation of appropriate universes, and the building of theories.

Hypothesis Testing. Hypothesis-testing investigations may concern within-level comparisons as well as transformations from one stage to another or trends through levels such as Leslie White's proposal (1959) that the harnessing of energy becomes more effective as culture evolves through time, that is, through successive stages. In addition, types of cultures and levels of integration raise interesting empirical problems themselves. For example, Does a taxonomy actually mirror real-world temporal sequences? What is the ontological status of a culture type? Why are some variables correlated with particular levels of integration while others vary independently? What is it about different levels of integration that alters the relationship between variables? Suggested taxonomies merit testing, too. For example, the evolutionary sequence of settlement types proposed in Beardsley et al. (1956) was compared by McNett (1973) with cross-cultural data to determine its degree of empirical support.

The Delineation of Appropriate Universes. Structural types, levels of integration, and measures of social development have also been used to control for level of development during hypothesis-testing investigations. Some anthropologists have maintained that variables cannot be compared cross-culturally by indiscriminate selection of any random set of societies. Level of sociocultural integration must be controlled. Cultures at different levels of integration are different by definition. Their types of social organization, political controls, and technoeconomic adaptations to the natural environment are not the same. If level of integration were not controlled, how could we determine whether low correlations were merely a reflection of differences in levels of integration? Or, again, whether high correlations were a reflection of similarity in developmental level? A research objective of comparative studies, and by implication scientific archaeology, is demonstrating when comparisons are legitimate between levels as well as within levels and when they are not (e.g., Cohen 1968).

Building Models and Theories. Although they are often hypothetical, the results of cross-cultural evolutionary studies are a stimulating source of ideas in theory building and model construction. In summarizing cross-cultural results concerning directional tendencies, Naroll (1970), for example, points out that there is strong evidence for a regular progression of a worldwide nature from generalists to occupational specialization, from simple organization to complex organization, from rural to urban settlement, from wealth-sharing to wealth-hoarding, from consensual leadership to authoritative leadership, from responsible elite to exploitative elite, and from vengeance war to political war. He also notes that such apparently distantly removed aspects of culture as perception, art styles, games, song and dance styles, theology, and deference patterns are believed related to stages of cultural evolution (also see Erickson 1977 and Levinson 1977). Besides suggesting long-term trends in cultural development that can be incorporated into theories and models, cross-cultural evolutionary studies suggest associations between cultural elements that are not usually apparent in the archaeological record but that may be equally valuable in theory building and model construction.

Structural types, measures of societal complexity and levels of sociocultural integration are particularly relevant to the process of theory building, a process that is the focus of chapter 10. Every measure and taxonomy implicitly contains a theory. For instance, a primary research activity of many evolutionary studies is the search for causes. But structural-functional analysis is concerned with a moment in time or a very short span in the life-way of a community rather than with development through time. Furthermore, this strategy of analysis assumes as methodological principles the interdependent relationships of the various parts of a culture and the equivalent interdependency of its parts. Therefore, causal significance cannot be assigned to one part of culture or another. In contrast, developmental or evolutionary analysis, such as Guttman scale analysis, can produce new ideas about the primary, or initiatory, features in culture change, ideas about the processes that "caused" one culture to transform into another in a taxonomy. This is so because these types of analysis are designed to answer questions such as, Under what conditions did specific culture types or organizational structures arise? What processes led to their transformation? Were the processes or causes ideological, structural, or technological? Theorists in anthropology have disagreed on the answers to these questions. However, both White and Steward, for example, maintained that the primary role (the causative factor, the prime mover) in evolutionary development was played by the technoeconomic subsystem. Suggestions like these, while based on the analysis of culture types and stages, may eventually lead to the building of processual theories of culture change.

Summary

Chapter 9 introduces the cross-cultural comparison of sociocultural systems made possible by the identification of common denominators of all cultural systems. Useful for testing general statements, as conceptual and methodological tools, and for constructing inferential histories, the comparisons concentrate on what is shared, ordered, and discoverable, assuming common human problems, predictable variability, and constant psychobiology for the past 40,000 years. Archaeological studies add time depth to these comparisons. Units of analysis used for comparison should have fairly precise theoretical and operational definitions, be explicit, cross-culturally applicable, and depend on a taxonomy of valid structural types, depending on the goals of a project. The properties studied should be universal and culture-free, rather than culture-bound, and be expressable as measurements on ordinal, interval, or ratio scales. How to measure and how to make measures applicable universally are formidable problems.

Hypotheses should relate two or more variables that are universal in scope and that are deducible from a systematic and consistent body of theory. Most units should be selected for comparison through general, stratified, rather than simple, random sampling. Geographic or cultural areas or levels of sociocultural integration are the most common criteria for stratifying universes. Comparisons should be made on the theoretical basis of testable general statements. Most cross-cultural statements are tendency statements that only apply to most cultures at most times and in most places.

A vast amount of systematic information on human societies on a worldide basis has been coded in the Human Relations Area Files (HRAF), then broken into categories and used for exploratory searches for frequency and percentage correlations. Another approach is to distribute societies among basic types and then to search for significant associations between societal characteristics and types. Another way is to survey societal characteristics by distributing societies into major ethnographic regions on the basis of geographic location and to determine characteristic and distinguishing cultural traits. A fourth approach attempts to define cross-cultural regularities between material culture and social systems on the association between floor plan or size and other cultural features. Cross-cultural information can be used to test hypotheses or to discover the possible existence of more than one system or temporal and functional differences within a system.

Comparative studies associated with evolutionary theories raise many questions for archaeologists. A short history of the interrelated growth of evolutionary theory and comparative anthropology, preevolution to classical evolution to neoevolution theory, is presented. The research strategies of specific and general evolution approaches prove relevant for different types of problems. General evolution theory must provide a typology of societies organized within an evolutionary scheme of stages, must provide criteria for determining evolutionary directions, and the framework of stages must be fruitful in comprehending transitions of actual societies. A widely adopted strategy has been to measure complexity by some absolute criterion, then group the resulting types into levels of sociocultural integration. Different sequences focus on different complexes of traits and must be considered within particular constructs. Freeman's scale of societal complexity and Naroll's social development index illustrate the construction of evolutionary scales. All these methods suggest associations between cultural elements not usually apparent in the archaeological record, but they may be valuable in theory building and model construction.

Suggested Readings

Discussions of cross-cultural comparisons in anthropology are provided by:

Adler, L. L., ed. 1982. *Cross-Cultural Research at Issue*. New York: Academic Press.

Driver, H. and R. Chaney. 1970. Cross-cultural sampling and Galton's problem. In R. Naroll and R. Cohen, eds., *A Handbook of Method in Cultural Anthropology*, pp. 990–1003. Garden City, N.Y.: Natural History Press.

Leach, E. 1968. The comparative method in anthropology. *International Encyclopedia of the Social Sciences* 7:340–341. New York: Free Press.

McNett, C., Jr. 1970. A cross-cultural method for predicting nonmaterial traits in archaeology. *Behavior Science Notes* 5:195–212.

—— 1979. The cross-cultural method in archaeology. In M. Schiffer, ed., *Advances in Archaeological Method and Theory*, Vol. 2, pp. 39–76. New York: Academic Press.

Naroll, R., G. Michik, and F. Naroll. 1974. Hologeistic theory testing. In J. Jorgensen, ed., *Comparative Studies by Harold E. Driver and Essays in His Honor*, pp. 121–148. New Haven, Conn.; HRAF Press.

——. 1976. *Worldwide Theory Testing*. New Haven, Conn.: HRAF Press.

Schaefer, J., ed. 1974. *Studies in Cultural Diffusion: Galton's Problem*. New Haven, Conn.: HRAF books.

Udy, S. H., Jr. 1973. Cross-cultural analysis: Methods and scope. In B. Siegel, ed., *Annual Review of Anthropology*, Vol. 2, pp. 253–270. Palo Alto, Calif.: Annual Reviews.

CHAPTER TEN

Formalizing Archaeological Theories

A scientific theory is a structured system of interrelated ideas that explains some aspect of the phenomenal world. The subject matter of scientific theories is general phenomena, such as falling apples or expanding balloons. One of the principal goals of science is the construction of ever more inclusive theories that include less general phenomena within more comprehensive explanatory frameworks. More comprehensive theories explain less general phenomena like falling apples and expanding balloons by referring to more general concepts, such as the pull of gravity or the pressure of gas molecules. In archaeology the transformation of hunter-gatherers to sedentary agriculturalists might be subsumed within a more inclusive theory that also explains the transformation of agricultural villages to urban centers. In the latter example, each individual transformation of one community type into another, no matter how diverse they may appear to us as observers, could be understood and explained by referring to this more general theory, if it existed, just as the movements of individual planets can be explained and become understandable by referring to Newton's theory of gravitation. Whether these theories are regarded as idealized but true approximations to the way the real world actually works (the realist perspective) or as handy fictions that merely help us make sense of our observations (the conventionalist perspective), they are considered the end products, the sine qua non, of science. As Mario Bunge (1967:384) has succinctly stated, "No theory, no science."

All theories in archaeology, however, and nearly all theories in the other social and behavioral sciences are discursive theories. They are expatiating narratives that lack the logical and predictive rigor of formal theories in the physical sciences. As a result, they tend to be ambiguous, incomplete, and often logically inconsistent. Formalizing discursive theories has become, therefore, an ideal goal of some archaeologists (e.g., Watson, Leblanc, and Redman 1971) and other social scientists (Gibbs 1972; Willer 1967; Hage 1972; Hudson 1969, 1972), for the advantages of formalizing a theory are many. Besides helping us tell a better, more coherent, story, the formalization process helps eliminate logical inconsistencies and unfalsifiable "metaphysical fluff." More positively, scientific theories organize seemingly undifferentiated masses of information, establish lawlike regularities between phenomena, expose gaps in our narratives, provide explanations of recognized empirical regularities, predict other possible regularities that hold between observable phenomena, and suggest tests and other research activities. Formal systematic theories perform these tasks by being explanatorily forceful, economical of thought, and heuristically fertile. If these arguments are valid, it is fair to conclude that without integrating theories, archaeological knowledge will continue to be a thing of "shreds and patches."

Although archaeologists have been calling for new types of theory, they have not been producing them. There are, therefore, few guidelines within archaeology itself for formalizing theories. For this reason, I have borrowed ideas from other social and behavioral sciences to provide a brief glimpse of what formal theories in archaeology might look like. The first section of chapter 10 introduces the parts of a theory; the second section discusses some of the many ways of generating theory; and the third section provides an axiomatic sketch of a general theory of sociocultural evolution as an example of the formalization process. Theory builders differ widely in the criteria they apply in evaluating theories. In this chapter, three principles of theory evaluation will be advocated (Gibbs 1972): (1) theories should be stated formally; (2) theories should be testable; and (3) predictive power should be the primary criterion for assessing theories. These are only ideal goals whose stringent application should not be used to eliminate emergent theories in their initial phases of construction.

Social and behavioral scientists have been reluctant to formalize their theories; archaeologists will undoubtedly be no different. The formalization process is very hard work, and it can and most likely will expose the often fatal flaws and untestable statements in a theory. Since formalizing theories is so risky, we are almost certain to be shown to be inconsistent, irrational, or just factually wrong—and who wants to suffer this fate? Furthermore, since building formal theories involves the construction of explanatory structures far more complex than hypotheses themselves, it should not be surprising that formalizing theories is a process engaged in less often and with less success than the construction and testing of hypotheses. Finally, as Amitai Etzioni (1970) has noted, there is a deep-rooted tendency in America to be fact-crazy and theory-shy. If none of these arguments for building more coherent and testable theories is appealing, then regard formal theory construction as a heuristic game, an alternative route to generalization and the testing of general hypotheses.

Parts of a Theory

What is a scientific theory? Does a scientific theory have a characteristic structure or set of criteria? How does a theory provide understanding and explanation? Answers to these questions must remain a matter of personal evaluation and choice, for there is no effective consensus among scientists and philosophers of science on the best answers to these questions at present. It is probably fair to conclude that there is no commonly agreed upon interpretation of what a scientific theory is or how it is to be characterized or what the criteria for the terms are (e.g., Suppe, 1977). A similar lack of consensus is reflected in the social and behavioral sciences in the diversity of strategies proposed for building formal theories (e.g., Amedeo and Golledge 1975; Blalock 1969, 1970; Dubin 1969; Gibbs 1972; Hage 1972; Mullins 1971; Reynolds 1971; Stinchcombe 1968; Willer 1967). Each of these strategies is somewhat different, and each reflects the author's own conception of what science and a scientific theory are. Jerald Hage's *Techniques and Problems of Theory Construction in Sociology* (1972) provides a clear and interesting introduction to the tasks of theory construction in sociology. Although there are obvious differences between the data of sociology and those of archaeology, the scheme is simple and general enough to be adapted to archaeology.

A theory is defined by Hage as consisting of six parts, the first four of which provide the basic ingredients of a well-formed theory. Each part has a unique role in a complete theory, and each makes a separate contribution to our understanding of archaeological and social phenomena. The six parts and the role each plays in a theory are listed in table 10.1. Theoretical concepts or concept names focus our attention on some part of the archaeological or systemic context: they tell us what properties of infinite classes of

Table 10.1 Parts of a Theory and Their Contribution to
Theory Construction

Theory Part	Contribution
1. Concept names	Description and classification
2. Verbal statements	Analysis
3. Theoretical definitions	Meaning
Operational definitions	Measurement
4. Theoretical linkages	Plausibility
Operational linkages	Testability
5. Ordering into primitive	Elimination of tautology
and derived terms	
6. Ordering into premises	Elimination of inconsistency
and equations	

SOURCE: J. Hage, *Techniques and Problems of Theory Construction in Sociology*, p. 173. Copyright © 1972 by J. Hage. Reprinted by permission of John Wiley & Sons, Inc.

events and things a theory is about. Verbal statements connect two or more concepts. These interrelationships permit analysis in addition to the descriptions and classifications provided by concept names. Analysis in turn allows prediction and explanation. Theoretical and operational definitions provide meaning and measurement as discussed in chapter 2. Finally, plausibility and testability are added by theoretical and operational linkages, while tautologies and inconsistencies are eliminated or minimized by the ordering of primitive and derived terms and of premises and equations.

An idealized form of a scientific theory, such as the form presented here, is generally thought of as being composed of two parts, a *text* and a *dictionary*. Other terms that have been used for these two parts include formal and substantive and intrinsic and extrinsic. The text is composed of the first two parts of a theory, the concepts and theoretical or verbal statements. Together these two parts represent a formal system of propositions, the hypotheses of the theory that account for particular characteristics of past systemic contexts. The dictionary is the remaining parts of a theory: the definitions, linkages, and ordering of terms. Since it is the text that is mainly presented and discussed in the literature, it is often mistakenly considered the completed theory. But the usually unwieldy dictionary is an essential part of a theory, too, for it provides among other things meaning, testability, plausibility, measurement, and consistency. In archaeological theory the dictionary interrelates the contents and events of archaeological and systemic contexts. Developing the text and dictionary of a theory is nearly always a slow and laborious project, a project that is a long-term objective of a community of scholars.

From this brief description of a scientific theory, it should already be apparent what theories are not. They are not conceptualizations of any kind, such as classificatory systems of community types or of ideal historical types such as Neolithic and Mesolithic. Nor are they theoretical orientations, such as the ecological approach or the systems approach. Each of these conceptualizations may play a role in theory construction, for each has a role in the research process, as discussed in chapter 2. But a theory, as defined here, is a deductive web—a text—and a dictionary that together account for the contents of the archaeological sites we study.

The Text of a Theory

The text of a theory consists of concept names and verbal statements.

Concept Names. The story told in a theory is usually narrated with theoretical concepts such as *force, volume, population pressure,* and *social status.* Concepts such as these represent phenomena or properties of phenomena that are not directly observable or fictions introduced to explain observations. Theoretical concepts provide economy and abstraction from individual instances, as mentioned in chapter 2. An example of a discursive theory of agricultural development under primitive agricultural conditions that has had an important impact on archaeological theorizing is Ester Boserup's *The Conditions of Agricultural Growth* (1965). The theoretical concepts used in the theory tell us what Boserup thinks is important in agricultural development. Among the concepts are annual food supply, population size, agricultural complexity, need to till less suitable land, output per worker-hour, number of people available for nonagricultural activities, frequency of cropping, production per land unit, and individual productivity per unit of labor. These concepts and several others supply the building blocks, the atoms, of Boserup's theory.

Verbal Statements. Theoretical concepts are related in theories in verbal statements. Besides concept names, verbal statements contain other parts of speech, such as connectives, adjectives, verbs, and adverbs. Verbal statements assert relationships among the concepts of a theory. Examples using concepts from Boserup's theory are "The greater the population size, the greater the degree of agricultural complexity" and "The greater the degree of agricultural complexity, the more people become available for nonagricultural activities." Scientific theories are systematic in part because their verbal statements have concepts in common, as in the above two examples. This is a significant requirement, for one of the goals of theorizing is to explore the deductive implications of interlinked statements like these. The statement "The greater the population size, the more people become available for nonagricultural activities" follows deductively from the two earlier verbal statements. As a rule each verbal statement must contain at least one concept that also appears in at least one other verbal statement in a theory; otherwise, there are no logical connections holding the theory together. Thus every statement in a theory will contain terms related to other terms, which, when taken as a whole, compose the text of the theory.

Verbal statements play many roles in a theory, such as axiom, theorem, hypothesis, and proposition. Even though all of these statements state empirically relevant hypotheses as clearly, concisely, and unambiguously as possible, the role that is played is determined by a statement's position in a theory and its function in the theory-building process. In formal physical science theories, axioms are generally unproved assumptions that are more abstract and of greater scope than the theorems that are derived from them. Their function is to provide a basis for deriving theorems and to help prove that a theorem is a valid member of the set of statements of a theory. Since axioms are generally more abstract than theorems, the justification of any axiom is obtained by noting how the theory's derived theorems perform in the real world. Furthermore, the fact that a law or regularity can be derived from a theory as a theorem lends support to the law by accounting for the relationship expressed in it and by showing why it takes the form it does.

The Dictionary of a Theory

The dictionary of a theory consists of theoretical and operational definitions and linkages and the ordering of primitive and derived terms and premises and equations.

Theoretical and Operational Definitions. The term *population size* is ambiguous: it could refer to "the average number of people resident within a community during a year" or to "the average number of members of a society over a five-year period," among many possible definitions. Many terms encountered in the archaeological literature are very often "raw" in that they are not very clearly defined. Meaning is assigned to a concept term by giving it a clear theoretical definition. Theoretical definitions can be readily borrowed from other social science disciplines, but archaeologists must nearly always develop their own operational definitions because of the peculiarity of their subject matter. As mentioned in chapter 2, operational definitions provide the operations used to measure a term; they provide theoretical definitions with at least partial empirical definitions by indicating what observations or what procedural steps stand for or represent them among the jumble of artifacts and features at a site. The operational definition of population size of a community as "living floor area of a component times 2.3" has already been mentioned. In some cases operational definitions are composed of a composite of observations, not all of which must be present to provide a measurement for a concept. For instance, plow fragments, stress marks on the shoulders of oxen, and furrowed fields are indicators with different values of plow agriculture and a short fallow system.

Explicit operational definitions ensure that archaeologists observe or measure comparable phenomena. However, the primary role of operational definitions in theory building is to point to what would count in some way for or against the truth or falsity of a verbal statement. Since an operational definition expresses a causal relation between theoretical entities and observational phenomena, it provides the means of indirectly testing the truth or falsity of theoretical statements. Theories are never directly testable themselves: their truth or falsity must be inferred from tests of statements of relations between measures.

Theoretical and Operational Linkages. The dictionary of a theory also contains a rationale for connections or linkages between theoretical concepts and an interpretation of the linkages between operational definitions. Why, for example, are annual food supply and population size ordinally related in a positive or negative direction within the context of Boserup's theory? Boserup presents an "argument of relevance" for this relationship: an increased annual food supply permits the survival of a greater number of people, while a sharp decrease in annual food supply leads to starvation, birth control practices, population dispersion, or other mechanisms of population reduction. Theories are made plausible by providing reasons for the relationship expressed in their theoretical statements, as in this example.

Linkages between operational definitions ensure the testability of a theory by grounding theoretical statements in archaeological reality. Operational linkages detail what is to be measured in relation to what else; that is, by relating measures to measures. As an example, take the statement "The greater the population size, the greater the need to till less suitable soil." A positive test of the statement would show a high correlation between larger floor areas in communities and increased percentages of fields on poorer agricultural lands. If this correlation was not supported by a number of tests, the statement as expressed or interpreted was false or there were other intervening variables. As a result, some aspect of the theory would have to be altered. However, if the operational system was validated at a useful level, its formal system would become a confirmed scientific theory.

Ordering Primitive and Derived Terms and Premises and Equations. According to Hage (1972), a theory is fairly complete if it consists of the four parts already discussed in this section. Ordering into primitive and derived terms and into premises and equations, however, helps eliminate tautologies and inconsistencies when the elements in a theory become large. Primitive terms are the basic, initial, concepts in a theory; they are either intuitively obvious or defined by illustration or by some other procedure outside the theory. Derived terms are defined within the theory by using primitive terms or other derived terms. The advantages of ordering concepts into primitive and derived terms are that (1) tautologies are eliminated or minimized; (2) new definitions for familiar terms may be located; and (3) the primitive terms are identified and exposed to critical scrutiny. When two or more operational definitions or theoretical definitions overlap, a tautology probably exists. A tautology is a fault in conception or labeling, for it is the saying of the same thing twice in different words. A simple way of determining whether there is a conceptual tautology is to see whether the indicators of two concepts are the same or cognate ideas. Arranging ideas into some ordered system also promotes the discovery of new definitions or meanings for familiar ideas, for theoretical definitions are systematically derived when concepts are ordered, too (table 10.2).

Just as it is advantageous to order concepts into primitive and derived terms when they begin to proliferate, it is as advantageous to order theoretical statements into premises and equations when they begin to proliferate. Although a formal system is not always composed of deductively related statements in the sense that one set must be deducible from another, the relations must be stated in a consistent and unambiguous manner. Conclu-

Table 10.2   Ordering Primitive and Derived Terms

	A. Primitive Terms
Structural differentiation	The absolute number of functionally specialized system parts
Energy level	The absolute amount of energy harnessed by the sociocultural system
Information level	The absolute number of different symbols (ideas) in the system
	B. Derived Terms
General evolutionary progress	The absolute amount of energy harnessed by the sociocultural system
Level of sociocultural integration	A configuration of values on the three criteria of general evolutionary progress (i.e., the three primitive terms)
Structural transformation	The transformation of a system's structure to higher or lower levels of integration
Thermodynamic efficiency	The ratio of the total amount of energy harnessed to the amount of energy expended in production of the total

SOURCE: Segraves 1974.

sions obtained from one part of a formal system must not contradict conclusions from another part. Ordering statements helps eliminate inconsistent reasoning and makes it easier to follow complex arguments or a flow of events. Premises are the axioms or postulates of a theory; they are the basic or core statements from which all other statements in a theory are derived through deductive reasoning. Equations, which are also called theorems, corollaries, or derived hypotheses, are statements that can be derived from the axiom core. Table 10.3 illustrates the ordering of statements into premises and equations. Ordering statements is advantageous to theory construction for several reasons. First, it facilitates criticism by exposing faulty and inconsistent lines of reasoning. Second, it facilitates creativity by revealing previously hidden relationships between concepts and statements. The premises summarize the story of a theory; the fewer there are, the better and more elegant the theory.

Each of the six parts of a theory plays its own role in the formalization process. The first two parts form the text of a theory. The text of Boserup's

Table 10.3 Ordering Statements into Premises and Equations

A. Premises
1. Sudden increases in degree of complexity produce increases in conflict rate.
2. Increased conflict creates greater centralization of organizations.
3. The greater the centralization of an organization, the greater its efficiency.

B. Derived Statements
1. Sudden increases in degree of complexity produce greater centralization of organizations.
2. Sudden increases in degree of complexity produce more efficient organizations.
3. Increased conflict creates more efficient organizations.

theory, although it has only been briefly sketched here, tells us why agricultural complexity increases under primitive agricultural conditions. The text isolates phenomena for study and analyzes their relationships. It does this by indicating which concepts are worth investigating if we are interested in studying the development of agricultural complexity, and it indicates how these concepts are related. The text also contains additional, hidden, logical relations between concepts. For example, if "The greater the population size, the greater the degree of agricultural complexity" and "The greater the degree of agricultural complexity, the more people become available for nonagricultural activities," it logically follows that "The greater the population size, the more people become available for nonagricultural activities."

The dictionary of a theory contains definitions of theoretical terms along with operational formulas, procedural instructions, arguments of revelance, techniques for ordering concepts and statements, and specifications of kinds of data pertinent to the test of the theory. Boserup's interesting and thought-provoking theory is a discursive theory that consists primarily of a text and a few elements that belong within the dictionary. As a result, the meaning and measurement of terms are not always clear and testability of statements is often ambiguous. Furthermore, the systematic ordering of statements would make the derivation of theorems in the theory more straightforward. For instance, the premise "The greater the degree of agricultural complexity, the more people become available for nonagricultural activities" implies that there should be more nonagricultural specialists among plow-based agriculturalists than among hoe-based agriculturalists, or among the Celts rather than the Siriono. The variety of derivative hypotheses even within this partial reconstruction of Boserup's theory is obviously very great. The dictionary of a theory is, therefore, an essential component of a scientific theory.

Principles of Theory Construction

How are theories constructed? Can discursive theories be formalized with the same procedures? Where are lawlike statements to be found? What form should these statements have? Each of the books on theory construction cited in the last section provides a strategy for answering these questions and a host of techniques for building scientific theories. These strategies and techniques are as applicable to building new theories as they are to formalizing discursive theories. Some of the many principles of theory construction that apply to concepts, theoretical and operational definitions, and theoretical statements are described in this section to further introduce the theory-building process in archaeology. Again, the main ideas have been borrowed from Hage (1972), who has written one of the clearest, most easily understandable introductions to the construction of ideal axiomatic theories in the social sciences.

Searching for Theoretical Concepts

One easy way to initiate the theory-building process is to search for theoretical concepts that describe or make understandable those archaeological phenomena that interest us. As chapter 2 stressed, every concept focuses on only some aspects of the real world as we perceive it and ignores other aspects. In searching for theoretical concepts we might begin by asking, What key concepts describe or make understandable the archaeological phenomena that interest us? Are the concepts associated with the technoeconomic, social, or ideological subsystems? What is our unit of analysis? Basically, there are two general kinds of concepts: categories, or either-or concepts, and variables, or dimensions of phenomena. Categorical concepts are nominal either-or measures that lack dimension. They are class concepts that either include an object or event or do not. Familiar categorical concepts in archaeology are site, projectile point, hunter-gatherer, urban, egalitarian, old, specialist, civilization, social status, and society. Like all nominal scales, either-or concepts permit only the measure of presence or absence. Perhaps their most constricting condition is that they often can be applied only to some groups of people and to particular time periods and not to others. Variables, by contrast, are culture-free and timeless continua that measure dimensions of phenomena. Concepts previously reconstructed from Boserup's theory, such as agricultural complexity, population size, output per worker-hour, and frequency of cropping, are variables because they represent continua. Extent of reliance on hunted and gathered foods, population density, years of age, and degree of social stratification are other common variables in archaeology. Table 10.4 lists examples of nonvariable and variable concepts.

Concepts expressed in variable form have a number of advantages in theory construction over those expressed in either-or form. First, they do not deny the complexity of reality but recognize the many shades that exist between either-or extremes. This allows an almost infinite variety of measures and a greater precision of measurement, which in turn makes possible a clearer differentiation between societies within a sample. Second, they permit the discovery of universal lawlike statements, for they are applicable to all human societies at all time periods. By contrast, the scope of an either-or generalization or hypothesis is limited by its nonvariable concept, such as Neolithic, Mississippian Culture, or rectangular house. Third, variables are often less complicated than nonvariable concepts. Nonvariable concepts, especially ideal types such as Neolithic or hunter-gatherer, tend to have numerous connotations that detract from their measurement. As a result, it is difficult to test hypotheses containing these concepts. In these cases, too, research tends to focus on finding the best or an agreed upon meaning of the term, its essence, rather than on exploring how some of its properties relate to the properties of other concepts. Finally, more complex descriptions of ideal types and other units of analysis become possible when a large number of variables are used. As Hage says, "Everyone's favorite definition becomes [just] another dimension."

One general strategy in initiating the theory-building process, then, is to search for variables. There are a number of techniques available for quanti-

Table 10.4 Examples of Nonvariable and Variable Concepts

Nonvariables	Variable Concepts
Old	Years of age
Urban	Population density
Totalitarian	Degree of centralization
Ranked societies	Degree of stratification
Warfare	Conflict rate
Large	Size in cubic meters

fying most properties of a society. For instance, a nonvariable such as *old* can easily be converted into a variable by searching for an appropriate dimension, such as, in this case, *years of age*. The presence of an analogy in a model also suggests the presence of a more abstract dimension. Listing diverse examples of a particular unit of analysis, such as *town,* and then searching the examples for shared dimensions can lead to the discovery of new, often unsuspected variables, too.

One of the primary goals of science is the development of ever more comprehensive theories. In the social sciences these would be theories that encompassed an ever greater range of societies. A technique that can accomplish this goal involves making some variables even more variable, for not all variables are as variable as others. For example, Boserup's theory can be made more comprehensive by converting some concepts, such as agricultural complexity and fallow period, into more abstract or general terms. Economic productivity and environmental recuperation period are possible abstractions. Just such an extension of Boserup's theory has been suggested by Cohen (1977), who extended the theory to include hunters and gatherers.

Not all concepts in a theory can be variable concepts, however. Nonvariable or categorical concepts are also necessary. One essential categorical concept is the analytical unit, the unit that is being analyzed or that is the focus of study. The behavior of these units is described and explained by variables and their interrelationships. Not all analytical units are as equally proficient in theory building, however. Some, such as peasant society, town, and religious bureaucracy, are confined in their application to only some human groups. Others, such as community, society, sociocultural system, organization, and role set, are more general. The latter terms are more or less applicable to all human groups, while the former apply to only some of them. Other categorical concepts define critical qualities that are useful in differentiating between analytical units or ideal types. For instance, measures along the variable scale of conflict may be broken down into quantitative zones to help identify the qualities *consensus, competition, protestation,* and *rebellion.* But the main goal of theory construction remains the search for culture-free and timeless variables. These variables not only increase the precision of theories but improve our chances of building ever more inclusive theories. Major advances have occurred in scientific disciplines when the shift was made from categorical to variable concepts (e.g., Cassirer 1953); perhaps similar advances will be made in archaeology, for this shift now seems to be under way.

Specifying Definitions

The three components of a concept—name, theoretical definition, and operational definition—have already been discussed in several previous chapters. A name is a label for a theoretical definition that specifies the meaning of a concept; an operational definition indicates what is actually to be measured or observed. All three components of a concept are essential components of the text and dictionary of a theory. One of the goals of concept definition in any science is to increase the validity of concepts; that is, to increase the correspondence between theoretical and operational definitions.

Specifying theoretical definitions results in greater clarity and helps us think more precisely and accurately about concepts and their interconnections. Because the meanings of terms are not commonly provided in the archaeological literature, definitions must be searched for in synonyms and indicators that imply definitions. In other cases, theoretical definitions must be provided for clusters of artifacts "discovered" through statistical analyses such as factor analysis. In the latter case, observations are suggesting the presence of a theoretical construct for which a theoretical definition is not yet available.

One of the bêtes noires of the logical positivists' research program was concepts that did not designate measurable phenomena. Their program was dedicated to the identification and elimination of metaphysical terms such as *world mind* and *vital force,* which, because they were not measurable or grounded in reality, were regarded as empty and meaningless. No measurement, then, no theory. Despite the efforts of the logical positivists, operational definitions are still rarely explicitly formulated in archaeology. Instead, individual indicators are occasionally mentioned. Some archaeologists collect these scattered indicators and file them under specific concept names. This process provides valuable insights into the use of some terms in archaeology, and it may even lead to a change in a theoretical definition. Indicators can also be discovered by searching the implications of theoretical definitions, for theoretical definitions, when present, usually point to or delimit some portion of the archaeological record.

Theoretical definitions guide the selection of valid indicators. But indicators also guide the selection of appropriate theoretical definitions, for the resources of a field may be inadequate in terms of time, money, and required data to actually carry out some measurements that are for the moment, at least, feasible only in principle. Take as an example the concept of *occupational differentiation*. Gibbs (1972) has provided a theoretical and operational definition for the concept, and a specified unit of analysis (a population). His theoretical definition is "a function of the number of occupations in a population and the evenness of the distribution of members of that population among the occupational categories," and his operational definition is $[1 - \Sigma X^2/(\Sigma X)^2]/[1 - (1/N)]$, where X is the number of members of a population in a given occupational category and N is the number of occupational categories in that population. The operational definition, the formula and other procedural specifications detailed in the dictionary of the theory, was developed within sociology. Is it empirically applicable within archaeology? Do presently available archaeological resources permit the measurement of the Xs and Ns? Would published cross-cultural data satisfy the terms of the formula or must fresh data be gathered through new excavations? If fresh data must be gathered, how much would it cost? It should be clear by now that the testability of an archaeological theory containing both of these definitions would probably be minimal. As the example implies, there is a constant interaction within the research process between the formulation of theoretical and operational definitions.

The adequacy of an operational definition may be assessed in many different ways. For example, the extent to which an operational definition agrees with other operational definitions of the same thoeretical definition of a concept is a measure of its degree of *concordance*. Degree of concordance is an important trait of operational definitions in archaeology, where slightly different indicators may have to be used for different geographical areas and for different time periods. Another trait of an operational definition is the relative ease with which it can be applied. This is a measure of its *feasibility*. Will it take five years or only one to measure the concept? Will it cost a large amount of money or can the measurement be done as part of a classroom project? Still another trait of an operational definition is its *intelligibility*, the ease with which its application can be understood. For example, is there room for ambiguity in the interpretation of the definition? Would two people reading the same definition understand it in the same way? Finally, the *universality* of an operational definition refers to its scope of application among a set of unit terms. For instance, will different definitions have to be developed for the same concept term in different parts of the world and for different time periods, or will this definition suffice? All of these traits of an operational definition together help to determine the testability of a theory and its derivative hypotheses.

As previously mentioned, very few archaeological terms have explicitly been given operational definitions. One result is that discussive grand theories are not grounded in the archaeological record. This means that systematic tests are precluded and that the theories must be evaluated on the basis of majority conviction rather than on their degree of empirical corroboration. When negative test results of a theory do occur, the results may be solely the product of the inconsistent application of theoretical definitions whose operational definitions have not been explicitly specified. This error may lead to the premature rejection of a theory or to the modification of one of its components rather than to the modification of the theory's measurement system. All of these are decisive errors that may easily occur when definitions have not been adequately specified. Shearing (1973) has with tongue-in-cheek discussed other procedures for making theories untestable.

Formulating Theoretical Statements

Theoretical statements permit analysis, explanation, and prediction by connecting two or more concepts. Some theoretical statements are *logical statements* in a syllogistic format, such as "All men are mortal" or "All A's are B's." Logical statements contain some form of the verb *to be:* "The Mesolithic is . . ."; "hand axes are . . ."; and so forth. Just as there are advantages to using variable concepts rather than categorical concepts during theory construction, so there are similar advantages to using *mathematical statements* rather than logical statements. Even though both connect concepts, mathematical statements permit concepts to be connected through addition, subtraction, multiplication, and other arithmetical devices, such as constants, powers, and coefficients in a continuous formulation. For instance, the Ideal Gas Law is a theoretical statement ($PV = RT$) that relates pressure (P), temperature (T), volume (V), and a constant (R). This statement clearly provides more information than "Gases expand when heated," for it provides precise measures of each variable as one or the other varies.

In archaeology, as in most social sciences today, the quality of data and the degree of understanding of the basic subject matter permit only relative or ordinal connections between concepts. The concepts taken from Boserup's theory in the last section were expressed in variable or quantitative form and related with an ordinal scale of measurement. "Among primitive agricultural communities, the greater the population size, the greater the degree of agricultural complexity" was an example. Although theoretical statements like this one are only expressed in an ordinal form, as are most theoretical statements in the social sciences, this less precise and somewhat inelegant method of stating relationships has the advantage of precluding premature falsification of theories in archaeology. Whether the relationship in the statement is really an interval or ratio relationship is just not known. The relationship could be made more precise by making it linear. For instance, "Among primitive agricultural communities, as population size increases, agricultural complexity increases collaterally in a linear relationship." But we cannot presume that the relationship is linear, for not many variables within the social sciences are probably related linearly. Their relationship could be curvilinear, through a power, inverse square, and so on.

Turning theoretical statements into continuous statements has other advantages, too. Continuous statements are more precise and contain more information; they tell us something about the expected change in variables as one or another varies. For example, agricultural complexity *increases* as population expands among primitive agricultural communities. The potential even exists for making more complex statements if the form of the relationship (linear, curvilinear, etc.) can be discovered; more information would become available because each relationship between variables would have large if not infinite numbers of separate measures. Continuous statements are ideal for studying culture change, too, for each links change in one variable with change in others.

Continuous theoretical statements or mathematical statements can be formulated through several techniques. The easiest technique is to search the literature for logical statements and ideal types and then to convert their contents into continuous statements. For example, the hypothesis "Communities that have a high degree of division of labor are more likely to have a high degree of effectiveness than communities with a low degree of division of labor" can be changed into the following continuous statement: "The greater the division of labor, the greater the societal effectiveness among communities." Redfield's folk-urban ideal types, which were discussed in the last chapter, can be searched for variables that define one type or the other, and then these variables can be related: "The greater the extent of trade with other societies, the greater the degree of social stratification among communities" and "The greater the number of secondary tools (tools fashioned exclusively for the manufacture of other tools), the greater the number of full-time religious or magical specialists" are examples. The pathways of systems models and other continuous flow models may also be searched for continuous statements. For instance, "The greater the number of small objects in a community, the greater the number of small objects that become lost" is a continuous statement that follows from one of the transformation processes discussed in Schiffer (1976).

Historically, the trend in theory building has been from the particular to the general, and from the less abstract to the more abstract (e.g., Bunge 1967:399). In this pathway, axioms of theories are formed by generalizing from low-level hypotheses in the following manner. First, low-level generalizations (which are future theorems) are established. These generalizations are then made more general, and logical or mathematical relations are searched for among those statements sharing common concepts. Even more abstract premises can then be invented from which presently known statements would follow as deductive conclusion. Alternatively, it may be discovered that some of these more abstract statements are already able to serve as axioms. In this process of ever increasing abstraction, axioms are commonly adopted in order to see what empirical assertions must be true if they are, rather than because the axioms are self-evident or otherwise strongly supported. Finally, the body of statements is systematized and, perhaps, eventually formalized into a deductive net. The deductive net not only controls the ideas within the theory but enriches existing knowledge by generating new hypotheses in the form of unexpected generalizations that logically follow from the axioms through the relationship of implication.

Evaluating Theories

Theories may be wrong for a variety of reasons. As we have seen, theoretical and operational definitions may not correspond well at all, the mechanism of a model may inaccurately conceptualize the regularities between empirical phenomena, and concepts and statements may not be formulated sharply and clearly. All of these potential problems and others must be evaluated in the research process through trial formulations. Trial formulations guide the decision-making process when choices must be made among concepts, definitions, theoretical statements, and other components of theories. A number of criteria have been suggested to guide this decision-making process, including simplicity, comprehensiveness, fertility, plausibility, logical consistency, predictive power, truthfulness, and elegance.

Simplicity refers to the number of axioms and other basic assumptions in a theory; a theory that contains numerous axioms and qualifying assumptions is not a simple theory. The *comprehensiveness* of a theory refers to the range in variety of the societies or other units of analysis which it includes within its scope. As we have seen, it is often possible in the theory-building process to make a theory more abstract by making its units of analysis more abstract. A theory's *fertility* refers to the numbers of interesting new avenues of research and surprising new relationships between variables that it suggests. Even when a theory is false, it can lead to exciting new avenues of research that might in the end prove its lack of truthfulness. The *plausibility* of a theory refers to our common-sense understanding of what is possible in the real world. For instance, does the theory of "vital forces" make sense in light of what we now know about the working of living organisms? *Logical consistency* is a criterion for clear, unmuddled thought. In trial formulations we ask, Does our theory contain logical ambiguities? Do our equations follow from our axioms? and so on. *Predictive power* refers to the ability to forecast the values of variable relationships from the statements within a theory. As mentioned earlier, this criterion is one reason why mathematical statements are preferred over logical statements in theory construction. The degree of a theory's *truthfulness* is the extent of its agreement with observations. Finally, *elegance* refers to the aesthetic beauty of a theory. Elegance is generally a product of all of the other traits that have been named when considered together.

Each of these criteria has been emphasized by some theorists and neglected by others, depending on their understanding of social phenomena and their interests. Gibbs (1972), for example, maintains that predictive power is more important in evaluating a theory than whether or not it is testable or falsifiable in principle. An archaeologist who is presently interested in Neolithic societies may not be particularly concerned with the comprehensiveness of his or her theory. In all of the social sciences, truthfulness and predictive power may not be as important as fertility, plausibility, and other criteria, for few theoretical statements are likely to be true for all societies or other units of analysis. In fact, theoretical statements in the social sciences are generally regarded as *tendency statements,* statements of what should happen if there were no interfering conditions (e.g., Gibson 1960:140). In other words, we should expect many exceptions to a statement or theory. As a result, theories in archaeology and most other social sciences are actually *factor theories* (Gibson 1960:144–155) or "concatenated theories" (Kaplan 1964:298), theories formed by interrelated sets of tendency statements. The predictive power of factor theories is uncertain, and their truth content or testability will be difficult if not impossible to determine, for each new falsification may just point to another exception. Still, they may be plausible, fertile, simple, comprehensive, logically consistent, and elegant. Chapter 11 explores several reasons why most theoretical statements in the social sciences are tendency statements.

Two Axiomatic Sketches

No theory within archaeology has ever been formalized. As a result, archaeological theories have not been systematically tested for logical consistency and correspondence with archaeological fact. One argument for this state of affairs has been that anthropological archaeology, which is concerned with what is general as well as with what is distinctive among sociocultural systems, is still an immature discipline. Many discursive theories within archaeology and anthropology, however, have been used to explain archaeological phenomena and would benefit from the formalization process. Examples are Boserup's theory (1965) of agricultural development, Karl Wittfogel's theory (1957) of the emergence of highly centralized political structures in preindustrial societies, Julian Steward's trial formulation (1949) of the development of early civilizations, V. Gordon Childe's theory (1951a) of social evolution, Kent Flannery's theory (1972) of the development of civilizations, and numerous other theories concerning culture change and the emergence of food production or civilization. The formalization of any of these theories would systematize their statements and concepts, allowing both logical inconsistencies and unanticipated, surprising, new ideas to become more easily apparent. Other theories and laws can be borrowed from other behavioral or social sciences, too, for they should in principle be applicable to past sociocultural systems. Formalization would permit systematic empirical tests of these theories and laws, and the separation of grand theories and empty laws without empirical foundation from those firmly rooted in the archaeological record as it is understood at this time.

The Marketing Process as a Theory: An Axiomatic Sketch

In chapter 7 the marketing process was presented as a mechanism in a model that was capable of explaining the distribution of certain prehistoric archaeological sites. What would a partial formalization of Walter Christaller and August Lösch's theory about spatial marketing look like? An axiomatic sketch of the marketing process as a theory has been presented by Douglas Amedeo and Reginald Golledge (1975:193–222), and a brief synopsis of their sketch is offered here as an example of the formalization process. Some definitions and axioms that attempt to capture the major assumptions of the theory are listed in table 10.5.

Table 10.5 Theory of the Marketing Process: Some Definitions and Axioms

Some Basic Definitions

1. *Marketing center.* Any size population center containing establishments primarily concerned with offering retail goods and services to consumers dispersed around the center.
2. *Space.* Undefined, but essentially refers to any extent in any direction from any point on the surface of the earth. Interpreted distance essentially reflects the effects of space in our context.
3. *Range of a good or service.* The maximum distance a consumer would be willing to travel to purchase a good or service offered by a seller. From the viewpoint of sellers, it is defined as the maximum distance from their establishment from which they will be able to attract consumers to purchase their goods or services.
4. *Trade area.* Any sized polygon-shaped area on the surface of the earth around an establishment that offers goods and services to consumers contained in the area.
5. *Threshold.* Used in reference to a trade area big enough (i.e., containing enough demand) to cover the costs (including opportunity costs) incurred by the establishment to offer the good or service.
6. *Order of a good, service, or center.* An ordinal designation indicating the relative importance of the good or service. In general, the less basic a good or service, the higher its order. Also, the higher the order of a good or service, the greater the threshold requirements. With respect to a center, the greater the number of goods and services offered, the higher its order.

Axioms

A_1. No boundaries enclose the plain upon which marketing process takes place.
A_2. For the area in which this marketing process operates, every place is like every other place and all places are perfectly flat.
A_3. The difficulty of movement over this plain is equal in all directions from any location.
A_4. The cost of transport is directly proportional to distance.

A_5. There is a single uniform transportation system servicing this plain.

A_6. Initially, the population on the plain is distributed uniformly.

A_7. Consumers on the plain earn identical incomes.

A_8. The propensity to consume is the same for every consumer on the plain.

A_9. Consumers on the plain have identical demand schedules.

A_{10}. All individuals on the plain have perfect knowledge of market conditions.

A_{11}. With respect to this knowledge gained about market conditions, individuals behave rationally and optimally. That is, consumers will try to minimize their expenditures to meet their consumption needs and producers will attempt to maximize their profits.

A_{12}. Human decisions about locations and spatial interactions reflect a fundamental desire to minimize the frictional effects of space.

A_{13}. There exists a large number of buyers and sellers on the plain.

A_{14}. For any *specific* good or service, one established price will prevail at the location of every center offering the good or service.

A_{15}. Every unit of a particular good is of the same quality.

A_{16}. There are no discounts in price for large quantity purchases.

A_{17}. The further consumers live from the store location, the greater the effective price to them for a good or service.

A_{18}. For any consumer, the quantity consumed declines with increasing distance from the store location because effective price increases. How much consumers are "willing" to consume, then, is a function of the price of the good or service to them *at* their place of residence.

A_{19}. As long as there exists surplus profits to be made, new entrepreneurs will enter the plain and establish stores offering this good.

A_{20}. Assume that the first network developed consists of centers offering the highest order good or service and, therefore, trade areas of the largest threshold size.

A_{21}. Assume that if a marketing center offers a good or service ranked, say, n, it also offers all other goods or services below it, that is, $n-1, n-2, n-3, \ldots . n-(n-1)$.

SOURCE: D. Amedeo and R. G. Golledge, *An Introduction to Scientific Reasoning in Geography.* Copyright © 1975 by D. Amedeo and R. G. Golledge. Reprinted by permission of John Wiley & Sons, Inc.

By viewing the marketing process as a theory, we can begin to comprehend why it generates certain spatial distributions. A number of theorems can be derived from the axioms in table 10.5. For instance, it can be reasoned from the axioms that the trade area around a center will be a perfect circle when no competition exists (figure 10.1A). This follows from axioms 2 through 10 and 15 through 18 and from at least the definitions of *range of a good* and *trade area*. Amedeo and Golledge present this conclusion as their first theorem, T_1: "In the ideal case with no other store or competition considered, the trade area around the store, *m,* is a perfect circle with a maximum radius *r*" (1975:201). If we assume further that all consumers must be served, that the number of establishments on the plain offering a particular good or service will be at a maximal level, and that competition exists throughout the plain, an overlapping of trade areas will occur (figure 10.1B).

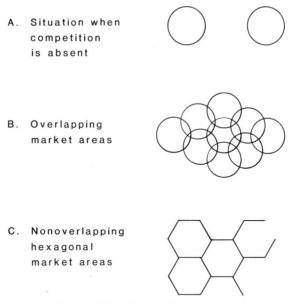

A. Situation when
   competition
   is absent

B. Overlapping
   market areas

C. Nonoverlapping
   hexagonal
   market areas

Figure 10.1   Forms of market areas.

According to these assumptions and axioms 2 through 5 and 10 through 16, all trade areas will change in shape to regular hexagons (figure 10.1C). Axioms 2 to 5 ensure that the process occurs uniformly across the plain, axiom 13 that the plain is "filled" with buyers and sellers, and axioms 14 to 16 that both price and goods exist uniformly from place to place. This conclusion is Amedeo and Golledge's second theorem, T_2: "All trade areas change in form from perfect circles tangent to one another to regular hexagons tangent to one another" (1975:204).

Now, if all consumers have to be served and the implication of axiom 19 is added, a third theorem follows from the second, T_3: "When surplus profits are no longer possible and competition essentially ceases, the offering of this good to consumers on the plain will be achieved by a regular distribution of a maximum number of identical minimum-scale establishments, each of which will charge an identical selling price to an identical, minimally sized, hexagonally shaped trade area" (p. 209) (figure 10.1C).

We already begin to see in this partial formalization of the marketing process how a process (marketing) begins to generate through time the form of the distribution of stores or communities given a set of basic assumptions (axioms) and some constraints. Now the spatial arrangements illustrated in figure 10.1 are for centers and their trade areas when only one good or service is considered. The implications of the theory can be extended by considering what would happen when other goods or services are introduced. Axioms 20 and 21 plus theorem 3 lead to theorems 4 and 5, which assert something about the locations of new businesses, the size and shape of their trade areas, the goods and services they will offer, and the evolution of new networks of centers and trade areas. These theorems, as stated by Amedeo and Golledge, are as follows:

> T_4. Businessmen offering new goods or services will locate exactly at the *midpoint* of a triangle formed by every three of the previously established higher order centers. The highest order good or service they will offer will be of a lower order than the highest order good or service offered by the centers forming the triangles. For example, if the highest order good offered by the centers forming the triangles is ranked n, then the new businessmen will offer a good ranked $n - k$ and will have an associated hexagonal-shaped trade area of threshold size equal to the trade area for the same good as offered by the centers forming the triangles.
>
> T_5. With time, a second, a third, a fourth, etc. network of marketing centers will evolve on the plain. Each network will completely cover the plain and will have marketing centers and maximum hexagonal-shaped trade areas smaller than those in previously established networks. Thus the smaller the marketing center and its associated trade area, the larger the number of them on the plain or the finer the network to which they belong. (1975:211; see figures 10.2 and 10.3)

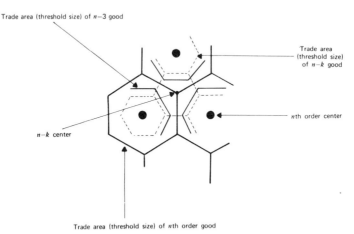

Figure 10.2 Trade areas and threshold sizes of nth, $n - 3$, and $n - k$ order goods. Source: D. Amedeo and R. G. Golledge, *An Introduction to Scientific Reasoning in Geography,* figure 7.12. Copyright © 1975 by D. Amedeo and R. G. Golledge. Reprinted by permission of John Wiley & Sons, Inc.

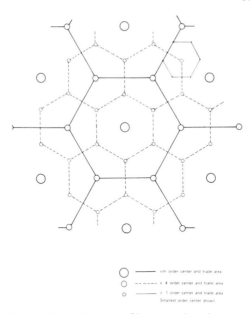

Figure 10.3   Systems of hexagonal trade areas.

Amedeo and Golledge (1975:211–222) rationalize theorems 4 and 5 and follow out the implications of the marketing theory in greater detail than will be presented here. However, the partial formalization already presented does illustrate many of the features of theory building in the social sciences. For instance, theories are generally about ideal situations: featureless plains, identical incomes, and so on. Furthermore, most social science theories are not well formed, to use Amedeo and Golledge's term. The axioms and theorems are not bound together within a tight deductive net. Instead, there are "meaningful" connecting relations between concepts that produce a logically connected structure, although not necessarily a logically deductive one. The basic assumptions of the theory have been made explicit. This procedure opens the theory to constructive criticism and its possible modification or falsification.

An Axiomatic Sketch of a Theory of Sociocultural Evolution

An interesting example of the formalization process in anthropology is B. Abbott Segraves partial formalization (1974) of some of the basic theoretical notions presented in *Evolution and Culture* (1960), a classic text edited by Marshall Sahlins and Elman Service. Together, the theoretical notions in *Evolution and Culture* form a discursive theory that endeavors to explain structural continuity and transformation among sociocultural systems. According to Segraves, the full impact and further development of the theory was being impeded by its discursive form. Her study was an attempt to provide the theory with increased rigor and greater clarity by explicitly presenting theoretical statements and definitions of key terms.

For our purposes here, the defining elements of a sociocultural system may be considered to be (1) a human population, (2) patterned interactions within the human population that form a functionally interdependent network of relations, (3) a material technology that effectuates the network and connects it with its environment, and (4) languages that serve to transmit information throughout the network. Certain basic assumptions are generally made in anthropology about sociocultural systems as defined above. First, they are open, dynamic systems having information and energy exchanges with their environments. Second, they are adaptive systems in that their structures remain stable or change depending on the nature of their information-energy transactions with their environments. Third, the environments with which they interact include other sociocultural systems as well as the physical and biotic realms. It is the variable properties of states of these systems that theories of sociocultural systems are about.

As in the construction of other theories, the concept terms in a sociocultural theory are restricted to those dimensions of sociocultural systems that are relevant to a particular problem area. Thus, in an evolutionary theory, terms are about very general properties of system structures, their relationships with their environments, and their classification along some scale of evolutionary development. Examples of concept terms in Segraves' partial formalization are survival probability, general evolutionary progress, structural stability, and level of sociocultural integration. Many of the primitive and derived terms in the formalization are listed in table 10.6 along with their theoretical definitions. Other undefined primitive terms, such as time, resources, and environmental change, are considered intuitively obvious. *Sociocultural system,* the unit of analysis, has already been defined.

Variables in the partially formalized theory were related by Segraves in tendency or probabilistic statements. The axioms or premises from which all other statements in the theory should be derivable are:

Axiom 1: Structural differentiation is an increasing function of absolute energy level in the system, and vice versa.

Table 10.6 The Theory of Sociocultural Evolution: Concept Names and Theoretical Definitions

Concept Name	Theoretical Definition
	A. Primitive Terms
Structural differentiation	The absolute number of functionally specialized system parts
Absolute energy level	The absolute amount of energy harnessed by the socio-cultural system
Absolute information level	The absolute number of different symbols (ideas) in the system.
	B. Derived Terms
Level of sociocultural integration	A configuration of values on the three criteria of general evolutionary progress: absolute structural differentiation, absolute energy level, and absolute information level
Structural stability	The requisite degree of fit in the intercorrelation of the three criteria of general evolutionary progress
External structural stability	The tendency of the system's principal defining parameters to stabilize within identifiable regions of their energy, information, and structural differentiation scales
Structural transformation	A shift from one scale region of external structural stability to another
Internal structural stability	Instances of within-zone variation which occur in regular patterns
Specific evolutionary progress or thermodynamic efficiency	The ratio of the total amount of energy harnessed to the amount of energy expended in production of the total
General evolutionary progress	The absolute amount of energy harnessed by the socio-cultural system
Degree of ecological generalization	Degree of heterogeneity in its resource base, i.e., the number of different kinds of resources upon which the system relies
Probability of an environmental destabilization	Any environmental change of sufficient magnitude to threaten the system's continued use of a basic resource. Lesser changes are uninteresting unless their long-term cumulative effect is the same, in which case they would be so classified
Survival probability	The likelihood that a sociocultural system will survive an environmental destabilization
Structural alteration	The failure of a system's structure to survive in its present form
Structural transformation	The transformation of a system's structure to higher or lower levels of integration

SOURCE: Segraves 1974. Reproduced by permission of the American Anthropological Association from *American Anthropologist* 76(3):530–552.

Axiom 2: Structural differentiation is an increasing function of absolute information level in the system, and vice versa.

Axiom 3: Absolute information level is an increasing function of absolute energy level in the system, and vice versa.

Segraves derived thirteen theorems or propositions from these three axioms (table 10.7). The text of her study contains arguments of relevance or theoretical linkages for each axiom and theorem. Together the theoretical statements partially account for or explain the structural continuity and transformation of sociocultural systems. Of course, the theory may be false in whole or in part, but the partial formalization is intended after all to open the theory to constructive criticism through an exploration of its empirical implications.

One frequent result of the formalization process, even a partial formalization, as in this case, is the discovery of unanticipated and interesting conclusions. The Fourth Law of Evolutionary Potential (proposition 12) is such an unanticipated conclusion, for it seems to run counter to what evolutionists intuitively feel to be correct. Nonetheless, it is a conclusion that is logically implied by theoretical statements within the theory. Furthermore, the proposition is testable, for it implies that systems higher on the evolutionary scale have a greater potential for further advance than those lower on the scale. The successful corroboration of this test implication would not only lend support to the proposition but to the entire theory as well. The theory implies other test implications, too. For example, proposition 9 leads to the expectation that the vast majority of these (sociocultural) systems will exhibit a marked degree of resource heterogeneity and that ecologically specialized systems will be rare; proposition 6 implies that the majority of significant societal transformations in history will have originated in ecologically generalized systems; and proposition 11 leads to the expectation that the higher a system is on the evolutionary scale, the more ecologically generalized it will be. Segraves summarizes available evidence in support of each of these real-world expectations.

Formalizing a theory is nearly always a long-term process that involves a community of scholars. In fact it is a process that may take generations of persistent effort, assuming that theory construction in the natural sciences is a reliable guide to what we might expect when building theories in the social sciences. In this example Segraves has partially formalized the text of a theory of sociocultural evolution. Elements of the dictionary of the theory have been provided, including theoretical definitions, theoretical linkages,

Table 10.7 The Theory of Sociocultural Evolution: Theoretical Statements

Proposition 1 (First Law of System Stability)
  External structural stability is a decreasing function of internal structural instability.

Proposition 2 (First Law of Structural Transformation)
  The probability that a sociocultural system will undergo a structural transformation to a higher level of sociocultural integration is an increasing function of its degree of internal structural instability.

Proposition 3 (Second Law of System Stability)
  Internal structural stability is an increasing function of the degree of specific evolutionary progress.

Proposition 4 (First Law of Evolutionary Potential)
  The likelihood that a sociocultural system will undergo a structural transformation to a higher level of sociocultural integration is a decreasing function of its degree of specific evolutionary progress (from propositions 1–3).

Proposition 5 (Third Law of System Stability)
  Internal structural stability is a decreasing function of degree of ecological generalization.

Proposition 6 (Second Law of Evolutionary Potential)
  The probability of a structural transformation to a higher level of sociocultural integration is an increasing function of the system's degree of ecological generalization (from proposition 5).

Proposition 7 (First Law of Environmental Instability)
  The likelihood of an environmental destabilization is an increasing function of time.

Proposition 8 (First Law of System Survival)
  The likelihood that a sociocultural system will survive an instance of environmental destabilization is an increasing function of its degree of ecological generalization (redundancy in the resource base).

Proposition 9 (First Law of Cultural Dominance)
  The relative frequency of ecologically generalized sociocultural systems is an increasing function of time (from propositions 7 and 8).

Proposition 10 (Third Law of Evolutionary Potential)
  In a population of sociocultural systems, the probability that at least one of them will experience a structural transformation to a higher level of sociocultural integration is an increasing function of time (from propositions 6–9).

Proposition 11 (Second Law of Cultural Dominance)
  The relative frequency of ecologically generalized sociocultural systems is an increasing function of absolute evolutionary progress (from proposition 10).

Proposition 12 (Fourth Law of Evolutionary Potential)
  The likelihood that a sociocultural system will undergo a structural transformation to a higher level of sociocultural integration is an increasing function of its degree of general evolutionary progress (from proposition 11).

Proposition 13 (Second Law of System Survival)
  The survival probability of a sociocultural system is an increasing function of its degree of general evolutionary progress (from proposition 11).

SOURCE: Segraves 1974. Reproduced by permission of the American Anthropological Association from *American Anthropologist* 76(3):530–552.

and some ordering into primitive and derived terms and premises and theorems. But other theorems implied by the axioms await discovery, and operational definitions and linkages, which provide measurement and testability, have not yet been specified. The interested reader is encouraged to read Segraves (1974) and other attempts to formalize discursive theories in the behavioral and social sciences (e.g., Debreu 1959; Blalock 1969, 1970; Dubin 1969; Gibbs 1972; Stinchcombe 1968).

Only a brief indication of what the formalization process would be like in archaeology has been presented here because of space limitations. But let us proceed. As mentioned in the introduction to Part Three, another goal of science is the ever increasing generalization of theories in order to subsume more and more phenomena under them. Cohen's generalization of Boserup's theory of agricultural development to include hunter-gatherers has already been mentioned in an earlier section. Can the theory of sociocultural evolution be generalized in this sense? The answer to this question is unknown at present, but one obvious possibility is the synthesis of the theory of sociocultural evolution and the theory of biological evolution, or perhaps the subsumption of the former under the latter as a special case. Although such a synthesis is not seriously attempted here, it is worth discussing the direction it might take.

Mary B. Williams (1970, 1973) has presented an axiomatic mathematical model of Darwin's theory of biological evolution. Her text contains seven axioms from which all other statements of the theory can be deduced, including a number of falsifiable predictions. Although her theory is too complex to present here, it is worth considering how the theory of biological evolution and the theory of sociocultural evolution might be synthesized. A first step would involve the generalization of the two units of analysis (sociocultural system and biological unit) to form a more abstract unit of analysis that subsumed both (such as unit of interaction). Or one might try to subsume one unit under the other. Common variables might then be listed, and existing theoretical statements made more abstract. Perhaps the two theories will never be fruitfully synthesized. They might be about things that are too disparate, or the resulting theorems and axioms might be so abstract that they do not account for the problems and archaeological phenomena of most immediate interest to the community of archaeologists. Nevertheless, important insights may be gained about the similarities and differences between biological and sociocultural evolution.

Summary

Chapter 10 introduces the process of building formal theories—structured systems of interrelated ideas that explain some aspect of the phenomenal world. All theories in archaeology are discursive, lacking the logical and predictive rigor of formal theories in the physical sciences. The author advocates that theories be assessed for formal statement, testability, and predictive power. Hage's concept of the tasks of theory construction is useful: a theory must first have a text, consisting of concept names related by verbal statements. Each verbal statement must contain at least one concept that also appears in at least one other statement, with the statements functioning as axioms, theorems, hypotheses, or propositions. Second, a theory must have a dictionary, consisting of theoretical and operational definitions and linkages. Archaeologists must nearly always develop their own operational definitions because of the peculiarity of their subject matter. Linkages between operational definitions ensure testability by grounding theoretical statements in archaeological reality. Finally, the ordering of primitive and derived terms and premises and equations minimizes tautologies, allows new definitions for familiar terms to be created, and identifies and exposes primitive terms to critical scrutiny.

The text isolates phenomena for study and analyzes their relationships. The dictionary contains definitions of theoretical and operational formulas, procedural instructions, arguments of relevance, techniques for ordering concepts, and statements and specifications of kinds of data pertinent to testing. Hage suggests that theory building start with the search for theoretical concepts that describe or make understandable archaeological phenomena that interest us. There are two kinds of concepts: categories (either-or) and variables. Either-or concepts are nominal-scale concepts, while variables are continuous, culture-free, and timeless. Variables are more useful in recognizing shades between extremes and in the discovery of universal lawlike statements. The search for culture-free and timeless variables remains the main goal of theory construction.

Concept definition (increasing the validity of name, theoretical definitions, and operational definitions) is essential to the text and dictionary of a theory. Theoretical definitions guide the selection of valid indicators and vice versa. The adequacy of operational definitions may be assessed by degree of concordance, feasibility, intelligibility, and universality. The formulation of theoretical statements permits analysis, explanation, and prediction. They are logical or mathematical. In archaeology the quality of data and degree of understanding permits only relative or ordinal connections between concepts. Historically, the trend in theory building has been from particular to general, from less to more abstract. Criteria for theory evaluation include simplicity, comprehensiveness, fertility, plausibility, logical consistency, predictive power, truthfulness, and elegance. Theoretical statements in the social sciences are generally regarded as tendency statements. As a result, theories in archaeology are factor theories.

No theory within archaeology has ever been formalized. Doing so would systematize statements and concepts, as well as allow inconsistencies and new ideas to become more easily apparent. Brief axiomatic sketches of the marketing process and of sociocultural evolution as theories are presented as examples of the formalization process.

Suggested Readings

Formal theory building in science is discussed by:

Amedeo, D. and R. G. Golledge. 1975. *An Introduction to Scientific Reasoning in Geography*. New York: Wiley.

Dubin, R. 1969. *Theory Building*. New York: Free Press.

Hage, J. 1972. *Techniques and Problems of Theory Construction in Sociology*. New York: Wiley.

Mullins, N. 1971. *The Art of Theory: Construction and Use*. New York: Harper and Row.

Read, D. and S. Leblanc. 1978. Descriptive statements, covering laws, and theories in archaeology. *Current Anthropology* 19:307–335.

Stinchcombe, A. 1968. *Constructing Social Theories*. New York: Harcourt, Brace and World.

Suppe, F., ed. 1977. *The Structure of Scientific Theories*, 2d ed. Urbana: University of Illinois Press.

Willer, D. 1967. *Scientific Sociology*. Englewood Cliffs, N.J.: Prentice-Hall.

CHAPTER ELEVEN

Is a Science of Archaeology Impossible?

We have assumed so far in Part Three that anthropological archaeology is, or at least some day can become, a science. But is anthropological archaeology a science or is the possibility of becoming a science really an attainable goal for the discipline? If social sciences like anthropological archaeology and social anthropology are already sciences, then why have they not made the same progress we associate with the natural sciences? Are there really contingent or a priori logical reasons, as some argue, why archaeologists and other social scientists will never discover laws of social phenomena analogous to the laws of physics? If anthropological archaeologists believe that they can discover scientific laws, where are their scientific laws of society? Are not the social phenomena studied by anthropological archaeologists so fundamentally different from physical phenomena, so much more complex and grounded in the realm of consciousness, that their study necessitates the adoption of different methodologies and goals than those of the natural sciences? If anthropological archaeologists cannot discover laws of social phenomena, why do they not stop attempting the impossible and give up the pretense of being scientists engaged in the discovery of empirical historical laws?

Anthropological archaeologists and other social scientists still do not agree on the most appropriate answers to these questions today. Opponents of a scientific archaeology point out that explicitly scientific archaeologists have produced very meager results indeed. They justify their position that a science of archaeology is either a contingent or an a priori improbability by pointing to the uniqueness of individual archaeological cultures or to the irredeemably subjective nature of social phenomena. The new archaeology is a new orthodoxy, they maintain, a new dogma that is intended to legitimize the activities of its adherents by the use of such persuasive concepts as logic, law, objectivity, fact, relevance, and science. Finally, even if a science of society were possible, they argue, it would be fundamentally different from that of the natural sciences, which has served as a model for new archaeologists. Scientific archaeologists have defended their position with vigorous proclamations of intent and plans for action. But they have continued to point the way rather than test propositions or formalize theories. In fact, no theories have ever been formalized and few if any propositions or laws have ever been systematically corroborated in archaeology. Still, they remind their critics that scientific archaeology is very young and though the results have been meager they do illustrate the promise of this approach to the study of the material culture of human societies. If archaeology is to contribute to the understanding of human social groups, it must become explicitly scientific.

These are not new arguments in the social sciences. Analogous arguments extend back to the very roots of social science and reverberate loudly throughout its history. None of these arguments will or could be conclusively answered here, of course. Rather, it is my intent to raise issues and to explore alternative interpretations of the social sciences as they apply to anthropological archaeology. Since the answers to the questions raised in the preceding paragraphs will depend in part on the conception of science that one adopts, three conceptions of science and their somewhat different approaches and goals are introduced in the first section of the chapter. These conceptions are positivism, realism, and conventionalism. A major goal of each of these views of science is the discovery of laws. Therefore, criteria for scientific laws are discussed in the second section along with some of the main barriers that have been suggested to the discovery of social science laws in archaeology. The final section explores in greater detail the fundamental role that concepts such as *meaning, intention,* and *purpose* have played in this debate.

Although only selected issues are introduced in this chapter, they do raise questions about the possibility of a scientific archaeology that must eventually be resolved by scientific archaeologists. Their exploration of these central issues will, it is hoped, lead them to a broader and deeper awareness of the dimensions of anthropological archaeology.

Conceptions of the Natural and Social Sciences

What kinds of activity does the adoption of a scientific perspective generate? As chapters 9 and 10 have demonstrated, one widely held answer is the search for general statements and their integration into scientific theories. But do social scientists agree on the kinds of general statements that they should be formulating? Do they agree on the most appropriate form for scientific theories? Do all social scientists agree on the function of general statements and theories, on what scientific activity is directed toward? Obviously, disagreement over the answers to these questions will generate different kinds of scientific activity. Unless the principles that generate these different kinds of scientific activity are made explicit, communication among social scientists generally becomes hobbled through misunderstandings rooted in divergent but uncomprehended research programs. It is beneficial, then, to have some idea of the various methodological principles and rules that generate different kinds of scientific activity. These issues are as relevant to the development of a science of archaeology as they are to the potential development of any other social science.

There are widely differing conceptions of the natural sciences. Each of these conceptions—which have names like positivism, realism, conventionalism, and rationalism—has a long history in both science and philosophy. All of these conceptions have been adopted at one time or another in the social sciences. A major recurrent issue in the social sciences, however, has been whether or not these research programs for doing natural science are, or at least to what extent they are, appropriate models for the social sciences. This has been called the issue of the methodological unity of the natural and social sciences. The issue has also been phrased in terms of naturalist (pro-unity) and antinaturalist (antiunity) positions. Whether the social sciences are or can become real sciences depends in part, of course, on the conception of the natural sciences that is adopted and on the position taken in the naturalism-antinaturalism debate.

Three conceptions of the natural sciences are introduced in this section: positivism, realism, and conventionalism. Since the names and definitions of the conceptions of natural science vary widely from one author to another, the names and definitions proposed by Keat and Urry (1975) are adhered to as closely as possible in this brief review. Each conception and position is presented as neutrally as possible, and the implications of each conception and position for research activity in anthropological archaeology when conceived as a social science are briefly drawn out. Since this is a brief review, the conceptions as presented are simplified composite constructions that do not necessarily represent the views of any single individual. Adherents to each of these three conceptions of science in the social sciences have generally been committed to a naturalist position. Some problems for the naturalist position are raised in the following section, and possible solutions to these problems and several antinaturalist perspectives are discussed in the third and final section.

The Positivist View

Elements of positivism can be found in the writings of medieval philosophers, such as Ockham. But positivism experienced its most significant development early in the eighteenth century through the writings of Hume and Berkeley, two British philosophers. Although the views of positivists have been many and varied, only three main characteristics of these views will be stressed here. First, positivism developed primarily as a counter to extreme metaphysical speculations that had little or no anchor in the realm of the observable. As a result, scientists of a positivist persuasion came to reject any concept as scientific that did not have clearly specified empirical (observable) referents. In a wider context, they even rejected questions of values and metaphysics as meaningless and insisted that the only legitimate form of human knowledge is scientific knowledge. Second, positivists came to defend what has been called the regularity view of causation and explanation and to deny the existence of causal necessity in nature. For the positivist, for one event to cause another is for the first event to regularly precede the other. Causation is the regular succession of one event by another. Although all possible instances, such as future instances, of the relationships of two events cannot be observed, the regular succession of one event by the other can be observed in individual instances. According to the positivists, to postulate any "necessary" link between events is an unnecessary, "metaphysical," assumption. The development of this second characteristic can be viewed in part as a natural consequence of the first characteristic of positivism mentioned above. Third, if the social sciences are to be sciences, they must be developed along the lines of the natural sciences. This is the naturalist position. Now let us see how these characteristics transfer into a program of scientific activity.

According to positivism, the goal of science is to gain predictive and explanatory knowledge of observable phenomena. This goal is to be accomplished by formulating and testing general statements, or laws, that express the regular relationships that are found to exist in the external world. Laws are causal empirical relations between observables. They are empirical discoveries of the relations between the elements of experience. Theories consist of interrelated, highly general statements like these. Observable events and things in the external world are explained by showing that they are instances of the regularities expressed in the general statements. Predictions are made on the same basis. This is the covering-law position, discussed in chapter 3.

The truth or falsity of the general statements that play an essential role for the positivist in explanation and prediction is not a matter of logical necessity. Nor can their truth or falsity be known by a priori means, by pure reasoning alone. Each is a purely empirical, universal, conditional statement whose truth must be objectively tested by means of observation and experiment. In fact, the criterion for being a scientific statement for positivists is the possibility of determining the truth or falsity of the statement through objective empirical observations, for observation and experiment are regarded as the only source of certain empirical knowledge. The pathway to formulating and testing general statements and theories is the scientific method, the logic of science, a process somewhat similar to the research process presented in chapter 2. The end product of this positivist research program is the gradual accumulation and growth of scientific knowledge, of laws and theories.

Science progresses according to positivism by honing away meaningless metaphysical concepts wherever they are found and by systematically testing statements of the regular relationships that exist between observable phenomena. This concept of scientific progress does not mean that positivists do not believe that essences, deep structures, and other mechanisms lying beyond observable phenomena do not exist. They only reject an ontological commitment to unobservable entities, for it is not the purpose of science to attempt to get behind the phenomena experienced through our sensory equipment. To do so would be to plunge science into the meaningless morass of claims that characterize metaphysics and theology. Even though scientific theories contain both theoretical and observational terms, these terms according to positivists do not refer to different entities or events. Theoretical terms are just shorthand symbols for observational phenomena. Positivism strictly interpreted has no ontological commitment to unobservable entities like culture, social structure, or the subjective states of individuals. A social structure, for example, does not exist in some real sense for the positivist. It is only a shorthand concept for the patterned social activities of people living within a society. In a similar sense, necessary connections do not exist in nature. There are only regular successions between physical phenomena. We might think of laws as causing things to happen, but in a positivist interpretation laws just describe observable regularities. To attempt to postulate unobservable phenomena or to attribute necessity to a relationship is, again, to plunge science into the meaningless morass of unverifiable claims.

Positivist approaches have dominated the development of the social sciences. The predominant methodological orientation in the development of the new archaeology has also been a positivist conception of science called logical positivism/empiricism. Although positivism did not enter archaeology as a well thought out research program, only against the background of logical positivism/empiricism do many of the fundamental concepts and endeavors of the new archaeology become intelligible. At a general level the following characteristics of the new archaeology all indicate the essential indebtedness it owes to the positivist conception of science: the equation of laws with relational statements expressing observable regularities; acceptance of the covering-law model of explanation as both a standard and goal of scientific inquiry; belief in the symmetry of explanation and prediction, and their equation with control; the belief that testing is primarily a matter of predictive success; an operationalist interpretation of concepts and theories; the belief in autonomous facts that serve as a means of objectively evaluating theories; the theory-fact dichotomy; the view that archaeology has progressed both historically and logically from description to theoretical explanation; and, not the least, the correspondence between the language of positivist philosophy and the language of archaeological theory. Statements characteristic of a positivist conception of science can be found in Binford (1972), Watson, Leblanc, and Redman (1971), Fritz and Plog (1970), and Martin (1971).

The influence of positivism on the new archaeology is also apparent in its present drift toward the behavioral sciences. Positivism and a behavioral approach to human social studies have been closely associated throughout their mutual histories. The epistemologically and ontologically privileged position of the observational language in positivism places an emphasis on the measurability of the observable, on the possibility of its quantification, and, therefore, on a behavioral interpretation of the social sciences. Measurability and quantification are especially important processes to positivists, for by performing these processes they support the assumption that an impartial given is being studied, that science itself is an objective process controlled by observation. Furthermore, both positivism and the behavioral approach stress the elimination of mentalistic concepts and explanations, the ideal of nomothetic explanation as compared to idiographic explanation, and concentration on overt behavior and its by-products, among other shared goals.

The Realist View

Elements of realism extend back at least to Aristotle and can be traced through various medieval philosophies. Significant contributions to this perspective were made by John Locke in the seventeenth century. Realism and positivism share many of the same conceptions of science, including the vision of science as providing true explanatory and predictive knowledge of the world we live in. Both research programs assume as methodological principles that sicence is objective, empirically based, and rational, and both share a common interest in formulating general statements, building theories, accumulating knowledge, and following the general guidelines of a "logic" of science. But there are at least two major differences between realism and positivism. First, realists emphasize explanation as a more primary objective of science than prediction because they believe in the existence of underlying structures and mechanisms that work to produce necessary connections between observable phenomena. An essential activity of science, according to realists, is the accumulation of knowledge of the often unobservable underlying structures and mechanisms that causally generate observable phenomena. Second, realists explain events and entities by showing not only that they are instances of well-established regularities but that they are instances of necessary connections between phenomena as well.

Realists' emphasis on making causal explanations through the discovery of underlying structures, mechanisms, and "essences" has often meant the postulation of the existence of types of entities and processes that we cannot see in the ordinary sense of that term. Unobservable theoretical entities such as a culture or a social structure are regarded as real in much the same way that we regard a stone or a house as real. Realists, then, make ontological commitments to theoretical terms in a manner that positivists find mystical and metaphysical. However, realists argue that this is an essential scientific strategy, as exemplified by such terms as *force* and *gravity,* for observable regularities can only be meaningfully explained by going beyond mere appearances to the underlying nature, mechanism, or essence of a situation.

Positivists, by analyzing only the superficial, apparent aspects of the natural and social worlds, fail to discover those deeper mechanisms and structures that cause observable natural and social phenomena. Most cross-cultural studies are misdirected and trivial for the same reason: they concentrate on the superficially observable rather than the deeper underlying substatum of social life. This same basic disagreement between realists and positivists is apparent too in their differing conceptions of the role of models in the research process and in their interpretation of scientific theories. For a realist, a model attempts to depict and transfer actual mechanisms from one better-known realm of study to another. The positivist, on the other hand, typically regards models only as heuristic aids that help one better grasp or represent a theory. Realists construct scientific theories consisting of general statements that describe the structure and mechanisms that causally generate the observable phenomena that are the subject of a study, while positivists adopt an instrumentalist interpretation of theories.

Even though most sociocultural anthropologists who believe that a science of anthropology is possible tend to be realists, a realist conception of science has been greatly overshadowed in anthropological archaeology by positivism. An example of a realist position in archaeology is Childe's Marxism. More recently, a realist structural archaeology has openly challenged positivist conceptions of archaeology in Europe (e.g., Friedman 1974; Friedman and Rowlands 1978; Spriggs 1977). Within anthropological archaeology, James Deetz (1967, 1977) probably comes closest to exemplifying a realist perspective.

The Conventionalist View

Conventionalist is a general term for a diverse group of scholars who are joined more by their rejection of many features common to realism and positivism than by a shared set of views about the process of science. What they basically reject is the general realist and positivist conception that science is an objective, rational enquiry that aims at true explanatory and predictive knowledge of an external reality (Keat and Urry 1975:5). In rejecting this general conception of science, conventionalists are united in rejecting (1) the idea that things exist in the external world independently of our beliefs and theories about them, (2) the idea that scientific statements and theories must be or even can be objectively tested and compared by experiment and the observation of empirical evidence, and (3) the idea that there are external and universal standards of scientificity that are independent of particular substantive theories and explanations.

These three interrelated negative statements provide the core assumptions of the conventionalist perspective. The reasons that conventionalists have stated for rejecting these ideas are varied. Only three of these reasons will be mentioned here. First, it has been argued that it is impossible to determine the truth or falsity of theories by appeal to observation, since no useful distinction can be maintained between theory and observation. There may be an external reality that exists independently of our theoretical beliefs and concepts, but our comprehension of that reality is inevitably distorted by the theory-ladenness of our perceptions. As a result, science cannot provide true descriptions and explanations of an external reality, nor can its theories be objectively assessed by reference to empirical evidence. Second, since there is no rock-hard observational base to help us rationally choose between different theories, criteria based upon moral, aesthetic, or even instrumental values must in reality play a fundamental role in helping us make such choices. We might just as well choose one theory over another because of its greater mathematical elegance, for example, than because of its greater degree of truthfulness. Third some conventionalists have even taken the extreme position that there is no external reality that can be said to exist independently of our theoretical beliefs and concepts.

Although conventionalists do not share a homogeneous set of views about science, their conception of science is generally associated with the idea that the adoption of a scientific theory is mainly a matter of convention. This view of science has had a long history, particularly in astronomy. In this view a theory is a computational device, an instrument, which helps us make correct and useful predictions about phenomena, such as the movements of the heavenly bodies. Since theories are only computational devices, they do not actually describe physical reality. Nor does it make much sense to talk about their truth or falseness: they are either useful or they are not. Their value is primarily that of calculi that help us use and control things and events as they appear to us. It is for these reasons that partly aesthetic criteria, such as simplicity or mathematical elegance, rather than truth are used to choose between theories that account for appearances.

Two examples of influential conventionalist philosophies of science during the last two decades are those of Kuhn (1970) and Feyerabend (1975). Both deny the existence of a theory-neutral observational language, as well as the existence of universal methodological rules and standards. According to Kuhn, every science alternates between phases of normal science and phases of revolutionary change. Each phase of normal science is governed by a paradigm that determines which problems and solutions are acceptable. The scientific community concentrates on solving those acceptable puzzles that are known to have solutions within the assumptive base of their paradigm. Theories within the paradigm are only computational devices that are elaborated until they are no longer able to resolve increasing numbers of anomalies. As anomalies grow in numbers, unrest emerges, young scholars uncommitted to the prevailing paradigm call for change, and a scientific revolution leading to the establishment of a new and of course a "better" paradigm ensues. The break to a new paradigm is generally not the result of critical assessment of accumulated arguments. Instead, it is more often a conversion experience, similar to that of a change in religious belief. Therefore, the explanation of these changes is to be sought through sociological and psychological studies. Furthermore, since theories are computational devices adopted for their proficiency in prediction and control, it is meaningless to search for the explanation of these changes in the growth of objective knowledge, for knowledge does not grow in some objective sense (e.g., Popper 1972) outside the parameters of paradigms.

Feyerabend, too, has attacked the image of science as a completely rational and objective process. In fact he has advocated an anarchistic epistemology founded on the methodological principle "anything goes" (1970:26; 1975). According to Feyerabend, an examination of the historical development of the sciences clearly shows that no methodological rule or standard can be justified. Advances have been made in more than one discipline by individuals who have done just the opposite of that required by a rule (Feyerabend 1970:22). Besides the principle of anything goes, Feyerabend advocates another principle that also contrasts with Kuhn's concept of normal science. According to this principle, the principle of proliferation, many and diverse competing theories should always be formulated. By concentrating solely on the development and testing of a single theory, scientists tend to avoid the discovery of counterevidence. In evaluating rival theories we must rely on our own subjective preferences and aesthetic tastes, for universal criteria for assessing theories do not exist (Feyerabend 1970:90). If we choose to do so, we can regard science as a rational and objective enterprise with universal principles and standards. But this is really just a subjective choice, a choice in fact that should be resisted by everyone who values human freedom and individuality (Feyerabend 1970:21). Science should be a truly human activity based on human values—a free enterprise unfettered by rigidly held methodological rules and principles.

Archaeologists *qua* archaeologists have probably never held a conventionalist philosophy of science. The absence of this conception of science in the discipline can be accounted for by two characteristics of archaeology. First, most archaeologists are and have been devoted to writing culture histories. A culture history, broadly defined, involves the explanation of past human behavior by reference to events and processes that actually took place. Culture histories are not intended to be fictions. Second, scientific theory about general classes of events and processes, about settlement location or subsistence intensification, for example, is poorly developed in archaeology. As scientific theories proliferate in archaeology, it is quite possible that at least some archaeologists will adopt a conventionalist conception of science. Although many archaeologists may now regard this as an unlikely possibility, even a distasteful possibility, the present rapid adoption of mathematical rationales as processual mechanisms in model building may actually hasten this development.

Each of the three conceptions of the natural and social sciences briefly reviewed here in simplified form has different implications for the activities of anthropological archaeologists who conceive of themselves as social scientists. The activities that follow from a positivistic or realistic conception of science are really quite close, with positivists focusing on observable regularities and realists searching for hidden structures and mechanisms. Differences between these two conceptions of science are based on a fundamental disagreement about what exists and is knowable in the world. Despite these differences, positivists and realists are often lumped together as positivists because of their common agreement on many other issues. Scientific activities that follow from conventionalists positions are varied, even though the positions reviewed here both support a naturalist perspective. Conventionalists who support a naturalist perspective formulate general statements and build theories, too, but the way in which these activities are conceived differs from that of either a positivist or a realist.

Can Archaeologists Discover Laws?

As we have seen, positivists, realists, and conventionalists disagree on several critical issues. They do not agree on what should be the primary focus of scientific study: observable regularities, the often unobservable structures and mechanisms that purportedly underlie these regularities, or imaginary computational devices that account for appearances. Nor do they agree on what scientific theories represent: approximations to what actually exists in external reality or only handy fictions that allow us to make accurate predictions. Despite these and other disagreements, most social scientists who hold one of these conceptions of science also adopt the naturalist position in the methodological unity debate. They agree that the general methods and goals of the natural and social sciences can be, should be, and must be the same; they agree that, as social scientists, their goal is to formulate theories and general statements. But problems exist within the naturalist position, problems that antinaturalists claim preclude the very idea of a social science and, by implication, a science of archaeology.

Several of the many problems that exist within the naturalist position are introduced in this section by examining an essential element of most conceptions of science, the concept of a scientific law. The formulation of laws is a goal of many scientists for a number of reasons: (1) they adhere to the covering-law model of explanation; (2) they view knowledge as an interlocking set of general laws; (3) they have adopted a deterministic or at least orderly view of the universe; (4) they believe that the search for laws and predictions based on laws is the very measure of a science; and, perhaps most importantly, (5) they believe that knowledge of laws will enable them to state something about a whole class of phenomena (all falling apples, for example) from what is known about a part of the class (the apple that struck Newton on the head).

In the social sciences, fundamental problems with the law concept revolve around two questions: Can archaeologists and other social scientists discover laws analogous to those in the natural sciences? If they can, where will they be found and what will be their subject matter? These questions raise problems about (1) the most appropriate set of criteria for separating scientific laws from other general statements and (2) the most appropriate location and subject matter of social science laws. The first problem is approached here by examining criteria for scientific laws, the second by reviewing two well-known debates in the philosophy of social science, that between objectivism and subjectivism and that between methodological individualism and methodological collectivism. Both of these sets of questions have provoked arguments among people who support a naturalist position in the social sciences. The questions also raise issues that antinaturalists have been responding to throughout the history of social studies. Scholars holding an antinaturalist position have generally argued that the questions are basically meaningless, since the subject matter of the social and natural sciences is so fundamentally different that their approaches and goals *must* be different. The variety of views discussed in this section provides a foundation, then, for understanding the issues that naturalists and antinaturalists debate, issues that are reviewed in the third section of this chapter.

What Is a Scientific Law?

A set of commonly agreed upon criteria that clearly separate scientific laws from general statements that are not laws is conspicuously absent from the philosophy of science. As Peter Achinstein remarks, "A tidy set of necessary and sufficient conditions cannot, I think, be produced for laws" (1971:1). Therefore, a degree of arbitrariness and justification must enter into the selection of any such set of criteria. While the criteria listed below have this uncertain characteristic, they do provide an explicit set of conditions that can serve as a standard against which purported laws in archaeology and the social sciences can be compared. Others may disagree with these criteria but at least they serve as a basis for discussion and disagreement.

Scientific laws may be defined as "statements which relate variables or phenomena in nature to each other and which describe the processes involved in these relationships" (Stickel and Chartkoff 1973:664). Although there are various kinds of laws (table 11.1), all of them are said to share a number of characteristics. Peter Achinstein (1971) has grouped what he considers the shared characteristics of laws under three key features: *generality, necessity,* and *regularity.* Achinstein not only presents his analysis of scientific laws in a systematic and thorough manner, but—unlike most discus-

Table 11.1 Kinds of Laws

Kinds of Laws	Examples from Science (after Nagel 1961)	Potential or Actual Archaeological Examples
1. Causal laws	1. Laws of quantum mechanics	1. Binford's tension-zone hypothesis for the origin of food production (Binford 1968b)
2. Statistical or probabilistic laws	2. Hardy-Weinberg law of genetics	2. Carneiro's quantitative law in anthropology (1970)
3. Determinable properties laws	3. The atomic elements	3. Semenov's *Prehistoric Technology* (1964)
4. Functional dependence laws a. with time element b. without time element	4a. Galileo's laws for freely falling bodies in a vacuum; the second law of thermodynamics 4b. Boyle's law; Venturi's principle	4a. Deetz and Dethlefsen's "Doppler effect" (1965) and archaeological diffusion; Steno's law 4b. Naroll's relationship (1962) between floor space and population size; Cook and Heizer's relationship (1968) between house size, settlement size, and population size
5. Developmental or historical laws	5. Principle of biological evolution; Marx's economic theory of history	5. Adams' *The Evolution of Urban Society* (1966); White's *Energy and the Evolution of Culture* (1943)

SOURCE: Stickel and Chartkoff 1973, table 1.

sions of laws in the philosophy of science—bases it on an examination of actual scientific laws as well. It is only possible here to briefly summarize some of the criteria that Achinstein discusses at length.

First, *laws are statements of universal form*. They are "unrestricted universals" that hold for all particular samples or instances in which all items satisfying the subject terms of the laws are present. Whenever and wherever conditions of a specific kind occur, so will without exception other conditions of another kind. In addition, their subject terms are general, as is their syntactical form (that is, they refer to "all" or "no" rather than to "some"). Laws must not be restricted in their application to any finite region of space and time: they must hold for all times and places. For example, the statement "As Pueblo societies in the Southwest nucleated, their agricultural systems intensified" would not qualify as a law, because of the spatial and temporal restrictions in the statement. For this reason, too, none of the terms occurring in scientific laws can refer only to particular, individual items; that is, they cannot contain names, such as Pueblo or Southwest. If the law is statistical, all things or events of some kind have a known chance of being related to something else. It is, for example, a law that the pressure and volume of a gas are inversely proportional; and "it is a statistical law that all atoms of the most common isotope of radium have the same chance (fifty-fifty) of turning into something else within their half life of 1622 years" (Mellor 1980:106).

Second, *laws describe what is nonaccidental and necessary.* They are not accidental generalizations. This can be demonstrated by showing that they support what are called counterfactual conditionals (If A *had been* the case, then B would have been the case, where in fact A has not been the case) and subjunctive conditionals (If A *should come to pass,* then so would B). Laws are generally surrounded by a constraining belt of necessary and sufficient conditions that provide an explanation of why, if the law is true, certain consequent conditions will follow if certain antecedent conditions exist. Third, *laws describe regularities.* These may be regularities in the behavior properties or characteristics that certain phenomena exhibit. However, the regularities that laws express underlie "other regularities in such a way that the latter can be analyzed and explained [in the natural sciences] in physical terms by the former" (Achinstein 1971). The regularities are expressed in as complete, precise, and simple a manner as possible. In addition, statements that satisfy the criteria expressed under these three general features are not considered laws unless there are reasons to assume that they are true: they must have survived systematic and severe tests, otherwise they are regarded only as hypotheses.

The criteria for scientific laws suggested by Achinstein are based as mentioned above on an examination of actual scientific laws. This approach has the advantage of excluding general statements that many philosophers of science call laws but that no scientists would. For example, statements like "All ravens are black" are commonly used by philosophers of science to illustrate what a covering-law statement would look like. Unlike scientific laws, statements such as these do not tell us *how* the relationships are produced and *why* they have the values they do. An analogous near-law is, "All bodies fall when unsupported." What is missing can be illustrated by stating Galileo's law ($s = \frac{1}{2} gt^2$): "All bodies fall when unsupported in such a way that the distance traversed is proportional to the square of the time." Galileo's law tells us how fast bodies fall and why they have the speed they do by introducing the concepts of distance and time to that of body.

As another example, consider Boyle's law. Boyle's law ($p = 1/v$) states that "the pressure and volume of a gas are inversely proportional." The law analyzes and explains the observable regularity between the height of mercury in the long leg in a glass J-tube and the distance between the mercury and the top of the short leg by introducing the physical ideas of pressure, volume, and compressibility of gas. What explains why changes in the long leg are inversely proportional to those in the short leg in the J-tube is the more fundamental regularity between pressure and volume of air expressed in Boyle's law. Notice too that the subject term of the law (gas) is general, that the syntactical form of the statement is general, and that the relationships are simply, precisely, and completely expressed in the formula $p = 1/v$.

Do the generalizations archaeologists use as laws in covering-law deductive explanations satisfy these criteria? Do the statements explicitly proposed as laws by archaeologists satisfy the criteria? A brief discussion of some of the problems involved in answering these questions will serve to introduce a few of the difficulties social scientists in general have encountered in formulating acceptable laws. Lawlike statements can easily be found in the archaeological literature. Many of these statements refer to regularities within or between sociocultural systems; that is, to regularities between elements of ecological, demographic, social, economic, ideational, and other subsystems. "The greater the degree of sedentism, the greater the accumulation of material possessions" is an example expressed in the form of a "the greater the A, the greater the B" statement. Other statements refer to the deposition of materials into the archaeological record or to the transformation of archaeological contexts through time. "Small objects tend to be lost more readily than large objects" is an example of the former. Are these general statements scientific laws? While most are general and do describe regularities, few provide a constraining belt of necessary and sufficient conditions that analyze and explain less abstract regularities. Related to this absence is the fact that few if any attempts have ever been made to falsify or confirm any of these statements. Systematic attempts to falsify statements like these would most likely lead to the identification of constraining conditions and the reformulation of the statements into acceptable law candidates.

If archaeologists who support a naturalist position are to demonstrate that they can discover laws, that there is more to explicitly scientific archaeology than just the pretense of being scientific, they must subject their hypotheses that qualify as law candidates to critical tests or their statements remain merely hypotheses whose truthfulness is questionable. In the third section of this chapter we will review why some scholars think that statements like these will never be demonstrated to be true of the external world in the social sciences. Here some of the problems involved in testing lawlike statements are briefly discussed under four topical headings: (1) the problem of the operational applicability of particular predicates; (2) the lack of statements of initial conditions; (3) the problem of relational terms and temporal qualifiers; and (4) the absence of theories from which the statements can be derived. The purpose of this brief discussion is to demonstrate that proving that lawlike statements are most likely true or most likely false is a very difficult task indeed—assuming of course that anthropological archaeologists can discover social laws and that they do care to test those that they have proposed as law candidates.

The Operational Applicability of Predicates. A still largely unexplored research frontier in archaeology is the critical examination of the empirical applicability of those sociocultural concepts presently in common use. Although lawlike statements and theoretical definitions of concepts are common in the archaeological literature, operational techniques of measurement are difficult to locate, as mentioned in earlier chapters. Even when operational rules of interpretation have been proposed, they generally remain so vague, ambiguous, and inconsistent that they only provide measures with low reliability and validity. One problem, therefore, in testing lawlike statements in archaeology is the construction of valid and reliable empirical or procedural interpretations for measuring the value or presence of concepts in specific instances. This process has already received considerable attention in recent decades in other social sciences.

Statements of Initial Conditions. Initial conditions define the boundaries or domain within which a law holds. A consistently important research task in the natural sciences is the delimitation of these boundaries. However, most generalizations in archaeology are expressed as though they are unrestricted, as though they hold in all societies or all sites under any condition at all times. Other generalizations are restricted to particular broad classes of society, such as hunters and gatherers or food producers. When generalizations are unqualified or only broadly restricted, they imply that they hold equally well for all types of social unit. As a result the lack of constraints introduced by initial conditions usually produce inaccurate predictions and the premature falsification of possibly correct generalizations. Consider, for example, the following general statement adapted from Boserup (1965:11): "Among food-producers, the greater the population size, the greater the intensity of agricultural development." Does the apparent falsification of this assertion in one instance (e.g., Wailes 1972) demonstrate that it is false or that qualifying conditions are finally being located?

Relational Terms and Temporal Qualifiers. Ambiguous relational terms and temporal qualifiers also limit the testability of lawlike statements in anthropological archaeology. Consider the general statement: "Whenever agricultural production intensifies, energy output per work hour of labor increases." This statement asserts an absolute relation between two predicates: whenever agricultural production intensifies by X amount, energy per work hour of labor increases by an equivalent amount. But is our knowledge generally that precise? Examination of other relational statements in the social sciences suggests that predicates such as these are more frequently connected by power or other nonabsolute algebraic relations, if they are regularly related at all (e.g., Hage 1972). For this reason, ordinal relational terms such as *greater . . . greater* and *greater . . . less* are commonly used to preclude premature falsification of general statements.

Ambiguity in testing also arises when temporal qualifiers that stipulate the length of the period within which the relation asserted in the generalization is consumated are not stated. When agriculture intensifies, does energy output per work hour of labor increase at that time, in ten years, in the next two hundred years? Temporal qualifiers aid testability by delimiting the temporal domain within which a test is relevant.

Theoretical Derivation of Generalizations. The remaining problem that arises in testing archaeological generalizations that will be discussed here is the absence of theories from which generalizations can be derived. That there are such theories is exemplified by Boserup's theory of agricultural development or by the theory of sociocultural evolution. When theories like these are absent, it is difficult to determine whether regularities in archaeological contexts are the result of accidental trends or whether there are sound theoretical arguments why they should be the necessary outcome of human actions. In other words, it is difficult to distinguish between trends, accidental associations, and true law candidates, when correlation hunting is the main method of searching for general statements.

Let us assume for now that an understanding of criteria for scientific laws and the introduction of rigorous testing procedures will allow archaeologists to discover laws themselves. Where will they be found? What will they be about? Boas (1940:436), for example, thought that anthropologists should strive to discover the psychical laws of the human mind. Julian Steward and Leslie White sought to discover laws in cultural ecological factors, that is, in economic and environmental conditions (Hatch 1973:10, 113). The debate among naturalists in the social sciences over the locus of laws is introduced below in a brief review of two issues: *objectivism* versus *subjectivism* and *methodological collectivism* versus *methodological individualism*. Other issues involving the locus of laws will be introduced in the third section.

Objectivism and Subjectivism

Unlike natural scientists, social scientists have a special problem: the people they study operate within a conceptual framework just as they, the social scientists, do. What implication does the existence of these two different frameworks have for our understanding of the activities of social groups and their material remains? Should we describe and interpret another culture in our terms or in theirs: in terms of our conceptual categories (the *etic* approach) or their conceptual categories (the *emic* approach)? Whether social scientists should study the outside or the inside view of a culture has been a perennial problem of the social sciences. This problem has been encapsuled within the debate between objectivism and subjectivism or mentalism.

Many social scientists have maintained that the social sciences are irredeemably subjective, that their proper subject matter is human opinions and attitudes, and, therefore, that mental categories cannot be dispensed with in the explanation of social phenomena. As a methodological rule, the subject matter of the social sciences, whether it is street corner gangs or artifact assemblages, can only be adequately known through a subjective method, through introspection: human institutions are to be explained by reference to familiar individual mental processes. Franz Boas, as mentioned above, assumed that evolutionary laws were to be found in the "psychical laws of the human mind" (1940:436). Boas was interested in the subjective side of culture, in how culture appeared to the native. In his work he assumed that "behavior is largely 'irrational' and emotional, and that it is precisely these subjective elements which must be taken into account in order to understand human affairs" (Hatch 1973:39). Subjectivism relies on our inside understanding of what it is to be human to intuit what money, mothers-in-law, or ceremonial rites might have meant to some other cultural group. This approach is effective because we are human: we have an innate understanding of human nature that an extraterrestrial observer can never have. Therefore, another methodological rule of subjectivism is: Further your understanding of human nature by working toward an ever greater rapprochement between anthropology and psychology.

Objectivism is based on the principle that the social sciences are not dependent on the knowledge we think we derive from introspection: successful social science is possible without having to rely on our subjective knowledge of the working of the human mind. Objectivists have adopted this principle for a variety of reasons. For instance, individual people often have a distorted and very limited view of their own culture, and they do not always do what they "ought" to do. Furthermore, according to Karl Popper and others, the proper subject matter of the social sciences is the *unintended* consequences of the actions of many people interacting together. Finally, if social scientists are to build theories that explain shared patterns of culture, they cannot rely on diverse inside views of different cultures: they must rely on one conceptual framework, on the etic framework of the observer. An example of an anthropologist who worked within an objectivist framework is Leslie White. White viewed the principles governing cultural systems as "generally beyond the awareness of the people themselves" (Hatch 1973:150–151). According to White, culture determines people's behavior and not vice versa. As a result, a science of culture must be about autonomous evolutionary processes rooted in the technoeconomic subsystem. While Boas reduced the objective sphere of culture to the subjective, White reduced the subjective sphere to the phenomenal or objective.

The objectivism-subjectivism dispute raises particularly interesting problems for archaeologists. It also helps explain why many social and cultural anthropologists maintain that archaeology will never become a science or, indeed, why archaeologists will never be able to adequately explain past human behavior. I will suggest later, however, that what is important for archaeologists and other social scientists to determine is which questions must be answered by referring to mental entities, and which, if any, can be answered without making such a reference. That some archaeologists have been subjectivists will also be seen in the third section of this chapter.

Methodological Collectivism and Methodological Individualism

A dispute closely related to the objectivism-subjectivism issue is that between methodological collectivism and methodological individualism. In the preceding chapters I have assumed that social institutions are organized and have structure, and that one of the primary goals of anthropological inquiry is to account for the stability and change that may take place in such structures. Methodological individualists generally maintain that the use of macroscopic, collective, nonpsychological concepts is always illegitimate in the explanation of social events. As a methodological rule, explanation in the social sciences must be in terms of *individual* motivation and behavior. Collective concepts such as culture, social structure, and class are only convenient fictions that have no reality independent of the individuals who make them up: the only reality is individual people. It follows, then, that collective behavior and sociocultural institutions must be explained in terms that refer to individuals. As we have seen in the subjectivist-objectivist dispute, these explanatory statements may be about intraorganismic psychic mechanisms and processes (subjectivism) or about observable behavior (objectivism). According to methodological individualists, a basic research activity of the social sciences must be the reduction of sociocultural phenomena to statements about the basic needs, the thought processes, the activities, and so on, of individuals.

Can and should sociocultural phenomena be "reduced to" statements about the behavior or psychological states of individuals? Although this goal is not realizable yet in many of the social sciences, methodological individualists assume that a true science of human social groups must be based on such statements. Indeed, they argue that nothing is being reduced since collective concepts such as culture and social structure are only handy fictions. Methodological collectivists, such as Kroeber, White, and Durkheim, reject reductionism and maintain that sociocultural phenomena constitute an autonomous level of analysis in which individual variables, especially psychological variables, are irrelevant or, at least, inessential to the development of a vigorous social science. In anthropology, methodological collectivism has often been associated with the superorganic view of culture. Leslie White, for instance, regarded culture as a sector of reality in its own right; since culture is governed by laws of its own, culture must cause culture through the medium of human biological organisms. However, not all methodological collectivists, such as Kroeber, support the naturalist position in the methdological unity of science dispute.

The methodological individualism–methodological collectivism issue is a dispute in part over where laws in the social sciences will be discovered. Again, the dispute has important implications for the possible existence of a science of anthropological archaeology. This dispute, however, seems to have less serious implications for archaeologists than the subjectivist-objectivist issue, for even if social science laws must be expressed in some fundamental sense in terms of individual behavior or psychological states, archaeologists would still be able to formulate laws in collective terms. Although not fundamental or rock bottom, these laws would be reducible in principle to statements about individuals. Archaeology might never be able to become a fundamental social science in this sense, but it would be able to contribute to the development of the social sciences by discovering fictive laws about the collective that other social scientists could reduce and test.

Is a Science of Archaeology Impossible?

Lawlike regularities are commonly used by archaeologists in "explanation sketches" to make sense of the archaeological record. But, as mentioned earlier, few if any of these general statements have ever been subjected to severe tests. For this reason, they must remain hypotheses. The question naturally arises whether these statements can ever be highly confirmed. In general, scholars who defend an antinaturalist position in the methodological unity debate maintain that social scientists will never be able to highly confirm such statements, nor should they waste their time pretending that they can, for social laws do not exist. Lawlike statements in the social sciences *must* fail to satisfy the generality and necessity criteria for laws. At the very least, their relation of implication must be different from that of natural science laws.

If lawlike statements in the social sciences are not valid law candidates, what kinds of statement are they according to antinaturalists? One sugges-

tion is that they are statements that summarize tendencies or trends that result as unforeseen consequences of rule-following, rule-making, and rule-
breaking behavior in social groups. Behavioral regularities in social groups
are evidence only for the existence of social rules. In fact, determining which
of this behavior is the unintended consequences of following social rules, of
rule breaking, or of rule making has been the primary research goal of the
social scientist and not the discovery of social laws. It follows, then, that it
is these social regularities of behavior that result from rule following, breaking, and making that social scientists must explain by means of underlying
social laws—if they exist.

The implication of this distinction for archaeological research can be illustrated by an example. As we now know from earlier chapters, anthropological archaeologists ask a wide variety of questions about social institutions
and other cultural systems. For example, chapter 5 argued that standardized
ways of behaving cluster into roles, that roles in turn cluster into institutions, and that institutions in turn cluster into systems, such as the social or
political system. It is an understatement to say, therefore, that a great deal
of an anthropological archaeologist's research activity is focused on the existence, function, relationship, and history of particular rule-related activities
and on the social regularities which such activity produces. Anthropological
archaeologists *are* interested in what the subsistence or exchange system of
a prehistoric culture was: how it worked, whether it was effective or not,
how it developed, and so on. But all of these questions, and others, char-
acteristically provide answers that describe the operation of a set of cultural
conventions, for these conventions and their violation are exhibited in the
behavior of particular social groups. By learning all of this, archaeologists
have only learned a lot about the regular course of rule-related activity. As
mentioned above, knowledge about social regularities does not ensure the
discovery of social laws. As Brown has stated, "An interest in [social] regularities is . . . not an interest in social laws" (1973:118).

According to this account, a confusion exists in archaeology between
statements of social regularities and statements of social laws. It is the presence of social regularities that result from the rule-related behavior of the
members of human groups that social laws are to explain. Social regularities
of behavior are not themselves exemplifications of social laws. However, "the
fact that a certain rule is adhered to or not under certain conditions may be
an instance of the operation of social laws" (Brown 1973:98). Again, according to Brown, social scientists "have to distinguish genuine social laws

from social rules, and to distinguish both from the social regularities of behavior, which are the putting into practice of social rules and which are evidence for the latter's presence" (p. 98).

Why are social regularities or tendencies not social laws? We can all agree
that social rules and practices generally result in regular behavior, and that
when this behavior occurs within groups it produces social regularities, which
represent the intended or unintended consequences of rules. But no regular
behavior need ensue, since, unlike natural laws, social rules can be internally
inconsistent, and two or more rules can be incompatible. Furthermore, no
rules are invariably followed; while laws must be discovered, rules depend
on the choices of people: they can be obeyed or violated, introduced, or
withdrawn. For these reasons, straightforward generalizations from social
regularities are not plausible law candidates, for they cannot satisfy the generality and in particular the necessity criteria for scientific laws. Does this
mean that attempts to formulate formal social theories using social regularities as axioms are predestined to failure? Are comparative studies that search
out cross-cultural regularities meaningless?

Some scholars have treated statements of social regularities as laws (e.g.,
Helmer and Rescher 1959) or at least as a special type of law unique to the
social sciences (e.g., Scriven 1959). Others have maintained that the social
laws underlying social regularities *can* be discovered (e.g., Brown 1973).
Antinaturalists argue that there is an element in this debate that destines all
attempts to discover social laws to failure. This element involves the concepts *action, purpose, motive,* and *intention.* The relevance of these concepts
to the debate can be demonstrated by briefly discussing some of the general
assumptions made by antinaturalists. Again this is a composite, oversimpli-
fied picture of complex arguments. Antinaturalists are united in their claim
that the human disciplines, including the social sciences, have aims, concepts, and methods of their own. Some of their principal assumptions are
expressed in the following methodological principles: the use of natural science principles in the social sciences is an exercise in self-deception (Chom-
sky's thesis); explanations of what people do can avoid any reliance on covering laws (Donagan's thesis); human actions are value charged: the physical
behavior of human beings cannot be considered in abstraction from the
thoughts they express; the phenomena of human behavior differ essentially
from those of inert matter in that they have a dimension of meaningfulness
that the latter do not (Winch's thesis); it is obviously absurd to claim to
have explained a sequence of social behavior without having any idea of what

it means to the participants. It thus follows that human behavior and its products must be explained by reference to actions, purposes, and intentions, that the categories in terms of which we are to analyze and explain social life must involve these concepts, for they are the concepts in whose terms the agents themselves understand their own behavior.

What are the implications of this antinaturalist view for social science research? To begin with, the task of the social scientist must be to acquire an understanding of what the intentions of the people they are studying are or were, what their conception of the facts is or was, and what their knowledge systems for getting things done are or were. This understanding will allow social scientists to account for a social action by showing that there was a reason for doing it, that it was the most appropriate thing to do within the framework of that knowledge system. Social scientists are not attempting to explain natural events but the actions of human beings who are free at least to some extent to order their activities in accordance with the demands of reason. There is a fundamentally different way of understanding in the social sciences from that sought in the natural science paradigm: while natural events can only be explained from the outside, human beings can and must be understood from the inside. And, while the natural scientist may attempt to demonstrate that what happens is inevitable or highly probable by subsuming natural events under general laws, explanations of human actions do not require the subsumption of particular acts under general laws. The proper form of explanation in the social sciences is reason-giving or rational explanation that endeavors to make clear the point or rationale of a behavioral act by showing that from the agent's point of view it was the thing to do. As far as explanation is concerned, if the subject matter of social science is human actions, its explanations must be in thoroughly purposive terms, for to discover the thought of the agent is to already understand the events expressed in her or his actions.

If we accept these arguments, what is the goal of empirical research in the social sciences? The main concern of the social sciences is now seen as the *interpretation* of social life and the establishment of the rules we should have to follow to be members of some particular society or subsection of society. The goal of establishing social regularities plays only a minor role now, if it plays any role at all. In fact, many antinaturalists are simply not interested in the apparent cross-cultural regularities that comparativists dredge out with their statistical draglines. They are much more interested in the significance that people themselves attach to the actions that created—perhaps unintentionally—these regularities, for the depth of understanding that this makes possible far exceeds anything possible in those sciences where causal regularities are the only object of inquiry.

What implications does this view of the social sciences have for the study of prehistory by anthropological archaeologists? Some scholars have implied that it renders archaeology an interesting diversion, for anthropological archaeologists do not have reasonable access to the inside perspective of the people whose remains they study. This conclusion implies more than the impossibility of an explicitly scientific archaeology: it implies the very impossibility of *understanding* in archaeology. At most, archaeology is the "science" of the artifact, a discipline that attempts to explain the patterning of artifacts without reference to the thoughts of past people and their group-produced sociocultural systems. To attempt more would be pretentious or methodologically naive. The view that archaeologists face implacable barriers to understanding past human actions helps make sense of some sociocultural anthropologists' devaluation of archaeology as a serious potential contributor to the understanding of human behavior.

Not all antinaturalists have adopted this pessimistic view. Some have thought it possible to rethink or reenact the thoughts of the people responsible for discarding archaeological materials. The main exponent of this interpretation of the archaeologist's task has been R. G. Collingwood, who demonstrated this approach in the interpretation of some sites in England. A more widely adopted approach has been the construction of ideal types based on the methodological insights of Max Weber, another antinaturalist.

Naturalists also can respond to these arguments by raising a series of questions. For instance, Although most anthropologists regard regularities within a social group as evidence for the existence of cultural norms, does this necessarily mean that social groups can only be studied by elaborating their conceptual structures? Can we really think like Winnebago, Neanderthals, or *Homo erecti* (and how would we know we could or were)? Are there not many different ways of expressing truths about a particular phenomena? Do all of the social sciences have to answer the same questions? Is not the fact that they do not one of the reasons why there is so little communication between archaeologists and sociocultural anthropologists? Why must we stop at the level of understanding that the participants themselves have of their actions? Are all actions motivated by consciously entertained reasons? Do we not need to understand the social forces acting on people through, for example, their institutions and economic conditions as well as through those psychological predispositions that operate more, as it were, from within? Why should not the explanation of the collective behavior of people from the outside supplement that from the inside, and vice versa? Can we not imagine two levels of theories, one about the thoughts of participants and one about external observable behavior and its material remains?

Even though it is clear that certain kinds of anthropology are dominated by the kinds of concerns described by antinaturalists and that these arguments appeal more readily to some people than to others, is this all that an anthropologist can do? For example, the antinaturalist account has little relevance to the work of the demographer. As Alan Ryan has maintained "Like the economist, [the demographer] takes for granted the conceptualization of the world employed by the people whose behavior he is studying, and seeks to elicit the consequences of their behavior which they generally neither foresee nor exercise any control over. Although it is true that population trends, like the growth rate of the Gross National Product, have their roots in the intended behavior of individual people, it is not the case that they are themselves intended, and for the most part they can be studied without attending to the intentions of anyone" (1970:158).

It can be claimed, then, that most social scientists are concerned with the *results* of human action, rather than with the purpose or intention of the person or persons involved.

Finally, are we always to believe the accounts people give of their actions? Do they always know why they do what they are doing, or even what it is they are doing? Are all actions carried out for consciously entertained reasons? Are not the social sciences "the study of the unintended results of human actions," as Popper claims (1963:93, 1969:342, 1972:125)? Why can we not substitute an account of our own? Even though an outside account that a prehistoric archaeologist suggests is not rooted in an account of the people that are being studied, are there not a wide variety of questions that can be asked about any social group? Is not an insistence on a normative focus on only one area—the purposes and intentions of individuals—constraining and potentially harmful to the development of the social sciences?

These arguments and counterarguments begin to assume the appearance of a clash between competing methodological research programs. Listen: the very idea of a nomothetic social science is unintelligible and self-defeating; social explanations of human behavior do not have to be couched in terms already available to the people being studied; the past can be studied for its own sake, in its own terms, for what it tells us about people in sociocultural systems. Let us examine again the two questions Does the meaningfulness of social action make a social science impossible and by implication a science of archaeology impossible? and Is it possible to discover social science laws? Is it not reasonable to conclude that there are only contingent rather than a priori reasons why a social science is impossible and that social science laws cannot be discovered? Whether social science laws exist or not is a matter that cannot be decided by fiat—the question must be empirically determined. Furthermore, if anthropological archaeologists took every methodological stipulation seriously, prehistoric archaeology might well grind to a halt. Consider, for instance, Kenneth Clark's dictum in *Civilisation* that "one should not try to assess a culture without knowing its language," since "so much of its character is connected with its actual use of words" (1969:xvii).

Are there not other methods of assessing a culture? Might not anthropological archaeologists and other social scientists discover social science laws after all? As Runciman has discerningly pointed out, "It is salutary to remember that when Boyle of Boyle's law was working on gases, plenty of people were ready to tell him on good *a priori* grounds that he was wasting his time: how, after all, can one possibly weigh air? (1969:19). Moreover, as Popper (1961) has concluded, it is impossible to predict future developments in a discipline, for such a claim is a claim to be able to see into the future. Whether or not a generalizing science of anthropological archaeology is possible must eventually be demonstrated by those archaeologists who have accepted the methodological principles and rules of that paradigm of research.

Summary

In general, anthropological archaeologists have rejected what they interpret as mere fact gathering as a desirable goal of archaeological research. Among their new goals is the explanation of past human behavior, in particular explanation cast in forms that it is thought characterize successful explanations in the physical sciences. A more overriding new goal is the reorientation of the methodological foundations of archaeology in such a manner that it is capable of becoming a science. Anthropological archaeology is nothing, so it has been argued, if it is not a generalizing science of human behavior. Chapter 11 is concerned with the status of this claim, the claim that anthropological archaeology can become, is, or ought to be a theoretical science. Possible examples of scientific activity within archaeology were presented in chapters 9 and 10, and possible answers to this claim are approached in chapter 11 by first considering various conceptions of what it means to be a science. The feasibility of discovering scientific laws—a goal of all of these conceptions—is then considered by listing criteria for scientific laws and by discussing the possible locus of social science laws. Finally, possible barriers to the very existence of such laws are considered.

There has been only minimal debate within anthropological archaeology concerning competing conceptions of science, the locus of social science laws, or the possibility of their very existence. Instead, a general positivist conception of science has been adopted, and professional prestige has been conferred upon those who have argued for a naturalist position in the methodological unity of science debate. At the same time, descriptive studies and cautious empiricism have become unfashionable. Still, scholars in other social science disciplines have not been content with a positivist, or even a naturalist, stance. They have concluded that there are contingent objections to the possibility of social science theorizing and, indeed, that these objections are strong enough for such activity to be labeled as pretense, that attempting to obtain the unobtainable can only hinder the development of social science proper. As Dixon has concluded, a natural science pretense "devalues significant empirical work by giving status to research findings only in so far as they relate to often arbitrarily conceived 'theoretical' concerns; it leads to a systematic neglect of the historical dimension in the explanation of human behavior . . ." (1973:viii). Other scholars have offered counterarguments, and some of these rejoinders are mentioned in this chapter. These arguments are not entirely about the preferences of scientists, whether they prefer system, clarity, and structure or enjoy complexity, fluidity, and disorder, for example, but about an alleged ontological difference between the phenomena they study.

Neither the naturalist nor the antinaturalist position has been supported here. Instead, it has been suggested that the debate between the two positions can be fruitfully regarded as a clash between competing research programs and that each must be evaluated on the basis of its usefulness in providing new insights into human existence as it was in the past.

SUGGESTED READINGS

Conceptions of science and their implications for research activities are discussed in:

Chenhall, R. G. 1971. Positivism and the collection of data. *American Antiquity* 31:372–373.

Dunn, J. 1978. Practising history and social science on "realist" assumptions. In C. Hookway and P. Pettit, eds., *Action and Interpretation*, pp. 145–175. New York: Cambridge University Press.

Harré, R. 1972. *The Philosophies of Science*. New York: Oxford University Press.

Keat, R. 1971. Positivism, naturalism, and anti-naturalism in the social sciences. *Journal of the Theory of Social Behaviour* 1:3–17.

Keat, R. and J. Urry. 1975. *Social Theory as Science*. Boston: Routledge and Kegan Paul.

Among the few attempts in anthropology to state scientific laws are:

Kaplan, D. 1960. The law of cultural dominance. In M. Sahlins and E. Service, eds., *Evolution and Culture*, pp. 69–92. Ann Arbor: University of Michigan Press.

Meggers, B. 1960. The law of cultural evolution as a practical research tool. In G. Dole and R. Carneiro, eds., *Essays in the Science of Culture*, pp. 302–316. New York: Crowell.

Service, E. 1960. The law of evolutionary potential. In M. Sahlins and E. Service, eds., *Evolution and Culture*, pp. 99–122. Ann Arbor: University of Michigan Press.

—— 1968. The prime mover of cultural evolution. *Southwestern Journal of Anthropology* 24:396–409.

Stickel, E. and J. Chartkoff. 1973. The nature of scientific laws and their relation to law-building in archaeology. In C. Renfrew, ed., *The Explanation of Culture Change*, pp. 663–671. London: Duckworth.

Readable accounts of the philosophical doctrines of objectivism and subjectivism can be found in:

Kimmerman, L., ed. 1969. *The Nature and Scope of Social Science*. New York: Appleton-Century-Crofts.

O'Neill, J., ed. 1973. *Modes of Individualism and Collectivism*. London: Heinemann.

The methodological unity of science issue is debated in:

Bunge, M., ed. 1973. *The Methodological Unity of Science.* Boston: Reidel.

A variety of positions in the often acrid debate over the very possibility of a social science are illustrated by the following:

Berlin, I. 1979. The concept of scientific history. In H. Hardy, ed., *Concepts and Categories,* pp. 103–142. New York: Viking.
Dixon, K. 1973. *Sociological Theory: Pretence and Possibility.* Boston: Routledge and Kegan Paul.
Gibson, Q. 1960. *The Logic of Social Enquiry.* New York: Humanities Press.
Kimmerman, L., ed. 1969. *The Nature and Scope of Social Science.* New York: Appleton-Century-Crofts.
Leach, E. 1973. Concluding address. In C. Renfrew, ed., *The Explanation of Culture Change,* pp. 761–771. London: Duckworth.
—— 1977. A view from the bridge. In M. Spriggs, ed., *Archaeology and Anthropology: Areas of Mutual Interest,* pp. 161–176. British Archaeological Reports, 5.19. London: BAR Publications.
Leaf, M. 1979. *Man, Mind, and Science: A History of Anthropology.* New York: Columbia University Press.
Stent, G. 1975. Limits to the scientific understanding of man. *Science* 187:1052–1057.
Thomas, D. H. 1979. *Naturalism and Social Science: A Post-Empiricist Philosophy of Social Science.* New York: Cambridge University Press.
Winch, P. 1958. *The Idea of a Social Science.* London: Routledge and Kegan Paul.
—— 1970. Understanding a primitive society. In B. Wilson, ed., *Rationality,* pp. 78–111. New York: Harper and Row.

Glossary

Abduction thought processes that connect *observations* with ideas; in the cycle of science these processes interpret *sample summaries* and *empirical generalizations* (chapter 2).

Abstraction thought processes such as *abduction* that connect observations with ideas or ideas with observations (chapter 3).

Activity area in archaeology, the smallest spatial unit of patterned social behavior in a community; an area where a specific task was carried out by a single individual (chapter 5).

Analogue model a model whose images, properties, and concepts are derived by analogy from better known and more familiar situations (chapter 4).

A posteriori in logic, reasoning backward from effects, consequences, or facts, to causes.

A posteriori model an interpretation of existing theory that facilitates the testing process; a posteriori models perform their function by simplifying the content and relationships among elements in complex *culture histories* or *scientific theories* (chapter 4).

A priori in logic, reasoning from cause to effect or from a generalization to particular instances; based on theory instead of experience or experiment.

A priori model a conceptual device for developing theory; a priori models function in the context of discovery by providing sets of rules that order data, structural schema suitable for explanation, and images for the interpretation of archaeological phenomena (chapter 4).

Archaeological context the material remains of past *sociocultural systems*— the pottery fragments, stone flakes, and crumbled house foundations that exist in the present (chapter 1).

Axiom generally unproved assumptions in *scientific theories* that are more

---

Italicized words are defined in separate entries.

abstract and of greater scope than the theories and other verbal statements that are derived from them (chapter 10).

Burial program   a reconstructed pattern of mortuary activities that is used in archaeology to identify the degree of social complexity of a past society (chapter 5).

Central place theory   a theory that explains the size and spacing of settlements (central places) in a region by assuming that settlement functions have important influences on *settlement patterning* in complex societies (chapters 7 and 8).

Cognitive archaeology   the study of the cognitive or ideological component of an artifact form or system (chapter 5).

Community plan   the spatial arrangement of roadways, empty spaces, *household clusters,* and other building complexes in a settlement (chapter 5).

Confirmation   support for a theory provided by a successful test of a *test implication* of the theory (chapter 2).

Conventionalism   a conception of science that rejects the *realist* and *positivist* contention that science is an objective, rational enquiry that aims at true explanatory and predictive knowledge of an external reality (chapter 11).

Covering-law model of explanation   the model of explanation in which all sufficient explanations involve the *deductive* subsumption of events to be explained under propositions consisting of hypothetically assumed general *laws* of nature and initial conditions (chapters 1 and 3).

Crude mortality rates   estimates of the average number of people who die per thousand each year (chapter 6).

C-transforms   processes such as the number of times that tools are used that affect the depositional rates of material items and, as a result, the composition of the archaeological record (chapter 6).

Cultural ecology   the study of the ecological relationships between a *sociocultural system,* the physical landscape, the biological environment, and other adjacent human groups (chapter 1).

Cultural historical reconstruction   a *research program* whose primary goal is the reconstruction and interpretation of the flow of past sociocultural events; usually associated with a normative view of culture and descriptive chronicle (chapter 8).

Cultural materialism   the view that technoenvironmental change is the most basic determining factor in cultural evolution (chapter 1).

Cultural processual approach   a *research program* whose primary goal is the explanation of sociocultural change through the discovery of those processes that generated change; usually associated with a *deductive* methodology and the goal of explaining rather than describing (chapter 8).

Culture   the central organizing concept of anthropology; an ideational design for living, a pattern of shared meanings, a system of knowledge and belief (chapter 1).

Culture Area   a geographical region within which a fairly large number of historically and ecologically related societies exist or have existed (chapter 9).

Culture-free concept   universally applicable terms, such as sharp point, that could have meaning in any social system (chapter 9).

Culture history   stories of what life in a community was like or narrative accounts of specific sociocultural changes; culture histories are about unique sequences of events, about particular peoples, cultures, or regions.

Cumulative mortality profile   a technique for providing reasonable estimates of population size from skeletal material (chapter 6).

Deduction   in logic, the process of reasoning from a premise to a logical conclusion (chapter 2).

Deductive-nomological explanation   a form of *covering-law explanation* in which the *explanandum* and the lawlike statements in the *explanans* are universal or deterministic statements (chapter 3).

Deductive statistical explanation   a form of *covering-law explanation* in which the *explanandum* and the lawlike statements in the *explanans* are probabilistic or statistical statements (chapter 3).

Demography   the study of human population parameters such as size and density (chapter 7).

Derived measurements   *measurements* defined on the basis of relations between *fundamental measures* (chapter 2).

Derived term   a term in a *scientific theory* that is defined within the theory by using *primitive terms* or other derived terms (chapter 10).

Descriptive statistics   mathematical techniques that display systematic order among *observations* (chapter 2).

Descriptive study   a strategy of investigation whose goal in archaeology is generally the systematic description and classification of a sample of the archaeological record (chapter 3).

Diachronic analysis   in the *systems approach,* analysis that is concerned with the mechanisms rather than the structural end products of changing subsystem relationships (chapter 1).

Dictionary of a theory   definitions of terms, procedural instructions, and other parts of a *scientific theory* not found in the *text* (chapter 10).

Distance-decay model   a *model* for measuring the amount of interaction between communities that is based on a gravity depletion *rationale* (chapter 7).

Ecological fallacy   the mental error committed by assuming that properties strongly (or weakly) associated at one level of analysis will be as strongly (or weakly) associated at other levels (chapter 9).

Empirical generalization   in the cycle of science, isolated descriptive statements that are made through the process of *induction* to a denumerable set called a population from a smaller randomly selected set called a sample (chapter 2).

Empirical interpretation   the *operational definition* of a concept or hypothesis (chapter 2).

Empirical research   analysis; research that pursues problems of *measurement* or *descriptive studies* (chapter 3).

Epidemiological research   the study of epidemics (chapter 6).

Equation of a theory   statements such as theorems, corollaries, or derived hypotheses that can be derived from the *axiom* core of a *scientific theory* (chapter 10).

Ethnoarchaeology   the study of material relationships within contemporary or historic societies, in order to provide tentative explanations of material relationships found in the archaeological record (chapter 5).

Explanandum   a statement that is to be explained (chapter 3).

Explanans   the premises of an explanatory argument (chapter 3).

Explanatory hypotheses   statements that relate two or more abstract notions (chapter 2).

Exploratory investigation   a strategy of investigation that accounts for *sample summaries* and *empirical generalizations* by generating *identities* and *explanatory hypotheses* (chapter 3).

Factor theory   a *scientific theory* formed by interrelated sets of *tendency statements* (chapter 10).

Falsifiable   capable of empirical refutation. According to Karl Popper, scientific statements or assertions are falsifiable at least in principle, while metaphysical statements or assertions are not (chapter 1).

Fiat measurement   a proxy *measurement* of an abstract concept such as degree of social stratification (chapter 2).

Formal models   *models* that are idealized descriptions of data (chapter 4).

Functional argument   the argument that cross-cultural comparisons are impossible, since traits are inseparable elements within unique *sociocultural systems* (chapter 9).

Fundamental measurements   measures of easily observable and relatively simple general properties such as length (chapter 2).

Galton's problem   in cross-cultural comparison, the problem resulting from the requirement of independence in statistical testing (chapter 9).

Game theory   a decision-making mechanism for dealing with situations of uncertainty (chapter 6).

General evolution   the formulation of grand theory about culture and the cumulative, collective experience of humankind (chapter 9).

Graph theory   a theory that provides a set of assumptions and procedures for viewing "places" in terms of wholes and for viewing networks as wholes (chapter 7).

Gravity model   a *model* for interpreting the size and distribution of settlements that is based on the *rationale* that larger centers, rather than smaller ones, tend to attract interaction from larger areas (chapter 7).

Household cluster   a spatial concentration of house remains, pits, burials, workshops, ovens, and other features and artifacts in an archaeological site that is assumed to be the material manifestation of a past household (chapter 5).

Hypothesis testing   a research strategy that compares the empirical implications of *explanatory hypotheses* with new observations (chapter 3).

Hypothetico-deductive approach   the strategy of science that deduces testable consequences from *explanatory hypotheses* and confronts them with data (chapters 1 and 3).

Iconic model   a *model* constructed to directly represent properties of empirical phenomena by subjecting them to a transformation in scale or importance and emphasis (chapter 3).

Identity   in archaeology, a statement that interprets an artifact by assigning it to a class of familiar tools and labeling it with an abstract universally applicable term, such as projectile point (chapter 2).

Ideological subsystem   the common denominator of every human *culture* that is especially concerned with the world of symbolic thought (chapter 4).

Idiographic studies   in archaeology, studies that are concerned with the uniqueness of individual archaeological cultures and with regional differentiation (chapter 3).

Indicator   an empirical *observation* that points to the presence of a theoretical concept or relationship (chapter 2).

Induction   in logic, the process of reasoning or drawing a conclusion from particular facts or individual cases (chapter 2).

Inductive statistical explanation   a weaker form of *covering-law explanation* that does not guarantee the (logical) truth of an *explanandum* (chapter 3).

Inferential statistics   techniques for reasoning from sample descriptions to population descriptions using the principles of probability (chapter 2).

Information component   in the cycle of science, *observations,* theories, predictions, and other types of information that are systematically transformed by methodological controls (chapter 2).

Instrumental-nomological investigation   a strategy of research whose goal is to construct, standardize, and validate instruments of *measurement* (chapter 3).

Interpretive-theoretical studies   strategies of research that synthesize existing sets of data, hypotheses, and other types of established information in new ways (chapter 3).

Interval scale   a measurement scale that has the properties of symbolic representation, rank, and distance (chapter 2).

Level of sociocultural integration   a rough continuum of broad stages of culture types (chapter 8).

Life tables   tables that provide typical profiles of the expected distribution of individuals in common types of cemeteries by age and sex (chapter 6).

Local aggregates   sets of people who cooperatively perform sets of activities in distinct locations (chapter 5).

Material model   a *model* that is an analogue for data or theories that are being interpreted (chapter 4).

Measurement   the application of a set of procedural rules for comparing sense impressions with a scale and for assigning symbols such as letters or words to the resulting observations (chapter 2).

Mental model   in archaeology, *models* of archaeology, such as *positivism* or *realism* (chapter 4).

Methodological collectivism   the philosophical position that the use of macroscopic, collective, nonpsychological concepts such as *social structure* is legitimate in the explanation of social events (chapter 11).

Methodological individualism   the philosophical position that the use of macroscopic, collective, nonpsychological concepts such as *social structure* is always illegitimate in the explanation of social events (chapter 11).

Methodological principles   in archaeology, the assumptions that archaeologists adopt concerning the nature of being human, science, or the fundamental structure of society, culture, and the natural world (chapter 3).

Methodological rules   admonitions or strictures about what are acceptable procedures and what are not that follow from *methodological principles* (chapter 3).

Methods   in the cycle of science, *processes* such as defining, measuring, and modeling that transform one *information component* into another (chapter 2).

Model   an *abstractive* tool that connects theories with empirical data (chapter 4).

Mortality curves   plots of the percentages of individuals in each age category in a mortuary site (chapter 6).

Narrative explanation   a form of *what-explanation* that answers the question, What happened here and in what order? (chapter 3).

Nearest neighbor analysis   a *descriptive statistic* used in archaeology to obtain a quantitative and systematic expression of the pattern of settlement distribution (chapter 7).

Nominal scale   the lowest order measurement scale in the Campbell system; it simply specifies the presence or absence of an attribute or quality (chapter 2).

Nomothetic studies   investigations that concentrate on domains of study unbounded by temporal and spatial restrictions; their main concern is the discovery of patterns that repeat themselves (chapter 3).

Nonvariable concepts   categorical concepts; *nominal* either-or measures that lack dimension (chapter 10).

N-transforms   natural processes such as oxidation which disrupt items deposited in the archaeological record (chapter 10).

Objectivism   the philosophical position that successful social science is possible without having to rely on our subjective knowledge of the working of the human mind (chapter 11).

Observation   an interpreted perceptual experience (chapter 2).

Operational definitions   definitions that provide the operations used to measure a term (chapter 2).

Operationalization   in the cycle of science, the process of providing a concept with an *operational definition* (chapter 2).

Operational models   simplified, often idealized, interlinked guesses about the processes and objects that either now exist or have existed in the past (chapter 4).

Ordinal scale   the measurement scale in the Campbell system that includes both symbolic representation and rank order (chapter 2).

Osteobiography   the reconstruction of the life histories of individuals through the analysis of their skeletons (chapter 6).

Paleopathology   the study of ancient diseases (chapter 6).

Pattern explanation   a form of *what-explanation* that answers the question, What sort of pattern was this object or event a part of? (chapter 3).

Positivism   a conception of science that is based solely on the positive data of sense experience (chapters 1 and 11).

Practical inference   a form of *reason-giving explanation* that has the following schema: A intends to bring about p; A considers that he cannot bring about p unless he does x; therefore, A sets himself to do x (chapter 3).

Premises of a theory   the basic or core statements from which all other statements in a *scientific theory* are derived through *deductive* reasoning (chapter 10).

Primitive terms   the basic, initial concepts in a *scientific theory;* they are either intuitively obvious or defined by illustration or by some other procedure outside the theory (chapter 10).

Process   a repetitive pattern of similarly organized flows of matter, energy, or information (chapter 1).

Random walk model   a class of movement *models* whose *rationale* is the Yule process (chapter 4).

Rank-size rule   a hypothesis based on the assumption that there is a relationship between the sizes of settlements and their importance in rank within a region (chapter 7).

Rationale of a model   the point of view, the picture of reality, or the basis of abstraction behind the selection of the concepts and process of a *model* (chapter 4).

Ratio scale   the measurement scale in the Campbell system that includes symbolic representation, rank order, and a point of natural origin (chapter 2).

Realism   a conception of science that emphasizes the discovery of the often unobservable underlying structures and mechanisms that causally generate observable phenomena (chapter 11).

Reason-giving explanation   a form of explanation that explains by stating why a person or a group of people thought that an action or belief was correct or proper (chapter 3).

Reciprocal exchange   most simply defined as the system of exchange that involves neither markets nor administrative hierarchies (chapter 7).

Redistributive exchange   a system of exchange in which goods are collected in an administrative center and then reallotted downward to consumers (chapter 7).

Reliability   the probability that, if repeated by the same or an independent observer, *measurement* procedures will give the same result (chapter 2).

Research designs   sets of instructions or strategies of investigation that clarify the goals and guide the procedures of research projects (chapter 2).

Research programs   plans for research that are founded on a core of essentially unchallenged *methodological principles* (chapter 3).

Sample summary   in the cycle of science, a summary of a sample of observations (chapter 2).

Scientific laws   "statements which relate variables or phenomena in nature to each other and which describe the processes involved in these relationships" (Stickel and Chartkoff 1973:664) (chapter 11).

Scientific theory   a theory formed by universal hypotheses or declarative sentences unbounded by spatial or temporal restrictions (chapters 2 and 10).

Settlement pattern   the number, size, and spatial distribution of the entire range of sites that a people occupied (Chapter 7).

Settlement pattern analysis   in archaeology, the study of the spatial organization of social activities at any level (chapter 5).

Settlement system   a *system* defined by the functional role and pattern of integration of each of a people's communities within an adaptive strategy (chapter 7).

Site catchment analysis   a method of determining land use patterns that is based on the assumption that rational people do not normally pursue energy-expensive economic activities (chapter 6).

Social organization   the way people actually interact within a community; their patterns of actual observable behavior (chapter 5).

Social structure   the set of norms that structure interpersonal relationships within a community (chapter 5).

Social subsystem   a *system* of common denominators of every human culture such as the social, technoeconomic, or ideological (part two).

Sociocultural system   the social realizations or enactments of ideational (cultural) designs for living in particular environments (chapter 11).

Socioeconomic system   the social arrangements employed in applying *technology* to the production, distribution, and consumption of goods and services in a social system (chapter 6).

Specific evolution   the parallel adaptive changes of *cultures* in somewhat similar structural-ecological niches (chapter 9).

Status   the ease of access of an individual or social unit to single commodities like food or to a variety of commodities (chapter 5).

Stochastic process   in model building, a process based on random developments or chance (chapter 8).

Structural functionalism   the view that each unit and relation in a *sociocultural system* helps maintain the cohesiveness and integrity of the whole system, while the whole functions to supply the biological needs of individual human beings (chapter 1).

Structural space   the facilities that coexist at any one time in a community together with other materials, natural features, and their spatial relationships (chapter 5).

Subjectivism   the philosophical position that successful social science must refer to mental categories in the explanation of social phenomena (chapter 11).

Survivorship curve   estimates of the percentage of individuals in subgroups of a theoretical population of 100 people that will still be alive at the end of a five-year period (chapter 6).

Symbolic model   a *formal model* composed of interconnected symbols, such as mathematical notation (chapter 4).

Synchronic analysis   in the systems approach, the study of the structure of the functional linkages of a *system* (chapter 1).

System   a set of units with relationships between them (chapter 1).

Systematic empiricism   in the cycle of science, an overemphasis on data collection and analysis (chapter 3).

Systemic context   past *sociocultural systems,* their web of interrelationships, and their position along the dimension of time (chapter 1).

Systems approach   the theoretical orientation that views the world as a complex living system in which individuals, social groups, and institutions are dynamically interrelated actors involved in continuing processes of decision making (chapter 1).

Technoeconomic subsystem   the subsystem of every human culture that is especially concerned with the inevitable relationships that form between humans and their natural surroundings (part two).

Technology   the material equipment and technical knowledge components of a technoeconomic system (chapter 6).

Teleological explanation   a form of *what-explanation* that answers the question, What goal was this action directed toward? (chapter 3).

Tendency statements   theoretical statements in the social sciences of what should happen if there were no interfering conditions (chapter 10).

Test implications   in the cycle of science, statements in a theory that say something about the archaeological record or its environmental context (chapter 2).

Text of a theory   that part of a *scientific theory* composed of concepts and theoretical or *verbal statements* (chapter 10).

Theoretical definition   a definition that assigns meaning to a concept term (chapters 2 and 10).

Theorizing   in the cycle of science, research that concentrates on interpretation through the use of *abductive* or *deductive* reasoning (chapter 3).

Tool-kits   spatial associations of archaeological materials that are assumed, as a working hypothesis, to be meaningfully related to a specific task (chapter 5).

Transformation process   a *process* involved in the formation of the archaeological record as the archaeologist finds it (chapter 6).

Trial formulation   in the cycle of science, thought experiments that mentally trace the consequences of transforming one *information component* into another or of applying a particular methodological control (chapter 2).

Universal culture pattern   a set of categories that Clark Wissler thought was necessarily present in every *culture* (part two).

Validity   the extent to which *theoretical* and *operational definitions* correspond (chapter 2).

Variable concepts   culture-free and timeless continua that measure dimensions of phenomena (chapter 10).

Verbal statements   statements that assert relationships among the concepts of a *scientific theory* (chapter 10).

What-explanations   explanations that explain by making clear what something is or by showing how something fits within a sequence of events (chapter 3).

World view   the way a people see themselves in relation to the universe and the things that they think are within it (chapter 5).

References

Achinstein, P. 1971. *Law and Expectation.* London: Oxford University Press.

Acsadi, G. and J. Nemeskeri. 1974. History of human life span and mortality: A book review. *Current Anthropology* 15(4):495–507.

Adams, R. M. 1966. *The Evolution of Urban Society.* Chicago: Aldine-Atherton.

Allen, W. L. and J. B. Richardson III. 1971. The reconstruction of kinship from archaeological data: The concepts, the methods, and the feasibility. *American Antiquity* 36:41–53.

Amedeo, D. and R. G. Golledge. 1975. *An Introduction to Scientific Reasoning in Geography.* New York: Wiley.

Ammerman, A. J. and L. L. Cavalli-Sforza. 1971. Measuring the rate of spread of early farming in Europe. *Man* 6:674–688.

—— 1973. A population model for the diffusion of early farming in Europe. In C. Renfrew, ed., *The Explanation of Culture Change,* pp. 343–358. London: Duckworth.

—— 1979. The wave of advance model for the spread of agriculture in Europe. In C. Renfrew and K. Cooke, eds., *Transformations: Mathematical Approaches to Culture Change,* pp. 275–293. New York: Academic Press.

Ammerman, A. J. and M. W. Feldman, 1974 On the "making" of an assemblage of stone tools. *American Antiquity* 39:610–616.

Ammerman, A. J., D. P. Gifford, and A. Voorips. 1978. Towards an evaluation of sampling strategies: Simulated excavations of a Kenyan pastoralist site. In I. Hodder, ed., *Simulation Studies in Archaeology,* pp. 123–132. New York: Cambridge University Press.

Ammerman, A. J., C. Matessi, and L. L. Cavalli-Sforza. 1978. Some new approaches to the study of the obsidian trade in the Mediterranean and adjacent areas. In I. Hodder, ed., *The Spatial Organisation of Culture,* pp. 179–96. Pittsburgh: University of Pittsburgh Press.

Anderson, A. D. and L. Zimmerman. 1976. Settlement/subsistence variability in the Glenwood locality, southwestern Iowa. *Plains Anthropologist* 21:141–154.

Anfinson, S. 1979. Fox Lake Phase. In S. Anfinson, ed., *A Handbook of Minnesota*

Prehistoric Ceramics, pp. 79–86. Occasional Publications in Minnesota Anthropology, No. 5. Fort Snelling: Minnesota Archaeological Society.

Angel, L. 1947. The length of life in ancient Greece. *Journal of Gerontology* 2:18–24.

—— 1972. Ecology and population in the eastern Mediterranean. *World Archaeology* 4:88–105.

Ascher, R. 1959. A prehistoric population estimate using midden analysis and two population models. *Southwestern Journal of Anthropology* 15:168–178.

Beardsley, R., P. Holder, A. Krieger, B. Meggers, and J. Rinaldo. 1956. Functional and evolutionary implications of community patterning. In R. Wauchope, ed., *Seminars in Archaeology: 1955*, pp. 129–157. Memoirs of the Society for American Archaeology, No. 11. Salt Lake City: Society for American Archaeology.

Beckman, M. J. 1958. City hierarchies and the distribution of city size. *Economic Development and Cultural Change* 6:243–248.

Beer, S. 1959. *Cybernetics and Management.* London: English University Press.

Bender, M. M. 1971. Variations in the $^{13}C/^{12}C$ ratio of plants in relation to the pathway of photosynthetic carbon dioxide. *Phytochemistry* 10:1239–1244.

Bender, M. M., D. A. Baerreis, and R. L. Steventon. 1981. Further light on carbon isotopes and Hopewell agriculture. *American Antiquity* 46:346–353.

Berry, B. J. 1961. City size distribution and economic development. *Economic Development and Cultural Change* 9:573–588.

—— 1967. *Geography of Market Centers and Retail Distribution.* Englewood Cliffs, N.J.: Prentice-Hall.

Bidney, D. 1953. *Theoretical Anthropology.* New York: Columbia University Press.

Binford, L. R. 1962. Archaeology as anthropology. *American Antiquity* 28:217–225.

—— 1964. A consideration of archaeological research design. *American Antiquity* 29:425–441.

—— 1965. Archaeological systematics and the study of culture process. *American Antiquity* 31:203–210.

—— 1968a. Archeological perspectives. In S. Binford and L. Binford, eds., *New Perspectives in Archeology*, pp. 5–32. Chicago: Aldine.

—— 1968b. Post-pleistocene adaptations. In S. Binford and L. Binford, eds., *New Perspectives in Archeology*, pp. 313–341. Chicago: Aldine.

—— 1971. Mortuary practices: Their study and their potential. In J. A. Brown, ed., *Approaches to the Social Dimensions of Mortuary Practices*, pp. 6–29. Memoirs of the Society for American Archaeology, No. 25. Washington, D.C.: Society for American Archaeology.

—— 1972. *An Archaeological Perspective.* New York: Seminar Press.

Binford, L. R. and J. B. Bertram. 1977. Bone frequencies—and attritional processes. In L. R. Binford, ed., *For Theory Building in Archaeology*, pp. 77–153. New York: Academic Press.

Binford, S. R. and L. R. Binford, eds. 1968. *New Perspectives in Archeology.* Chicago: Aldine.

Bishop, C. A. and M. E. Smith. 1975. Early historic populations in northwestern

Ontario: Archaeological and ethnohistorical interpretations. *American Antiquity* 40:54–63.

Blake, J. and K. Davis. 1964. Norms, values, and sanctions. In R. E. Faris, ed., *Handbook of Modern Sociology*, pp. 456–484. Chicago: Rand McNally.

Blalock, H. M., Jr. 1969. *Theory Construction*. Englewood Cliffs, N.J.: Prentice-Hall.

—— 1970. The formalization of sociological theory. In J. McKinney and E. A. Tiryakian, eds., *Theoretical Sociology*, pp. 271–300. New York: Appleton-Century-Crofts.

Blaut, J. M. 1962. Object and relationship. *Professional Geography* 14:1–7.

Boas, F. 1940. *Race, Language and Culture*. New York: Macmillan.

Bohannan, P. 1963. *Social Anthropology*. New York: Holt, Rinehart, and Winston.

Bökönyi, S. 1970. A new method for the determination of the minimum number of individuals in animal bone material. *American Journal of Archaeology* 74:291–292.

Bonini, C. P. 1963. *Simulation of Information and Decision Systems in the Firm*. Englewood Cliffs, N.J.: Prentice-Hall.

Bonnichsen, R. 1973. Millie's Camp: An experiment in archaeology. *World Archaeology* 4:277–291.

Boserup, E. 1965. *The Conditions of Agricultural Growth*. Chicago: Aldine.

Bourguignon, E. and L. Greenbaum. 1973. *Diversity and Homogeneity in World Societies*. New Haven, Conn.: HRAF Press.

Braybrooke, D. 1970. The logic of the succession of cultures. In H. E. Kiefer and M. K. Munitz, eds., *Mind, Science, and History*, pp. 270–283. Albany: State University of New York Press.

Bridgman, P. W. 1927. *The Logic of Modern Physics*. New York: Macmillan.

Brothwell, D. and E. Higgs, eds. 1969. *Science in Archaeology*, 2nd ed. New York: Praeger.

Brown, A. B. 1963. Bone strontium content as a dietary indicator in human skeletal populations. Ph.D. dissertation, University of Michigan.

Brown, J. A., ed. 1971. *Approaches to the Social Dimensions of Mortuary Practices*. Memoirs of the Society for American Archaeology, No. 25. Washington, D.C.: Society for American Archaeology.

Brown, J. A., R. E. Bell, and D. G. Wyckoff. 1978. Caddoan settlement patterns in the Arkansas River drainage. In B. D. Smith, ed., *Mississippian Settlement Patterns*, pp. 169–200. New York: Academic Press.

Brown, R. R. 1973. *Rules and Law in Sociology*. Chicago: Aldine.

Brumfield, E. 1976. Regional growth in the Eastern Valley of Mexico: A test of the "population pressure" hypothesis. In K. V. Flalnnery, ed., *The Early Mesoamerican Village*, pp. 234–249. New York: Academic Press.

Buckley, W. 1967. *Sociology and Modern Systems Theory*. Englewood Cliffs, N.J.: Prentice-Hall.

Buikstra, J. 1976. Hopewell in the Lower Illinois Valley: A regional study of human biological variability and prehistoric mortuary behavior. Northwestern University Archaeological Program, *Scientific Papers*, No. 2. Evanston, Ill.

Bunge, M. 1967. *Scientific Research.* 2 vols. New York: Springer-Verlag.

Campbell, N. 1957. *Foundations of Science.* New York: Dover.

Carneiro, R. L. 1970. A theory of the origin of the state. *Science* 169:733–738.

Carneiro, R. L. and S. L. Tobias. 1963. The application of scale analysis to cultural evolution. *Transactions of the New York Academy of Sciences* (Series II) 26:196–207.

Cassirer, E. 1953. *Substance and Function, and Einstein's Theory of Relativity.* New York: Dover.

Casteel, R. W. 1971. Differential bone destruction: Some comments. *American Antiquity* 36:466–469.

—— 1972. Two static maximum-population-density models for hunter-gatherers: A first approximation. *World Archaeology* 4:19–40.

—— 1976. *Fish Remains in Archaeology and Paleo-Environmental Studies.* New York: Academic Press.

—— 1977. Characterization of faunal assemblages and the minimum number of individuals determined from paired elements: Continuing problems in archaeology. *Journal of Archaeological Science* 4:125–134.

—— 1978. Faunal assemblages and the "weigemethode" or weight method. *Journal of Field Archaeology* 5:71–77.

Cavalli-Sforza, L. L. 1974. The genetics of human populations. *Scientific American* 231 (22):80–89.

Caws, P. 1969. The structure of discovery. *Science* 166:1375–1380.

Chadwick, A. 1978. A computer simulation of Mycenaean settlement. In I. Hodder, ed., *Simulation Studies in Archaeology,* pp. 47–57. Cambridge: Cambridge University Press.

Chamberlain, T. C. 1897. The method of multiple working hypotheses. *Journal of Geology* 39:155–165.

Chang, K. C. 1958. Study of the neolithic social grouping: Examples from the New World. *American Anthropologist* 60(2):298–334.

—— 1962. A typology of settlement and community patterns in some circumpolar societies. *Arctic Anthropology* I:28–41.

—— 1967, *Rethinking Archaeology.* New York: Random House.

Chaplin, R. E. 1971. *The Study of Animal Bones from Archaeological Sites.* New York: Seminar Press.

Chapman, G. 1970. The application of information theory to the analysis of population distributions in space. *Economic Geography* 46:317–331.

Childe, V. G. 1951a. *Social Evolution.* New York: Henry Schuman.

—— 1951b. *Man Makes Himself.* New York: New American Library.

—— 1954. *What Happened in History.* Baltimore: Penguin.

—— 1956. *Piecing Together the Past.* London: Routledge and Kegan Paul.

—— 1958. *The Prehistory of European Society.* Harmondsworth, Middlesex, England: Penguin.

Clark, J. G. D. 1965a. Radiocarbon dating and the expansion of farming culture from the Near East over Europe. *Proceedings of the Prehistoric Society.* 31:58–73.

—— 1965b. Traffic in stone axe and adze blades. *The Economic History Review* 18:1–28.

—— 1966. The invasion hypothesis in British archaeology. *Antiquity* 40:172–189.

Clark, K. 1969. *Civilisation: A Personal View.* New York: Harper and Row.

Clark, P. and F. Evans. 1954. Distance to nearest neighbor as a measure of spatial relationships in populations. *Ecology* 35:445–453.

Clarke, D. L. 1972a. Models and paradigms in contemporary archaeology. In D. L. Clarke, ed., *Models in Archaeology,* pp. 1–60. London: Methuen.

—— 1972b. A provisional paradigm of an Iron Age society. In D. L. Clarke, ed., *Models in Archaeology,* pp. 801–869. London: Methuen.

—— 1978. *Analytical Archaeology,* 2nd ed. New York: Columbia University Press.

Cohen, M. N. 1977. *The Food Crisis in Prehistory.* New Haven, Conn.: Yale University Press.

Cohen, Y. 1968. Macroethnology: Large scale comparative studies. In J. A. Clifton, ed., *Introduction to Cultural Anthropology,* pp. 403–448. Boston: Houghton Mifflin.

Collingwood, R. G. 1964. *The Idea of History.* Oxford: Clarendon Press.

—— 1966. *Roman Britain.* Oxford: Clarendon Press.

Conacher, A. J. 1969. Open system and dynamic equilibrium in geomorphology: A comment. *Australian Geographical Studies* 7:153–158.

Cook, S. F. and R. Heizer. 1968. Relationship among houses, settlement areas, and population in aboriginal California. In K. C. Chang, ed., *Settlement Archaeology,* pp. 79–116. Palo Alto, Calif.: National Press.

Cowgill, G. 1968. Archaeological applications of factor, cluster, and proximity analyses. *American Antiquity* 33:367–375.

Crumley, C. 1976. Toward a locational definition of state systems of settlement. *American Anthropologist* 78:59–73.

Curry, L. 1964. The random spatial economy: An exploration in settlement theory. *Annals of the Association of American Geographers* 54:138–146.

Daly, P. 1969. Approaches to faunal analysis in archaeology. *American Antiquity* 34:146–153.

Daniel, G. 1975. *A Hundred and Fifty Years of Archaeology.* Cambridge: Harvard University Press.

Dean, J. 1969. Chronological analysis of Tsegi Phase sites in northeastern Arizona. *Papers of the Laboratory of Tree-Ring Research,* No. 3. Tucson: University of Arizona Press.

—— 1970. Aspects of Tsegi Phase social organization: A trial reconstruction. In W. Longacre, ed., *Reconstructing Prehistoric Pueblo Societies,* pp. 140–74. Albuquerque: University of New Mexico Press.

Debreu, G. 1959. *Theory of Value: An Axiomatic Analysis of Economic Equilibrium.* Cowles Foundation Monograph, No. 17. New Haven, Conn.: Yale University Press.

Deetz, J. 1965. *The Dynamics of Stylistic Change in Arikara Ceramics.* Illinois Studies in Anthropology, No. 4. Urbana: University of Illinois Press.

—— 1967. *Invitation to Archaeology*. Garden City, N.Y.: Natural History Press.

—— 1974. A cognitive historical model for American material culture: 1620–1835. In C. Moore, ed., *Reconstructing Complex Societies*, pp. 21–24. Supplement to the Bulletin of the American Schools of Oriental Research, No. 20. Cambridge, Mass.: American School of Oriental Research.

—— 1977. *In Small Things Forgotten: The Archaeology of Early American Life*. New York: Anchor Press/Doubleday.

Deetz, J. and E. Dethlefsen. 1965. The Doppler effect and archaeology: A consideration of the spatial aspects of seriation. *Southwestern Journal of Anthropology* 21:196–206.

Divale, W. 1977. Living floor area and marital residence: A replication. *Behavioral Science Research* 12:109–116.

Dixon, J., J. Cann, and C. Renfrew. 1968. Obsidian and the origins of trade. *Scientific American* 218:38–46.

Dixon, K. 1973. *Sociological Theory: Pretence and Possibility*. Boston: Routledge and Kegan Paul.

Doran, J. and F. Hodson. 1975. *Mathematics and Computers in Archaeology*. Cambridge: Harvard University Press.

Drennan, R. 1976. Religion and social evolution in Formative Mesoamerica. In K. V. Flannery, ed., *The Early Mesoamerican Village*, pp. 345–368. New York: Academic Press.

Dubin, R. 1969. *Theory Building*. New York: Free Press.

Dumond, D. 1965. Population growth and cultural change. *Southwestern Journal of Anthropology* 21:3021–324.

Edynak, G. 1976. Life-styles from skeletal material: A medieval Yugoslav example. In E. Giles and J. Friedlaender, eds., *The Measures of Man*, pp. 408–432. Cambridge, Mass.: Peabody Museum Press.

Einstein, A. 1934. *Essays in Science*. New York: Philosophical Library.

Elliott, K., D. Ellman, and I. Hodder. 1978. The simulation of neolithic axe dispersal in Britain. In I. Hodder, eds., *Simulation Studies in Archaeology*, pp. 79–87. New York: Cambridge University Press.

Ellis, B. 1968. *Basic Concepts of Measurement*. Cambridge: Cambridge University Press.

Ember, M. 1971. An empirical test of Galton's problem. *Ethnology* 10:98–106.

—— 1973. An archaeological indicator of matrilocal versus patrilocal residence. *American Antiquity* 38:177–181.

Englebrecht, W. 1974. The Iroquois: Archaeological patterning on the tribal level. *World Archaeology* 6:52–65.

Erickson, E. 1977. Cultural evolution. *American Behavioral Scientist* 20:669–680.

Etzioni, A. 1970. Fact-crazy, theory-shy? *Science* 170 (3956):391.

Feyerabend, P. K. 1970. Against method. In M. Radner and S. Winokur, eds., *Minnesota Studies in the Philosophy of Science*, No. 4, pp. 17–130. Minneapolis: University of Minnesota Press.

—— 1975. *Against Method*. London: Verso.

Fischer, J. 1961. Art styles as cultural cognitive maps. *American Anthropologist* 63:79–93.

Fitting, J. 1965. A quantitative examination of Virginia fluted points. *American Antiquity* 30:484–491.

Flannery, K. V. 1972. The cultural evolution of civilizations. *Annual Review of Ecology and Systematics* 3:399–426.

Flannery, K. V., ed. 1976. *The Early Mesoamerican Village*. New York: Academic Press.

Freeman, L. 1957. An empirical test of folk-urbanism. Ann Arbor: University Microfilms No. 23, 502.

Fried, M. 1967. *The Evolution of Political Society*. New York: Random House.

Friedman, J. 1974. Marxism, structuralism, and vulgar materialism. *Man* 9:444–469.

Friedman, J. and M. Rowlands, eds. 1978. *The Evolution of Social Systems*. Pittsburgh, Pa.: University of Pittsburgh Press.

Fritz, J. 1972. Archaeological systems for indirect observation of the past. In M. Leone, ed., *Contemporary Archaeology*, pp. 135–157. Carbondale: Southern Illinois University Press.

—— 1973. Relevance, archeology and subsistence theory. In C. Redman, ed., *Research and Theory in Current Archeology*, pp. 59–82. New York: Wiley.

Fritz, J. and F. Plog. 1970. The nature of archaeological explanation. *American Antiquity* 35:405–412.

Geertz, C. 1965. The impact of the concept of culture on the concept of man. In J. Platt, ed., *New Views of the Nature of Man*, pp. 93–118. Chicago: University of Chicago Press.

Gerard, H. 1968. Basic features of commitment. In R. Abelson, E. Aronson, W. McGuire, T. Newcomb, M. Rosenberg, and P. Tannenbaum, eds., *Theories of Cognitive Consistency: A Sourcebook*, pp. 456–463. Chicago: Rand McNally.

Gibbon, G. 1974. A model of Mississippian development and its implications for the Red Wing area. In E. Johnson, ed., *Anthropology of the Upper Great Lakes*, pp. 129–137. Minnesota Prehistoric Archaeology Series, No. 11. St. Paul: Minnesota Historical Society.

—— 1980. Positivism and the new archaeology. Paper read at the 45th annual meeting of the Society for American Archaeology, Philadelphia.

Gibbs, J. 1972. *Sociological Theory Construction*. Hinsdale, Ill.: Dryden Press.

Gibson, Q. 1960. *The Logic of Social Enquiry*. New York: Humanities Press.

Gilbert, R. 1975. Trace element analyses of three skeletal amerindian popluations at Dickson Mounds. Ph.D. dissertation, University of Massachusetts, Amherst.

Goldstein, M. and L. Goldstein. 1978. *How We Know: An Exploration of the Scientific Process*. New York: Plenum Press.

Gouldner, A. 1967. Reciprocity and autonomy in functional theory. In N. Demerath and R. Peterson, eds., *System, Change and Conflict*, pp. 141–169. New York: Free Press.

Grayson, D. 1973. On the methodology of faunal analysis. *American Antiquity* 38:432–439.

—— 1979. On the quantification of vertebrate archaeofaunas. In M. Schiffer, ed., *Advances in Archaeological Method and Theory*, Vol. 2, pp. 199–237. New York: Academic Press.

Green, E. 1973. Locational analysis of prehistoric Maya sites in northern British Honduras. *American Antiquity* 38:279–293.

Green, S. 1980. Broadening least-cost models for expanding agricultural systems. In T. Earle and A. Christenson, eds., *Modeling Change in Prehistoric Subsistence Economies,* pp. 209–241. New York: Academic Press.

Grigg, D. 1976. Population pressure and agricultural change. *Progress in Geography,* Vol. 8, pp. 133–176. London: Edward Arnold.

Groot, A. D. de. 1969. *Methodology.* The Hague: Mouton.

Gumerman, G., ed. 1971. *The Distribution of Prehistoric Population Aggregates.* Prescott, Ariz.: Prescott College Press.

Hage, J. 1972. *Techniques and Problems of Theory Construction in Sociology.* New York: Wiley.

Haggett, P. 1965. *Locational Analysis in Human Geography.* London: Edward Arnold.

Hall, R. L. 1976. Ghosts, water barriers, corn, and sacred enclosures in the eastern woodlands. *American Antiquity* 41:360–364.

—— 1977. An anthropocentric perspective for eastern United States prehistory. *American Antiquity* 42:499–518.

Hallowell, A. I. 1959. Behavioral evolution and the emergence of the self. In B. Meggers, ed., *Evolution and Anthropology: A Centennial Appraisal,* pp. 36–60. Washington, D.C.: The Anthropological Society of Washington.

Hanson, J. 1975. Stress response in cultural systems: A prehistoric example from east-central Arizona. Chapters in the Prehistory of Eastern Arizona, IV. *Fieldiana: Anthropology* 65:92–102. Chicago: Field Museum of Natural History.

Hanson, N. R. 1958. *Patterns of Discovery.* Cambridge: Cambridge University Press.

Harner, M. 1970. Population pressure and the social evolution of agriculturalists. *Southwestern Journal of Anthropology* 26:67–86.

Harré, R. 1970. *The Principles of Scientific Thinking.* Chicago: University of Chicago Press.

Harris, M. 1968. *The Rise of Anthropological Theory.* New York: Crowell.

Harvey, D. 1969. Pattern, process, and the scale problem. *Transactions, Institute of British Georgraphers* 45:71–78.

Harsanyi, J. 1960. Explanation and comparative dynamics in social science. *Behavioral Science* 5:136–145.

Hassan, F. 1981. *Demographic Archaeology.* New York: Academic Press.

Hatch, E. 1973. *Theories of Man and Culture.* New York: Columbia University Press.

Hawkes, C. 1954. Archaeological theory and method. *American Anthropologist* 56:155–168.

Hearn, M. 1979. An ancient Chinese army rises from underground sentinel duty. *Smithsonian* 10:38–51.

Helmer, O. and N. Rescher. 1959. Exact and inexact sciences. *Management Science* 6:25–52.

Hempel, C. 1965. *Aspects of Scientific Explanation and Other Essays in the Philosophy of Science.* New York: Free Press.

Hempel, C. and P. Oppenheim. 1948. Studies in the logic of explanation. *Philosophy of Science* 15:135–175.

Hesse, M. 1966. *Models and Analogies in Science.* Notre Dame, Ind.: University of Notre Dame Press.

—— 1976. Models versus paradigms in the natural sciences. In L. Collins, ed., *The Use of Models in the Social Sciences,* pp. 1–15. Boulder, Colo.: Westview Press.

Hill, J. 1966. A prehistoric community in eastern Arizona. *Southwestern Journal of Anthropology* 22(1):9–30.

—— 1970a. Broken K Pueblo: Prehistoric social organization in the American Southwest. *Anthropological Papers of the University of Arizona,* No. 18. Tucson: University of Arizona Press.

—— 1970b. Prehistoric social organization in the American Southwest. In W. Longacre, ed., *Reconstructing Prehistoric Pueblo Societies,* pp. 11–58. Albuquerque: University of New Mexico Press.

Hill, J. and F. Plog. 1970. Research design for twelfth Southwestern Ceramic Conference. Manuscript, Dept. of Anthropology, University of California, Los Angeles. Mimeograph.

Hodder, I. 1972. Locational models and the study of Romano-British settlement. In D. Clarke, ed., *Models in Archaeology,* pp. 887–909. London: Methuen.

—— 1974. Regression analysis of some trade and marketing patterns. *World Archaeology* 6:172–189.

——. 1979. Simulating the growth of hierarchies. In C. Renfrew and K. Cooke, eds., *Transformations,* pp. 117–144. New York: Academic Press.

Hodder, I., ed. 1978. *The Spatial Organisation of Culture.* Pittsburgh, Pa.: University of Pittsburgh Press.

Hodder, I. and C. Orton. 1976. *Spatial Analysis in Archaeology.* New York: Cambridge University Press.

Hoffman, M. A. 1974. The social context of trash disposal in an Early Dynastic Egyptian town. *American Antiquity* 39:35–49.

House, J. 1975. A functional typology for Cache Project surface collections. In the Cache River Archeological Project, assembled by M. Schiffer and J. House. *Arkansas Archeological Survey, Research Series* 8:55–73.

Howells, W. 1960. Estimating population numbers through archaeological and skeletal remains. In R. Heizer and S. Cook, eds., *The Application of Quantitative Methods in Archaeology,* pp. 158–180. Viking Fund Publication in Anthropology, No. 28. New York: Quadrangle Press.

Hoyme, L. and W. Bass. 1962. Human skeletal remains from Tollifero (Ha-6) and Clarksville (Mc-14) sites, John H. Kerr Reservoir Basin, Virginia. *Bulletin of the Bureau of American Ethnology* 82:329–400. Washington, D.C.

Hudson, J. 1969. A location theory for settlement. *Annals of the Association of American Geographers* 59:365–381.

—— 1972. *Geographical Diffusion Theory.* Studies in Geography, No. 19. Evanston, Ill.: Northwestern University.

Jantz, R. 1974. The Redbird Focus: Cranial evidence in tribal identification. *Plains Anthropologist* 19:5–13.

Jarvie, I. C. 1965. Limits to functionalism and alternatives to it in anthropology. In D. Martindale, ed., *Functionalism in the Social Sciences,* pp. 18–34. Philadelphia: American Academy of Political and Social Science.

—— 1967. *The Revolution in Anthropology.* Chicago: Henry Regnery.

Jochim, M. 1976. *Hunter-Gatherer Subsistence and Settlement: A Predictive Model.* New York: Academic Press.

Johnson, G. A. 1977. Aspects of regional analysis in archaeology. In B. Siegel, ed., *Annual Review of Anthropology,* Vol. 6, pp. 479–508. Palo Alto, Calif.: Annual Reviews.

Kaplan, A. 1964. *The Conduct of Inquiry: Methodology for Behavioral Science.* Scranton, Pa.: Chandler.

Kaplan, D. and R. Manners. 1972. *Culture Theory.* Englewood Cliffs, N.J.: Prentice-Hall.

Kearney, M. 1975. World view theory and study. In B. Siegel, ed., *Annual Review of Anthropology,* Vol. 4, pp. 247–270. Palo Alto, Calif.: Annual Reviews.

—— 1976. *World View.* New York: Holt, Rinehart and Winston.

Keat, R. and J. Urry. 1975. *Social Theory as Science.* Boston: Routledge and Kegan Paul.

Keesing, R. M. 1974. Theories of culture. In B. Siegel, ed., *Annual Review of Anthropology,* Vol. 3, pp. 71–97. Palo Alto, Calif.: Annual Reviews.

Kidder, A. V. 1932. *The Artifacts of Pecos.* Papers of the Southwestern Expedition, No. 6. Andover, Mass.: Phillips Academy.

—— 1958. *Pecos, New Mexico: Archaeological Notes.* Papers of the R. S. Peabody Foundation for Archaeology, Vol. 5. Andover, Mass.

Knudson, S. 1978. *Culture in Retrospect: An Introduction to Archaeology.* Chicago: Rand McNally.

Koestler, A. 1967. *The Ghost in the Machine.* London: Hutchinson.

Krantz, D., R. D. Luce, P. Suppes, and A. Tversky. 1971. *Foundations of Measurement.* New York: Academic Press.

Kroeber, A. 1939. *Cultural and Natural Areas of Native North America.* University of California Publications in American Archaeology and Ethnology, No. 38. Berkeley: University of California Press.

Kuhn, T. 1970. *The Structure of Scientific Revolutions,* 2nd ed. Chicago: University of Chicago Press.

Lakatos, I. 1970. Falsification and the methodology of scientific research programmes. In I. Lakatos and A. Musgrave, eds., *Criticism and the Growth of Knowledge,* pp. 91–196. Cambridge: Cambridge University Press.

Lane, R. and A. Sublett. 1972. The osteology of social organization: Residence pattern. *American Antiquity* 37:186–201.

Langton, J. 1972. Potentialities and problems of adopting a systems approach to the study of change in human geography. *Progress in Geography* 4:125–179.

Leach, E. 1973. Concluding address. In C. Renfrew, ed., *The Explanation of Culture Change,* pp. 761–771. London: Duckworth.

—— 1977. A view from the bridge. In M. Spriggs, ed., *Archaeology and Anthropology: Areas of Mutual Interest,* pp. 161–176. British Archaeological Reports, 5.19. London: BAR Publications.

Leblanc, S. 1971. An addition to Naroll's suggested floor area and settlement population relationship. *American Antiquity* 36:210–211.

—— 1973. Two points of logic concerning data, hypotheses, general laws and systems. In C. Redman, ed., *Research and Theory in Current Archeology,* pp. 199–214, New York: Wiley.

Lenski, G. and J. Lenski. 1974. *Human Societies.* New York: McGraw-Hill.

Leone, M., ed. 1972. *Contemporary Archaeology.* Carbondale and Edwardsville: Southern Illinois University Press.

Levinson, D. 1977. What have we learned from cross-cultural surveys? *American Behavior Science* 20:757–792.

Longacre, W. 1963. Archaeology as anthropology: A case study. Ph.D. dissertation, Department of Anthropology, University of Chicago.

—— 1964. Archaeology as anthropology:A case study. *Science* 144:1454–1455.

—— 1966. Changing patterns of social integration: A prehistoric example from the American Southwest. *American Anthropologist* 68:94–102.

—— 1968. Some aspects of prehistoric society in east-central Arizona. In S. Binford and L. Binford, eds., *New Perspectives in Archeology,* pp. 89–102. Chicago: Aldine.

—— 1970. *Archaeology as Anthropology: A Case Study.* Anthropological Papers of the University of Arizona, No. 17. Tucson: University of Arizona Press.

—— 1974. Kalinga pottery-making: The evolution of a research design. In M. Leaf, ed., *Frontiers of Anthropology,* pp. 51–67. New York: Van Nostrand Reinhold.

McKern, W. C. 1939. The Midwestern taxonomic method as an aid to archaeological study. *American Antiquity* 4:301–131.

McKinley, K. 1971. Survivorship in gracile and robust australopithecines: A demographic comparison and a proposed birth model. *American Journal of Physical Anthropology* 39:471–426.

MacNeish, R. 1967. An interdisciplinary approach to an archaeological problem. In D. Byers, ed., *The Prehistory of the Tehuacan Valley, Vol. 1: Environment and Subsistence,* pp. 14–24. Austin: University of Texas Press.

McNett, C. Jr., 1973. A settlement pattern scale of cultural complexity. In R. Naroll and R. Cohen, eds., *A Handbook of Method in Cultural Anthropology,* pp. 872–886. Garden City, N.Y.: Natural History Press.

Marquardt, W. 1978. Advances in archaeological seriation. In M. Schiffer, ed., *Advances in Archaeological Method and Theory,* Vol. 1, pp. 257–314. New York: Academic Press.

Marsh, R. 1967. *Comparative Sociology.* New York: Harcourt, Brace & World.

Marshack, A. 1972. Upper Paleolithic notation and symbol. *Science* 178:817–827.

Martin, P. 1971. The revolution in archaeology. *American Antiquity* 36:1–8.

Meehan, E. 1968. *Explanation in Social Science: A System Paradigm*. Homewood, Ill.: Dorsey Press.

Mellor, D. 1973. On some methodological misconceptions. In C. Renfrew, ed., *The Explanation of Culture Change*, pp. 493–498. London: Duckworth.

—— 1980. Necessities and universals in natural laws. In D. H. Mellor, ed., *Science, Belief and Behavior*, pp. 105–125. Cambridge: Cambridge University Press.

Miller, J. 1965. Living systems: Basic concepts. *Behavioral Sceince* 10:193–237.

Mills, C. 1967. Grand theory. In N. Demerath and R. Peterson, eds., *System, Change and Conflict*, pp. 171–183. New York: Free Press.

Modderman, P. 1971. Bandkeramiker und Wanderbauertum. *Archaëologische Korrespondenzblatt* 1:7–9.

Montague, W. 1925. *The Ways of Knowing*. London: Allen and Unwin.

Moore, C., ed. 1974. *Reconstructing Complex Societies: An Archaeological Colloquium*. Supplement to the Bulletin of the American Schools of Oriental Research, No. 20. Cambridge, Mass.: American Schools of Oriental Research.

Morgan, C. 1973. Archaeology and explanation. *World Archaeology* 4:259–276.

Morgan, L. 1877. *Ancient Society*. New York: Holt.

Mueller, J., ed. 1975. *Sampling in Archaeology*. Tucson: University of Arizona Press.

Mullins, N. 1971. *The Art of Theory: Construction and Use*. New York: Harper and Row.

Murdock, G. 1959. Evolution in social organization. In B. Meggers, ed., *Evolution and Anthropology: A Centennial Appraisal*, pp. 126–143. Washington, D.C.: The Anthropological Society of Washington.

—— 1967a. *Ethnographic Atlas*. Pittsburgh: University of Pittsburgh Press. First published 1962–1965 in *Ethnology*, vols. 1–4.

—— 1967b. Ethnographic atlas: A summary. *Ethnology* 6:109–236.

Murphree, I. 1961. The evolutionary anthropologists: The concepts of progress and culture in the thought of John Lubbock, Edward B. Tylor, and Lewis H. Morgan. *Proceedings of the American Philosophical Society* 105 (3):265–300.

Nagel, E. 1961. *The Structure of Science*. New York: Harcourt Brace Jovanovich.

Naroll, R. 1956. A preliminary index of social development. *American Anthropologist* 58:687–715.

—— 1962. Floor area and settlement population. *American Antiquity* 27:587–589.

—— 1964. On ethnic unit classification. *Current Anthropology* 5:283–312.

—— 1970. What have we learned from cross-cultural surveys? *American Anthropologist* 72:1227–1288.

Naroll, R. and L. Von Bertalanffy. 1956. The principle of allometry in biology and the social sciences. *General Systems* 1:76–89.

Naroll, R., G. Michik, and F. Naroll. 1974. Hologeistic theory testing. J. Jorgensen, ed., *Comparative Studies by Harold E. Driver and Essays in His Honor*, pp. 121–148. New Haven, Conn.: HRAF Press.

O' Shea, J. 1978. A simulation of Pawnee site development. In I. Hodder, ed., *Simulation Studies in Archaeology*, pp. 39–46. Cambridge: Cambridge University Press.

Payne, S. 1972. On the interpretation of bone samples from archaeological sites. In E. Higgs, ed., *Papers in Economic Prehistory*, pp. 65–81. New York: Cambridge University Press.

Peebles, C. and S. Kus. 1977. Some archaeological correlates of ranked societies. *American Antiquity* 42:421–448.

Peirce, C. S. 1932. *Collected Papers*. C. Hartshorne and P. Weiss, eds. Cambridge, Harvard University Press.

Pelto, P. 1970. *Anthropological Research: The Structure of Inquiry*. New York: Harper and Row.

Perkins, D., Jr. 1973. A critique on the methods of quantifying faunal remains from archaeological sites. In J. Matolsci, ed., *Domestikationsforschung und Geschichte der Haustiere*, pp. 367–370. Budapest, Akadémiai Kiadó.

Pires-Ferreira, J. 1976. Obsidian exchange in Formative Mesoamerica. In K. V. Flannery, ed., *The Early Mesoamerican Village*, pp. 311–326. New York: Academic Press.

Pires-Ferreira, J. and K. V. Flannery. 1976. Ethnographic models for Formative exchange. In K. V. Flannery, ed., *The Early Mesoamerican Village*, pp. 286–292. New York: Academic Press.

Plog, F. 1974. *The Study of Prehistoric Change*. New York: Academic Press.

—— 1975. Systems theory in archaeological research. In B. Siegel, ed., *Annual Review of Anthropology*, Vol. 4, pp. 207–224. Palo Alto, Calif.: Annual Reviews.

Plog, S. 1976a. Relative efficiencies of sampling techniques for archaeological surveys. In K. V. Flannery, ed., *The Early Mesoamerican Village*, pp. 135–158. New York: Academic Press.

—— 1976b. Measurement of prehistoric interaction between communities. In K. V. Flannery, ed., *The Early Mesoamerican Village*, pp. 255–272. New York: Academic Press.

Polanyi, K. 1957. The economy as instituted process. In K. Polanyi, C. Arensbert, and H. Pearson, eds., *Trade and Market in the Early Empires*, pp. 243–270. New York: Free Press.

—— 1959. Anthropology and economic theory. In M. Fried, ed., *Readings in Anthropology*, Vol. 2, pp. 215–233. New York: Crowell.

Popper, K. 1961. *The Poverty of Historicism*. London: Routledge and Kegan Paul.

—— 1963. *The Open Society and Its Enemies*, 4th ed. 2 vols. New York: Harper and Row.

—— 1969. *Conjectures and Refutations*, 3rd ed. London: Routledge and Kegan Paul.

—— 1970. *The Logic of Scientific Discovery*. New York: Harper and Row.

—— 1972. *Objective Knowledge: An Evolutionary Approach*. Oxford: Oxford University Press.

Quine, W. and J. Ullian. 1970. *The Web of Belief*. New York: Random House.

Rappaport, R. 1968. *Pigs for the Ancestors*. New Haven, Conn.: Yale University Press.

Redfield, R. 1947. The folk society. *American Journal of Sociology* 52:293–308.

—— 1953. *The Primitive World and Its Transformations*. Ithaca, N.Y.: Cornell University Press.

Redman, C. 1974. *Archaeological Sampling Strategies.* Addison-Wesley Module in Anthropology, No. 55. Reading, Mass.: Addison-Wesley.

——. 1978. Multivariate artifact analysis: A basis for multidimensional interpretations. In C. Redman, M. Berman, E. Curtin, W. Langhorne, N. Versaggi, and J. Wanser, eds., *Social Archeology,* pp. 159–192. New York: Academic Press.

Redman, C., M. Berman, E. Curtin, W. Langhorne, N. Versaggi, and J. Wanser, eds. 1978. *Social Archaeology: Beyond Subsistence and Dating.* New York: Academic Press.

Reed, C. 1963. Osteo-archaeology. In D. Brothwell and E. Higgs, eds., *Science in Archaeology,* pp. 204–216. London: Thames and Hudson.

Reed, E. 1956. Types of village plan layouts in the southwest. In G. R. Willey, ed., *Prehistoric Settlement Patterns in the New World,* pp. 11–17. *Viking Fund Publications in Anthropology,* No. 23. New York: Wenner-Gren Foundation for Anthropological Research.

Reichenbach, H. 1951. *The Rise of Scientific Philosophy.* Berkeley: University of California Press.

Reid, J. 1978. Response to stress at Grasshopper Pueblo, Arizona. In P. Grebinger, ed., *Discovering Past Behavior,* pp. 195–213. New York: Gordon and Breach.

Renfrew, C. 1974. Beyond a subsistence economy: The evolution of social organization in prehistoric Europe. In C. Moore, ed., *Reconstructing Complex Societies,* pp. 69–96. Supplement to the Bulletin of the American Schools of Oriental Research, No. 20. Cambridge, Mass.: American Schools of Oriental Research.

—— 1979. Systems collapse as social transformation: Catastrophe and anastrophe in early state societies. In C. Renfrew and K. Cooke, eds., *Transformations: Mathematical Approaches to Culture Change,* pp. 481–506. New York: Academic Press.

Renfrew, C., J. Dixon, and J. Cann. 1966. Obsidian and early cultural contact in the Near East. *Proceedings of the Prehistoric Society* 32:30–72.

—— 1968. Future analysis of Near Eastern obsidians. *Proceedings of the Prehistoric Society* 34:319–331.

Reynolds, P. 1971. *A Primer in Theory Construction.* New York: Bobbs-Merrill.

Rickert, H. 1926. *Kulturwissenschaft und Naturwissenschaft,* 7th ed. Tübingen, W. Germany: Mohr.

Robbins, L. M. 1977. The story of life revealed by the dead. In L. Blakely, ed., *Biocultural Adaptation in Prehistoric America,* pp. 10–26. Southern Anthropological Society Proceedings, No. 11. Athens: University of Georgia Press.

Robbins, M. 1966. House types and settlement patterns: An application of ethnology to archaeological interpretation. *Minnesota Archaeologist* 28:3–26.

Roe, D. 1976. Typology and the trouble with hand-axes. In G. Sieveking, I. Longworth, and K. Wilson, eds., *Problems in Economic and Social Archaeology,* pp. 61–70. London: Duckworth.

Rohn, A. 1965. Postulation of socioeconomic groups from archaeological evidence. Assembled by D. Osborne, *Contributions of the Wetherill Mesa Archaeological Project,* pp. 65–69. Memoirs of the Society for American Archaeology, No. 19. Washington, D.C.: Society for American Archaeology.

—— 1971. *Mug House*. National Park Service, Archaeological Research Series, No. 7-D. Washington, D.C.: U.S. Department of the Interior.

Roper, D. 1979. The method and theory of site catchment analysis: A review. In M. Schiffer, ed., *Advances in Archaeological Method and Theory*, Vol. 2, pp. 119–140. New York: Academic Press.

Rowe, C. J. Rolfe, R. Dearden, A. Kent, and N. Grenger. 1974. The Neolithic game. *Oxford Geography Project. 2: European Patterns*. Oxford: Oxford University Press.

Runciman, W. C. 1969. *Social Science and Political Theory*, 2d. ed. Cambridge: Cambridge University Press.

Ryan, A. 1970. *The Philosophy of the Social Sciences*. London: Macmillan.

Sahlins, M. 1960. Evolution: Specific and general. In M. Sahlins and E. Service, eds., *Evolution and Culture*, pp. 12–44. Ann Arbor: University of Michigan Press.

—— 1968. *Tribesmen*. Englewood Cliffs, N.J.: Prentice-Hall.

—— 1972. *Stone Age Economics*. Chicago: Aldine.

Sahlins, M. and E. Service, eds., 1960. *Evolution and Culture*. Ann Arbor: University of Michigan Press.

Saul, F. 1972. *The Human Skeletal Remains of Altar de Sacrificios. An Osteobiographic Analysis*. Papers of the Peabody Museum, Harvard University, Vol. 63, No. 2. Cambridge, Mass.

—— 1976. Osteobiography: Life history recorded in bone. In E. Giles and J. Friedlaender, *The Measures of Man*, pp. 372–382. Cambridge, Mass.: Peabody Museum Press.

Saxe, A. 1970. Social dimensions of mortuary practices. Ph.D. dissertation, University of Michigan, Ann Arbor.

Schaefer, J., ed. 1974. *Studies in Cultural Diffusion: Galton's Problem*. New Haven, Conn.: HRAF books.

—— 1977. The growth and development of hologeistic cross-cultural research. *Annals of the New York Academy of Sciences* 285:75–89.

Schaefer, J., M. Antoine, H. Carroll, J. Devitt, T. Haberman, B. Herda, M. Moyer, R. Rechlin, and L. Ward. 1971. Sampling methods, functional associations and Galton's problem: A replicative assessment. *Behavior Science Notes* 6:229–274.

Schiffer, M. 1972. Archaeological context and systemic context. *American Antiquity* 37:156–165.

—— 1976. *Behavioral Archeology*. New York: Academic Press.

—— 1983. Toward the identification of formation processes. *American Antiquity* 48(4):675–706.

Scriven, M. 1959. Explanation and prediction in evolutionary theory. *Science* 130:477–482.

Segraves, B. A. 1974. Ecological generalization and structural transformation of sociocultural systems. *American Anthropologist* 76:530–552.

Sellars, W. 1963. *Science, Perception and Reality*. New York: Humanities Press.

Semenov, S. 1964. *Prehistoric Technology*. London: Adams and Dart.

Service, E. 1962. *Primitive Social Organization: An Evolutionary Perspective.* New York: Random House.

Sharer, R. and W. Ashmore. 1979. *Fundamentals of Archaeology.* Menlo Park, Calif.: Benjamin/Cummings.

Shearing, C. 1973. How to make theories untestable: A guide to theorists. *The American Sociologist* 8:33–37.

Shennan, S. 1975. The social organization of Branc. *Antiquity* 49:279–288.

Skellam, J. 1951. Random dispersal in theoretical populations. *Biometrika* 38:196–218.

Smith, B. and S. Epstein. 1971. Two categories of $^{13}C/^{12}C$ ratios for higher plants. *Plant Physiology* 47:380–384.

Smith, M. A. 1955. The limitations of inference in archaeology. *Archaeological Newsletter* 6:3–7.

Smith, P. E. L. 1972. Changes in population pressure in archaeological explanation. *World Archaeology* 4:5–18.

—— 1976. *Food Production and Its Consequences.* Menlo Park, Calif.: Cummings.

Spaulding, A. 1968. Explanation in archeology. In S. Binford and L. Binford, eds., *New Perspectives in Archaeology,* pp. 33–40. Chicago: Aldine.

—— 1973. Archaeology in the active voice: The new anthropology. In C. Redman, ed., *Research and Theory in Current Archaeology,* pp. 337–354. New York: Wiley.

Speth, J. and G. Johnson. 1976. Problems in the use of correlation for the investigation of tool kits and activity areas. In C. Cleland, ed., *Cultural Change and Continuity,* pp. 35–57. New York: Academic Press.

Spooner, B., ed. 1972. *Population Growth: Anthropological Implications.* Cambridge, Mass.: MIT Press.

Spriggs, M., ed. 1977. *Archaeology and Anthropology: Areas of Mutual Interest.* British Archaeological Reports, 5.19. London: BAR Publications.

Squier, E. and E. Davis. 1848. *Ancient Monuments of the Mississippi Valley.* Smithsonian Contributions to Knowledge, Vol. 1. Washington, D.C.: Smithsonian Institute.

Stanislawski, M. 1973. Review of Archaeology as Anthropology: A Case Study. *American Antiquity* 38:117–121.

Steward, J. 1937. Ecological aspects of southwestern society. *Anthropos* 32:87–104.

—— 1949. Cultural causality and law: A trial formulation of the development of early civilizations. *American Anthropologist* 51:1–27.

—— 1955. *Theory of Culture Change.* Urbana: University of Illinois Press.

Steward, J. and F. Setzler. 1938. Function and configuration in archaeology. *American Antiquity* 4:4–10.

Stickel, E. and J. Chartkoff. 1973. The nature of scientific laws and their relation to law-building in archaeology. In C. Renfrew, ed., *The Explanation of Culture Change,* pp. 663–671. London: Duckworth.

Stier, F. 1975. Behavioral chain analysis of yucca remains at Antelope House. *The Kiva* 41:57–64.

Stinchcombe, A. 1968. *Constructing Social Theories.* New York: Harcourt, Brace and World.

Struever, S. 1968. Problems, methods and organization: A disparity in the growth of archaeology. In B. Meggers, ed., *Anthropological Archaeology in the Americas,* pp. 131–151. Washington, D.C.: Anthropological Society of Washington.

—— 1971. Comments on archaeological data requirements and research strategy. *American Antiquity* 36:9–19.

Struever, S. and G. Houart. 1972. An analysis of the Hopewell Interaction Sphere. In E. Wilmsen, ed., *Social Exchange and Interaction,* pp. 47–79. Anthropological Papers of the Museum of Anthropology, University of Michigan, No. 46. Ann Arbor: University of Michigan Press.

Suppe, F., 2d ed. 1977. *The Structure of Scientific Theories,* ed. Urbana: University of Illinois Press.

Symmes, O. 1962. *Ecology and Cultural Continuity as Contributing Factors in the Social Organization of the Plains Indians.* University of California Publications in American Archaeology and Ethnology 48:1.

Tatje, T. and R. Naroll. 1973. Two measures of societal complexity: An empirical cross-cultural comparison. In R. Naroll and R. Cohen, eds., *A Handbook of Method in Cultural Anthropology,* pp. 766–833. Garden City, N.Y.: Natural History Press.

Taylor, D. M. 1970. *Explanation and Meaning.* Cambridge: Cambridge University Press.

Taylor, W. W. 1948. A study of archeology. *American Anthropologist,* Memoir No. 69, Rpt. 1967. Carbondale: Southern Illinois University Press.

Thomas, D. 1979. *Naturalism and Social Science: A Post-Empiricist Philosophy of Social Science.* New York: Cambridge University Press.

Thomas, D.H. 1969. Great Basin hunting patterns: A quantitative method for treating faunal remains. *American Antiquity* 34:393–401.

—— 1971. Distinguishing natural from cultural bone in archaeological sites. *American Antiquity* 36:366–371.

—— 1972. A computer simulation model of Great Basin Shoshonean subsistence and settlement patterns. In D. Clarke, ed., *Models in Archaeology,* pp. 671–704. London: Methuen.

—— 1976. *Figuring Anthropology.* New York: Holt, Rinehart, and Winston.

Thomas, F. N. 1967. Additional comments on population size relationships for sets of cities. In W. Garrison and D. Marble, eds., *Quantitative Geography,* pp. 167–190. Northwestern University Studies in Geography, No. 13. Evanston, Ill.: Northwestern University Press.

Tidswell, W. and S. Barker. 1971. *Quantitative Methods: An Approach to Socio-Economic Geography.* London: University Tutorial Press.

Tiffany, J. 1983. Site catchment analysis of southeast Iowa Oneota sites. In G. Gibbon, ed., *Oneota Studies,* pp. 1–13. Publications in Anthropology, No. 1. Minneapolis: University of Minnesota Press.

Todd, I. 1974. Comments on Prof. Renfrew's paper. In C. Moore, ed., *Reconstructing Complex Societies,* pp. 85–88. Supplement to the Bulletin of the American Schools of Oriental Research, No. 20. Cambridge, Mass.: American Schools of Oriental Research.

Tortellot, G. and J. Sabloff. 1972. Exchange systems among the ancient Maya. *American Antiquity* 37:126–134.

Toulmin, S. 1953. *The Philosophy of Science.* New York: Harper and Row.

—— 1958. *The Uses of Argument.* Cambridge: Cambridge University Press.

Trigger, B. 1968. Major concepts of archaeology in historical perspective. *Man* 3:523–541.

Trinkaus, E. 1978. Hard times among the Neanderthals. *Natural History* 87:58–63.

Tuggle, H. 1970. Prehistoric community relationships in east central Arizona. Ph.D. dissertation, University of Arizona, Tucson.

Tuggle, H., A. Townsend, and T. Riley. 1972. Laws, systems, and research designs: A discussion of explanation in archaeology. *American Antiquity* 37:3–12.

Tylor, E. B. 1871. *Primitive Culture.* London: J. Murray.

—— 1889. On a method of investigating the development of institutions applied to the laws of marriage and descent. *Journal of the Royal Anthropological Institute* 18:272.

Ubelaker, D. 1978. *Human Skeletal Remains.* Chicago: Aldine.

Uerpmann, H.-P. 1973. Animal bone finds and economic archaeology: A critical study of "osteoarchaeological" method. *World Archaeology* 4:307–322.

van der Merwe, N. and J. Vogel. 1 1978. ¹³C content of human collagen as a measure of prehistoric diet in woodland North America. *Nature* 276:815–816.

Vita-Finzi, C. and E. Higgs. 1970. Prehistoric economy in the Mount Carmel area of Palestine: Site catchment analysis. *Proceedings of the Prehistoric Society* 36:1–37.

Vogel, J. and N. van der Merwe. 1977. Isotopic evidence for early maize cultivation in New York State. *American Antiquity* 42:238–242.

Vogt, E. 1974. Aerial photography in Highland Chiapas ethnography. In E. Vogt, ed., *Aerial Photography in Anthropological Field Research,* pp. 57–77. Cambridge: Harvard University Press.

Wailes, B. 1972. Plow and population in temperate Europe. In B. Spooner, ed., *Population Growth: Anthropological Implications,* pp. 154–179. Cambridge, Mass.: MIT Press.

Wallace, W. 1971. *The Logic of Science in Sociology.* Chicago: Aldine.

Watson, J. P. N. 1972. Fragmentation analysis of animal bone samples from archaeological sites. *Archaeometry* 14:221–227.

Watson, P. J. 1973. The future of archaeology in anthropology: Culture history and social science. In C. Redman, ed., *Research and Theory in Current Archaeology,* pp. 113–124. New York: Wiley.

Watson, P. J., S. Leblanc, and C. Redman. 1971. *Explanation in Archaeology: An Explicitly Scientific Approach.* New York: Columbia University Press.

Watt, K. 1972. Man's efficient rush toward deadly dullness. *Natural History* 81(2):74–82.

Wauchope, R. 1962. *Lost Tribes and Sunken Continents.* Chicago: University of Chicago Press.

Weis, K. 1973. Demographic models for anthropology. *American Antiquity,* Memoir No. 27, Vol. 38 No. 2, Part 2.

White, J. and N. Modjeska. 1978. Where do all the stone tools go? Some examples and problems in their social and spatial distribution in the Papua New Guinea Highlands. In I. Hodder, ed., *The Spatial Organisation of Culture*, pp. 25–38. Pittsburgh, Pa.: University of Pittsburgh Press.

White, L. 1943. Energy and the evolution of culture. *American Anthropologist* 45:335–356.

—— 1959. *The Evolution of Culture*. New York: McGraw-Hill.

White, T. E. 1953. A method of calculating the dietary percentages of various food animals utilized by aboriginal peoples. *American Antiquity* 18:396–398.

Whiting, J. and B. Ayres. 1968. Inferences from the shape of dwellings. In K. C. Chang, ed., *Settlement Archaeology*, pp. 117–133. Palo Alto, Calif.: National Press.

Wiessner, P. 1974. A functional estimator of population from floor area. *American Antiquity* 39:343–350.

Wilford, L. A. 1955. A revised classification of the prehistoric cultures of Minnesota. *American Antiquity* 21(2):130–142.

Willer, D. 1967. *Scientific Sociology*. Englewood Cliffs, N.J.: Prentice-Hall.

Willer, D. and J. Willer. 1973. *Systematic Empiricism: Critique of a Pseudoscience*. Englewood Cliffs, N.J.: Prentice-Hall.

Williams, M. B. 1970. Deducing the consequences of evolution: A mathematical model. *Journal of Theoretical Biology* 29:343–385.

—— 1973. Falsifiable predictions of evolutionary theory. *Philosophy of Science* 40:518–537.

Wilmsen, E. 1973. Interaction, spacing behavior, and the organization of hunting bands. *Journal of Anthropological Research* 29:1–31.

Wing, E. and A. Brown. 1979. *Paleonutrition*. New York: Academic Press.

Winter, M. C. 1972. Tierras Largas: A Formative community in the Valley of Oaxaca, Mexico. Ph.D. dissertation, University of Arizona, Tucson.

—— 1976. The archaeological household cluster in the Valley of Oaxaca. In K. V. Flannery, ed., *The Early Mesoamerican Village*, pp. 25–31. New York: Academic Press.

Winter, M. C. and J. Pires-Ferreira. 1976. Distribution of obsidian among households in two Oaxacan villages. In K. V. Flannery, ed., *The Early Mesoamerican Village*, pp. 306–311. New York: Academic Press.

Winters, H. D. 1968. Value systems and trade cycles of the late Archaic in the Midwest. In S. Binford and L. Binford, eds., *New Perspectives in Archeology*, pp. 175–221. Chicago: Aldine.

Wissler, C. 1923. *Man and Culture*. New York: Crowell.

—— 1936. Changes in population profiles among the Northern Plains Indians. *Anthropological Papers of the American Museum of Natural History* 36:1–67.

Wittfogel, K. 1957. *Oriental Despotism: A Comparative Study of Total Power*. New Haven, Conn.: Yale University Press.

Wobst, H. M. 1974. Boundary conditions for paleolithic cultural systems: A simulation approach. *American Antiquity* 39:147–178.

Wood, W. R. 1965. The Redbird Focus and the problem of Ponca prehistory. *Plains Anthropologists*, Memoir 2, No. 10(28).

Wood, W. R. and D. Johnson. 1978. A survey of disturbance processes in archaeological site formation. In M. Schiffer, ed., *Advances in Archaeological Method and Theory* 1:315–381. New York: Academic Press.

Wright, G. E. 1974. The tell: Basic unit for reconstructing complex societies of the Near East. In C. Moore, ed., *Reconstructing Complex Societies,* pp. 123–130. Supplement to the Bulletin of the American Schools of Oriental Research, No. 20. Cambridge, Mass.: American Schools of Oriental Research.

Wright, G. H. von. 1971. *Explanation and Understanding.* Ithaca, N.Y.: Cornell University Press.

Wright, H. Y. and M. Zeder. 1977. The simulation of a linear exchange system under equilibrium conditions. In T. Earle and J. Ericson, eds., *Exchange Systems in Prehistory,* pp. 233–253. New York: Academic Press.

Zarky, A. 1976. Statistical analysis of site catchments at Ocos, Guatemala. In K. V. Flannery, ed., *The Early Mesoamerican Village,* pp. 117–128. New York: Academic Press.

Ziegler, A. C. 1973. Inference from prehistoric faunal remains. *Module in Anthropology,* No. 43. Reading, Mass.: Addison-Wesley.

Zimmerman, L. J. 1977. Prehistoric locational behavior: A computer simulation. Report 10. Iowa City: Office of the State Archaeologist.

—— 1978. Simulating prehistoric locational behaviour. In I. Hodder, ed., *Simulation Studies in Archaeology,* pp. 27–37. Cambridge: Cambridge University Press.

Zipf, G. K. 1949. *Principle of Least Effort.* New York: Hafner.

Index

Abduction, 46-47, 75, 80, 105, 417
Abstraction 46-47, 52, 54, 57, 68, 75, 77, 83, 105, 115-16, 132, 417
Achinstein, Peter, 397, 399
Activity area, 141-44, 162, 175, 198, 417
Aggregation problem, 186
Amedeo, Douglas, 372-76
Ammerman, A. J., 193, 195-97, 260, 282-85, 303
Anderson, A. D., 299
Archaeological context, 10-11, 39, 47-48, 51, 54, 68, 77, 103, 118, 142-43, 191, 312, 325, 354-55, 400, 402, 417
Ascher, R., 213
Ayres, B., 332-35

Bacon, Francis, 46
Baerreis, D. A., 187-88
Beardsley, R., 347
Beckman, M. J., 295
Beer, S., 20
Behavioral stream, 4
Bell, Robert E., 234-35
Bender, M. M., 187-88
Berry, B. J., 295-96
Bertram, J. B., 184
Bidney, David, 17
Binford, Lewis R., 1, 6, 31, 81, 138, 160, 164, 184, 390
Binford, Sally R., 1, 31
Bishop, C. A., 224
Boas, Franz, 3, 403-4
Bökönyi, S., 184
Bonini's paradox, 121

Bonnichsen, Robson, 161, 175
Boserup, Ester, 356, 358, 360-62, 364, 368, 371, 381, 402
Bourguignon, E., 328-32
Brown, A. B., 160
Brown, James A., 234-35
Brown, R. R., 407
Brumfield, Elizabeth, 277-81, 302
Buikstra, Jane, 159, 166, 168, 210-12, 216
Bunge, Mario, 352
Burial program, 164-68, 176, 418

Cann, J., 255, 259
Carneiro, R. L., 342-43
Casteel, R. W., 184
Catastrophe theory, 298
Categories, 41
Cavalli-Sforza, L. L., 260, 282-85, 303
Central place theory, 231-34, 246, 263, 290-95, 297, 303, 418
Chang, K. C., 137
Chaplin, R. E., 184
Childe, V. Gordon, 169, 340, 342, 371, 392
Christaller, Walter, 231, 372
Clark, J. G. D., 261
Clark, Kenneth, 412
Clarke, David, 108, 125-31, 133, 146, 239, 281
Class intervals, 41
Cognitive archaeology, 171-72, 176, 183, 418
Cohen, M. N., 364, 381
Collingwood, R. G., 88, 410

Community plan, 150, 175, 262, 418
Comte, Auguste, 27
Confirmation, 58, 418
Context of discovery, 66, 68, 75, 80, 112, 116
Context of justification, 66, 68, 75, 80, 113, 116
Cook, S. F., 334
Cross-cultural comparison, 63, 119, 135, 138, 164, 308-51, 392
Crude mortality rate, 214-18, 418
Crumley, C., 296
C-transform, 193, 195, 418
Cultural ecology, 1, 7-8, 13, 28-29, 104-5, 268, 418
Cultural materialism, 1, 7-8, 13, 29, 97, 180, 418
Culture area, 323-24, 343, 349, 419
Culture-bound term, 316, 319, 349
Culture concept, 1-11, 15-19, 24, 29-30, 35, 46, 96-97, 100, 106-7, 115, 136, 150, 156, 170, 217, 220, 223, 268, 270, 274, 313-14, 321, 390-91, 405-6, 419; normative interpretation, 3-4, 6, 9, 16-17; utilitarian interpretation, 6-8
Culture-free concept, 316, 349, 419
Culture history, 8-9, 45, 47-50, 57, 63, 68-69, 73, 75-76, 92, 103-4, 106-7, 112-14, 120, 123, 125, 131, 268-69, 302, 319, 325, 395, 418-19
Cumulative mortality profile, 216, 419
Curry, L., 294

Daly, P., 184
Davis, E., 78
Dean, Jeffrey, 149
Deduction, 50, 57, 68, 75, 86-87, 119, 122-24, 357, 360, 369, 376, 419
Deductive-nomological explanation, 84-85, 99, 419
Deductive paradox, 123
Deductive statistical explanation, 85-86, 99, 419
Deetz, James, 173-74, 176, 392
Demography, 18, 212-18, 271, 286, 411, 419
Derived measurement, 55-56, 70, 419
Derived term, 355, 357, 359, 377, 381-82, 419

Descriptive statistics, 43, 67, 77, 419
Diachronic analysis, 22, 221, 267, 419
Dictionary of a theory, 355-61, 365, 379, 382, 419
Discursive theory, 352-53, 356, 361-62, 367, 371, 377, 381-82
Distance-decay model, 118, 244-45, 263, 419
Divale, W., 155
Dixon, J., 255, 259
Dixon, K., 413
Drennan, Robert, 271-74, 302
Durkheim, Emile, 404

Ecological fallacy, 261, 315, 419
Ecological niche, 7, 340
Edynak, G., 205-6
Einstein, Albert, 46
Elliot, K., 260-62
Ellman, D., 260-62
Ember, M., 153-55, 332
Emic approach, 403
Empirical generalization, 36, 44, 46-49, 54, 57, 59, 69, 79-80, 84, 103, 131, 420
Empirical interpretation, 36, 39, 52-54, 56-60, 69-70, 83, 108, 112, 249, 278, 420
Empirical research, 74, 420
Enumeration, 43
Environment, 10, 16-19, 22-24, 61, 169-70, 182-83, 189-90, 217, 262, 270, 272-73, 286, 348, 377
Epidemiological research, 205, 420
Equation of a theory, 355, 357, 359-61, 382, 420
Ethnoarchaeology, 420
Etic approach, 403-4
Etzioni, Amitai, 354
Explanandum, 26, 84-85, 420
Explanans, 26, 84-85, 420
Explanation, 3, 5, 7, 10, 12, 15, 21-23, 25-30, 33-35, 37, 46, 49, 66, 68, 73, 75, 83-91, 93, 95, 99, 102, 104-5, 107, 112-13, 141, 182, 232, 267-71, 282, 285, 294, 303, 309, 312, 321, 338-40, 352-53, 355, 364, 367, 372, 377, 379, 383, 388-95, 403-7, 409-13; covering-law model, 12-13, 26, 28-29, 84-88, 90-91, 309, 325, 389-90, 396, 399-400, 418; practical inference, 88, 423; reason-giving, 88, 90,

99, 409, 424; sketch, 87, 90, 406; symmetry thesis, 91; systems model 89, 93; what-explanation, 88-91, 99, 427
Ex post facto approach, 62-63

Factor theory, 371, 383, 420
Feldman, M. M., 193
Feyerabend, Paul, 35, 394
Fiat measurement, 55-56, 70, 420
Fitting, James, 336
Flannery, Kent, 31-32, 144-46, 257, 293-94, 303, 371
Freeman, L., 318, 342-43, 350
Fried, M., 165, 168, 342
Fritz, J., 390
Functional argument, 319-20, 420
Functionalism, 25-27, 30, 97, 104-5, 111, 298, 340
Fundamental measurement, 55-56, 70, 420

Galton, Sir Francis, 321-23
Game theory, 111, 201-4, 217, 237, 263, 420
General evolution, 341, 350, 421
General systems theory, 24, 114-15
Gibbs, J., 366, 370
Gilbert, R., 207
Golledge, Reginald, 372-76
Goodenough, Ward, 17
Gouldner, A., 23
Graph theory, 111, 250-53, 263, 421
Gravity model, 110-11, 242-44, 248-49, 263, 421
Grayson, D., 184, 186
Green, E., 237, 303
Green, Stanton, 286-90
Greenbaum. L., 328-32
Guttman scale, 343-44, 349

Hage, Jerald, 354, 359, 362-63, 382
Haggett, Peter, 291
Hall, Robert L., 171-72
Hallowell, A. Irving, 274-76, 302
Hanson, J., 190
Hanson, N. R., 37
Harré, R., 110
Harris, Marvin, 4
Harsanyi, J., 320

Heizer, R., 31-32, 334
Hempel, Carl, 87
Higgs, E., 198
Hill, James, 153, 190
Hodder, Ian, 245-46, 260-62, 296-98, 303
Hoffman, M. A., 160-61
Houart, G., 246
Household cluster, 144-48, 151, 175, 253-54, 421
Human population, 39, 130, 136, 155, 180, 182, 187-89, 204-18
Hypothesis, 37-39, 44-59, 61-63, 68-69, 74-76, 78-82, 86, 91-92, 96-97, 105, 117, 119, 123, 141, 150, 160-61, 171, 188, 191-93, 209-11, 217, 228-29, 233-34, 243, 247, 277-78, 281, 291, 301, 311-12, 318-21, 324, 332, 335-37, 347, 349-50, 354, 357, 361, 363, 367, 369, 399, 401, 406, 420
Hypothetico-deductive approach, 12-13, 28-29, 82, 421

Identity, 45, 47-49, 57, 68-69, 76, 78-81, 140, 143-44, 172, 175-76, 193, 209, 253, 421
Ideological subsystem, 136-37, 139, 169-76, 212, 340, 362, 421
Idiographic study, 92, 99, 391, 421
Index, 56, 157, 344
Indicator, 53, 55, 149-50, 153-54, 157-61, 166, 169, 185, 190, 205, 213, 228, 246, 253-54, 274-76, 278, 332, 342, 344-45, 358-59, 365-66, 382, 421
Induction, 44, 57, 104, 421
Inductive analogical argument, 46, 69
Inductive statistical explanation, 85-87, 99, 421
Information component, 36, 69-70, 421
Instrument, 39, 54-55, 57, 59, 70, 76-77, 141, 154
Instrumental-nomological investigation, 76-77, 422
Interval scale, 40-43, 69, 316-17, 349, 368, 422

Jantz, R., 209-11
Jarvie, I. C., 25
Jochim, M., 326

Kaplan, A., 113
Keat, R., 387
Keesing, R. M., 17-18
Kidder, A. V., 78, 213
Koestler, A., 220
Kroeber, A. L., 217, 405-06
Kuhn, T., 394
Kus, S., 157

Lane, R., 155
Law, lawlike, 12-13, 15, 30, 48-49, 58, 84-
    88, 90, 92, 97-98, 106, 111, 123, 190,
    308-9, 312, 353, 357, 362-63, 367, 371-
    72, 382, 385-86, 389-90, 396-408, 412-
    13, 424
Leblanc, S., 1, 32, 213, 390
Lenski, G., 326-28
Lenski, J., 326-28
Leone, M., 1, 32
Liddy, Willard, 9
Life-table, 215, 218, 422
Local aggregates, 149, 422
Location analysis, 14, 169, 225
Longacre, W., 32, 152-53, 156, 175
Lösch, August, 231, 372

McNett, Charles, 342-43, 347
Markov process, 129
Marsh, R., 314-15
Martin, P., 32, 390
Matessi, C., 260
Measure, measurement, 12, 14, 21, 24, 28,
    36, 38-43, 49, 52-57, 60, 62, 69-70, 74,
    76-77, 79, 117, 141, 164, 181, 184, 186-
    88, 190-92, 207-9, 217, 225-27, 230,
    234, 236, 245, 248, 250, 252, 254, 262,
    274, 277-78, 282, 308, 314, 316-18,
    322-23, 341-42, 347, 349, 355, 358-59,
    361, 363-68, 381, 391, 401, 422
Method, methodology, 1, 11-13, 16, 25-26,
    28-29, 35-36, 38, 44, 50-52, 57-60, 62-
    63, 66-67, 69-70, 73, 77, 91, 125, 171,
    198, 308, 320, 340-42, 385, 390, 410-12,
    422
Methodological collectivism, 397, 403, 405-
    6, 422
Methodological individualism, 397, 403,
    405-6, 422
Methodological principle, 93-99, 136, 169,
    190, 221, 268-70, 298, 319, 338, 348,
    387, 391, 394-95, 404, 408, 412, 422
Methodological rule, 93-99, 136, 171, 181,
    198, 268, 270, 319, 387, 394-95, 403-5,
    412, 422
Midwest taxonomic system, 4-5
Model, modeling, 14, 24-25, 34, 36, 41, 43,
    46-47, 62, 66-69, 74, 78-79, 91, 97, 140,
    163, 166, 173, 176, 181, 183, 193, 198-
    99, 206, 217-18, 221, 223, 228, 230,
    232-33, 236-37, 239, 241-48, 255, 257-
    63, 267, 271-74, 276, 281-82, 284-86,
    288, 290-92, 294, 297-98, 301-3, 325-
    26, 348, 350, 364, 369, 372, 392, 395,
    422; analogue model, 108-11, 132, 417; a
    posteriori model, 112-13, 116, 132, 417;
    a priori model, 112-13, 116, 132, 417;
    iconic model, 108-11, 124, 126, 132,
    421; form of, 104-7, 109-11, 114-15,
    120, 122, 124-25, 127, 132; formal
    model, 108, 111, 116, 132, 420; material
    model, 108, 110, 116, 132, 422; mental
    model, 102, 422; operational model, 102,
    105-6, 110, 259, 423; process of, 104-7,
    109-11, 114-15, 117-18, 120, 122, 124-
    28, 132; rationale of, 104-6, 109-11, 125,
    127, 131, 228, 230, 237, 239, 242, 244,
    281, 288, 291, 293, 303, 424; source of,
    110-12, 115, 125, 242; subject of, 110-
    12, 115, 118; symbolic model, 108-9,
    111, 132, 426
Moh's scale, 42
Moore, C., 168
Mortality curve, 213-14, 218, 423
Murdock, G. P., 135, 321, 332
Murphree, Idus, 38
Myth of the given, 58

Narrative explanation, 89, 423
Naroll, R., 77, 213, 318, 335, 342-46, 348,
    350
Natural history chronicle, 78, 80, 269
Nearest neighbor analysis, 225-27, 230,
    262, 423
Nominal scale, 40-43, 54, 69, 187, 217,
    316-17, 319, 337, 342-43, 362, 382, 423
Nomothetic study, 92, 99, 391, 423

Nonvariable concept, 362-64, 367, 382, 423
N-transform, 193, 195, 423

Objectivism, 397, 403-05, 423
Observation, 27, 36-40, 43-47, 51-52, 57-59, 61-63, 66-70, 73, 75, 78, 82, 103, 106, 131-32, 365, 389-90, 393, 423
Operational definition, 52-54, 70, 77, 98, 299, 314, 317-18, 349, 355, 357-59, 362, 365-67, 369, 381-82, 423
Operationalism, 82
Operationalize, 52, 192, 261, 423
Ordinal scale, 40-43, 69, 157, 187, 189, 217, 316-17, 335-36, 349, 368, 383, 402, 423
Orton, C., 245-46, 260
Osteobiography, 205-6, 218, 423

Paleopathology, 205, 218, 423
Paradigm, 394
Pattern explanation, 89, 423
Payne, S., 184
Peebles, C., 157
Peirce, Charles, 46, 80
Perkins, D., Jr., 184
Pilot study, 60
Pires-Ferreira, J., 246, 253, 257
Plog, Fred, 190, 390
Plog, Stephen, 248-49
Polanyi, Karl, 253
Political system, 163-69, 176
Popper, Karl, 6, 16, 51, 404, 411-12
Positivism/logical empiricism, 12-13, 29-30, 66, 68, 102, 132, 170, 307, 365, 388-91, 423
Positivistic fallacy, 17
Post facto hypothesis, 45
Premise of a theory, 355, 357, 359-61, 377, 381-82, 424
Primitive term, 355, 357, 359-60, 377, 381-82, 424
Principle of proliferation, 394
Probability sampling, 44
Process, 8-11, 14, 20, 22-23, 29-30, 39, 102, 104-6, 109-11, 114-15, 117-18, 120, 122, 124-25, 128, 132, 141-42, 191, 193, 208, 217, 222, 226, 228-30, 236, 241-42, 245, 260, 268-69, 282, 285-86,

291, 296-97, 302-3, 312, 316, 324, 349, 374, 395, 404, 418, 424

Quine, W., 37

Random walk model, 127-30, 260-61, 281, 424
Rank-size, 233-35, 263, 294-98, 303, 424
Rappaport, R., 256-57
Rationalism, 46, 387
Ratio scale, 40-43, 69, 187, 189, 316-17, 342, 349, 368, 424
Reciprocal exchange, 246, 253-57, 261, 264, 424
Redfield, Robert, 343, 368
Redistributive exchange, 166, 246, 253-54, 261, 264, 424
Redman, Charles, 1, 32, 390
Reed, C., 184
Reid, J., 189-92
Regional approach, 23, 148, 163, 169, 176, 224-25, 323
Reliability, 54-56, 70, 77, 153, 184, 342, 401, 424
Renfrew, Colin, 157, 168, 213, 255, 259
Research design, 14, 39, 50, 60-66, 74, 76, 192, 424
Research program, 7, 73-74, 97-100, 102, 136, 180-81, 268-69, 302, 312, 320, 324, 338, 387, 391, 411, 413, 424
Residence group, 151
Residence rule, 151
Richert, H., 92
Robbins, L. M., 214
Robbins, M., 77
Rohn, Arthur, 149
Runciman, W. C., 412
Ryan, Alan, 411

Sabloff, J., 247
Sahlins, M., 342, 377
Sample summary, 36, 43-44, 50, 69, 79-80, 103, 131, 424
Scale, scaling, 39-43, 56-57, 60, 70, 83, 245, 263, 316-17, 343, 364, 377
Schaefer, J., 323
Schiffer, M., 31-32, 193, 369

Science, conceptions of, 1, 10-13, 38, 66-69, 82; conventionalist, 59, 352, 386-87, 392-96, 418; positivist, 12-13, 27-29, 66, 114-15, 386-92, 413, 423; realist, 114-15, 132, 352, 386-87, 391-92, 395-96, 424

Scientific method, 33-73, 82, 91, 94, 389

Scientific theory, 12, 45, 47-51, 57-59, 63, 68-70, 75-76, 103, 106-7, 112-14, 120-21, 123, 125, 131, 308, 312, 352, 354-55, 357, 359, 361, 387, 389, 392-93, 395-96, 425

Segraves, B. Abbott, 376-81

Sellars, W., 58

Service, Elman, 340, 342, 377

Settlement pattern, 18, 113, 140, 221-47, 292, 298, 300, 328, 425

Settlement system, 23, 221, 425

Shearing, C., 367

Shennan, S., 159

Site catchment analysis, 198-201, 204, 217-18, 228, 278, 425

Skellam, J., 282

Smith, M. E., 224

Social organization, 139-40, 150, 155-56, 159, 161, 168-69, 301, 338, 341, 425

Social structure, 62, 115, 139, 150-51, 156, 161, 171, 338, 390-91, 405, 425

Social subsystem, 136-37, 139-69, 175, 212, 274, 316, 332, 340, 350, 362, 425

Sociocultural change, 7, 10, 15, 30, 48, 61, 138, 181, 267-305

Sociocultural system, 6-11, 15, 17-18, 21, 23-25, 28, 30, 35, 47, 49, 51, 97, 104, 113, 117, 137, 143, 169-71, 181-82, 190, 193, 209, 218, 223, 267-70, 286, 298, 309, 311, 314, 316-17, 322, 336-38, 340-41, 343, 349, 364, 371, 377, 379, 381, 400, 410-11, 425

Socioeconomic system, 180, 425

Specific evolution, 340, 350, 425

Squier, E., 78

Stanislawski, M., 153

Stateless society, 163, 256

State-level society, 163, 165-66, 168, 176, 236, 277, 281, 308, 314-15

Statistical inference, 44, 69

Status, 56, 146, 156-61, 164-66, 169, 175, 188, 211-12, 246, 425

Steventon, R. L., 187-88

Steward, Julian, 336, 340, 342, 371, 403

Stochastic process, 61, 111, 123, 125, 127, 129, 133, 239, 294-95, 303, 425

Structural-functionalism, 1, 7-8, 13, 25, 29, 98, 348, 425

Structured space, 140, 143, 425

Struever, S., 246

Subjectivism, 397, 403-5, 425

Sublett, A., 155

Survivorship curve, 214-18, 425

Symmes, O., 323

Synchronic analysis, 22, 221, 262, 313, 426

System, 5-7, 18, 30, 39, 96, 136-37, 220, 259, 268-69, 298, 377, 379, 426; approach, 6, 8, 10, 13, 18-25, 29-30, 114, 308, 356, 426; strain, 189-92, 205, 272-73, 301

Systematic empiricism, 79, 82, 426

Systemic context, 10-11, 37, 39, 47, 49, 55, 59, 68, 77, 81, 88-89, 103, 118, 143, 191, 193, 302-3, 312, 319, 325, 354-55, 426

Systems duality, 24, 30

Tatje, T., 344

Tautology, 51, 319, 355, 359, 382

Technoeconomic subsystem, 61, 136-37, 171, 180-204, 212, 217, 221, 245-64, 340, 349, 362, 404, 426

Technology, 15-16, 20-21, 30, 180, 338, 377, 426

Teleological explanation, 89, 93, 426

Tendency statement, 325, 350, 371, 377, 383, 426

Test implication, 51, 57, 126, 192, 379, 426

Text of a theory, 355-57, 360-61, 365, 382, 426

Theoretical definition, 52, 54, 70, 77, 98, 277, 314, 317-18, 349, 355, 357-58, 362, 365-66, 369, 377-79, 382, 426

Theorizing, 75, 426

Theory building, 12, 45-49, 73, 81, 91, 308-9, 347-48, 350, 352-84

Thiessen polygon, 230-31, 263

Thomas, D. H., 32, 184, 237-39, 335-37

Thomas, F. N., 295

Thompsen, Christian, 2

Three-age sequence, 2
Three-degree rule, 323
Tobias, S. L., 342-43
Todd, I., 163, 168
Tool-kit, 81, 141-43, 175, 426
Tortellot, G., 247
Toulmin, Stephen, 80
Trace element analysis, 207, 218
Trend surface analysis, 141-42, 175
Trial formulation, 59-61, 70, 81, 117, 119, 369, 426
Tuggle, H., 326
Tylor, Sir Edward Burnett, 3, 321-22
Tylor-Galton problem, 321-24, 420

Uerpmann, H.-P., 184
Ullian, J., 37
Unity of scientific method thesis, 12, 27-30, 387, 396, 406, 413
Universal culture pattern, 15, 135-36, 270, 274, 427
Urry, J., 387

Validity, 54-56, 70, 77, 153, 184, 186, 190, 234, 246, 283, 314, 318, 342, 365-66, 382, 401, 427

Variable concept, 362-64, 367-69, 377, 382, 427
Vita-Finzi, C., 198

Wall abutment, analysis, 149
Watson, J. P., 184
Watson, P. J., 1, 32, 390
Watt, K., 190
Weber, Max, 410
White, Leslie, 340-41, 403-6
Whiting, J., 332-35
Wiessner, P., 213
Willer, David, 105
Williams, Mary B., 381
Wilmsen, E., 326
Winter, M. C., 144, 246, 253
Winters, Howard, 258
Wissler, Clark, 135, 216, 270
Wittfogel, Karl, 371
Wood, W. R., 209-10
Work-activity area, 81
World view, 170, 173-74, 176, 427
Wright, G. Ernest, 137
Wright, H. Y., 257-60
Wyckoff, D. G., 234-35

Zeder, M., 257-60
Zimmerman, L. J., 298-303